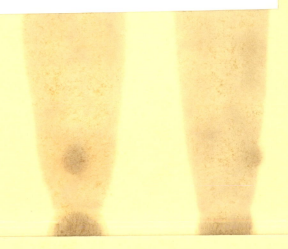

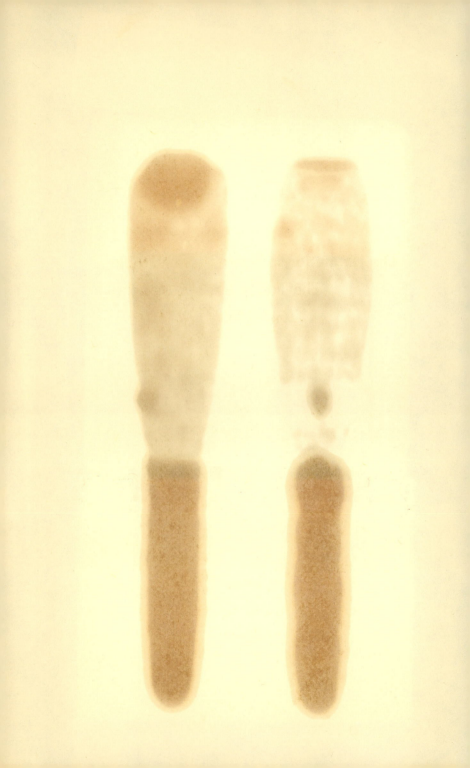

Discrimination in International Trade
The Policy Issues
1945–1965

DISCRIMINATION IN INTERNATIONAL TRADE THE POLICY ISSUES

1945–1965

BY GARDNER PATTERSON

PRINCETON, NEW JERSEY

PRINCETON UNIVERSITY PRESS

1966

To
E. R. P.

PREFACE

THIS is an examination of policy formulation. It is a non-quantitative empirical study. My concern is with the major policy issues that arose during the two decades following the end of World War II because many governments of the free world consciously chose to discriminate in their trade and payments, hoping thereby to further some important national objective. This book is an effort to find out what they hoped to accomplish by treating imports from some areas more favorably than from others and what some of the major consequences, on themselves, and especially on third countries, of such practices have been—or seem likely to be, since much of what is examined is still in train. Although the subject seems to me sufficiently interesting for its own sake to justify a long study of it, I must admit to the hope that my findings may provide some useful guides to future policy formulation.

The subject is vast. It has had to be limited at every turn. Theoretical work during the period has been merely cited or drastically summarized, and even such attention limited to that which was of direct, immediate, and major relevance to the policy issues. No effort has been made to discuss the techniques of discrimination, nor to provide a catalog of all discriminatory acts. Only passing attention has been given to discrimination on exports. Nothing has been said about the discrimination among the state controlled economies, or between them and the so-called free market economies. Each of these is a major study in itself. Attention here is focused on the conscious use of discrimination as a *major* tool of policy to accomplish some substantively important objective. Thus, no attention has been given to discrimination that was incidental, in the sense that it was not sought in order to accomplish something else but was merely a side effect, even though such side effects may have been important.

Most of the research was carried out in Europe in 1963–1964 while I held a Ford Foundation Faculty Research Fellowship and a research grant from the Social Science Research Council. Much the most important source of information was the archives and records in Geneva of the Contracting Parties to the General Agreement on Tariffs and Trade. Access to that primary material, usually in mimeographed form, was an absolute requirement for this study because most of the major acts of discrimination in the period studied here came under the purview of that remarkable organization. The GATT Secretariat is a unique source of primary materials on all manner of trade policy issues since World War II. I therefore owe a special debt to Mr. Eric Wyndham White, the Director General. He made that material available; he provided me for many months with an office at the Villa le Bocage, which was not only close to the material I needed but gave an unsurpassed view of Lake Geneva and the Alps beyond; and he gave me insights into many of the problems in which I was interested. Of the many members of the GATT Secretariat who helped me I must make special mention of Mr. Constant Shih, who for many years dealt with discriminatory issues; to the staff of the GATT Library; and, most of all, to Mr. Richard R. Ford. Mr. Ford not only went to great lengths in putting me on to documents I wanted, no matter how inconvenient the nature or timing of my request, but he was a constant source of information that I could not find elsewhere. Moreover, the GATT press releases, for which he bore much responsibility, were for many years models of accurate and remarkably full statements of complicated discussions and issues. In a massive understatement he once referred to himself as "a rag-bag of GATT history." He has, in fact, a rich and ordered source of knowledge about that institution and its works. These men bear no responsibility for the interpretation or the selection of the data presented here. That is mine alone.

Particular thanks must also go to the staff, and especially to Mr. Norman Field, of the United Nations Library in Geneva. And, as must be the case of all American economists who visit Geneva, I, too, owe much to Professor Jacques Freymond and his colleagues, especially Dr. Gerard Curzon, at the Graduate Institute of International Studies, for their generous hospitality and the chance they provided to try out some preliminary notions on their students.

Much help, on a nonattributive basis, was also given me by the officials of the United States Missions in Geneva and in Brussels, and by officers of the European Economic Community and the European Free Trade Association. Many persons in Washington have also similarly aided me. I would like to single out Dr. Irving Friedman. During most of the period covered by this study he was immersed in the problems of exchange restrictions; he has an unsurpassed knowledge of them, and I spent many extremely useful hours discussing with him all manner of economic questions touching on discrimination.

In one way and another, I have received help from a large number of my colleagues here at Princeton, but I must mention for special thanks Professor Benjamin J. Cohen. He offered many more criticisms than I was prepared to act upon.

GARDNER PATTERSON

Princeton
August 1965

TABLE OF CONTENTS

xi

ABBREVIATIONS FREQUENTLY USED

BISD	Basic Instruments and Selected Documents (GATT)
ECE	Economic Commission for Europe (UN)
ECLA	Economic Commission for Latin America (UN)
ECSC	European Coal and Steel Community
EEC	European Economic Community (Common Market)
EFTA	European Free Trade Association
EPU	European Payments Union (OEEC)
GATT	General Agreement on Tariffs and Trade
IMF	International Monetary Fund
ITO	International Trade Organization
LAFTA	Latin American Free Trade Area
OEEC	Organization for European Economic Cooperation
OECD	Organization for Economic Cooperation and Development
QR's	Quantitative Restrictions

Discrimination in International Trade

The Policy Issues

1945–1965

CHAPTER I

The Setting

THE YEARS between the two World Wars—to go no further back in a long history—saw a great deal of discrimination in international trade and payments.[1] But the gospel according to many of those who were destined to play a major role in establishing the post-World War II commercial policy rules was that this was an evil thing and that the world's economic efficiency and welfare suffered thereby. It was a textbook maxim that, prevalent as the abuses might be, unconditional-most-favored-nation treatment [2] was the most important single

[1] Jacob Viner believes that, taking the world as a whole, the general trend from the late 1870's to the outbreak of World War II was an increase in discrimination. See his "Peace as an Economic Problem" (1944), in *International Economics,* Glencoe, Ill., 1951, p. 259. For a short, general statement of the largely frustrated efforts between the wars to secure general adoption of the principle of nondiscrimination, together with a reduction of trade barriers, see Clair Wilcox, *A Charter for World Trade,* New York, 1949, pp. 3ff. More details on this period may be found in the League of Nations, Economic Committee, *The Most-Favoured-Nation Clause,* Geneva, 1936; League of Nations, *Commercial Policy in the Inter-War Period,* Geneva, 1942; League of Nations, Report of the Economic and Financial Committees, *Commercial Policy in the Post-War World,* Geneva, 1945; League of Nations Secretariat, *Quantitative Trade Controls: Their Causes and Nature,* Geneva, 1943. See also, R. C. Snyder, *The Most-Favored-Nation Clause; An Analysis with Particular Reference to Recent Treaty Practice and Tariffs,* New York, 1948; and Jacob Viner, *The Customs Union Issue,* New York, 1950, Chaps. 2 and 3.

[2] The unconditional-most-favored-nation clause in treaties provides in effect that each of the parties shall grant—automatically and without compensation—to the other any privilege or favor of commerce which it grants or may later grant to third countries. That is, it provides that each shall treat trade in any given good or service with the other as well as it treats the same kind of transaction with any third country, which of course may be very badly. The definition in the General Agreement on Tariffs and Trade (Art. I, Sec. 1) states: "With respect to customs duties and charges of any kind imposed on . . . imports or exports, . . . and with respect to all rules and formalities in connection with importation and exportation, . . . any advantage, favour, privilege or immunity

3

rule of conduct in international trade, because it proscribed discrimination: the granting of differential treatment to international transactions according to the nationality of the source or destination.

Many were the arguments that had been used to justify discrimination and, as we shall see, most of them, often in new dresses, were heard again in the period covered by this study. The more persistent were a group—variations on a theme—that were essentially political rather than economic. Granting "better" treatment to trade with former military allies and well-disposed neutrals than to former enemies and less friendly neutrals was often believed to be "reasonable" and "appropriate." It had long been held by many that exchanges of preferences among limited groups of nations would bring both political and sentimental gains. Such exchanges of favors, it was often said, would strengthen political ties and smooth the path toward political union, if this were desired. Although many students had concluded that it was easy to exaggerate the contributions here,[3] the view was widely held and played an important part in policy formulation. It had also long been generally accepted that there were often compelling political reasons for a mother country granting preferential treatment to the exports of her colonial areas. Once the economies of such areas had been developed on the basis of such preferences, then a case was found to exist for continuing the discriminatory arrangements lest, in the absence of other compensating measures, some of them become tropical slums or derelict areas.

The more strictly economic arguments for discrimination were usually short run and from the point of view of a single, or small, group of nations rather than from a long run and universal point of view. That most powerful argument for import barriers—outright protection of vociferous or for other reasons gently treated domestic producers against lower cost

---

granted by any contracting party to any product originating in or destined for any other country shall be accorded immediately and unconditionally to the like product originating in or destined for the territories of all other contracting parties."

[3] See especially, Viner, *Customs Union Issue*, pp. 91–105.

imports—was also a telling argument for discriminatory practices, especially since it was often justified in terms of alleged labor exploitation by those against whom discrimination was practiced. Although professional economists frequently doubted the fact of such exploitation, and saw this as a devious and self-serving argument that played on public ignorance and prejudice, it was a very hardy one indeed.

Adam Smith noted another "economic" thesis that has long appealed to politicians: It is only "fair" to discriminate in favor of those who buy from you. His famous answer—"The sneaking arts of underling tradesmen are thus erected into political maxims for the conduct of a great empire; for it is the most underling tradesmen only who make it a rule to employ chiefly their own customers. A great trader purchases his goods always where they are cheapest and best, without regard to any little interest of this kind." [4]—was found convincing by most economists but not always by men who were wielding power.

The "fair," "unfair" consideration was also one of the most commonly cited reasons for favoring conditional over unconditional-most-favored-nation-treatment clauses in trade agreements. The argument here was that it was unfair on the face of it that one country should receive "free" what others had to "pay" for in terms of increasing access to their markets. Most professional economists also found this unconvincing because it looked at a particular transaction as if it were an isolated event. If one looked at the whole range of international trade over a reasonably long period of time, then, although A's concessions to B under a nondiscriminatory system might be "free" to, say, C, C's later concessions to D (or to A and B) became "free" to B and A and so some sort of balance would be struck. [5] Policy makers, however, were not always convinced.

---

[4] Adam Smith, *The Wealth of Nations*, Modern Library edition, New York, 1937, p. 460.

[5] In the extreme case where C granted no concessions to anyone, a case, most economists agreed, could be made for others withdrawing most-favored-nation treatment from *it*, principally on the bargaining grounds that this might cause it to follow the same practices as the

Experience had also been that governments sometimes could not resist the temptation to discriminate, in the hope that they could thereby get double return for any tariff cuts they made: the first in the form of concessions to their exports by the country with which it was originally negotiating; the second in the "pay" others would offer for relief from the discrimination they were now suffering. While not denying that this could happen, many observers doubted that it had often been successful, although no serious empirical study seems to have been made of it. Their skepticism rested on the fact that an obvious response by those who suffered from this discrimination would be to retaliate by putting on new and discriminatory restrictions against the first nation. Exports of each would then suffer. Nations also sometimes discriminated in the hope this would help solve a domestic unemployment problem: increase exports by exchanging tariff cuts with another nation while maintaining imports at the old level by diverting them away from a nonfavored to a favored source. Apart from the probability of retaliation and lower trade all around, this policy too had little appeal to those who looked at the problems of the benefits of trade and levels of employment from the worldwide point of view.

Discriminatory policies were sometimes defended on the much wider grounds that they fostered freer trade. In a world in which there are problems of unemployment and in which tariff barriers exist and are reduced by a process of negotiation and exchange of "concessions," in such a world a policy of nondiscrimination (unconditional-most-favored-nation treatment) by A and B reduces their future bargaining power in the quest for larger markets in C and D. The consequence, many held, could easily be a slowing down in tariff reductions all around the world. This case for discrimination was more

---

others. For a discussion of this question, as well as several of the other pre-1945 discrimination issues, see Jacob Viner, "The Most-Favored-Nation Clause in American Commercial Treaties" (1924), "The Most-Favored-Nation Clause" (1931), and "The American Interest in the Colonial Problem" (1944). All of these are reprinted in his *International Economics.*

difficult to deal with by those who favored more liberal trade policies and it was commonly accepted as a potent case for discrimination. Ways were found to partially meet the problem —notably, the development of the "principal supplier" rule and specialized tariff classification [6]—but at the cost of impairing the most-favored-nation principle.[7]

There were other arguments too that nondiscrimination reinforced protectionist tendencies. Especially in times of slack demand, it was asserted, the nondiscriminatory rule worked to prevent an exchange of concessions between just two countries; but this might be as far as each was prepared to go in risking the adverse effects on its import-competing industries. It was sometimes said in response to this policy that a somewhat greater reduction in import barriers extended to all might be no more disruptive and might better serve a given nation via the terms of trade effect.[8] It was replied that the benefits to a nation's exports that could be expected from an exchange of bilateral concessions might be much longer in coming about if

[6] The principal supplier—or chief source—rule requires that a nation negotiate reductions in import barriers on a given product only with the country which had been supplying the greatest portion of the former's import of that product. It is thus intended that each concession will be negotiated with the country having the greatest interest in it. This practice preserves bargaining power when the unconditional-most-favored-nation practice is followed, because there is a tendency under it for some products of prime interest to other countries (those goods for which each is a major supplier) not to be the subject of negotiation between other pairs of countries. Specialized tariff classification facilitates the application of the principal supplier rule by so defining products for trade barrier cutting purposes that fewer, rather than more, of the exports important to those not participating in a given bilateral negotiation qualify for the bilaterally agreed cuts.

[7] The argument lost some more of its potency when, immediately after World War II, arrangements were made for simultaneous bilateral negotiations, a procedure which Germany had followed before World War I, and which became the hallmark of the General Agreement on Tariffs and Trade.

[8] If the preference-receiver cannot supply all of the preference-granter's market at the prices it previously charged prior to duty, then the terms of trade worsened for the preference-giver, unless this is offset by its being able similarly to raise its prices in the partner country.

7

one had to wait for the benefits of others lowering their barriers, and during depressions time was important.

Discrimination was also frequently defended on the grounds that the most-favored-nation rule introduced lethargy into tariff reduction negotiations because it encouraged many countries to wait, hoping to obtain automatically the benefits of others lowering their tariffs.[9] Nor should we overlook the argument sometimes used that the practice of nondiscrimination could be and was used to buttress a policy of raising tariffs, because a nation doing so has some immunity against reprisal, stemming from the fact that such retaliation by others would have to apply to all countries.

Finally, even this briefest of catalogs of the major reasons for the widespread discriminatory practices in the inter-war period must note that governments sometimes believed that by discriminating they could introduce a monopsonistic principle into their imports and so improve their terms of trade. Most economists agreed that this was possible. But apart from the fact that, even if successful, the improvement in welfare by the country practicing discrimination would be at the direct expense of those with whom she traded, with little likelihood that general welfare would be increased, most were very bearish on the probability of any government being able to successfully carry out such a policy. The skepticism arose on several counts. Experience had shown that retaliation was likely, which of course tended to reduce the total quantity of trade and leave the terms of trade unaltered, or even worsened, from the point of view of the country starting the process For most countries and for most commodities, given a few years to work things out, the reciprocal demand curves were believed likely to be very elastic, thus greatly limiting the possibility of changing the terms of trade in this way. In any case, many observers

---

[9] For a recent statement of these and other arguments against most-favored-nation treatment, see Gerard Curzon, *Multilateral Commercial Diplomacy,* London, 1965, Chap. 3. See also, Harry C. Hawkins, *Commercial Treaties and Agreements, Principles and Practices,* New York, 1951, Chaps. 8–11.

doubted that governments had the skill to pick those commodities and those nations where export elasticities were sufficiently low to make discrimination for this purpose effective.

Although those responsible for determining their government's policies had no trouble finding some justification for discrimination, the inter-war experience and analysis had also developed powerful support—especially among those who were to play a major role in setting the post-war rules—for a new effort to adopt international rules proscribing discrimination. As they saw it, the case for nondiscrimination was not merely that the case *for* discrimination often was weak. Nor was it just that it served to prevent direct injury to third countries. Nor was it merely a reflection of the fact that the eagerness of many individual nations to obtain a preferential position was often matched by their eagerness to put obstacles in the way of others getting such favored treatment. The more solid basis for their position was that nondiscrimination secured major benefits to those who practiced it and to the world as a whole. This conclusion rested on the same line of reasoning that had for so long led many to advocate freer trade, only applied now just to a nation's dealings as *among* the parts of the trading world *outside* its own frontiers. If persons and nations were free to buy in the cheapest foreign market and sell in the dearest, each would specialize where his advantages were greatest or disadvantages least, and could thus convert his own efforts into the maximum possible amount of desired goods and services. All careful proponents of this thesis recognized that such a conclusion rested on a series of heroic assumptions, including, but not limited to, all those necessary to ensure that for all products and at all times the marginal social values equalled marginal social net costs, or, in more homely and a bit less precise terms, that relative money prices equalled relative real costs.[10] As a guide to policy it also assumed that welfare depends on private

[10] The reader wishing a detailed, precise, formal statement of the case for nondiscriminatory trade is referred to James E. Meade, *The Theory of International Economic Policy*, Vol. II, *Trade and Welfare*, London, 1955, Chaps. 2, 9, and 30.

consumption of goods and services. So the goal was to maximize this "real product"; that is, that no value should be attached to noneconomic objectives, or to such economic objectives as a diversified economy.[11]

No thoughtful advocate of nondiscrimination denied that there were many departures in fact from such an assumed, nicely ordered world—the more important being ignorance, external economies and diseconomies, monopolistic and monopsonistic practices, and a host of governmental interferences with the mechanisms, resulting in arbitrary exchange rates, government-fixed prices, subsidies, nonconvertible currencies, etc.—or that national goals which included more than maximizing real product were appropriate. But in the absence of a well-developed body of theory to replace it, the classical doctrine still kept its hold on many men's minds, and on few more firmly than those Americans who were to exercise such great influence on the shape of post-war, international economic institutions and commitments. A commonly held view amongst this group was that, in spite of the doctrine's fragile and faulty moorings, there was no better guideline to policy. Their conviction was strengthened by many specific arguments *against* discrimination.

High on that list was the political argument that discrimination generates a lot of international ill will. There was considerable evidence that persons and governments could adjust themselves quite quickly to high nondiscriminatory foreign tariffs, but that resentment against tariff discrimination, even when of little commercial importance, was often bitter and lasting. Viner's studies during the 1920's led him to conclude that the United States' application of conditional, rather than unconditional-most-favored-treatment during the previous century had probably led to more diplomatic controversy and more international ill will than had developed under all the unconditional-most-favored-nation pledges of all other countries com-

[11] For a path-breaking article developing a theory of protectionism which departs from this assumption, see H. G. Johnson, "An Economic Theory of Protectionism, Tariff Bargaining, and the Formation of Customs Unions," *The Journal of Political Economy*, June 1965.

bined.[12] The Economic and Financial Committee of the League of Nations, in its 1945 report on post-war commercial policy, anticipated that widespread discrimination, if permitted, would sap the basis of political cooperation and so of world peace.[13] Lionel Robbins found here a compelling argument against perpetuating the dollar discrimination favored by so many of his countrymen after World War II. He feared that the price England might pay for continued dollar discrimination after the post-war "emergency" had passed might include not only a contracting out of the Commonwealth by such members as Canada and South Africa but also a reduction in United States willingness to cooperate on political and military matters.[14]

On more strictly economic grounds, Viner, in his teaching and writing, had for many years been pointing out, although his seminal work on *The Customs Union Issue* did not appear until several years after the end of World War II, that discriminatory barriers might be more costly to economic efficiency than a higher level of uniform barriers because of their trade-diverting effects. It was more or less accepted doctrine before the war that a discriminatory system was more unstable than a nondiscriminatory one. Any system that attempted to force A to buy from B and/or B to buy from A, goods A and B did not particularly want or which were at relatively high prices, was not thought to have a high survival value. Such instability increases the hazards and risks, and thus the costs, of production for export. So a nation whose exports were favored by discrimination was seen as running the risk not only that the import country may raise tariffs—a risk all exporters face—but also the further risk that the preference might be withdrawn, or what from its point of view can amount to much the same thing, be given to a competitor in a third country. Moreover, the

---

[12] Viner, "The Most-Favored-Nation Clause in American Commercial Treaties," *International Economics,* p. 25.

[13] League of Nations, Report of Economic and Financial Committees, *Commercial Policy in the Post-War World,* p. 33.

[14] See Lionel Robbins, "Inquest on the Crisis," *Lloyd's Bank Review,* October 1947; "The Sterling Problem," *ibid.,* October 1949; "Towards the Atlantic Community," *ibid.,* July 1950.

nation receiving a preference would probably have to stand alone in its opposition, or even find the action of preference withdrawal being applauded by others, while a threat to increased tariffs applicable to all would find those adversely affected with many allies.[15]

A more important economic argument for nondiscrimination by those favoring freer trade was that nations often would not be willing to exchange concessions unless each could be assured that what it was receiving in the way of larger markets for its exports would not be nullified by large concessions later to a rival. Many, indeed, regarded this as an overwhelmingly important consideration, outweighing all others, and sufficient by itself to dictate a policy of nondiscrimination. Finally, to those actually implementing a nation's commercial policy, a discriminatory policy has the additional, very substantial defects of involving large administrative costs associated with its implementation, plus the much more complicated and costly negotiations that must be undertaken if imports are to be treated differently according to source.

For all these reasons the virtues of a general policy of nondiscrimination were firmly—even passionately—advocated by many men in places of influence, especially in the United States, and to a much lesser extent in those of the other governments who were making plans for the post-war world.[16] This became apparent in the 1941 Atlantic Charter, in which, at United States insistence, was included the declaration that the British and United States governments would "endeavor . . .

---

[15] To the extent that this risk leads the preference-receiver to check its investment and lessen its capacity to supply efficiently the preference-giver's needs, the latter also loses. The preference-granter can also lose, of course, if the preference-receiver cannot meet all the granter's demands and so the latter continues to import from other sources. In this case, prices will presumably remain the same, or nearly so, inside the preference-granting country, and that country's loss is measured by the foregone customs revenue which becomes a bounty to the preference-receiver.

[16] The general flavor of the approach and attitudes of American officials on this can be found in Hawkins, *Commercial Treaties and Agreements, Principles and Practices.*

with due respect for their existing obligations, to further the enjoyment of all States . . . of access, on equal terms, to the trade . . . needed for their economic prosperity." A few months later, in the famous Article VII of the Master Lend Lease Agreement between the United States and the United Kingdom, these two governments agreed to work towards "the elimination of all forms of discriminatory treatment in international commerce. . . ." [17] The Atlantic Charter was subsequently adopted by a great many other nations and Article VII was included in the long list of Lend Lease Agreements. Nondiscrimination, then, was to be a major aspect of post-war commercial policy.

But in the lengthy negotiations that were to precede concrete agreements on institutions and rules intended to govern the post-war world, there was to be much debate on the matter. One economist, a veteran trade negotiator, found that during those years four quite distinct approaches or points of view emerged. [18]

Many professional economists, as well as most of the concerned officials of the United States, Canada, Belgium, Holland, and the Scandinavian countries, were convinced of the virtues of a world trading system based on individual initiative, free markets, convertibility, and nondiscriminatory multilateralism. They wanted agreement on, and commitments to, these principles. At the other extreme, largely represented by spokesmen from Eastern Europe, were those who saw the future of their nations best assured by resort to central planning and controls. For them, logic required bilateralism, and so discrimination, in their international economic relations. A third group, including official spokesmen from most of the countries of Latin America, the Middle East, and Asia, were those preoccupied with the problems of economic development,

[17] See R. N. Gardner, *Sterling-Dollar Diplomacy*, Oxford, 1956, Chaps. 3 and 4, for an account of the negotiation of these commitments.

[18] See Wilcox, *Charter for World Trade*, Chap. 4, for a short, authoritative general discussion of these negotiations. Aspects of these have also been carefully chronicled by, among others, Roy Harrod, *The Life of John Maynard Keynes*, London, 1951, Chaps. 12 and 14; and Gardner, *Sterling-Dollar Diplomacy*, Chaps. 6, 8, 14, and 17.

already frequently equated with industrialization. Their views on discrimination at that time can perhaps be characterized as: "If rapid economic development and industrialization requires, as we expect, many government controls and if this in turn means discrimination, then so be it. We do not now advocate discrimination, but neither are we willing to rule it out as undesirable." The fourth group, most prominently represented by the officials, as well as many of the professional economists, of the United Kingdom and France, acknowledged the force of the arguments for nondiscrimination, provided the assumptions on which they were based did in fact coincide reasonably well with reality and, perhaps more important, provided one could afford to take the long-run point of view. But, they argued, for some years after the war the world would be in a state of acute economic crisis, international disequilibrium would be great, and the economies of most nations would be severely disjointed in the sense that relative money prices would bear but little systematic relation to relative real costs. During this period at least, they insisted, they must not be bound by rules designed for quite other circumstances. Running throughout these planning discussions was the fear of what came to be called the "chronic dollar shortage" and, more generally, prolonged non-convertibility of many trading currencies. From this there developed a new and important "balance of payments argument" for discrimination, and complex provisions intended to cope with it were incorporated in the rules. This is the subject of Chapter II and nothing more need be said about it here.

Several preferential systems, short of customs unions or free trade areas, existed at the time of the war and early post-war negotiations.[19] The most important were those among the members of the British Commonwealth and the French Union. Less important were those between Benelux and their dependent territories, and between the United States, on one hand, and Cuba and the Philippines on the other. There were also some among a few neighboring states in Latin America and the Middle East, and between Spain and Portugal and their respective colonial empires. No serious attempts were made to

[19] Some earlier ones involving Germany, Italy, Japan, and their overseas conquests were regarded as no longer existent.

obtain agreement to abolish outright any of these,[20] it being found that there were such strong, vested interests and political considerations involved that the most that could be agreed to was that the existing margins of preference could not be increased and in principle should be reduced as part of future tariff negotiations. But neither did most of the negotiators take seriously the rather modest efforts by delegations from Central America, South America, Northern South America, Southern South America, from the Arab League, the Middle East, and Southeast Asia, to get permission to establish *new* preferential arrangements. Indeed, at the time of the IMF and ITO negotiations, spokesmen for these latter countries were given short shrift. This was to change, and, as we shall see in Chapters IV, V, and VII, a great deal of attention was destined to be given to amending and modifying the rules and practices so as to use discrimination as a tool for facilitating the economic development of the less developed states.

From the outset, the planning for the post-war world in-

---

[20] The United States Congress had already passed (1934) the Philippine Independence Act, under which, by 1946, trade between the two countries would be accorded the same treatment as that with other nations. This was revised in the 1946 U.S.–Philippine trade agreement, extending until 1974 the period for the gradual elimination of mutual customs preferences.

The United States began reducing its preferences to Cuba in 1949 as a consequence of tariff reductions negotiated with other countries under the GATT. Cuba protested in vain this loss of favors. (See U.S. Department of State, *Department of State Bulletin,* Nov. 21, 1949, p. 776.) Following the rise to power of Fidel Castro and the rapidly worsening political relations between the two countries, the United States not only withdrew the remaining old preferences, but instituted reverse preferences. In late 1962 the United States declared a virtual total embargo on trade with Cuba and the 1962 Tariff Classification Act, as well as the 1962 Trade Expansion Act, suspended most-favored-nation· treatment to Cuban goods. This placed Cuba in the same category as Russia, Mainland China, and other countries controlled by the "world communist movement" which had been denied most-favored-nation treatment from the United States by acts of Congress.

As we shall see later, especially in Chapters IV, V, and VII, the Commonwealth preferences and those of the French Union have been the subject of much discussion, dispute, and change in recent years.

15

cluded approval of customs unions—to which was soon added free trade areas—but at the time it was anticipated that there would be relatively few efforts in this direction, involving only a few countries. Nothing like the growth of regionalism that has taken place, the subject of Chapters III, IV, and V below, was then foreseen. Even those who argued most strongly against preferential arrangements and for nondiscrimination as the major guidelines for post-war trade policies, usually favored, in principle, the establishment of customs unions. There are, as has often been pointed out, some logical inconsistencies in this position. Part of the explanation was simply the tradition that customs unions were "a good thing" because they involved some reductions of trade barriers and because their political implications might override the demands of economic consistency. Part of the explanation was that the full complexities of customs unions and free trade areas, especially their impact on third areas, was not fully appreciated at the time by many of the negotiators. This is not surprising, since little systematic theoretical work on the problem had yet been published. Part of the explanation also lies in the fact that those favoring freer trade clearly saw in customs unions their possibilities for trade creation (shifting the locus of production from higher cost to lower cost areas), but saw only dimly the possibilities for trade diversion (shifting the locus of production from lower cost to higher cost areas), while the latter possibilities were clearly seen in preferential arrangements.[21] Related to this was the recognition by some that while *any* preferential system has the possibility of creating trade in some products and diverting trade in

---

[21] Thus it was said in justification of the distinction that "A customs union creates a wider trading area, removes obstacles to competition, makes possible a more economic allocation of resources, and thus operates to increase production and raise planes of living. A preferential system, on the other hand, retains internal barriers, obstructs economy in production, and restrains the growth of income and demand. It is set up for the purpose of conferring a privilege on producers within the system and imposing a handicap on external competitors. A customs union is conducive to the expansion of trade on the basis of multilateralism and nondiscrimination; a preferential system is not." Wilcox, *A Charter for World Trade,* pp. 70–71.

others, a *complete* discriminatory system rules out the possibility, which is permitted in a *partial* system, of picking and choosing for preferential treatment only those commodities where the effect will be to divert trade. In other words, as one of those who played a prominent part in making the post-war plans has written, a preferential system, as distinct from a full customs union, "does harm to outsiders by diverting trade away from them, without sufficient compensating benefits in the form of an enlargement of the total market of the participating countries." [22] This central critical point was formalized in the ITO-GATT [23] provision requiring that "substantially all trade" must be covered if a regional bloc were to be blessed. This requirement was also insisted on by those trying to proscribe discrimination because it was seen as likely to deter many attempts to form regional groups. To fulfill it would almost certainly require that some domestic producers suffer new competition from partner countries.

In the end, those subscribing to the International Monetary Fund committed themselves to making their currencies convertible at unitary rates and to abandoning exchange controls on current transactions, thus eschewing most discriminatory practices. But in recognition of the chaotic conditions expected to follow the war's end, members were given a period of grace during which they could discriminate, it being anticipated that this would be short, about five years. It was also provided in the Fund Agreement that if one country should run such a persistent surplus that its currency became "scarce" in the Fund, then others might be authorized to discriminate against the offender. It was, however, assumed by most that this condition was not likely to arise and that the rule would become applicable only if the cause were that the scarce currency country so mishandled its internal affairs as to have a severe and long internal depression.

Those who acceded to the GATT committed themselves in

---

[22] Hawkins, *Commercial Treaties and Agreements,* p. 125.

[23] In this book, the General Agreement on Tariffs and Trade is usually referred to as GATT or General Agreement.

Article I to follow unconditional-most-favored-nation treatment.[24] This was generally regarded as the cornerstone of the GATT, and was a major extension of the principle because the General Agreement is a many-faceted multilateral commitment. This meant that for a member to back out of its nondiscriminatory obligations would threaten an unraveling of a huge package—not just a few commitments with one other country, as had been possible when the most-favored-nation clause was only part of a bilateral accord. But to this general rule there were exceptions, in addition to the one that the obligation formally extended only to transactions with other members of the GATT club.[25] One of the more important, reflecting the considerations noted above, was that a contracting party was authorized to impose discriminatory, quantitative restrictions so long as it suffered acute balance of payments problems (and the major trading currencies were inconvertible) (Article XIV). Existing preferential systems could be maintained, but (Article I, Paragraph 2) the preferential margins were not to be increased and no new preferences were to be created.[26] Customs unions and free trade areas were blessed (Article XXIV), provided they were consummated "within a reasonable length of time"; they covered, as we have noted, "substantially all the trade" among the members; and provided

[24] Art. II, Para. 1, provides considerable reinforcement to the principle.

[25] In practice, most countries have extended most-favored-nation treatment to most nonmembers in the free world, Japan being a major exception, as we shall see in Chapter VI. The General Agreement also includes a few specific exceptions to the most-favored-nation clause, which are of no interest to us here because major policy issues are not involved. Thus, anti-dumping duties (Art. VI) are exempted, as is the application of certain sanctions applied by one party against another in the case of nonfulfillment of obligations (Art. XXIII) and actions necessary to protect public morals, health, to carry out obligations under international commodity agreements, etc. (Art. XX).

[26] The ITO Charter had Article 15, which would permit certain carefully circumscribed preferential arrangements designed to facilitate economic development, but these were not included in the General Agreement. In 1965, for reasons outlined in Chapter VII below, a move was underway to incorporate this old Article 15 in the General Agreement.

that the duties and restrictions on trade applied by the new institutions against trade with third countries was not "on the whole, higher or more restrictive than the general incidence" of those that individual members had applied before they entered the new regional arrangements.[27]

There was, finally, that great loophole, Article XXXV, which specified that any contracting party[28] had the option of not applying the GATT to a new contracting party. This was put in originally at the request of India, so that she could avoid being bound by the GATT rules in her relations with the Union of South Africa, but, as we shall see in Chapter VII, it opened the door to widespread discriminatory practices for protective purposes.

As the post-war world began, the two major international agreements on the rules for conducting foreign trade and finance had something for everybody. That nondiscrimination should be the major policy guideline was written in bold type. But it had been drafted in the face of doubts and worries by many and against the background of a long history of discrimination. It was possible to negotiate this only because several exceptions were specifically permitted. These exceptions and this background opened the possibility that the future would bring such a host of discriminatory practices and affirming decisions that the new institutions would come to embody a codification of new discrimination.

Before taking up the task of looking at what has since happened, it is well to restate what was said in the preface as to the limited focus of this study. It is an empirical study of policy formulation. It is concerned only with examining two decades of efforts by free world governments, as a matter of major calculated policy, to make imports from certain geographic

---

[27] This free trade area, customs union, article (Art. XXIV) also exempted from the nondiscriminatory rule advantages accorded by any contracting party to adjacent countries in order to facilitate frontier traffic.

[28] Throughout this study, as has become the general custom, the expression "contracting parties" is written with capitals "C" and "P" when used in the collective sense of the contracting parties acting jointly.

areas easier or less costly than imports from other regions, with the explicit aim of accomplishing thereby some other important and explicit policy objective. All of the adjectives are important. Thus, my concern is limited to discrimination as among nations, not as among commodities or services even though any import restriction, other perhaps than a uniform ad valorem duty on all products from all sources, involves discrimination among nations.[29] At times this "incidental" discrimination can be important. In the early post-war years it was a common practice to restrict imports of what officials regarded as "non-essentials" more severely than those of "essentials." Certain countries—Italy for a time was an example—which numbered among their major exports such items as fresh fruits, wines, and handmade goods, thus suffered a form of discrimination. In recent years much attention has been paid to the fact that in the more industrialized countries duties often go up as the degree of processing increases. Such practices bear with particular severity on the exports of the less-developed countries.[30] Important as this was, and is, to the latter, it falls outside the terms of reference of this study, for it was not a conscious, intended policy of those imposing these restrictions to discriminate against *particular* foreign sources. Rather it was to protect certain domestic producers from foreign competition, no matter what the source, and the discrimination was incidental, though important. Also excluded from this study is any systematic concern with the mechanics of discrimination. Similarly, no effort has been made to provide a catalog of all

[29] See Meade, *Theory of International Economic Policy,* Vol. I, *The Balance of Payments,* London, 1951, Chap. 28; and League of Nations Economic Committee, *The Most-Favoured-Nation Clause.*

[30] For a recent, critical look at the extent to which both tariff and non-tariff import restrictions seem to bear especially heavily on the less-developed countries, even when they are not discriminatory in the sense used here, see the report prepared by the United Nations Bureau of General Economic Research and Policies for the 1964 United Nations Conference on Trade and Development. UN, *Doc. E/Conf. 46/6,* 14 Feb. 1964. See also the United Nations *World Economic Survey, 1962, Part 1,* New York, 1963, the Chapter, "Expansion of Markets for Exports of Manufactures from Developing Countries."

discriminatory acts,[31] for our interest is in the use of discrimination as a major policy tool, a tool to help achieve some other major policy objective. Finally, the study is limited to policy with respect to imports and to relations among the so-called free-market economies. To examine export discrimination, discrimination within the so-called controlled-market economies, and between the controlled-market economies and the rest of the world are major studies in themselves. Even such limiting of the field of inquiry leaves a vast area to cover.

---

[31] Several of the interesting, more or less traditional, specific violations of most-favored-nation commitments that have periodically occupied the Contracting Parties to the GATT, are described by I. B. Kravis, in his *Domestic Interests and International Obligations,* Philadelphia, 1963, pp. 121–29.

CHAPTER II

Discrimination for Balance of Payments Reasons

INTRODUCTION

S INCE 1945, balance of payments difficulties, cum inconverti-bility, have been the least contested justification for dis-crimination.[1] Quantitative trade and monetary restrictions and exchange controls—the favorite devices for implementing bal-ance of payments discrimination—enjoyed great popularity in World War I and in Europe in the 1930's. Discrimination is almost always a by-product of the use of such instruments,[2] but

[1] It is not necessary in this chapter to make any general distinction between developed and underdeveloped countries. The International Monetary Fund Articles of Agreement make no such distinction. The General Agreement does have separate provisions (notably Art. XVIII) and the new (1965) Chapter entitled "Trade and Development," for dealing with some of the particular problems of nations in the "early stages of development." So far as *discrimination* for balance of payments reasons is concerned, however, the provisions in the GATT are essentially the same for both groups. The major difference is that, especially after the 1955 revisions, the GATT specifically recognizes that balance of payments difficulties tend to be generated by economic development efforts. It follows that the balance of payments case for imposing quantitative restrictions can be honored for a longer time in countries undergoing economic development than in others. While this carries no special authorization for applying such restrictions in a discriminatory manner, in practice other countries being adversely affected have been less critical of the discriminatory activities of the less-developed countries than they were of others. For an official statement of the GATT provisions, and their implementation as they affect the less-developed countries, see GATT, *The Role of GATT in Relation to Trade and Development,* Geneva, March 1964. (Throughout this study publications by the Contracting Parties to the General Agreement on Tariffs and Trade are referred to simply as publications by GATT.)

The theme of the 1964 United Nations Conference on Trade and Development was that many of the established commercial policy rules and practices needed to be changed in order to facilitate the economic growth of the less-developed areas. The role of discrimination in this is the subject of Chapter VII below.

[2] The Economic Committee of the League of Nations reported in 1936 that "no system has been discovered by which quotas can be allocated

22

in most of the inter-war period the purpose of the restrictions was more to provide protection to domestic industries, to advance self-sufficiency, to maintain an overvalued exchange rate (to "correct" a "short run" deterioration in the balance of payments), and to help implement government "planning" activities than to *discriminate* because of balance of payments difficulties.[3] There was relatively little in the pre-war literature defending, or even discussing, discrimination on balance of payments grounds.

THE PROBLEM FORESEEN

When the Articles of Agreement of the International Monetary Fund and the Charter for the International Trade Organizations were being negotiated, however, this question was much discussed. The chief architects of these accords: White, Keynes, Wilcox, Razminsky, Hawkins, Robbins, were convinced by the considerations outlined in Chapter I that over the long-run the world's economic welfare would be furthered by a general policy of nondiscrimination. Thus, not only do members of the Fund commit themselves to a policy of currency convertibility and the abandonment of exchange controls, but one of the major provisions specifies that its members should not engage in discriminatory currency arrangements. One of the chief reasons for permitting access to the Fund's resources is to help members meet balance of payments problems without recourse to such practices. The cornerstone of the GATT—

---

without injuring the interests of countries entitled to benefit under the most-favoured-nation clause." League of Nations, Economic Committee, *The Most-Favoured-Nation Clause,* Geneva, 1936, p. 14. Gerard Curzon states that "experience by the end of the Thirties showed that quantitative limitations on trade could not be applied in a non-discriminatory way." Gerard Curzon, *Multilateral Commercial Diplomacy,* London, 1965, p. 130.

[3] See International Monetary Fund, *First Annual Report on Exchange Restrictions,* Washington, D.C., 1950, pp. 1–44. This report also gives an excellent and authoritative account of the various devices used for restricting trade and payments. See also, Heinrich Heuser, *Control of International Trade,* London, 1939; H. J. Tasca, *World Trading Systems,* Paris, 1939; League of Nations, *Commercial Policy in the Inter-War Period,* Geneva, 1942; and F. A. Haight, *French Import Quotas, A New Instrument of Commercial Policy,* London, 1935.

which incorporates most of the commercial provisions of the ill-fated ITO—is that the contracting parties shall conduct their trade with each other on a nondiscriminatory basis. Not only does Article I of the General Agreement provide for general most-favored-nation treatment, but Article XI commits the members to the general elimination of quantitative restrictions, the handmaiden of discrimination.

It was found in negotiating these provisions, however, that while most believed, or at least would agree, that the abandonment of exchange controls and quantitative restrictions were proper long-term objectives, they were convinced that this would not do for the immediate post-war years. At the war's end they correctly anticipated facing acute balance of payments problems arising from accumulated domestic demands; productive capacities reduced below pre-war levels as regards both quality and quantity of production; a pattern of market demand for imports which did not coincide with what was regarded by many governments as socially desirable; depleted international reserves; the inconvertibility of many of the currencies they held or would earn; and disjointed or fractured international cost-price relationships. They insisted that in trying to resolve these many problems they could not rely only on changes in the exchange rate (for many, the problem for some time was the availability of supplies for export, not prices), or on monetary and fiscal policy, or employment policies—which most believed were too slow in making their effects felt or were politically unacceptable. They concluded that they must have in their arsenal the right to continue to use, or in some instances to introduce, exchange controls and quantitative restrictions.[4]

Permeating this concern with their short-run balance of

[4] The General Agreement also has other exceptions to the general prohibition of quantitative restrictions. Included are the well-established exceptions to cover matters of public morals, prison-made goods, arms, etc. (Arts. XX and XXI). In addition to the provisions authorizing direct controls to assist in economic development efforts (Art. XVIII), the most important provides that if a nation is restricting its domestic production or marketing of agricultural goods in order to support farm income, it may use quantitative restrictions to restrict imports to the same degree. These do not interest us here, for there is no provision authorizing such restrictions to be applied in a discriminatory manner.

payments problems was the then widely held belief that for a long—perhaps indefinite—period the United States would tend to run a large surplus in its international accounts. During the war years and immediately thereafter most thought this was likely to result from the United States so mismanaging its domestic affairs as to suffer a more or less persistent depression. It was not long, however, until many held the view that there were other, more structural, forces at work which, given employment, fiscal, and exchange rate policies that were highly valued, would result in other countries facing a chronic dollar shortage.[5] As a consequence, most governments anticipated that it might be quite some time before they could make their currencies convertible into dollars or gold.

Out of the fact of widespread nonconvertibility in the 1940's and this fear of continued nonconvertibility, a new and powerful case for discrimination developed. Accepting that a fixed exchange rate system had been selected; accepting that nations do find it "necessary" to impose restrictions on imports for balance of payments reasons;[6] accepting that many of the currencies earned in international trade, or borrowed, or held in reserve, are inconvertible; accepting too, as it generally was, initially at least, by those responsible for determining policy that the supply (earnings plus borrowings) of hard, or convertible currencies is otherwise determined—accepting all this, to insist on nondiscrimination would be to reduce trade below what it could otherwise be among the nonconvertible (soft) currency countries without thereby expanding it with hard currency areas.[7] This is so, because if country C has, compared to

[5] Two of the most extended discussions of the "chronic dollar shortage" thesis are given in Charles Kindleberger, *The Dollar Shortage*, New York, 1950; and G. D. A. MacDougall, *The World Dollar Problem*, London, 1957.

[6] That is, nations had chosen for reasons satisfactory to themselves that this was preferable to changing the exchange rate or pursuing deflationary domestic policies, or borrowing abroad.

[7] The most important, early theoretical demonstration that under some circumstances discrimination would involve less reduction of trade than nondiscrimination was R. Frisch, "On the Need for Forecasting a Multilateral Balance of Payments," *American Economic Review*, Sept. 1947, pp. 535–51.

demand for it, a relatively small supply of the hard currency of country A (dollars) and a relatively large supply of the soft currency of country B (sterling and most other non-dollar currencies) then a nondiscriminatory policy, requiring that the restrictions against imports from B be as severe as those against imports from A, would prevent C buying some goods from B which it wanted and which B was prepared to sell. But it would not thereby permit any increase in C's purchases from A because B's currency could not be spent in A.[8]

THE ARRANGEMENTS MADE

In recognition of these considerations, the Fund Articles of Agreement (Article XIV) provides a period of grace, then assumed to be no longer than five years but whose duration was not specified, during which members could maintain and adapt restrictions, including discriminatory ones, on international payments. Members were obliged to "have continuous regard" in their policies to the objective of achieving nondiscriminatory payments arrangements and were to withdraw these restrictions "as soon as conditions permit." [9] Any member keeping such restrictions after 1952 was required to consult periodically with the Fund "as to their further retention"; if the Fund found the member persisting in maintaining restrictions not justified

---

[8] See Clair Wilcox, *A Charter for World Trade,* New York, 1949, pp. 88–90. Little if any attention was given at this time to the case for discrimination increasing the level of world trade even if all currencies were convertible, but there were some surplus and some deficit nations. This was to come later, see below, pp. 49ff.

On consumption-effect grounds, the case for discrimination in these years was often stated as follows: If, in C, the spread between cost and marginal utility of a dollar spent on imports from B is greater than for a dollar spent on domestically produced substitutes, this trade should be permitted for it will increase welfare. The fact that the spread between cost and marginal utility of a dollar spent on imports from A is greater than either of the other two, does not argue for stopping the B-C trade so long as the dollar spent in B or C cannot be spent in A. This, of course, assumes that increased imports by C from B have no adverse effects on C's or B's exports to A.

[9] That is, when they found themselves, without such restrictions, able to settle their balance of payments without "unduly" encumbering their access to the Fund's resources.

by the conditions, that member could be required to withdraw from the Fund. Once a country had elected to make its currency convertible (to be governed by Fund Article VIII) it could engage in discriminatory arrangements only if it received prior approval from the Fund in each case.[10]

The provisions finally incorporated in the General Agreement (first in the International Trade Organization Charter) are corresponding but more complex in their details. They reflect the often bitter disputes between those, frequently led by the United States, who wanted to minimize the rights of participants to use discriminatory quantitative restrictions and those, including the United Kingdom and several of the West European participants, who were greatly worried about their dollar difficulties and their problems of reconstruction and who sought great latitude in the use of all kinds of controls, including quantitative restrictions, and in their discriminatory application.[11]

After committing itself in general to the elimination of quantitative restrictions, a participant was authorized (in Article XII) to use them "in order to safeguard its external financial

[10] The Fund also includes the famous Article VII "Scarce Currency" clause which provides that if a member runs such a surplus in its international transactions that the Fund's ability to supply its currency to other members is threatened, then the Fund may declare that currency "scarce"; this action authorizes other nations to discriminate against that country's exports. The "Scarce Currency" provision reflected the fear in 1944 that the United States would suffer a depression which would threaten the balance of payments position of other countries. It was hoped that this threat of discrimination would induce the United States to take action to prevent such a shortage from developing. It supported the principle that responsibility for correcting an international disequilibrium must be borne by creditors as well as debtors. The clause has not yet been invoked, and it is therefore of no further interest to us here. As noted below, it was referred to in the 1955 effort to extend "approved" discrimination to cases of balance of payments difficulties when currencies were convertible. For a discussion of this clause, see W. M. Scammell, *International Monetary Policy*, London, 1961 edition, pp. 139, 162–66; E. M. Bernstein, "Scarce Currencies and the International Monetary Fund," *The Journal of Political Economy*, March 1945; and Roy Harrod, *The Life of John Maynard Keynes*, London, 1951, pp. 543–48, 571–72.

[11] See Wilcox, *Charter for World Trade*, pp. 45ff.

27

position and its balance of payments. . . ." But these can be no more than necessary "to forestall the imminent threat of, or to stop, a serious decline in its monetary reserves," or to achieve "a reasonable rate of increase" in them.[12] The signatories agreed to accept the Fund's determination as to whether these conditions were met.[13]

They also agreed to the general principle that these quantitative restrictions would be applied on a nondiscriminatory basis.[14] But in recognition of the fact that with some major trading currencies inconvertible nondiscrimination probably would contract rather than expand trade that was otherwise desirable, the Contracting Parties were specifically permitted during the "transitional period" [15] to discriminate in the application of the authorized quantitative restrictions.

[12] In recognition that such an international reserve situation could easily result from domestic policies outside the purview of either the Fund or the Contracting Parties, each contracting party undertook in applying such restrictions to pay "due regard" to the need for maintaining or restoring equilibrium in its balance of payments "on a sound and lasting basis and to the desirability of avoiding an uneconomic employment of productive resources," and to avoid unnecessary damage to the economic interests of other countries.

[13] This important role given to the Fund was not unrelated to the fact that the United States had a particularly large voice in the Fund. See Wilcox, *Charter for World Trade*, p. 45.

[14] Article XIII. Even when not intended, as we noted above, quantitative restrictions almost always have some discriminatory effects. In an attempt to minimize these, this Article also spells out the practices contracting parties should follow in applying them, a prominent place being given to the use of global quotas and to the allocation of quotas on a "representative period" basis, due account being taken of "special factors." Though not part of the text, these "special factors" were understood to include such phenomena as changes in relative efficiencies and the development of new capacities to export. See GATT, *Analytical Index of the General Agreement*, Revised, Geneva, 1959, p. 62. For a discussion of some of the post-war problems of trying to apply quantitative restrictions on a nondiscriminatory basis, see GATT, *Liberating World Trade*, Geneva, June 1950. Since our concern is with discrimination as a conscious policy, not with incidental discrimination, we will not concern ourselves further with this problem.

[15] Defined as the period during which the contracting parties were availing themselves of the transitional period (Art. XIV) of the Fund or

Although the short-run case for discrimination under conditions of nonconvertibility was strong, it was feared by many that it might be costly to economic welfare over the longer-run. The danger most commonly seen at that time was that the more extensive the discrimination and the longer it lasted the greater the risk that those whose markets were thus protected would develop vested interests in a continuation of discrimination after the original justification for it had disappeared. Less concern was shown over the possible effects on hard currency exports. Efforts to establish rules for limiting both the scope and duration of the approved discrimination led to prolonged hassling, and, in the end, to a complex set of options and rules that permitted great freedom. A nation could choose the "Havana Option" and discriminate in its use of quantitative restrictions imposed for balance of payments reasons, in a manner having an equivalent effect to exchange restrictions which they might be applying under Article XIV of the Fund's Articles of Agreement [16]—which Article in turn includes no precise rules on this matter. In addition, they could also apply, and adapt to changing circumstances, any other discriminatory balance of payments import restrictions they were applying on March 1, 1948.[17] Alternatively, a nation could choose the so-called "Geneva Option" (or "Annex J"). This was more specific and stated that a participant could discriminate "to the extent necessary to obtain additional imports above the maximum total of imports" which it could "afford" had it not discriminated.[18]

This option further specified that the prices paid for such imports should not be "substantially" above those for comparable goods regularly available from other countries and that any excess be progressively reduced, that the discriminatory

---

analogous provisions in special exchange arrangements which were made with non-Fund members; that is, when their currencies were not convertible.

[16] Or analogous obligations in special exchange arrangements which were made if the country were not a member of the Fund.

[17] *General Agreement*, Art. XIV, 1(b) and 1(c).

[18] This last option was primarily designed to accommodate the Sterling Area countries.

arrangements should not divert exports away from markets where they could normally earn hard currency, and that the discrimination should not cause unnecessary damage to the commercial and economic interests of other nations.

Although a great deal of time had been spent in securing agreement on these alternative provisions, and nations did elect to be subjected to one or the other of them, in practice it made little if any difference in the policies followed or in the reactions of others which option applied. In 1955, therefore, it was agreed that these various options should be dropped and a single, more simple criteria (very similar to the Havana Option) established: namely, discriminatory application of quantitative restrictions would be permitted if the country would have been permitted to discriminate in a similar way by the International Monetary Fund had they chosen to use exchange rather than trade restrictions.[19]

The important fact was that the "rules" in the Fund and the GATT on discrimination for balance of payments purposes left great latitude to the nations concerned.[20] Each had, however, taken a general commitment not to discriminate and those who did were subject to provisions requiring periodic reporting, review, and consultation with the Fund and the Contracting Parties to determine if they were still justified. This reporting and consultation requirement proved to be an important means whereby pressure was applied and considerations raised, which helped hasten the end of this particular type of discrimination.

For several reasons the International Monetary Fund was to play the prominent role in the consultations. Its "findings" on the financial aspects of the justification for such restrictions (whether discriminatory or not) had to be accepted by the Contracting Parties. Trade restrictions and exchange controls

---

[19] See GATT, *Basic Instruments and Selected Documents, Third Supplement,* Geneva, 1955, pp. 176–78, for discussion of the changes made in 1955.

[20] They did not even formally specify that nonconvertibility of the major currencies earned was a necessary condition for balance of payments discrimination. This was, however, generally understood to be a requirement.

are often alternative devices for implementing a stated policy,[21] and, as we have just noted, the General Agreement, having been negotiated after the Fund Agreement was accepted, specifically states that the Contracting Parties may discriminate in their trade in a manner having an equivalent effect to that being condoned by the Fund. Finally, as events were to prove, only the Fund had a large enough professional staff to adequately prepare for the consultations. It soon developed that a common practice was for the Fund to supply the Contracting Parties the results of its consultations with the concerned countries, together with background materials prepared for these consultations. Indeed, it was not long before the Contracting Parties would hold consultations with the individual countries only if the Fund were ready to participate and for these GATT consultations in large measure to duplicate those held earlier, and in greater detail, by the Fund.[22]

[21] While quantitative import restrictions and parallel exchange allocations were the major tools for discrimination, much the same discriminatory effects could be, and sometimes were, obtained via such cost or price devices as multiple currency practices and disorderly cross rates. These latter financial tools were extremely complicated and had other consequences, too. They have not been carefully investigated in the preparation of this study because it is believed any discriminatory effects as between geographic areas were largely incidental and, where discrimination by source rather than commodity was intended, they do not seem to have raised important problems of discrimination other than those considered here.

[22] See GATT, *Basic Instruments and Selected Documents, Second Supplement,* Geneva, 1956, pp. 33–34. For an official discussion of the Fund's role in the GATT consultations, see International Monetary Fund, *Third Annual Report on Exchange Restrictions,* Washington, D.C., 1952, pp. 9–13, and *Fourth Annual Report on Exchange Restrictions,* Washington, D.C., 1953, Chap. 2, Sec. 1. For a less guarded statement showing that the Contracting Parties were sometimes resentful of the dominant role of the Fund, see GATT, *Doc. L/189,* 12 April 1954, and GATT, *Basic Instruments and Selected Documents, Third Supplement,* pp. 195–205. One of the reasons the Fund asked that its yearly consultations be continued after its members made their currencies convertible was that it would facilitate its work with the Contracting Parties. See International Monetary Fund, *Twelfth Annual Report on Exchange Restrictions,* Washington, D.C., 1961, p. 4.

THE BENEFITS ACHIEVED

For several years after the end of World War II most nations of the free world did discriminate for balance of payments reasons.[23] Although imports from many countries were often subject to such discrimination, especially as a consequence of the vast network of bilateral (and intra-Sterling Area) payments and trade agreements which had their roots in the 1930's and which had flowered during and just after the war,[24] quantitatively much the most important was that directed against the so-called Dollar Area.[25] By 1963 only a tiny part of international trade was being subjected to discrimination for these reasons.[26] The question of central interest is why this change came about.

[23] Details on the practices of individual nations may most conveniently be found in the regular International Monetary Fund, *Annual Report on Exchange Restrictions,* and in the periodic reports during the 1950's of the GATT, entitled *Report on the Discriminatory Application of Import Restrictions,* and the GATT's *International Trade* annual. Here we are concerned with the development of policies and doctrines, not with detailing the practices or particular methods of individual countries.

[24] For a discussion of the evolution and nature of these arrangements see Raymond F. Mikesell, *Foreign Exchange in the Postwar World,* New York, 1954, Part I.

[25] The list of countries considered as belonging to this Area differed somewhat from country to country, but for most during the 1940's and 1950's it included the United States, Canada, Belgium, Colombia, Costa Rica, Cuba, the Dominican Republic, Ecuador, El Salvador, Guatemala, Haiti, Honduras, Liberia, Mexico, Nicaragua, Panama, the Philippines, and Venezuela.

[26] Here we are concerned with discriminatory import and payments restrictions applied for balance of payments reasons, but it must be noted that restrictions—often discriminatory—have also been applied to *exports,* though far less extensively than to imports.

These discriminatory export restrictions have frequently been applied for strategic reasons: to curtail trade which it was believed, on balance, would increase the relative military strength of a potential enemy. In this category falls much of the export controls on East-West trade. Discriminatory export controls have also sometimes been used in an attempt to increase the internal difficulties of politically unfriendly nations, a recent case being United States restrictions on exports to Cuba. Restrictions on exports were also sometimes applied among

Let it be stressed at the outset that most of the explanation is to be found in the fact that during this period production and productivity increased throughout the world. The discrepancies between the relative prices and relative costs which were so prevalent in the early post-war years were greatly reduced. Internal measures restraining, though usually not eliminating, inflation were taken in most countries. Exchange rates were altered so that by the early 1960's for most countries they reflected with acceptable accuracy the relative demands for traded goods at the ruling prices. The private financial system and the International Monetary Fund provided more international reserves and credit. The United States replaced a large surplus with substantial deficits. All of these changes resulted in most of the industrialized nations at least finding their balance of payments at, or close to, what the authorities regarded as a tolerable balance, and their international reserve positions greatly improved. This permitted many to make their currencies convertible, including those widely used in international transactions. Once this happened, much of the justification for balance of payments discrimination disappeared.

Did the policy of discrimination contribute to the economic well-being of those practicing it and to this improvement in their international economic environment, which in turn removed this particular basis for discrimination? Both the levels of internal

---

politically friendly nations, especially in the early post-war years. Here the main purposes were: (1) to apply pressure on another country to buy your less-wanted exports; (2) to force another nation to sell you much-wanted goods; (3) by placing restrictions on exports of raw materials to protect or promote a domestic fabricating industry, either by granting a price advantage to that industry on the purchase of its raw materials or by reducing the supply of raw materials available to foreign competitors; and, finally (4) to improve the nation's terms of trade by reducing price competition among the country's exporters. For all practical purposes these practices were contrary to commitments under the General Agreement, but they do not seem to have been a major and continuing problem. The Contracting Parties to the GATT made a study of them in 1950, but at later sessions the topic was assigned a progressively lower priority and was not pursued. See GATT, *The Use of Quantitative Restrictions for Protective and Other Commercial Purposes,* Geneva, July 1950, pp. 5–9.

economic activity and the pattern of international trade were subject to so many other powerful influences in these years of great change that a confident answer is not possible. Still, the available evidence indicates that discrimination did for a time make at least a small contribution to each.[27] The GATT consultations in the early 1950's showed that governments believed (supporting quantitative evidence was not provided) the discriminatory application of import restrictions had, as expected, resulted in some trade that would not otherwise have taken place and that, *for a time at least,* this was not at the expense of exports to other countries. This additional exchange —additional over what was believed achievable under what most governments considered the only real alternative: the same exchange rate and domestic employment policies but import restrictions applied in a nondiscriminatory fashion— led to direct improvements in economic welfare. It probably also resulted in some increase in production, and possibly productivity, since there then were unemployed resources in most of these countries that were used to provide the goods for trade which discrimination made possible. In practice, the discrimination also probably resulted in many countries diverting some of their imports and so curtailing their hard currency expenditures even more than they would have under a nondiscriminatory system. So long as hard currency exports were not thereby adversely affected and so long as incomes, and so savings, were going up this permitted an increase in the hard currency holdings of the countries—a precedent condition in most of them for adopting more liberal trade and payments policies.

From the point of view of many governments another great benefit of discrimination in the early post-war years was that it permitted them to make many of the adjustments called for by the war and early post-war changes in their comparative advantages, without suffering either the reduced level of economic ac-

---

[27] The evidence relied upon here is primarily material in the GATT archives, which are not open to direct citation or quotation. Much of the same conclusions, however, emerge from a reading of the periodic GATT, *Report on the Discriminatory Application of Import Restrictions,* noted above.

tivity that they feared—almost pathologically—the full blast of competition from the Dollar Area would mean, or the sharper devaluations that might otherwise have been necessary. It is not clear from the available record that the total economic cost of adjustments made more rapidly would have been larger than those that discrimination permitted to be made more slowly, but the political costs of the former were probably more than most governments could survive. Neither is there sufficient evidence to be confident that the cost to countries in a deterioration of their terms of trade from a sharper devaluation would have been greater than the real costs of high and discriminatory import restrictions. But after the 1949 devaluations the ability of most governments to gradually restore their international competitive position at least strongly suggests that larger devaluations was not clearly a better solution.

Although the available evidence is particularly flimsy—being largely statements by government officials unsupported by other evidence—I have concluded that the shelter provided by the discriminatory restrictions gave officials some much-needed assurances that their balance of payments positions were, at least for a time, "under their control." The restrictions thus provided the oft-referred to "breathing spell," and this was used not just to postpone indefinitely adjustments that would otherwise have had to be made more quickly although there was some of that, too. The time was also frequently used for reforming internal monetary and fiscal policies which subsequently eased a nation's international economic position, permitting, finally, the dismantling of at least part of the discriminatory apparatus. Important in preventing a misuse of the time provided was the fact that under the Fund-GATT system those who did discriminate had periodically to explain why they continued to maintain discriminatory controls and what measures were being taken to remove the need for them.[28]

---

[28] For the text of the information requested for the GATT consultations see, for example, GATT, *Basic Instruments and Selected Documents, Fourth Supplement*, Geneva, 1956, pp. 44–46. The agenda for these consultations changed from time to time, but this is a representative one. The Monetary Fund has not published a similar agenda for its

SOME COSTS PAID

Whatever the contributions of discrimination, once those practicing it found that their internal and external economic position had greatly improved, few believed that continued discrimination was needed to maintain the new situation. On the other hand, virtually all observers became more and more impressed with the costs, and so the pressures for abandoning the practice mounted. The costs took many forms.

Those discriminated against saw themselves paying a price in terms of foregone sales each day the practices continued.[29] They often complained, even when acknowledging that the effects were the "approved" ones—certain commodities or services were discriminated against but the total level of exports was not thereby reduced. At no time, so far as I could find, did those practicing discrimination argue, as they were soon so often to do in defending their discrimination under the regional economic blocs, that the noted beneficial effects of the policy on their level of real income would result in at least partially offsetting gains in exports by those discriminated against. The explanation for the failure to stress this point probably lies in the fact that the effects on income levels of balance of payments types of discrimination were not all that important; and, also, any growth effects on imports often were dampened by the reluctance of the authorities to grant additional import licenses because they wished to protect their own producers and international reserves. In any case, the theory regarding these "dynamic effects" aspects of discrimination had not yet become a familiar tool to most government policy makers. Moreover, for those discriminated against, it was easy to know what was happening to particular exports and hard to know what might otherwise have been or to trace out generalized growth effects.

consultations, but it is common knowledge that typically these explored every important aspect of the nation's policy that had an impact on its international financial position.

[29] In the available recorded discussions the "costs" to those discriminated against were only rarely expressed in terms of the effects of discrimination on their subsequent ability to import or on their terms of trade.

Those discriminated against therefore conducted, in bilateral discussions and international meetings, especially those of the Contracting Parties to the GATT,[30] a relentless campaign for the reduction and the elimination of the practice.[31] The United States and Canada often took the lead in the multilateral discussions, but they were usually joined by many soft currency countries who were being discriminated against by others' bilateral agreements, and some of them by the OEEC trade liberalization procedures.[32] They usually presented their "case" in terms both of the general obligations of others to provide most-favored-nation treatment and the specific damage being caused particular firms or industries. Those doing the discriminating were thus placed on the defensive in matters of principle and concrete action.

Appearing regularly on the consultation agenda were the items "alternative measures to restore equilibrium" and "steps taken to avoid unnecessary damage [to others]." These questions, plus the fact that the GATT consultations and reviews were annual, meant that those discriminating could not easily rest their defense on broad, general answers but were under pressure to give an accounting of the particular steps they had taken, or if not, why not, since the last confrontation, to reduce the burden they were placing on others. And those complaining were usually well informed and seasoned spokesmen for

[30] Bilateral discussions were often held against the background of previous GATT consultations. Sometimes a government would raise the matter in the sessions of the GATT precisely because it had been unable to get satisfaction in its bilateral discussions and hoped for additional support from other contracting parties.

[31] This is not to suggest that redress was always sought by the aggrieved. Many times it was decided to say nothing. See Raymond Vernon, *America's Foreign Trade Policy and the GATT,* Essays in International Finance, Princeton University, 1954, p. 17.

[32] See, for example, Australia's statement in GATT, *Press Release Spec. (59) 237,* 28 Oct. 1959; and GATT, *International Trade 1955,* Geneva, 1956, p. 188. Members of the outer Sterling Area found especially galling the frequent failure of the OEEC countries to extend to them all of the intra-OEEC trade and payments liberalization measures, even though the former's currencies were freely transferable with those of the latter via the United Kingdom's participation in the EPU.

their own countries' interests. The discussions became increasingly blunt; advice as to reforms came more frequently and with greater specificity. The willingness of most to quietly acquiesce in discrimination against themselves declined as the balance of payments position of others improved and their reserves increased, and, as after the late 1958 convertibility moves, the *composition* of a country's reserves became a matter of less concern.[33]

Although the point must not be pressed, an important cost of discrimination therefore was the necessity of reporting on it and defending it periodically in semi-public forums before an essentially hostile audience of *many* governments, not just one or two, as in the old days of bilateral accords. It was costly not only in terms of time and effort, but perhaps more important, in terms of the embarrassment of having many members of the "club"—professional colleagues—charge that another member was not living up to some of its international commitments.[34] Another cost that seemed to become heavier as the years went by was the sheer expense of administering the controls and, though it too can easily be overemphasized, the cost represented by the incentive such controls gave to corruption amongst those responsible for administering them.

[33] The full flavor of these consultations can only be obtained from the unpublished records of the oral discussions, but an indication of their intense and blunt nature in two particular instances involving quantitative restrictions, some intentionally discriminatory and some not, is given in the published reports of the GATT discussions of the German and Belgian import restrictions during the last half of the 1950's and the early 1960's. These may be found in the *Fifth* through the *Tenth Supplement* of the GATT, *Basic Instruments and Selected Documents*. The German case is analyzed in some detail in Curzon, *Multilateral Commercial Diplomacy*, pp. 146–55.

The cost to those discriminated against received a great deal of attention in the meetings of the Contracting Parties to the GATT. This aspect of the question was given but little attention by the Monetary Fund; there the emphasis was on the cost to the country practicing discrimination.

[34] See GATT, *GATT In Action*, Geneva, Jan. 1952, p. 14 (mimeographed edition). This point is also made by Curzon, *Multilateral Commercial Diplomacy*, p. 145.

Much more important than these costs, however, was the steadily accumulating evidence that countries practicing discrimination often for that reason paid higher prices for their imports, taking account of quality and delivery dates.[35] Most of this of course was inherent; if prices for equivalent goods were lower in the favored areas there would have been no need for discrimination. But it was also found that countries practicing discrimination often tended to drive up the prices of their imports precisely because the discrimination concentrated their demands on particular areas of supply. This presumably not only moved the producers in those areas into higher cost positions but it was also often believed that by granting such shelter to certain foreign suppliers a nation sometimes had made itself vulnerable to noncompetitive pricing practices by those suppliers.[36]

The higher prices were from the outset a matter of concern to most governments who saw them as adversely affecting their real income and worsening the soft currency portion of their balance of payments. But for a few years they were accepted without much complaint because the only alternative seemed to be policies which would reduce their hard currency reserves below the levels regarded as tolerable. Any balance above this level was already being used to purchase what they regarded as "essential" goods not available elsewhere and to buy imports of less high priority goods or services when the price discrepancies between hard and soft currency markets were especially great. But before long it became apparent to many governments that the higher prices for imports were having—or threatening to have—a damaging effect on their exports. This effect was especially strong where substantial amounts of imports were directly incorporated in the exports, but it was present in other

[35] It is interesting to recall here that a frequent argument for practicing discrimination has been that it improves one's terms of trade. But this assumes, among other things, that one does in fact still buy a good bit from those he discriminates against.

[36] I have found no convincing data that such practices were in fact widespread, or that they were not; but many believed it to be the case and this is all that was needed for another "cost" to be assigned to the policy of discrimination.

imports as well, since higher domestic prices would be expected, through the wage rate, to be reflected in the price of exports.

It was this cost of discrimination which, once reserves had increased somewhat, was the most important single consideration leading to the relaxation of balance of payments discrimination. The cost became more apparent to some nations when others reduced their restrictions and reported that they had thereby gained "substantial benefits," both from lower prices for imports and increased competitive power because of the lower prices for their exports.[37] The International Monetary Fund put particular emphasis on this aspect of discrimination since its interest was not limited to the particular problem of the adverse effects of discrimination on a specific country. Furthermore, it was also worried lest the effect of discrimination on reducing the competitive ability of its members serve to prolong conditions perpetuating discrimination, and so postpone the day when it could come into its own.[38]

As more experience was gained, many nations found that their discriminatory practices were having harmful effects on their exports in other ways, too. To the extent that they kept out goods otherwise entering, nations were protecting domestic industries; thus there was a tendency to reduce competitive ability in other markets by reducing the pressure to increase efficiency.

But the problem went beyond this. For a great many countries the degree and form of discrimination exercised was not determined unilaterally, but was mostly the result of negotiated bilateral or group arrangements. The provisions of the hundreds of bilateral agreements which characterized these

[37] See the 1953 Report on the discriminatory application of import restrictions, in GATT, *Basic Instruments and Selected Documents, Second Supplement,* pp. 33–52. See also the statement by the Government of South Africa, in GATT, *Press Release 141,* 19 Oct. 1953, in which South Africa announced that it was abandoning its discriminatory practices for the specific purpose of reducing its costs.

[38] See International Monetary Fund, *Annual Report of Executive Directors,* Washington, D.C., 1950, pp. 60–61. The Fund's *Fourth Annual Report on Exchange Restrictions,* Washington, D.C., 1953, pp. 1–22, gives an excellent account of several aspects of discrimination in the early years.

years were extremely varied because they were usually designed and later amended under the influence of conditions peculiar to the time. Few general statements can be made about them to which some exception cannot be found. Still, they usually were first negotiated between soft currency countries. They normally did include import commitments and, often, export commitments ranging from targets to quotas. The agreements were designed to encourage the partners to trade quite freely with each other in what were regarded as both essential and relatively nonessential goods, while imports from third countries were more severely restricted.[39] In addition to these bilateral trade and payments agreements there were the Sterling Area and the Organization for European Economic Cooperation (OEEC) arrangements (the EPU and the associated Code of Trade Liberalization), incorporating special facilities for payments and currency transferability among the members of each group, together with reductions in trade restrictions for members, which did not apply equally to commerce with outsiders.[40] That is, the group arrangements, too, were discriminatory, for they always involved giving some favors or opportunities to partners which were not extended to all. It needs emphasis that, although the balance of payments difficulties *cum* inconvertibility was the usual *raison d'être* offered for these group arrangements, soft currency countries often also suffered from the discrimination inherent in bilateral or regional arrangements to which they were not a party.

In the early post-war years of shortages, discrimination based

---

[39] The bilateral trade agreements were often designed originally to reinforce the bilateral payments agreements and were intended to achieve a close balance in trade so as to limit any settlement in hard currency or any great extension of credit.

The degree of freedom permitted trade with each other was usually greater as trade tended toward balance and as one partner was willing to lend to another; this willingness to lend, of course, was reflected in the size of the swing margin. See Mikesell, *Foreign Exchange in the Post-War World,* Chaps. 2, 3, and 5; and the International Monetary Fund's *Annual Report on Exchange Restrictions* during the early and mid-1950's for many details on these bilateral arrangements.

[40] Most of the regional·aspects of these latter areas are discussed at some length in the following chapter.

41

on either bilateral or larger group arrangements were found to carry an important export-competitive cost to the participants which was not present in unilaterally determined discrimination. Once a group is involved, a nation granting preferences in its import market for less-essential, higher-priced, or otherwise less-competitive goods, was tempted to ask in return that its partner deliver some more-essential (competitive) goods as well. The existence of a protective market in a partner also made it less necessary for affected producers to make the efforts to export elsewhere. Moreover, an exchange of preferences, by reducing competition, encouraged still higher prices in the countries engaging in such practices, which contributed an additional pressure for the partners to export to each other. From these tendencies followed the risk that the soft currency country's exports to hard currency countries would fall—either absolutely or relatively.[41] Yet an expansion of exports to the hard currency areas was commonly regarded by those practicing balance of payments discrimination as the preferred way of reducing their balance of payments difficulties.[42]

By 1954, when the post-war shortages had been considerably eased and the widened transferability of several of the world's major trading currencies had removed much of the original justification for bilateral agreements, it was found that the

[41] The possibility of discrimination reducing the exports of deficit countries to surplus countries was one of the major reasons James Meade found for his grave doubts that a convincing case in real life could be made for discriminatory controls as a means of restoring equilibrium, though under favorable assumptions the case for such discrimination was strong. See his *The Balance of Payments,* London, 1951, p. 416.

[42] The level of hard currency exports of any nation depends on many other things as well, including most importantly, the import policy of the hard currency countries and the availability of export supplies in the soft currency countries. The officials of many governments apparently believed that *their* hard currency sales were not in fact suffering because of *their* discriminatory policy. But when they looked at others' problems, they often saw this danger as real. This view frequently appears in the records of the plenary sessions of the Contracting Parties to the GATT. See also, GATT, *First Report on the Discriminatory Application of Import Restrictions,* Geneva, 1950, pp. 11–12.

emphasis in many bilateral agreements was changing. In particular, some partners in, bilateral agreements were using their power to control imports to insure markets for their noncompetitive exports. To the partner, this was another possibly important cost of the arrangement. To other nations, whose exports were thus discriminated against, this was an additional reason to work for the abolition of the practice, especially since some saw as an alternative their own retreat to bilateralism, previously found too costly, in order to protect their exports.[43]

Although it was apparently not a major phenomenon, there were some instances where the discrimination against dollar countries forced them to curtail their trade—still another cost of the policy. Thus, when a non-dollar country discriminated against imports from a dollar country which itself was not running a surplus and did not have what it regarded as excess reserves, that dollar country was forced to restrict its imports.[44] In this case, the balance of payments deficit of the first country, which justified the discrimination, had merely been passed on to another and the total amount of trade had not increased, as the accepted justification for balance of payments discrimination demanded.[45]

THE "INCIDENTAL PROTECTION" PROBLEM

Still other kinds of problems appeared. Experience after the war soon verified the belief, often expressed during the negotiations of the Havana Charter and the Bretton Woods Agreement, that although imposing exchange controls and quantitative import restrictions might be justifiable on balance of payments

---

[43] South Africa often complained during these years that it found discrimination costly in terms of its imports but that others, by discriminating in favor of each other, were applying great pressure on it to re-enter into discriminatory bilateral arrangements in order to protect its exports. See GATT, *International Trade, 1954,* Geneva, 1955, pp. 119ff., for some specific details on these practices.

[44] Most affected were some of the Central American nations.

[45] See International Monetary Fund, *Annual Report, 1950,* Washington, D.C., 1950, p. 61. Once again, Meade had foreseen this possibility. See his *The Balance of Payments,* pp. 412–15.

grounds, they inevitably had an "incidental" protective effect on domestic producers of substitutable products. As expected, it was found that the most common criteria used by nations in developing their import restriction schemes intended to meet balance of payments problems was to restrict imports according to the ease with which alternative domestic sources could be built up.[46] It was also found that once such a system of trade and payments restrictions existed, governments were under constant pressure from domestic producers to adapt that system to the specific objective of protecting them rather than the nation's monetary reserves. Thus new, vested interests were easily created, strengthening the forces for a continuation of the restrictions. The problem was complicated because it was difficult in fact to distinguish protectionist from balance of payments considerations, since protectionism, by its adverse effect on productivity, could be a source of balance of payments difficulties.

This protective effect was present, whether the restrictions were discriminatory or not, and most of the great concern over the so-called "trade effects" of restrictions applied for "financial" reasons was without reference to their discriminatory aspects; however, by the early 1960's most of the restrictions that remained on nonagricultural products were directed against consumer goods produced in Asia, were intentionally discriminatory, and were a part of the "market disruption" problem, to be discussed in Chapter VI. We can therefore treat briefly here a matter that became known as the "hard core" problem and that occupied much of the attention of the Contracting Parties and the Fund for several years. Although the problem was primarily one of a nation imposing the restrictions, thereby encouraging internal investment the "profitability" of which required continued protection, when the restrictions were discriminatory, they had the further effect of favoring particular exporters in third countries who thus also developed vested interests in continuing the restrictions.

It was the nations, led by the United States, whose long-term export interests were threatened, that early took the initiative in

[46] GATT, *Liberating World Trade,* Geneva, 1950, p. 23.

bringing the hard-core problem out into the open and that insisted on keeping it on the agenda of international organizations, as well as for bilateral meetings. But leaving aside the cases where governments as a matter of policy wished to use this device to encourage new investments, in which case protection was no longer "incidental," it was soon generally recognized that here was an important cost, too, to those who were applying restrictions: an inefficient use of the nation's investment resources. This latter aspect was regularly emphasized by the Fund. The former aspect received relatively more attention in the GATT.

Early discussions in both the Fund and the GATT led to the conclusion that the costs could not altogether be avoided so long as restrictions for balance of payments reasons were accepted as necessary, but they could be reduced by governments taking measures to discourage investments which needed this type of protection to survive. The Contracting Parties, therefore, specifically recommended that governments seek frequent opportunities to remind domestic producers that the balance of payments restrictions were temporary; that they frequently adjust the restrictions so as to emphasize their impermanent character; allow at least token import of goods that would otherwise be excluded for balance of payments reasons so as to keep domestic producers aware of what they must ultimately face; avoid allocating import licenses to specific countries; and avoid narrow product classifications in their restrictions.[47] The Monetary Fund strongly supported such policies.

During the early 1950's the Contracting Parties gave more and more attention to this problem. It was found that all members were in fact taking some action along the recommended lines, be it often less than those whose exports were suffering thought desirable. It was also generally agreed, however, that such measures could at best be ameliorative. Only an abandonment of the restrictions could eliminate this cost.[48] At the time of the major review of the General

[47] GATT, *The Use of Quantitative Restrictions for Protective and Other Commercial Purposes,* Geneva, July 1950, p. 12.
[48] GATT, *Third Report on the Discriminatory Application of Import Restrictions,* pp. 15–16.

45 .

Agreement on Tariffs and Trade in 1955, most observers were convinced that the balance of payments restrictions, whether discriminatory or not, had in fact encouraged a large amount of "uneconomic" investment.[49] There was also a consensus that many nations would not remove their balance of payments restrictions when the financial considerations permitted unless arrangements were made giving such industries more time to adjust before this particular shelter was removed.[50] A "hard core" waiver decision was therefore taken, which provided that even though a contracting party no longer had any financial or balance of payments justification for retaining import restrictions, it could continue to apply them to particular products for a "comparatively short period of time" (not more than five years was foreseen) if the sudden withdrawal of the protection would result in "serious injury." A country requesting a waiver was to agree to carry out such policies as would insure progressive relaxation and removal of the restrictions. The decision also specified that any such restrictions should be administered in a nondiscriminatory fashion.[51]

In the event, Belgium was the only country that came under this arrangement before it expired in 1962, and she did so reluctantly. Several other countries maintained non-tariff restrictions on imports after it was formally found they no longer had any balance of payments justification for doing so. But they did not seek to have this sanctioned under the waiver. The reasons were partly their unwillingness to commit themselves to removing the protection in the short period specified, or to do so in a nondiscriminatory way. Probably more important, as some insisted it would be when the waiver was originally debated, was

[49] I have found no underlying data either to substantiate or to disprove this.

[50] Some countries were deeply worried lest any such action weaken the entire General Agreement and merely serve to postpone the adjustment, thereby making it more difficult and less likely.

[51] The text of this 5 March 1955 decision may be found in GATT, *Basic Instruments and Selected Documents, Third Supplement,* pp. 38–41. A brief explanation of the reasons for it can be found on pp. 191–95.

the fact that the protection in question was not merely the "incidental" effect of the balance of payments restrictions but was protection that would have been provided, and justified, on other grounds, had it not been easier in the first instance to justify it under the balance of payments provisions.[52]

Be that as it may, the extended discussion after 1954 of "hard core," later referred to as "residual," restrictions, provided much evidence that barriers to trade and payments justified on balance of payments grounds, whether discriminatory or not, did frequently create conditions tending to perpetuate themselves; that these new conditions were often recognized by the country imposing them as regrettable and costly in economic efficiency terms; that the substitution of one justification for another often lead not only to formal violations of international commitments [53] but also to the questioning of the good faith of a government, with consequent burdens on international comity; and, finally, that such situations involved huge amounts of time and effort in making charges and preparing answers.[54] All of

[52] The sources for this conclusion are GATT documents not open for citation.

[53] Such violations were not uncommon after 1959 and were recognized as such in the "residual import restrictions" procedures. See, for example, GATT, *Doc. L/1470*, 10 May 1961, and *L/2014*, 19 June 1963. (The many references throughout this book to GATT, *Doc. L/1111*, etc., are to mimeographed documents in the archives of the GATT in Geneva.) See also, GATT, *Basic Instruments and Selected Documents, Ninth Supplement*, pp. 19–20, and *Eleventh Supplement*, pp. 206ff. This continuing hard core problem has been met in some cases by countries seeking a waiver under the "exceptional circumstances" provision of Article XXV of the GATT and in others by what is nothing more than a tolerated violation of its rules.

Commodities subject to such illegal import restrictions constitute what are euphemistically called in the GATT "negative lists." In 1963 the Contracting Parties expressed the hope that all of these illegal restrictions would be removed by the end of 1965. Most of the non-agricultural ones had been done away with by early 1965; those that remained were aimed chiefly at Japanese and developing nations' exports. See GATT, *Doc. L/2336* and *Corr. 1 and 2*, 1965.

[54] For more data on the Belgian case, see GATT, *Doc. L/357 Add. 1*, 10 June 1955, when Belgium gave warning that it might use the time

47

these effects constituted "costs" of the original policy; as year after year they became more obvious, they too played a role in the movement toward abandonment of discrimination.

DISCRIMINATION IMPERILS ACHIEVING CONVERTIBILITY

Another cost also emerged. By the mid-1950's some governments, most notably that of the United Kingdom, had concluded that it was in their national interests to soon move more energetically toward making their currencies convertible. Such a prospect introduced another argument for these nations to abandon discrimination: the less the discrimination before convertibility the less the adjustment process afterwards, and the easier the process of adjustment the less the risk that there would be need to retreat later. But it was not just one's own discrimination that created problems. So long as others were discriminating against hard currency countries and the rules permitting discrimination were lax, any nation moving toward convertibility ran a great risk that, for some time at least, others would "take unfair advantage" of it and discriminate against its exports in order either to accumulate more of the new hard currency or, even more worrisome, to increase their net earnings of the newly convertible currency so as to be able to exchange them for gold or dollars. After all, well-established and tested convertible currencies were more valuable than new ones. The prospect of such a "convertibility drain" could only delay the

---

provided by the waiver to find alternative measures of protection. See also, GATT, *Basic Instruments and Selected Documents, Fourth Supplement,* pp. 102ff.; *Fifth Supplement,* pp. 115ff.; *Sixth Supplement,* pp. 135ff.; *Seventh Supplement,* pp. 118ff.; *Ninth Supplement,* pp. 236ff.; *Tenth Supplement,* pp. 236ff.; and *Eleventh Supplement,* pp. 220ff. for reports on discussion by the Contracting Parties of this case.

The conclusions of the last paragraph in the text above are even more strongly supported in the treatment of the German residual import restrictions. See GATT, *Basic Instruments and Selected Documents, Eighth Supplement,* pp. 160ff.; *Ninth Supplement,* pp. 243ff.; *Tenth Supplement,* pp. 244ff.; *Eleventh Supplement,* pp. 222ff. See also, GATT, *Basic Instruments and Selected Documents, Tenth Supplement,* pp. 117ff., for a report on the Italian residual restrictions.

moves toward convertibility, yet it was generally believed that making the major currencies convertible was in the economic interests of all. So, although 1954–1955 was, in the event, too early for such moves, still another "cost" of discrimination was noted.[55]

DISCRIMINATION NEEDED TO MAINTAIN CONVERTIBILITY?

It was while arguing that discrimination was a serious impediment to moves *toward* convertibility that the United Kingdom, supported by other members of the Sterling Area, made a case at the policy formulation level for discrimination, as a last resort, to expand trade and to *maintain* convertibility in the event that a major trading nation should develop a large and continuing surplus.[56] Some argued, as they had in 1942–1944 when the Monetary Fund "scarce currency" clause was being considered, that the *authority* to discriminate against a persistent creditor, even before there was a "shortage" of his currency, was desirable because it would be an effective way of safeguard-

[55] The question of tightening the rules permitting discrimination was discussed at some length in the 1954–1955 review of the GATT but, for reasons discussed below, the majority of the Contracting Parties were not yet willing to agree to any substantial changes in the rules. See the report of the "Review" Working Party in General Agreement on Tariffs and Trade, *Basic Instruments and Selected Documents, Third Supplement,* pp. 170–79. See also, E. Wyndham White, *The Achievements of the GATT,* GATT Secretariat, Geneva, March 1957.

[56] The abstract case for discrimination when currencies were convertible but the world had both persistent debtors and creditors, had been made earlier, of course, by Marcus Fleming in his important "On Making the Best of Balance of Payments Restrictions on Imports," *Economic Journal,* March 1951; Meade, *Balance of Payments,* Chap. 30; and *Trade and Welfare,* Chap. 34. See also, D. MacDougall, *The World Dollar Problem,* Chap. 16, for a later statement of more possibilities than were actually discussed at the GATT sessions. For details on the British case and the discussion, on which these paragraphs were written, see GATT, *Docs. W9/18,* 17 Nov. 1954; *W9/22,* 19 Nov. 1954; *W9/82,* 9 Dec. 1954; *W9/136,* 7 Jan. 1955; *W9/139,* 11 Jan. 1955; and *L/325,* 16 Feb. 1955. See GATT, *Press Release 174,* 8 Nov. 1954; and GATT, *Basic Instruments and Selected Documents, Third Supplement,* pp. 174–76, for a very muted account of the discussion.

ing one's economy from deflationary tendencies abroad. This was because the threat of discrimination would apply pressure on the creditor to take such internal measures as would remove its surplus. Much more attention was given in 1955 to the thesis that if a serious and prolonged international economic disequilibrium developed, in which there was at least one major country running a surplus, the deficit nations would in fact probably choose to protect their reserves by imposing direct controls on their imports. If such restrictions were applied on a nondiscriminatory basis, the deficit nations would also be forced to restrict their imports from other deficit—or balanced—countries whose international payments problems would thereby be increased. This would call forth still further trade and payments restrictions against everyone else. The result would be larger contraction of world trade than would have been needed merely to reduce the payments to the surplus countries to a level equal to receipts from them.

But this was not all. If a serious "scarcity" of a major hard currency developed, some countries, finding themselves short of it but being unable because of nondiscrimination requirements to be especially severe in their use of it, would probably try to convert their holdings of other convertible currencies into the scarce one to a greater extent than they otherwise would have done. They would be encouraged in this by the fear that others would be doing the same thing and that therefore the convertibility of the new currency could not be sustained. It was believed that this could easily so deplete the reserves of the countries suffering the run that convertibility would have to be abandoned. Once that happened to any major currency, others would be subjected to the same forces and a "general collapse" of the international monetary system would follow.

Worried over the direct effects on its exports, the United States—the acknowledged target of the proposal—strongly opposed writing any new provisions into the international agreements permitting such discrimination. The U.S. negotiators did not deny that there might be some "theoretical validity" to the argument. They did not want to discuss that. They did assert that the issue was an "artificial" one, for no government of a major country today could survive if it permitted a prolonged and severe depression of the sort which they said had been assumed by those advocating this new discrimination. U.S. negotiators also took the position that new rules were "unnecessary," because the protection sought was already in the Monetary Fund "scarce currency clause" and the related articles of the General Agreement.[57] Finally, they insisted that the proposals were "undesirable," that they would *in practice* permit discrimination even if the scarcity arose because of mismanagement, most notably inflation or maintenance of overvalued exchange rates, in other countries. They thus interpreted what was being proposed as authority for the rest of the world to "boycott" the United States, this at a time when the balance of payments *cum* nonconvertibility case for discrimination against the dollar was daily becoming weaker. Perhaps a more telling point was the negotiators' warning that if the rules were then changed for the acknowledged purpose of permitting discrimination against the United States even when the other major trading currencies were convertible, it would be difficult to convince the American Congress that the United States should still continue a liberal trade policy. If that should happen, it could easily more than offset any increase in trade among others that the discrimination might bring about.[58]

The sponsors acknowledged that the United States was not likely to suffer another severe and prolonged depression, but they said it could not be ruled out, that it was surely prudent to provide in advance for possibilities which, if they should come about, could have such severe consequences. Moreover, it was asserted, some of the internal opposition to making other currencies convertible could be more easily overcome if this safeguard were present. Other countries also had less confidence than the United States that the Fund "scarce currency" clauses were adequate. In part, this was because of doubt that

[57] Art. XIV, 5(a).

[58] Although looked at from a different angle, the importance of selecting the "right" countries to discriminate against if discrimination with convertibility were to maximize trade is emphasized by Meade. In practice, the difficulty of making such a selection constitutes for him a major reason for doubting the efficacy of discrimination under these conditions. Meade, *Balance of Payments,* Chap. 30.

the United States, which possessed so many votes in the Fund, could in fact vote for a decision that entailed discrimination against her. Partly, it was because they foresaw that there could be a "scarcity" of dollars in the sense discussed above, even though the Fund's holdings were not scarce simply because, for one reason or another, members chose not to borrow from the Fund, or the Fund found good reasons not to lend.

They also acknowledged that a "scarce currency" situation might arise because of inflation in the deficit areas and asserted that in this case the appropriate remedy would not. be discrimination against the creditor but deflationary policies, or exchange rate alterations, in the deficit countries.[59] But, they said, the cause of the scarcity, should it develop, would have to be determined at the time, and if the responsibility were found to lie in the surplus country then discrimination might be the best of all the available alternatives.

It did not prove possible to reach an agreement and, in the end, rather than exacerbate what was becoming a serious division among the governments concerned, the matter was left suspended. In the decade since, apparently no one has pressed this case for discrimination.[60] The official reports on the discussion, however, created a record which will permit the matter to be raised again should a "world shortage" of some major currency develop.[61]

[59] They did not argue the case that Fleming had made in the earlier cited 1951 *Economic Journal* piece, that if they for whatever reason chose not to follow these policies, there would still be a case (be it a second-best one) for discrimination against the surplus countries.

[60] The only exception seems to be the understanding reached by the Contracting Parties to the GATT that if a country still had balance of payments problems and was still imposing some discriminatory restrictions after the 1958 convertibility moves, it was not expected to achieve nondiscrimination by *re-imposing* some restrictions against those who had been treated more favorably than others up to then. It was understood that when such a country's balance of payments position permitted it to remove restrictions, it was expected to do so in a manner reducing discrimination.

[61] GATT, *Basic Instruments and Selected Documents, Third Supplement,* pp. 174–76.

WHY DID IT TAKE SO LONG TO ABANDON DISCRIMINATION?

By the mid-1950's the balance of payments positions of most countries had greatly improved, reducing much of the need for quantitative restrictions against imports.[62] A large amount of transferability, if not formal convertibility, of the world's major trading currencies had been achieved, which removed much of the justification for the discriminatory application of those import and payments restrictions that remained.[63] Moreover, as both the internal and external economic and financial position of most nations eased, government authorities in many countries began for the first time to seriously examine their discriminatory policies, usually begun in the harassed days of the war and early post-war chaos and often by other governments than themselves. When they did, they became more conscious of the many costs of discrimination discussed above.

Very modest moves toward a general relaxation of balance of payments discrimination could be seen in 1953 and 1954. These moves were given a substantial push during the 1954–1955 review sessions of the Contracting Parties to the GATT, when, although few substantive changes were made in the formal rules, the clear tone of the extended discussions was that the time had come for much more rapid progress in dismantling the discriminatory machinery.[64] At this time, the

---

[62] The improvement in balance of payments positions was uneven and did not extend to all countries. In general, the international economic position of the industrialized countries improved a great deal fairly steadily, while many of the less-developed countries continued to have what everyone regarded as acute balance of payments problems.

[63] Authoritative accounts of this backdoor convertibility can conveniently be found for these years in the *Annual Reports* of the Executive Directors of the International Monetary Fund or the *Annual Reports* of the Bank for International Settlements.

[64] See the Report of the Working Party (charged with reviewing the question of quantitative restrictions) which is reproduced in GATT, *Basic Instruments and Selected Documents, Third Supplement,* pp. 170–205.

Monetary Fund also made a major assault on the network of bilateral agreements (there were over 400 existing in 1955), under which not only much of the East-West trade but also a large part of the trade between the Western European countries and those of Latin America, and a substantial part of the trade among the Latin American countries and the Asian countries, was still being carried out. These agreements, as noted, were not only inherently discriminatory but by their many-pronged effects on costs tended to preserve or create conditions justifying discrimination. The Fund attack took the form not only of reminding members that the conditions justifying bilateral agreements under the Fund Articles were often no longer present, but of emphasizing the cost of bilateralism to those practicing it and of standing ready to consider making its resources available to members who might need them to meet problems created by such changes in their international arrangements—most notably the giving up of any credit facilities that might have been a part of the bilateral agreements.[65]

After 1955 there was a noticeable quickening in the tempo of relaxation in the discriminatory systems but there was nothing approaching a wholesale dismantlement.[66] In late December 1958 several West European countries made their currencies

[65] For the text of a formal Fund decision on this question see International Monetary Fund, *Annual Report, 1955,* Washington, D.C, 1955, pp. 123–24.

[66] For details on the changes in discriminatory restrictions, see International Monetary Fund, *Annual Reports on Exchange Restrictions,* for these years. See also, the *Seventh* through the *Eleventh Annual Report[s] of the Contracting Parties on the Discriminatory Application of Import Restrictions,* in the GATT, *Basic Instruments and Selected Documents, Fifth Supplement, Sixth Supplement, Seventh Supplement, Eighth Supplement, Ninth Supplement,* respectively, as well as GATT, *Review of Import Restrictions under Articles XII:4(b) and XVIII: 12(b),* Geneva, 1959. This last report, as do the Fund reports on exchange restrictions, especially those of 1955 and 1956, outlines the changes over the years in the methods and procedures of restriction. The movement was away from the direct and detailed control with broad discretionary power in the hands of central authorities that characterized the early post-war years, and in the direction of simpler, more routine and standardized methods that were thought to be less burdensome to

convertible. In October 1959, the Fund's Executive Directors made their famous "decision" that there was "no longer any balance of payments justification for discrimination by members whose current receipts are largely in externally convertible currencies." The Fund recognized that a short amount of time might be needed to get rid of discriminatory restrictions that had long been in effect, but stated Fund members "will be expected" quickly to cease their discriminatory practices.[67] Shortly thereafter, the Contracting Parties to the GATT, under strong U.S. urging, formally endorsed this policy.

This was a strong statement, as such statements go, but it was reached only after months of discussion and the difficulties in reaching it were, by and large, the same as the reasons why discrimination, though lessening, continued for so many years after 1955, when most of the benefits had been reaped and most of the costs were becoming apparent.[68]

After 1955 there was no great effort at the government policy formulation level to defend continued balance of payments discrimination in principle. There was both explicit and implicit acceptance of the view that abandoning discrimination

---

trade. These included permitting commercial banks to approve more transactions, issuing general rather than specific import licenses, raising the ceilings for certain types of goods, waiving all control procedures for transactions below a certain value, and transferring import functions from state organizations to private sectors.

[67] For text of the decision, see International Monetary Fund, *Annual Report, 1960,* Washington, D.C., 1960, p. 179. For statement by the United States and the Australian ministers strongly supporting this move, see GATT, *Press Release, Spec.* (59) 222, 27 Oct. 1959, and *Spec.* (59) 237, 28 Oct. 1959.

[68] Much of what is included in the following paragraphs describing the substance of the issues that were taken into account in reaching this decision, and which accounted for the slowness in getting rid of discrimination, are stated, or can easily be inferred, from the Fund's *Annual Reports On Exchange Restrictions* and the *Annual Reports* of Executive Directors, plus the cited periodic reports of the Contracting Parties on *The Discriminatory Application of Import Restrictions.* I have however, also benefited much from discussions with various governmental and GATT officials and from having been permitted to read some GATT documents which are not open for citation.

would, *over the longer-run,* and for the traditional reasons, improve economic welfare. But there were a great many concerns over the short-run costs and difficulties of quickly abandoning practices that had been in force for years—often well over a decade—and were deeply embedded. Well up on the list here were the practical problems of dismantling the often complex administrative machinery. More subtle were the matters of introducing new uncertainties, and of creating disruptive effects on the economic fabric by getting rid of arrangements which had become a part of the economic organization of the country; more concrete was the possibly unpleasant chore of reaching agreement on liquidating the credits often built up under discriminatory bilateral arrangements. Related to this, where the discrimination was tied up with bilateral or regional arrangements which were giving rise to no particular problems among the partners, was a reluctance to take the initiative in raising with the partners the matter of dropping an established arrangement lest the latter regard this as an unfriendly act. It sometimes turned out that each partner took this view. Here the Fund, and to a lesser extent the Contracting Parties, was often able to play the role of honest broker.

Many governments hesitated to move quickly because they feared that domestic full employment—a major national objective—was incompatible with worldwide competition. Often, they also believed that their international reserves, while much increased, were still not adequate to meet the drain that might result from rapidly removing discrimination against goods from countries for which no near substitutes had been available.[69] These considerations led to a consensus that restrictions should be removed only gradually, to reduce the risks by progressively testing the effects. The fear that there would be unemployment-creating competition and serious drains on reserves gradually subsided as more and more evidence was accumulated that those who did remove their discriminatory restrictions usually

[69] It had been found that it was hard to reverse liberalization measures, for both consumers and producers who benefited from the removal of discrimination had a strong interest in seeing the new situation continued.

did not in fact so suffer. This finding, repeatedly noted and commented on in the GATT and the Fund over the years, reflected the fact that nations frequently kept their restrictions much longer than necessary for short-run financial reasons. It also supported the thesis that most industries had a greater power of adaptation to competition than their officials knew, or would acknowledge, and that shifts in sources of supply because of price discrepancies often are slow to take effect, and frequently never happen, because of the many nonprice advantages home industries enjoy on the home market.[70]

Countries were often reluctant to abandon their bilateral accords because they feared that to do so would subject them to discrimination in the partner countries. Their concern was that if they gave up their reciprocal bilateral commitments with a former partner, while others did not, the latter would then pre-empt a preferential position in the former partner's market. This fear, too, was gradually reduced as more and more countries made their currencies convertible and so found it increasingly difficult to grant effective preferences, and more importantly, as the number of bilateral agreements was reduced. Again, the Fund and the GATT were sometimes able to assist this trend by arranging for discussions leading to the simultaneous elimination of several bilateral agreements involving countries having competitive exports.[71] There were, of course, some countries that relied on their bilateral agreements for more than mere protection against discrimination. We have noted that some found part of their exports were not competi-

[70] The then Dutch Minister of Economic Affairs drew this general conclusion from the Benelux experience. See GATT, *Press Release 182,* 10 Nov. 1954.

[71] As we shall see in Chapter III, the Fund had a good many reservations about the European Payments Union, but it did welcome the fact that it greatly reduced the incentives for bilateral accords within Europe and, for the same reasons, it welcomed the formation of the so-called "Hague Club" and "Paris Club," under which the currencies of several European countries earned by Brazil and Argentina, respectively, were fully transferable among the currency areas of the European signatories. These complicated arrangements fell into disuse when the European currencies were made convertible.

57

tive and openly used preferential access to their markets as a bargaining lever to gain export markets for themselves. In some cases both partners' exports were priced above world market levels: here, each argued that bilateral accords served to increase the total amount of world trade. It was acknowledged that using bilateral agreements for these purposes served to perpetuate rather than solve the problems, but countries offering this case for continued bilateralism were preoccupied with the short run.

The cumulative effect of these considerations was often considerable, but they were not the major reasons for the reluctance of most governments to quickly abandon discrimination after 1955, or even after 1958. More serious was the problem of what to do about those producers who had for so long been receiving protection under the balance of payments discriminatory restrictions: the "hard core" problem. Spokesmen for countries which believed they had this problem sometimes stated that they could not remove the protection offered by the balance of payments restrictions until they had found other means of providing equivalent shelter.[72] Others did not make a case for indefinitely continuing such restrictions, but insisted that lots of adjustments would be needed in their economies as the incidental protection was removed and that time was needed to make them. The available record provides no demonstration that the identifiable economic costs of spreading an adjustment over a longer period would be less than if they were done in a shorter time but it was generally accepted that this was true.[73] Present here, also, was the hope that if there

---

[72] This was the problem for some products in both the Belgian and German cases, for example. See the sources cited in footnote 54 above.

[73] In another connection, Pierre Uri has asserted that once trade has begun to expand and international competition is felt, the relationships between production costs is no longer what it was at the outset, and so the adjustments called for by a rapid liberalization would be far more than would be induced by a gradual one. Pierre Uri, *Partnership For Progress,* New York, 1963, p. 15. This seems to be true if one ignores the possibility that early adjustment by the *liberalizing* country may so change cost relationships that smaller adjustments are ultimately needed. But even ignoring this, the economic cost of more rapid though larger

were time some unforeseen development would solve the difficulties. The controlling aspect, however, was the argument that the political opposition to a vast and quick adjustment would likely be so great as to preclude it.

The other major consideration against abandoning all of the discriminatory arrangements originally justified on balance of payments grounds, was the belief of several of the smaller countries that to do so would greatly reduce their trade with the Soviet Bloc countries, especially Russia. Soviet Bloc countries usually insisted that their foreign trade be carried out under bilateral agreements with mutual import and export commitments. They frequently required the free market economy country to agree to import some goods from the Soviet Bloc which in a free market they would have bought from other sources. For many of the nonbloc countries, including not only Finland and Iceland but most of the Middle Eastern countries and many other less-developed nations as well, the Soviet Bloc was an important market for goods that they were finding exceedingly difficult to sell elsewhere at anything like comparable prices. Their bargaining power was therefore small. They believed that if they did not discriminate in favor of imports from the Bloc, either their exports would remain unsold, their terms of trade would seriously deteriorate, or they would find themselves building up ruble balances—lending to the Soviet Bloc, which most of them did not wish to do. Even if the Soviet Bloc were to pay in convertible currencies, it was asserted, the non-Soviet nations would still wish to discriminate in favor of Soviet imports. If they did not, their imports from the Soviet Bloc would fall and, if payments in hard currency were involved, this would likely lead to a decline in the Soviet imports from the non-Soviet countries, creating balance of payments problems for the latter. The outcome was that virtually all member governments, as well as the Fund and the Contracting Parties, acting as separate institutions, accepted that the existence of state-trading countries does present, especially for

---

adjustments may still be less than slower, smaller ones, once time is included in the costs.

small, market-economy countries which have important trade with them, problems of a sort that sometimes justify continued discrimination.[74]

The reasons offered for going slow in abandoning discrimination were many, but they could not offset for long the demonstrated burdens and costs of the policy. After the convertibility moves of late 1958, the process of reducing discrimination for balance of payments reasons quickened. By 1963 discrimination for these purposes had all but disappeared and that arising from bilateral agreements was heavily concentrated in trade involving at least one state-trading nation.[75] One important post-war episode in the use of discrimination as a tool of policy had ended.

CONCLUSIONS

The experience in the two decades following World War II demonstrates that under conditions of severe international disequilibrium and the inconvertibility of many of the major trading currencies, discrimination can—*in the short-run, and given national policies which place great value on internal full employment at all times and on fixed exchange rates*—directly improve welfare by permitting some trade that would be prevented under a firm policy of nondiscrimination. The experience also indicates—*proves* would be too strong a word —that the discrimination via this increase in trade; via its effect

[74] In 1960 Finland signed (reportedly as a condition of getting Russian approval for its associating itself with the European Free Trade Association) a bilateral agreement with the USSR in which Finland specifically abrogated its most-favored-nation obligations (other than to the EFTA countries) with respect to the reductions in import restrictions negotiated with Russia. There is no record available of the Contracting Parties having formally censured Finland for this flagrant violation of the General Agreement, but one must assume the matter was discussed, the action deplored, and others urged not to follow Finland's example.

[75] On March 31, 1964 there was a total of just over 300 active bilateral payments agreements involving the 102 nations which were members of the International Monetary Fund. In the great majority of these at least one of the partners was a state-trading economy. See International Monetary Fund, *Fifteenth Annual Report on Exchange Restrictions,* Washington, D.C., 1964, for details.

on facilitating an increase in international reserves of 'some countries; and by making it somewhat easier for government officials to turn their attention during times of acute international disequilibrium away from the day-to-day balance of payments problems and toward the longer-run determinants of a country's international position (monetary and fiscal policy, technological innovations, exchange rates, etc.); also made a modest contribution toward increasing production and, possibly, productivity. These, in turn, created conditions leading to a more tolerable balance of payments position, to currency convertibility, and to financial conditions removing the original justification for this type of discrimination.[76]

What is more clear from the record is that when, for whatever reasons, the internal and external position of a country had so improved, there was almost no evidence that its continuation demanded continued discrimination. But if the benefits of discrimination were thus found to taper off, the costs did not. Quite the contrary. New costs were being discovered all the time and old ones often seemed to be growing. The direct costs to particular exports of those discriminated against were acknowledged from the beginning as a price of the policy, but these costs were regarded by them as increasingly burdensome as time went on, both because they were less necessary for the original reasons, and, more important, because the costs of reestablishing markets for the discriminated-against goods went up as time passed. By far the most important and pervasive, however, were the costs to those practicing discrimination. The most widely recognized here were the higher prices for imports resulting from the practice and the adverse effect of this on the discriminating country's real income and on internal costs, and so, on exports. After a time the costs, in terms of relatively "uneconomic" investments, began to weigh even more heavily in the calculations of many. Less important, but not insignificant, were the costs in terms of time, effort, and talent in administering the discrimination and in defending the practices

---

[76] This is not to deny, as was noted on pages 34 and 35, that a system of flexible exchange rates *might* have been a preferred alternative to discrimination.

before the Contracting Parties and the International Monetary Fund. Sometime later costs appeared, in terms of the increased risks—and so delays—in some countries making their currencies convertible. Not to be ignored was the cumulative cost of the strains discrimination placed on international comity.

In sum, for a time the benefits of discrimination for balance of payments purposes exceeded the costs, but after awhile the benefits decreased, the costs increased, and there was a net cost to the policy. I find it encouraging that it only took about four or five years to unravel most of the policy after the scales had clearly shifted. Much of the credit for this belongs to the GATT and the International Monetary Fund.

Discrimination in international trade is not new and the observed economic consequences of the post-war discrimination for balance of payments reasons verify the theoretical expectations. What was new were the extent of the international commitments not to discriminate and the periodic consultations on discriminatory practices held with the governments of individual countries by the Fund [77] and by the Contracting

[77] The Fund consultations typically were held in the first instance between members of the Fund staff—largely professional political-economists—and officials of the government concerned, in the capital of that country. These annual consultations frequently lasted as long as three weeks and might be supplemented by shorter talks in Washington or in the field between the regular consultations. The usual Fund "team" numbered three or four persons, including at least one "country" expert, as well as persons who were expert in the subject to be discussed—which usually went far beyond the question of discrimination. The staff would submit a long report on the consultations to the Executive Directors of the Fund, often also officials of national governments, where it would be discussed and decisions, if any, taken after a spokesman of the country concerned was given an opportunity to join in discussing the report.

In the important staff consultations certain general principles were followed. Each Fund mission, whenever possible, contained some members who had taken part in several earlier consultations, and all were well informed on that country's problems. The legal obligations of members, while always noted, were not emphasized and the consultations avoided the overtone of a country being on trial. The Fund missions made great efforts to avoid publicity to their visit in the countries concerned; theory and doctrine had an important role in serving as guides to the Fund's appraisal and actions, but the consultations were not

Parties.[78] What can be said about the impact of these commitments and these consultations on the actual practices of governments? I believe that they appreciably hastened the relaxation of discrimination. Although based on the study of the printed reports and on discussions with many persons who participated, this conclusion must be labeled impressionistic, for these are not the sort of causal relationships that permit clearly demonstrable answers.

The general commitment in the Fund Articles of Agreement and in the General Agreement not to discriminate, despite all the exceptions, was in fact taken seriously by the staff of the Fund, by the contracting parties, and by the national govern-

---

couched in these terms; contacts were made and nurtured both with the most senior, politically responsible financial and economic officials, as well as with career men. If the jointly worked out actions were successful, credit was given to national officials. If they were not, the Fund usually attached no blame in public. In each consultation the Fund concentrated on only a few things—those which it believed were then, or soon would be, appropriate for action, and avoided "throwing the book" at the government concerned. For a recent account of Fund consultations by a Fund official, see J. van der Mensbrugghe, "Consultations With the Fund," *Finance and Development,* June 1965, pp. 90–96.

[78] The Contracting Party consultations, on the other hand, typically took the form of a working party, which included officials of the governments most concerned, examining in Geneva the practices and plans of countries which were discriminating. This examination was on the basis of replies to questionnaires which had been sent out, and sometimes analyzed, by the GATT Secretariat, the Fund's report on its consultations, and such other information as might be introduced at the time by those who were directly affected and which might have been submitted beforehand as more or less special papers. The government practicing discrimination was given a chance to make an opening statement, which might or might not have been circulated before the meeting. The spokesmen were subject, in important cases, to prolonged examination, both on the basis of the documents submitted and on any statements they might have made. The Working Party report on the consultations would later be placed on the agenda for a plenary session of the Contracting Parties and, in important cases, might be discussed at length there, though often these discussions were only perfunctory. The Working Party report, on the other hand, might involve several days of discussion. Often these multilateral meetings were followed by bilateral discussions between the governments most concerned.

ment representatives when they met as Executive Directors or as contracting parties. This meant that in the required consultations, the fact and extent of discrimination were made evident and the burden of proof for the practice was on those who wished to discriminate. They were in the open, and on the defensive—often an uncomfortable position worth paying something in the way of a policy change to get out of.

Contracting parties which discriminated did so with the certain knowledge that in the GATT consultations those whose exports suffered, and who therefore had an immediate and concrete concern, would ask "Is this still necessary?" and would have a "right" to expect a specific and detailed answer which said more than that the policy was an easy answer to the discriminating country's immediate problems.[79] The commitment to consult required that the interests of third countries be weighed. As it happened, the practice developed early of asking blunt and searching questions, and national spokesmen who year after year could not provide answers convincing to third countries often found themselves in acutely embarrassing positions. The replies given in successive years as to recent policy changes show that governments were responsive to findings that their actions conflicted with their international obligations and were hurtful to others.

The Fund gave much less attention than the Contracting Parties to the effects of discrimination on the exporting countries. But they always asked "Is this still necessary?" The question forced much attention to be given to alternative solutions and, the record shows, to the relationship between internal inflation and balance of payments problems. Early in the period both the Fund and many of the contracting parties began to believe that the reason for much of the balance of payments problems, and so much of this "case" for continuing discrimination, resulted from domestic inflationary policies. In both institutions deflationary policies were frequently recommended. It would be a gross mistake to suggest that had it not

[79] The fact that the consultations were periodic was important, too, for this meant that a superficial answer one year might create new problems the next.

been for these consultations the world would not have resorted in the manner it did after 1950 to monetary and fiscal restraints as methods of achieving balance of payments equilibrium. There can be little doubt, however, that the consultations contributed, perhaps importantly, by being the occasion where it was easy to discuss in detail the experience of others who had followed this route to success.

In almost every country practicing discrimination there were some officials who, quite independent of the Fund mission or the discussions in the Contracting Parties, wished to see discrimination removed faster than it was, usually for some combination of the cost considerations mentioned earlier. The Fund, and to a lesser extent the GATT, consultations generally served to strengthen the influence of such men. It provided them with supporting arguments and, especially in the less-developed countries, often increased the prestige and authority of these persons within their own governments.

The Fund rarely, if ever, specifically tied the relaxation of discrimination with immediate access to its resources. After all, it was not until 1957–1958 that most countries regarded the Fund as a place where one was likely to obtain much financial help. Nonetheless, some countries were influenced by the fact that they wanted their record at the Fund to look good against the day when they might have to ask for a drawing. More important was the fact that the Fund was able to reduce the risks of dropping discrimination. It was a common Fund position that if the country removed or relaxed discrimination and took other recommended measures, and, as a consequence, found itself in balance of payments trouble, the Fund would stand ready to help it with its resources.

As time went on and the prestige of the Fund and the GATT increased, national governments became more sensitive to their opinions and recommendations. They began to value a "good name" in those quarters. Nations wanted, in a manner of speaking, their flags respected in these international organizations. This consideration was the more potent because the atmosphere of these consultations, especially those involving the Fund, was not that of a court of law so much as a frank appraisal by peers, in which one could not "win" by trickery or by resort to legal technicalities. This moral pressure method of exercising influence was made more effective by the practice of the international institutions specifically giving recognition to "good behavior" in their reports and decisions.

A more important contribution of the consultations to the relaxation of discrimination was the fact that they facilitated one nation being exposed to the experience of another. It often turned out to be the case that this knowledge both impressed the first government with the high cost of continued discrimination and the relative ease with which it could be abandoned, especially if done before newly created, vested interests were strong and in a period of relatively full employment. We have already noted that the consultations also sometimes permitted the international staffs to act as honest brokers between two countries continuing to discriminate in favor of each other, usually via bilateral agreements, after each had independently concluded that the arrangements were no longer in its interests but was reluctant to take the initiative in cancelling or changing the arrangements because it thought the other still wanted it.

Perhaps the most important contribution of the Fund missions and the GATT consultations was that their coming usually but once a year, and after the early 1950's from prestigious international institutions, meant that the problem was brought to the attention of the top government authorities. At this level there was often little vested interest either in terms of a job, or a capital facility, or an intellectual investment in the discriminatory policy. It was possible, therefore, to focus attention on long-run policy. And in the long run the costs loomed larger and the benefits smaller than they often did to those who were preoccupied with day-to-day problems.

CHAPTER III

Discrimination as a Stepping-stone to Nondiscrimination: Temporary Regional Arrangements

INTRODUCTION

T HE balance of payments justification for discrimination was based primarily on individual nation economic welfare grounds; the consultations and discussions surrounding it were with individual countries. But much of the discrimination since World War II has grown out of *regional* efforts to solve pressing economic problems and, often more important, to achieve political objectives. Intermingled chronologically and in purpose, it is nonetheless analytically useful to distinguish two types of regional arrangements. The first are those intended to be transitional, which had as one of their objectives to facilitate the movement toward nondiscrimination. The second are those which were intended from the start to be permanent and whose supporters regarded any costs to themselves or to others of continuing discrimination as an acceptable price for the benefits they expected to reap from regionalism. Certain aspects of the Sterling Area and the European Payments Union, together with the associated Code of Trade Liberalization, were the major instances of the first type and are the subject of this chapter. The various "communities," "common markets," and "free trade areas" are examples of the second. They are the subject of Chapters IV and V.

THE STERLING AREA DOLLAR POOL

The Sterling Area has been a thing of constant change in membership, in practice, and in reason for being. Indeed, it has changed so often, so many of the arrangements are informal, its objectives and aims have been so rarely defined, that there is much disagreement as to when it began or what it is.[1] As a

[1] Several excellent accounts and analyses of the Sterling Area have been published since the war. See especially, Philip Bell, *The Sterling*

minimum in recent decades it has been a group of countries that use sterling as a normal means of external settlement, hold most of their reserves in sterling, and look to the United Kingdom as a major source of external credit. This is enough to lead members to favor, at least slightly, trade with each other over trade with nonmembers; but when sterling is convertible such "natural" preferences as are inherent in the system have not been important enough to cause much concern to third countries.[2] The United Kingdom in recent decades has also usually held a central reserve of non-sterling currencies for sale to the whole sterling area for non-sterling settlements. It is around the conditions for such sales and purchases, especially when sterling was inconvertible, that more acute problems of discrimination have arisen.

A central feature of the arrangements between 1939 and 1958 was that sterling was not freely convertible, and while payments within the area were largely unrestricted, those into and out of the area as a whole were strictly controlled by each country. Members sold their hard foreign currency earnings, especially dollars and gold, to the United Kingdom Treasury in exchange for sterling and agreed to limit their drawings on this so-called "dollar pool" to amounts required for agreed purposes. Members generally agreed to confine their dollar purchases to items that could not be obtained—or that were obtainable only under severely adverse price or delivery conditions—within the Area itself. The extent of the resulting discrimination could, and did, vary greatly from time to time and from country to country. But it was extensive, and was so as a matter of conscious policy.

Area and the Post-War World, New York, 1956; J. Polk, *Sterling,* New York, 1956; W. M. Scammell, *International Monetary Policy,* London, 1961, Chap. 9; and the relevant sections of the Committee on the Working of the Monetary System, *Report* and *Principal Memoranda of Evidence,* London, 1959 (hereinafter referred to as the Radcliffe Committee *Report* and *Memoranda of Evidence*).

[2] When this is combined with membership in the Commonwealth preference system the discrimination, of course, becomes much more serious, primarily because of the operation of the imperial preferences which are discussed elsewhere in this book.

The discriminatory dollar pool arrangements were set up in 1939 for the purpose of conserving dollars to meet war needs. During the war years there was little criticism of them, but some senior officials of the United States Government saw them as something to be abolished as quickly as possible after the war's end. The official British position was that they were temporary. They were dealt with in the 1946 Loan Agreement between the United States and the United Kingdom. Although the general commitment by Britain in that accord to undertake sterling convertibility was in effect a commitment to abolish the dollar pool, Article VII of the Agreement specifically stated that "any discrimination arising from the so-called sterling area dollar pool will be entirely removed. . . ." [3] The United States Government's position then was that, for the reasons outlined in Chapter II, the United Kingdom itself probably would have to retain some discriminatory restrictions against dollars for some time, but this policy should not be binding on those Sterling Area members who were, on their own account, in a more comfortable hard currency position. The argument acknowledged that such a change in policy might not increase the total amount of United States exports to the Sterling Area countries as a group, but it would change the composition of American exports, and this "does make a difference to us." [4] This change was also considered desirable by the United States Treasury because it would mean a larger *number* of national economies free from dollar discrimination. Even though this was at the price of more intense discrimination by some sterling countries, some of those convinced of the virtues of nondiscrimination saw the combination as an improvement in the general economic climate. The underlying reason, however, was that it was then the policy, born of the devotion by the men then in power to the doctrine of nondiscrimination and the reconstruction of a multilateral regime, combined with deep mistrust of the British Empire system, of the United States

---

[3] HMSO, *Financial Agreement between the Governments of the United States and the United Kingdom*, Dec. 6, 1945, cmd 6708.

[4] Bell, *Sterling Area and the Post-War World*, p. 53, quoting H. D. White, then a senior official in the United States Treasury.

Executive branch to break down British preferential arrangements wherever they were found.[5]

The policy at first backfired. The premature 1947 convertibility attempt failed; among the consequences of this debacle was closer cooperation among members of the Sterling Area with respect to trade policies as well as in the utilization of sterling assets. More, rather than less, uniformity was introduced into members' exchange and import controls; formal agreements were extended on questions of drawings upon the central reserves; and capital movement policies became more concerted.[6] But the issue was not settled.

In July 1949, two years later, there was a continuing and growing drain on the dollar pool. It was then agreed at a London conference of Commonwealth Finance Ministers that each member of the Sterling Area would reduce its demands on the central reserves during the next year by cutting dollar expenditures 25 percent below the calendar 1948 level.[7] As we saw in the last chapter, the GATT permits contracting parties to temporarily intensify restrictions—and to do so in a discriminatory fashion—if found necessary to forestall or stop a serious decline in monetary reserves, or to permit a reasonable rate of increase in them. Consultations with those adversely affected are required, however; so, in 1950, Australia, Ceylon, India, New Zealand, Pakistan, Southern Rhodesia, and the United Kingdom were invited by the GATT to discuss the policy at the forthcoming (Torquay) session. As provided in the General Agreement (Article XV, Paragraph 2), the International Mone-

[5] For an interesting account of the differences between American and British officials on this matter in 1945, see R. N. Gardner, *Sterling-Dollar Diplomacy,* Oxford, 1956, Chap. 10.

[6] In the late 1940's and early 1950's large amounts of war-accumulated sterling balances were released to buy goods within the Sterling Area only, and this, of course, constituted discrimination against others. By 1951 the needs of Sterling Area countries to hold larger monetary reserves because of higher prices and more trade sharply reduced this particular form of discrimination.

[7] *The New York Times,* July 19, 1949, p. 4, reproduces the text of the communiqué.

tary Fund was invited to participate and determine if there had been the necessary "serious decline in monetary reserves."

The Fund decided to take a broad view of its responsibilities and prepared reports including not only relevant statistical data but also opinions and recommendations on policy. It took the position that the Sterling Area was not a member of the Fund or the GATT, but that each of the members was, so each was subject to the rules of those institutions. The Fund acknowledged that the Sterling Area was a fact; its existence perhaps inevitably meant some discrimination; but, they held, this did not itself excuse the individual members from their international commitments in the Fund and the GATT. Starting from there, the Fund's investigation led it to conclude that, while the discriminatory restrictions were justified when they were first imposed, the subsequent improvements in the international economic positions of Australia, Ceylon, New Zealand, Southern Rhodesia, and the United Kingdom had been such that, with all due caution, it was now feasible and desirable for them to begin a progressive relaxation of their dollar import instructions. However, the other members of the Sterling Area involved, India and Pakistan, were found to be in a position justifying the continuation of the existing discrimination against dollar imports.[8]

These findings, approach, and recommendations were supported in the GATT by the delegates of Belgium, Cuba, Canada, and the United States—nations whose exporters were feeling the discrimination and which were in those years the

[8] For published accounts of these consultations, see *Department of State Bulletin*, March 12, 1951, pp. 415ff.; *The Banker*, London, Dec. 1950, pp. 347ff.; *The Economist*, London, Nov. 18, 1950, p. 832; International Monetary Fund, *Annual Report*, Washington, D.C., 1951, p. 69; *Statist*, Nov. 18, 1950, p. 265; *Parliamentary Debates* (Hansard), House of Commons, Nov. 14, 1950, pp. 137–38 of Written Answers; GATT, *The Use of Quantitative Import Restrictions to Safeguard Balance of Payments*, Geneva, Oct. 1951; International Monetary Fund, *International Financial News Survey*, Dec. 22, 1950; *Financial Times*, London, Nov. 11, 1950; and *The New York Times*, Nov. 12, 1950, p. 44, and Nov. 13, 1950, p. 6.

champions of nondiscriminatory policies—but were bitterly contested by those from the United Kingdom and other members of the Sterling Area, especially Australia and New Zealand, who urged that the Fund's report be dismissed "out of hand" as intolerable intervention in matters beyond their legitimate concern.[9]

Apart from differences as to what the facts were, what facts were relevant, what was "temporary" and what was not, and the resentment stemming from the irritation of having one's policies criticized by still another organization, one which had been providing no help in those difficult, early post-war years; apart from all these things, the fundamental objection of Britain and her supporters was the cavalier treatment being accorded the Sterling Area as a regional group. To argue, as the Fund representative and his supporters from various governments did, that some members could reduce restrictions while others could not was to come very close to destroying the arrangement of pooled reserves and common policies for drawing on them. But it was on this that the operation of the Sterling Area mechanism at that time hinged.

Britain and, so far as one can tell from the published records, the other members, were anxious to preserve and strengthen the regional financial arrangement and were determined to resist any efforts to dismantle any part of its machinery. It was prized by the United Kingdom, among other reasons, because it provided some nonsterling earnings, could on occasion facilitate borrowing from the Outer Sterling Area, helped provide a sheltered export market, and was a source of invisible sterling earnings. Moreover, it was seen as much more than "a narrow economic thing," it was an important link in Commonwealth

[9] Two months before these discussions the Commonwealth ministers had again met in London and agreed there might be some relaxation in the July 1949 "formula" for discrimination against dollar imports, but apparently they were not prepared at the GATT meetings to use this agreement as a means of avoiding the debate or of being willing to make formal commitments to reduce the discrimination. See statement by Chancellor of the Exchequer Gaitskill, in *Parliamentary Debates* (Hansard), House of Commons, Nov. 14, 1950, pp. 137–38 of Written Answers; and *Statist,* Nov. 18, 1950, pp. 624ff.

relationships. To the rest of the Sterling Area the arrangements also helped provide a sheltered market, meant easy access to the London capital market, and helped ensure that Britain would speak for them in various international gatherings. At the Torquay meetings the members of the Sterling Area chose not to belabor the importance of these advantages or to argue at length the "merits and demerits" of the system as a contribution to international liquidity and to more multilateral trade than would otherwise actually have been achieved. Instead, they generally took the position that the Sterling Area was a fact, its existence must be recognized, and to look at individual nations apart from their membership in the regional system was unrealistic and unhelpful.

Beyond this, it was asserted, though not much stressed at the time, that the discrimination in the dollar pool arrangements was defensible because it was an efficient and available method of helping to create conditions under which sterling could be made convertible and discrimination therefore relaxed, if not removed. Those making this stepping-stone argument believed sterling convertibility must await both a sizable increase in the area's hard currency reserves and an elimination or sharp curtailment in the then "dollar shortage." (It was held neither desirable nor feasible to devalue sterling again as a method of achieving these objectives.) It was assumed that the area's hard currency earnings would not be adversely affected in any serious way by this discrimination and so it would work to permit an accumulation of reserves. It was accepted that to restore international balance to the world economy would not be easy and would take time, since this would involve not just, or perhaps even primarily, changes in relative prices but also the elimination of demand backlogs, the making of many new investments, the re-establishment of foreign markets and sources of supply, etc. Making such structural readjustments inside the shelter of discriminatory payments restrictions admittedly ran the risk of misdirected investment and so a continued "political" case for discrimination. But this risk was reduced, it was argued, by its being recognized. In any event, and this was perhaps the major consideration, most of the spokesmen for the

Sterling Area countries believed dollar goods were so competitive that, in the absence of discrimination against them, the necessary structural adjustments in the Sterling Area if sterling were ultimately to become convertible would take place in an environment of deflation and much unemployment.[10] This was regarded as intolerable.

Those supporting the Fund's recommendations showed no interest at the time in discussing this stepping-stone approach, or in a searching examination of the discriminatory aspects of regional groups. This was not surprising, for it was being done in connection with the European Payments Union discussions. These Sterling Area dollar pool discussions, then, were inconclusive. The delegates from the Sterling Area countries stated they would report the views and opinions expressed to their governments. The Fund, having been bitterly criticized by several of its members, seems to have decided that political discretion, and the wish to have influence in the future, dictated no more frontal attacks on the Sterling Area or on the general *principle* of regionalism.

The available evidence does not permit a judgment as to the contribution this discrimination in fact made to progress toward nondiscrimination. In 1952 Britain and other members of the Sterling Area began a new drive to make the pound convertible. The drive suffered several setbacks and raised some important new matters of discrimination, which were discussed in Chapter II. But the options opened to holders of sterling were gradually increased, de jure convertibility for nonresident holders was declared in December 1958, and in early 1961 Britain assumed full responsibilities for the external convertibility of sterling under Article VIII of the International Monetary Fund Agreement.

The dollar pool as it had been known ceased to exist, although the United Kingdom continued to hold a central reserve of foreign currency to help Sterling Area members to

[10] Much of this rationale for continuing the Sterling Area dollar pool arrangements at the time later found its way into the Radcliffe Committee *Report* (e.g., p. 244), and the various reports in the *Memoranda of Evidence,* Vol. 1.

meet their nonsterling settlements. While discrimination against nonmembers as a matter of conscious policy ceased to be a major *raison d'être* of the system, the members continued to cooperate to maintain the external value of sterling and often followed generally comparable policies in their overseas financial dealings; but they did feel much freer than before to run deficits with the nonsterling area. The regional arrangements, known as the Sterling Area, have continued to involve some mild discrimination because of the tendency to favor dealings with area members, since this is less likely to involve a difficult foreign exchange problem and because of the intimate trading and political relationships among the members. But there have been virtually no complaints about this discrimination from third countries since 1958, and the Sterling Area as a regional system has continued to be whittled down by Britain's recurring economic crisis, while the underlying political and trading ties have been weakened by the effects of other regional arrangements. The growing pressures in the 1960's to reform the entire international monetary system so as, among other things, to reduce the role of sterling (and the dollar) as an international reserve currency seem destined to result in still further erosion.

EUROPEAN PAYMENTS UNION—OEEC TRADE LIBERALIZATION SCHEME

Origin of the Arrangements

Far more important issues over the use of discrimination as a stepping-stone to a nondiscrimination system arose out of the European Payments Union and the associated trade liberalization measures. The background of the EPU has been described and analyzed in detail in the literature and only the barest outlines need be given here.[11] In the economic and financial chaos during and following World War II, desperate reliance was placed by many European countries on bilateral payments

[11] See especially, William Diebold, Jr., *Trade and Payments in Western Europe*, New York, 1952; and Robert Triffin, *Europe and the Money Muddle*, New Haven, 1957.

arrangements, often accompanied by bilateral trade agreements.[12] A network of more than 200 had been negotiated by the European countries by 1947. They did remove for a time some of the pressure for strict barter trade, but since these nations usually did not want to lend much to each other (each wanted an import surplus), the credit margins in the payments agreements were relatively small. They were often quickly exhausted for one partner, although that partner sometimes still had credit available in his arrangements with another European country. The European countries were at that time also not willing to use much of their supply of dollars to pay for European deficits. As a consequence, the bilateral agreements soon tended toward a close bilateral balancing and so were considered by most governments to be both restrictive and distortive of trade.[13] In 1947 efforts were made to partially multilateralize the system by a "first category" compensation involving a round robin offsetting or cancellation of debit and credit balances and a "second category" compensation involving acceptance by a creditor of a new debtor in place of an old one. This came virtually to nothing, because the possible circuits were often short in the first category, and members often refused to engage in the second, seeing it as replacing debts in a relatively weak currency with debts in a stronger currency.[14]

In 1948, with strong United States support,[15] the first Intra-

[12] One of the best accounts of the early post-war economic situation in Europe remains United Nations, Economic Commission for Europe, *A Survey of the Economic Situation and Prospects of Europe*, Geneva, 1948. For an account of the development of this network of bilateral arrangements see Raymond F. Mikesell, *Foreign Exchange in the Postwar World*, New York, 1954, Part I.

[13] As we saw in Chapter II, these bilateral agreements might nonetheless have resulted in more trade than would a nondiscriminatory system at that time.

[14] For a description and discussion of this complicated scheme see R. W. Bean, "European Multilateral Clearing," *The Journal of Political Economy*, Oct. 1948.

[15] This stemmed in part from the desire to encourage the Europeans to get goods from each other rather than rely upon Marshall Plan aid to receive them from the United States.

European Payments and Compensations Scheme was introduced. This helped to avoid the threatened general resort to strict bilateral barter, by making some European Recovery Program aid to individual countries "conditional" on that country extending equivalent credit, "drawing rights," to its European debtors under the bilateral agreements. This scheme, while permitting an increase in intra-European trade as compared with the previous arrangement, was unsatisfactory on several counts. It rested on the periodic provisions of United States dollars and ameliorated only slightly the bilateral character of intra-European trade relations. In practice, the allocation of so-called conditional aid and drawing rights required the determination a year in advance of a pattern of intra-European deficits and surpluses, which often proved faulty and introduced more rigidities into the system. More serious was the fact that the mechanism not only did not provide incentives for creditors to import or for debtors to export, but it seemed to encourage debtors to continue their intra-European deficits, thus building a case for drawing rights from their European partners the next year, and for creditors to pile up intra-European surpluses —thus creating a "claim" for dollar "conditional aid" the following year. This was most regrettable, since a major problem for the group was one of increasing exports to the dollar area.[16]

Efforts were then made to overcome some of these deficits by devising a scheme whereby the "drawing rights" and associated "conditional aid" could be transferred among countries, thus following and not preceding trade, and so providing for more competition among European exporters with hoped-for benefi-

---

[16] JHW, "The Revision of the Intra-European Payments Plan," *Foreign Affairs*, Oct. 1949. There was some tendency for this to be partially offset, because in practice it did not prove possible to withhold the conditional aid if the actual trade balances so developed that the drawing rights were not used. The surplus countries therefore had some short-run incentive to discourage the use of the drawing rights that had been provided. See Triffin, *Europe and the Money Muddle*, p. 158.

For an authoritative account of developments under this scheme, see United Nations, Economic Commission for Europe, *Economic Survey of Europe in 1949*, Geneva, 1950, pp. 97–108.

cial effects on the area's dollar earnings. Because this would introduce new uncertainties both as to the dollar earnings and dollar payments of individual countries, negotiations were difficult and prolonged. In the end, only 25 percent of the drawing rights and conditional aid were multilateralized. Less than two weeks after agreement had been reached on this admittedly makeshift scheme the September 1949 devaluations came. The devaluations had the effect of falsifying many of the trade estimates on which the nonmultilateralized drawing rights and conditional aid of the revised Intra-European Payments Arrangement scheme were based. The exchange rate changes were also an important step toward the creation of conditions which would permit the reduction of U.S. aid. Conditions clearly demanded new payments arrangements.

Major Characteristics of the Scheme

Within about three months after the wave of devaluations, the general outline of the new European Payments Union had been worked out, although it took six months of difficult negotiations to settle all of the specific details.[17] The arrangements were technically complex but the fundamental principles behind them were simple. Once a month the central bank of each Union member, including its associated monetary area, if any, reported to the Bank for International Settlements, the EPU agent, the net surpluses or deficits of its current transactions with each of the other members—all the other OEEC countries. The Bank for International Settlements then offset each country's total net surpluses and total net deficits and arrived at a single net figure—surplus or deficit—for each member vis-à-vis all the other members as a group. The net balance for each member was accumulated month by month. This net accumulative credit or debit balance was then set off, month by month, against the "quota" assigned each country,

[17] For a running account of the extended discussions of the more important of these issues, see *The Economist* for late 1949 through July 1950. A concise and more analytically rewarding account will be found in A. O. Hirschman, "The European Payments Union—Negotiations and Issues"; and Randall Hinshaw, "Consideration of Some Criticisms"; both in *The Review of Economics and Statistics,* Feb. 1951.

generally fixed at approximately 15 percent of each member's total intra-European visible and invisible trade in 1949.[18] Accumulated balances against this quota were settled partly in gold and partly in credit, on a sliding scale. Initially, the percentages were so calculated that once the quota was exhausted creditors (debtors) had received (paid) 40 percent of the quota in dollars and extended (received) 60 percent in credit. The initial agreement also provided that if a debtor country exhausted its quota, it was to pay subsequent deficits 100 percent in gold or dollars. It was not possible to reach agreement on what to do about excessive creditors, a problem left for future determination. A relatively weak Managing Board was established. It could only make recommendations to members, but could back the recommendations up with special credits in support of agreed reforms.

Those responsible for determining Europe's international economic policies recognized from the beginning that monetary and trade restrictions were often alternatives and that payments liberalization might accomplish little unless accompanied by reduction in trade barriers. As contracting parties to the GATT, the European countries negotiated downward their tariffs in those years, at Geneva in 1947, at Annecy in 1949, and at Torquay in 1951. But in those days quantitative restrictions were also often restricting trade, and in the late 1940's a reduction of these barriers was not high on the GATT agenda. Evolving alongside the regional payments arrangements, therefore, were plans for reducing quantitative restrictions on intra-European trade.[19] In 1950 the various earlier decisions and recommendations, plus some new ones, were brought together

---

[18] Some members who were thought likely to be structural debtors or creditors were given modest, additional, initial credit balances, or saddled with modest, additional, debit balances, in return for some conditional American aid.

[19] Detailed accounts of these may be found in the periodic *Report to Congress,* by the United States Economic Cooperation Administration, Washington, D.C., during the late 1940's and early 1950's; and the annual *Economic Survey of Europe,* prepared by the United Nations, Economic Commission for Europe, Geneva. See also, Foreign Operations Administration, *Import Quotas in Western Europe* (mimeographed), Washington, D.C., Aug. 1953.

in a Code of Trade Liberalization which became effective when the EPU Agreement was signed. There were many exceptions and escape hatches, but the heart of the scheme was that members agreed, according to periodically negotiated time schedules, to progressively remove quotas so that at least a negotiated (increasing) percentage of each nation's imports on private account from other members *as a group* should be free of such quantitative restrictions. That is, there was to be no discrimination among the members. No comparable obligations were undertaken to reduce quantitative restrictions on imports from nonmembers.[20]

Improvements Over Earlier System

All this was clearly a great improvement on the previous arrangements for meeting the immediate trade and payments problems of Europe. The monetary arrangement was not dependent on outside financial help, although the United States did contribute $350 million for the capital fund and directly helped to finance some of the deficits of certain countries. The partial settlement in gold or dollars of net balances increased the amount of credit available to finance intra-European trade and so reduced the risk that countries would be forced to deliberalize that trade. The operation of the cumulative principle provided an effective substitute for international reserves for those nations which from one accounting period to another shifted between being net creditors and net debtors. Most important, to the extent it could achieve, and maintain, full transferability at the central bank level of current earnings within Europe and its associated monetary areas, the EPU effectively removed the financial justification for bilateralism and thus facilitated the increase in both the quantity and quality of trade among the participants. This was further supported by the specific obligations to reduce the quantitative restrictions on trade amongst themselves and by formally integrating the trade

[20] See Organization for European Economic Cooperation, *A European Payments Union and the Rules of Commercial Policy to be Followed by Member Countries,* Paris, 1950; and *Code of Liberalization,* Paris, July 1951.

and payments commitments, thus reducing the possibility of trade and monetary policy offsetting each other.[21]

But the arrangements were also discriminatory: earnings of European currencies could be freely spent only in Europe; the EPU credits were available only for European deficits; and the trade liberalization commitments did not extend to nonmembers. They were therefore a matter of great concern to third countries.

At this point, it is important to recall that in these years the problems of Europe *as a region* had gripped the attention of a large majority of those economists in the United States, the United Kingdom, and Western Europe who were concerned with international economic problems. Furthermore, there had not been, either in governmental or academic circles, any great concern voiced up to this time over the discriminatory aspects of the earlier European trade and payments arrangements. They were commonly accepted as a part of those post-war transitional arrangements which it had been agreed need not conform to the accepted long-run commitments. So it was, too, with those facile, competent, energetic, and dedicated men, charged, after the September 1949 devaluations, with working

---

[21] Given the actual differences in relative scarcities of members' currencies, Marcus Fleming subsequently argued that this policy of nondiscrimination *within* EPU was a defect for the same reason that nondiscrimination against the Dollar Area was an unwise policy so long as the dollar was relatively more scarce than other currencies. It would result in otherwise unnecessary curtailment of trade. This conclusion received little support at the policy level, presumably for several reasons. It specifically assumed that there was no feasible method of adjustments to a balance of payments deficit other than import restrictions (an assumption made explicit in Fleming's famous *Economic Journal* article). There were also doubts as to the feasibility of organizing discrimination within the EPU in the needed way. Many found a good bit of political and psychological value in a policy of nondiscrimination within Europe. Finally, some feared that automatic discrimination in favor of debtors would encourage the latter to follow inflationary policies. See J. M. Fleming, "Regional Organization of Trade and Payments," *American Economic Review, Papers and Proceedings,* May 1952, pp. 345–58; and the "Comments" thereafter by Hirschman and Triffin, pp. 359–68.

out new European payments and trade arrangements. They had an immediate problem to solve, a technically complex problem, and they did not have much time. They were convinced that a full-scale move toward worldwide trade liberalization and currency convertibility was not then a real alternative. Their approach was short-run, focused on Europe. Their task was that of bringing immediate improvement to a defective system of trade and settlements in a rapidly changing economic environment. They were responsible to their superiors in the executive branches and to their parliaments for European, not worldwide, problems. Their responsibility was not one of building an institution for the indefinite future.

Most of those involved hoped for a multilateral nondiscriminatory, worldwide system of trade and payments.[22] Although this was for the future, the increases in productivity, production, and hard currency exports, which it was hoped would stem from the new arrangements, were, they believed, the best feasible way of creating conditions making such a system possible. They formally stated, therefore, that the arrangements they had worked out should facilitate "a return to full multilateral trade, . . . and . . . to . . . the general convertibility of currencies";[23] that is, to a nondiscriminatory system. At the same time, they were not going to be either surprised or upset if this took quite some time.

[22] Taking into account only the usual economic considerations, internal consistency dictated this hope. The great stress put on the economic benefits of nondiscrimination *within* Europe, while some of these nations have a balance of payments problems vis-à-vis each other, implicitly assumes that the nations with such balance of payments difficulties have both feasible and more desirable alternatives than continued reliance on discriminatory import restrictions. Otherwise, as Fleming argued in the source cited in the preceding footnote, the case for systematic discrimination among the members of the Union is strong. But if one assumes this for balance of payments problems *within* an area, then one must also, on strictly economic grounds, assume it for balance of payments problems in relation to the rest of the world, too.

[23] *Preamble to the Agreement for the Establishment of A European Payments Union,* Organization for European Economic Cooperation, Paris, Sept. 1950.

There were others, however, who were much worried about the discriminatory aspects of the system, which was designed to extend beyond what had been thought in the past as a post-war transitional period, and who doubted that it would be a stepping-stone toward a wider system of nondiscriminatory trade and currency convertibility. Those who so believed were strongly represented in the International Monetary Fund and the United States Treasury Department, but they could also be found in some of the member governments, as well as in academia.

The question of interest here is *not* whether there were political or sentimental justifications for closer regional arrangements, and the attendant discrimination, in Europe. Nor are we concerned with whether there was a case for discrimination on the assumptions that the European currencies were not convertible into gold or dollars; that exchange rates were given, and that at those rates the demand for dollars relative to their supply was greater than the demand for European currencies; and that the dollar (hard currency) availabilities were *otherwise* determined than by the effects of this policy. In these circumstances (as we saw in Chapter II), there is a strong case for the members of a region freeing the flow of trade among themselves so that each could at least reap the welfare benefits of equalizing the marginal utility of equal expenditures on other European goods with home goods. What is interesting here is only the question of whether such regional preferential arrangements tend to perpetuate, and possibly increase, discrimination, or whether, as claimed, they facilitate a movement to full multilateral trade and currency convertibility.[24] In other words, under what conditions can regional discrimination be a step to nondiscrimination, rather than to the creation of a more or less permanent, protected, soft-currency area?[25]

---

[24] An early discussion of this general question may be found in H. S. Ellis, *et al., The Economics of Freedom,* New York, 1950, Chap. 9.

[25] Elements of this question were, of course, present in the discrimination for balance of payments reasons discussed in Chapter II, but the stepping-stone aspect was both more important and a more explicit policy objective in the EPU–OEEC Trade Liberalization arrangements.

Effects on Hard Currency Earnings?

It seems to have been generally agreed at the time that the answer hinged largely on the effects these particular regional arrangements would have on the hard currency earnings of the members. In the circumstances of the early 1950's all agreed that hard-currency earnings were *not* independently determined but were much influenced by the economic intercourse *among* the European nations. It was also agreed that if the regional arrangements were likely to retard the growth of dollar exports they probably would delay the achievement of convertibility by the EPU members [26] because both larger reserves and a better balance with the dollar area were prerequisites of convertibility and nondiscrimination.[27]

In the short-run, and it was on the short-run that most of the attention was focused, the EPU and associated trade liberalization measures could affect dollar exports in several ways. The enthusiasm or skepticism one had for it as a stepping-stone depended on the relative weight given these various factors.

At the beginning of the 1950's, the conviction was growing among economists and government officials alike that inflation

[26] Since the level of dollar imports was at that time closely related to the dollar earnings plus unilateral transfers, a decline in the rate of growth of exports would also adversely affect welfare within Europe, since it was almost certainly true that, at the existing level of restriction and exchange rates, the marginal utility of a dollar's worth of dollar goods was substantially greater than a dollar's worth of European imports.

[27] The need for dollar reserves might be less, and the balance might be achieved, by reducing the demand for dollar goods as well as by increasing dollar earnings. At the time, it was generally agreed that both were probably necessary to the achievement of convertibility and general nondiscrimination, but the latter was regarded as much the more desirable for the welfare reasons cited in the preceding footnote. Moreover, in the short run, at least, most observers saw little scope for these new arrangements *displacing* dollar imports with European ones, because even prior to the new arrangements there had been little incentive in Europe to restrict imports of European goods that were anything like close substitutes for dollar imports.

84

was an important cause of most West European nations' balance of payments difficulties, and so a major obstacle to a more rapid movement to convertibility and nondiscriminatory trade policy. The provisions for settling net EPU positions were therefore of great importance. To have provided no credit and so required each country to settle each month's net position entirely in gold or dollars would have meant that each EPU member's imports from its partners were in effect costing the same as the imports from the dollar area. In 1950 the result would almost certainly have been for each member to curtail imports from the others in a mutually defeating effort to earn dollars. On the other hand, as the settlement of net balances was made in credits, a train of events might be set in motion which would reduce hard currency earnings. Additional money was introduced into the European creditor countries, contributing to inflation and dollar export difficulties.[28] More credit was also seen as permitting debtors to postpone exchange rate changes and to delay instituting tighter internal fiscal and monetary policies, often prerequisites to the increase in exports required for more liberal import policies. The provision of credits also directly permitted deficit countries to siphon unto themselves exports from their partners that might otherwise have been sold for hard currency. Looked at somewhat differently, as the proportion of the net balance that had to be settled in gold or dollars was increased, the less the credit provided. The less the credit provided, the more each country would have to treat its European balance of payments as indistinguishable from its total balance, and the closer the EPU members would be to eliminating the discriminatory aspects of the scheme.

The problem was viewed as that of achieving the right degree of hardness, enough to keep debtors from indulging in inflation and to restrict to noninflationary levels the increase of money

[28] The individual exporter in the creditor country was normally paid in local currency even though his central bank only received a credit at the payments union. As noted below, this became a serious problem for several countries, particularly Belgium.

supply in the creditors, but not so hard as to intensify the import restrictions in intra-European trade to the point where total trade—intra-European plus extra-European—declined.

Some believed that the combination of quotas and gold/ credit ratios finally agreed upon erred seriously on the "soft" side and, via the adjustments outlined in the preceding paragraphs, would delay and impede, not faciliate, progress toward general convertibility. Others defended the payment terms, asserting that the amount of credit involved—originally, a theoretical maximum of about $1.2 billion, exclusive of extra-quota borrowing permitted—was modest when compared with the roughly $10 billion loss of gold and dollar reserves, measured in 1950 prices, suffered by the European countries since the prewar years [29] and that any tighter terms would have resulted in a contraction of intra-European trade without an increase in extra-European trade. Moreover, they insisted, to suggest that the availability of some additional credit would result in inflation was to underestimate the concern of governments with this problem and the ability of the economies to respond to more credit by increasing output.

By all odds, the most frequently offered argument in support of the EPU as a stepping-stone was that the abandonment of bilateralism within Europe would increase competition among European producers in European markets, tending to reduce prices to the level of the cheapest European source. These price reductions, it was insisted, were the first prerequisite for the restoration of convertibility because, via their effect on other costs, they could encourage dollar exports. In the short-run, it was believed, the price reductions would be mostly at the expense of profits previously protected by intra-European import restrictions and a general business climate of "live and let live," rather than by any substantial shifts in sources of supply from higher cost to lower cost areas. In addition, some thought that the increased competition would result in a considerable increase in efficiency by existing producers who, in the absence of such competition, had failed to be as energetic as existing knowledge permitted them to be in reducing their

[29] Triffin, *Europe and the Money Muddle,* p. 201.

costs. Any such increase in productivity would decrease the price of their exports and so increase their competitive ability with the United States.[30]

It was also alleged that since some members had more liberal dollar import policies than others, the increased multilateralism in Europe would expose—via indirect dollar imports—those with more severe import restrictions to somewhat more competition from the dollar world which also would have beneficial effects on their prices and thus exports to the outside world.[31] The other side of this coin was that such an indirect demand on their dollar resources might well force stronger EPU members to intensify their dollar import restrictions, thus creating a new shelter for their inefficient firms. On balance, this consideration, therefore, was not thought to be important.

The abolition of intra-European restrictions on trade and payments, underwritten by the additional credit, would of course tend directly to increase the demand of Europeans for each other's exports. Some saw here the strongest argument against the scheme, fearing that in the short-run at least only a small part of this increased demand would be met by increases in total supply and so there would tend to be a reduction of supplies available for export to dollar markets.[32] This adverse effect on exports was likely to be significant for goods the demand for which in the dollar area were more price elastic than in Europe. Under these conditions, small increases in

[30] It remained for others, especially Tibor Scitovsky some years later, to examine with care and make considerably more precise the cost-reducing possibilities resulting from an increase in regional competition, as distinct from an increase in trade. (See his *Economic Theory and Western European Integration*, London, 1958, pp. 19–48, 110–35.) Chapter IV below cites several of the other major contributors to the theory of the cost effects of economic integration.

[31] See Hinshaw, "The European Payments Union: Consideration of Some Criticisms," *The Review of Economics and Statistics*, Feb. 1951, pp. 55ff., for a discussion of this point.

[32] If the liberalization took place with no increase in money supply, the increased intra-area trade might release in the members some other production capacity, a part of the output of which might be exported. Apparently no one thought that this was likely to be important, in light of the "pent up" demands of the period.

European demands might raise prices and extinguish a lot of U.S. demands. Some thought this would be a common phenomenon because of the greater availability of close substitutes in the dollar area. This analysis, of course, was pertinent only as the effect of the regional arrangements was to raise prices in Europe.

Doubts that the EPU would be a stepping-stone and fears that instead it might be a new barrier to worldwide liberalization also stemmed from the very fact of its being regional.[33] Experience had been that there was no tendency for the international accounts of each EPU member to balance vis-à-vis all the other EPU countries as a group. Nonetheless, the EPU system could function well only under this condition and it introduced strong pressure on its members to achieve such a balance. To the extent those running European surpluses received only a partial payment for their surpluses in hard currency and had to finance the balance by extending credit, they would find themselves, it was anticipated, under pressure to divert imports from foreign to partner sources. Pressure would be especially strong if the country "normally" was in overall balance of payments equilibrium and used its net earnings in intra-European trade to settle a deficit with the rest of the world. If, on the other hand, the payments for the surplus were to be largely in gold, would not the Union then be tempted to apply pressure on the creditor to "correct" its European balances so as both to reduce the drain on the Union's reserves and to reduce the pressure on debtors to curtail European imports? The obvious way to correct such a balance would again be for the creditor, in one way or another, to divert imports from foreign to partner sources. This would mean not only a direct step away from general convertibility and nondiscrimination but, since it also meant substituting higher-priced

---

[33] For a more extended discussion of several of the points in these paragraphs, together with several bibliographical references, see the chapters on European Economic Integration in G. Patterson *et al.,* *Surveys of United States International Finance,* International Finance Section, Princeton University, Princeton University Press, Vols. for 1949–1951.

for lower-priced imports, it could adversely affect future production costs and thus ability to compete in third markets. The result would be to delay the return to convertibility and worldwide trade liberalization.

The EPU enthusiasts did not deny that the system had this built-in incentive toward more discrimination,[34] nor did they deny that the assumption in the system that all members' currencies were equally valuable was not true and that treating them as such would tend to encourage members to divert their exports to the weakest currency market—that with the highest prices at the official exchange rates. The consequence of this would be to reduce the pressures in the EPU strong currency countries to make their exports competitive in the extra-EPU hard currency markets. EPU proponents did not believe, however, that these factors were likely to prove quantitatively important and thought they would be outweighed by other considerations (noted above), which were favorable to larger dollar exports. They also insisted that the scheme must be judged on the basis of genuine alternatives, not against some unobtainable ideals. Although the terminology was not to become popular for some years, they defended it as a second-best optimum.

At the time the arrangements were negotiated and discussed relatively little attention was given to their long-run effects on the restoration of general convertibility. These effects were to bulk large later in connection with the European Common Market proposals and are discussed in Chapter IV. It is sufficient here to record that it seems to have been lightly assumed by those defending the EPU as a stepping-stone that the increased competition made possible by the multilateral payments arrangements and reduction of quantitative restrictions within the region would not only eliminate some of the

---

[34] A very modest attack on this problem was made when the EPU was created in the form of the "initial" positions accorded to the prospective net debtors and net creditors, whereby certain creditors received for one year more ECA aid than they otherwise would, in return for agreeing to cancel certain surpluses, and also, certain debtors had their deficits cancelled up to a certain amount.

high-cost firms and shift production to lower-cost ones, but, by enlarging the size of the market, would encourage greater amounts of both European and foreign investment into productive facilities to take advantage of newly available economies of scale and external economies. All this would result in greater production, increased productivity, and lower prices, which would in turn both reduce the rate of growth of dollar imports and increase that of dollar exports.

Detailed studies needed to determine whether in fact the necessary conditions existed for these benefits to develop had not been made. Of those who concerned themselves with these questions, the majority, however, apparently believed that this did not much matter, for such studies were almost certain to produce cases on both sides and any attempt to strike a net balance would be impossibly difficult and arbitrary. Moreover, technological changes would soon vitiate any conclusions that might be reached. In any event, there really wasn't much point in overly concerning oneself with estimating the uncertain long-run effects. The hoped-for increased international competitiveness of Europe, which would make it possible for those countries to adopt nondiscriminatory trade and payments policies, would arise less from any possible benefits of changing the locus of production within Europe and opening up new economies of scale possibilities, than from the manifold short- and long-run benefits growing out of the reinvigoration of the spirit of entrepreneurial initiative and business morale which would result from the increased competition and accompany the growth of this "new Europe." [35]

When the EPU began to function it was clear that it was possible for it to become a stepping-stone to general convertibility but that it might be so slippery as to be an obstacle. A priori analysis had shown that almost anything could happen; it

---

[35] As Scitovsky was to point out later, in his *Economic Theory and Western European Integration,* it was reasonable to expect that among the major benefits of the increased competition would be the taking advantage of the *available* economies of scale once European producers were forced by the competition into a more energetic pursuit of markets.

would all depend on what particular problems came up and how they were resolved.

Two Critical Episodes

GERMAN DEFICIT AND INFLATION ISSUE. In the event, the worries that the EPU would prove to be an inflation-generating engine proved unfounded. EPU debtors had received approximately $1 billion of credit by June 1952, but thereafter the total outstanding fluctuated between roughly $0.8 and $1.2 billion. Of the total net bilateral positions settled through the Union in its $8\frac{1}{2}$ years of existence, only about 6 percent were settled with credit; 70 percent via the compensation arrangements; and 24 percent via gold and dollars.[36] This aspect was put to a major concrete *policy* test in the first months for reasons that many had feared and anticipated and which were sketched in the preceding section: a major member—Germany— quickly exhausted her quota and reached an extreme debtor position. The details of the crisis and of the many facets of the "solution" need not delay us here.[37] For our purposes, the important facts are that the Organization for European Economic Cooperation and the Managing Board of the EPU in this critical case decided that help in the form of some additional credit from the Union, special efforts by other members to favor imports from Germany, plus commitments by other members of the club not to retaliate because Germany found it "necessary" for a time to reimpose some restrictions against imports from other members; these solutions, whose net immediate effect was to increase discrimination against third countries and which buttressed the case of the skeptics, were dependent on the manner in which Germany handled her internal affairs. In particular, these easy solutions were approved, provided Germany undertook not only to cancel a lot of outstanding import

[36] For more details, see Organization for European Economic Cooperation, *Final Report of the Managing Board of the European Payments Union,* Paris, Oct. 1959.

[37] For authoritative accounts, see OEEC, *European Payments Union, First Annual Report of the Managing Board,* Paris, 1951, pp. 21–24; Federal Reserve Bank of New York, *Monthly Review,* New York, April 1951; and *The Banker,* London, Sept. 1951, pp. 171–77.

licenses, but to put through a wide variety of fiscal and credit measures designed to reduce domestic demands: increases in certain taxes, a sharp rise in the discount rate, a doubling of the legal reserve requirements. These deflationary actions were all the more significant because the German import surplus that created its EPU problem was attributed not so much to overt inflationary policies as to an upsurge in personal consumption, the stockpiling of imports, prepayment of imports, ineffective exchange controls, and a relatively rapid removal of import restrictions, some of which were a consequence of the Korean War.

This crisis—and it was a genuine crisis in West European economic affairs—forcefully demonstrated that the skeptics had underestimated the determination of the EPU Managing Board and the EPU member governments to avoid inflation. It had been demonstrated that the Union need not (taking all of its aspects into account) be a force for inflation, commonly thought to be perhaps the most important short-run factor discouraging a move toward general nondiscrimination. A few months later Germany succeeded in actually reversing its EPU position—the result of many factors, including a fall in raw material prices, but it strengthened the faith of the EPU Managing Board in the virtues of noninflationary policies. It also seems to have had an emulative effect, encouraging other governments subsequently to rely more than they had in the recent past on financial and monetary measures to restrain their balance of payments deficits.

Although "proof" can never be had, it was believed by many at the time that in the absence of the OEEC regional arrangements and the pressures these institutions applied, Germany would have relied less on anti-inflationary means to correct her deficit and more on a raising of import barriers.[38] This would almost certainly have forced some of its European neighbors, whose balance of payments positions were weak and who were dependent on the German market, to deliberalize their import policies.

[38] This statement is based on conversations I had with several persons close to the scene.

BELGIAN SURPLUS AND FORCED REGIONAL BALANCE ISSUE. A more severe test at the policy level of the stepping-stone doctrine was soon to come, but this one did give support to the view that a regional system is biased in the direction of *forcing* regional balance at the price of increasing discrimination against others. Many had expected that the Belgium-Luxembourg Economic Union—given its pre-war trading pattern whereby it earned in Europe what was needed to settle its overseas deficits, plus its successful post-war anti-inflationary efforts—would be a creditor in the EPU. The Union soon became an extreme one, despite a much higher than average intra-European liberalization effort, and exhausted its quota in the summer of 1951.[39] The EPU gold and dollar pool was not big enough to allow full dollar payments for the extra-quota surpluses.[40] Although at that time Belgium enjoyed a strong hard-currency reserve position, this granting of large credits to other EPU members threatened to create serious inflationary pressures within the Belgian economy, which would endanger both the internal and the external value of the franc. Most thought that efforts to force the debtors to pay a larger proportion in gold would probably result in their reimposing restrictions on imports. To do nothing was to run the risk of Belgium deliberalizing its trade with Europe. After months of difficult negotiations, it was agreed that the extra-quota surpluses, up to certain agreed limits, would be settled half in gold and half in credit. In order to reduce future Belgian surpluses a "package" was worked out: licensing (restraining) of Belgian exports to Europe of some goods for which alternative markets could be found in the dollar area; new controls to ensure that only bona fide transactions entered the Belgian EPU accounts; imposition of tighter controls on capital imports into Belgium; special measures to encourage Belgian exporters themselves to carry some of the credit from their sale to EPU countries; and increased credit facilities to importers. But the package also called on Belgium

[39] Portugal and Italy were also extreme creditors at this time and so presented similar though less acute problems.

[40] There were several EPU debtors at that time; they were therefore in the lower tranches of their quotas, and thus of the gold-credit ratios.

to impose new restrictions on imports from the dollar area for the specific purpose of diverting imports to EPU suppliers.[41]

Belgium informed the Contracting Parties to the GATT of its actions, emphasizing that it hoped the new discrimination against the dollar imports would be needed only for a short time. It reported that it had done this reluctantly and only because it appeared that the alternative solutions it regarded as actually available—internal inflation in Belgium or much greater deliberalization of trade within Europe—would have been even more costly to Belgium's economic welfare and probably to that of the rest of the world as well.

United States and Canadian officials expressed great concern, asserting that this not only adversely affected their exports but was a step *away* from the goals of convertibility and nondiscriminatory multilateral trade by a country in a strong international economic position. They recognized that Belgium had a problem, but held that the choices were not limited to those posed. They noted that they too had extended foreign credits which had created internal financial pressures; they insisted that there were various ways other than those chosen by Belgium to deal with the problem, and emphasized that they had not felt obliged to resort to discrimination in favor of their debtors.[42] The discussions at that time were, however, inconclusive. The United States Government was divided in its position,[43] and the legal aspects of Belgian obligations under the General Agreements and the Fund Articles of Agreement were

[41] For an official statement of the Belgian problem and position, see Contracting Parties to the General Agreement on Tariffs and Trade, *Doc. CP6/44,* 22 Oct. 1951. See also, Organization of European Economic Cooperation, *European Payments Union, Second Annual Report of the Managing Board,* Paris, 1952, which virtually ignored the discriminatory aspects of all this.

[42] For an official U.S. statement, see GATT, *Doc. CP6/50,* 25 Oct. 1951.

[43] It was well known that ECA officials had played an active part in the decisions leading to the Belgian action. Moreover, having long supported the regional economic and political integration of Europe, the United States Government was not prepared to face squarely the possibility that it could not have both a more integrated Europe and nondiscriminatory treatment at all times for its exports.

in doubt. It was generally recognized that, *given the EPU arrangements,* Belgium did have a strong case for at least temporary discrimination against dollar imports. And at that time no government was prepared to argue that to destroy the EPU would speed the restoration of international equilibrium and nondiscrimination. Moreover, Belgium had a good record as a supporter of the GATT and Monetary Fund principles. For these many reasons, the decision was made not to pursue the matter to formal action, it being hoped that somehow or another the problem would disappear and Belgium would quickly remove the dollar discrimination.[44]

Shortly thereafter, Belgium held its first consultations under Article XIV with the International Monetary Fund. The latter has not published its findings or its decisions, if any, but subsequent public statements from other official sources encourage the conclusion that these consultations, to say the least, gave no support to the Belgian policy.[45] In light of this, plus new complaints by the United States that the Belgian action had nullified the benefits to which it was entitled from earlier tariff negotiations,[46] and because within Belgium itself there was a growing awareness of the cost to the nation of the discrimination in terms of higher priced and lower quality imports, the Belgians announced in October that they would gradually relax the discrimination.

---

[44] An excellent, long summary of this discussion in the GATT is given in the GATT, *Press Release, GATT/62,* Geneva, 29 Oct. 1951. Following these discussions the United States and Canada sought satisfaction in bilateral consultations with Belgium.

[45] GATT, *Press Release/101,* Geneva, 11 Nov. 1952, states: "In considering the Belgian dollar import restrictions . . . , the Contracting Parties had before them and made full use of the results of the Fund's consultation with Belgium as well as background material prepared in the Fund in connection with its consultation. The Belgian delegation have informed the Contracting Parties that the Belgian Government now feels that it is justified in proceeding in its return, albeit cautiously, to a regime of freedom from quantitative restrictions and therefore it proposes as a first step to institute shortly significant measures of relaxation in its dollar import restrictions."

[46] See GATT, *Press Release, GATT/71,* 27 Feb. 1952.

At this juncture, the question of whether the EPU and the associated trade measures were to facilitate, or to stand in the way of, progress by individual members toward universal nondiscrimination moved even more sharply to the fore. France, with varying amounts of support from Italy and the Netherlands, said that it was of course glad that the differences between Belgium and the United States and Canada were on the way to a settlement and that it was not in favor of permanent long-term discrimination against the dollar. Nonetheless, it went on, a reduction of discrimination against dollar imports by the Belgians threatened to damage the interests of other EPU members by making it more difficult for them to sell to Belgium, thereby worsening their balance of payments position vis-à-vis Belgium. The French spokesman emphasized that this certainly was not the way to promote European economic cooperation and that such cooperation was a major French objective.[47] This position raised the stepping-stone issue at once, and in concrete terms, to the political level.[48]

The United States and Canada, among others, expressed "shock" at this position and made strong statements in the GATT meetings to the effect that they (especially the United States) had contributed much to the EPU because it was thought to be a device that would help Europe increase production and productivity in a fashion consistent with the progressive relaxation of restrictions on trade and payments with the rest of the world. That is, they said, their support was based, and would continue to be based, on the belief that these were transitional institutions. The Belgians themselves added their support to the U.S.–Canadian thesis by stating that they had never regarded their traditional liberal trade and payments policy as being in conflict with their membership in the regional

---

[47] Listeners were also reminded that closer European economic cooperation had as one of its long-term aims the elimination of the dollar deficit.

[48] Those with a penchant for legal formulations defined the issue as whether a nation could be relieved of its obligations under the General Agreement and the Fund Articles of Agreement because of obligations under a regional arrangement.

organization, and that they planned to proceed gradually to remove the dollar restrictions.

By tacit, mutual agreement the debate did not continue in the Contracting Parties after the original positions were stated and clarified. The whole affair, nonetheless, was a sobering experience for many because it was concrete evidence that a temporary regional system easily runs the danger of drifting into a permanent, closed preferential area, and that vigilance is required to prevent it. More important, the affair was the occasion for a joining of the issue on a high political level with resulting insistence by a powerful group of nonmember nations that the EPU must be a transitional institution. The EPU governments were thus put on notice, and the others on guard.[49]

Mounting Costs of Discrimination

Soon after this episode, attitudes and policies toward the European arrangements by its members began to be greatly influenced by four major developments, all of which argued for terminating them. First, there were those, including many EPU architects and officials, who had always hoped and planned that EPU would be a way station, and who, as it became easier for them to take a longer-run view, began to have more concern lest the discrimination in the system become so consolidated in investments, distorted price relationships,[50] and attitudes that future dismantling would be progressively more difficult.[51]

Second, many EPU members were finding both their internal

---

[49] GATT, *Press Releases, GATT/101*, 11 Nov. 1952, and *GATT/139*, 14 Oct. 1953. See also, *The New York Times*, Nov. 2, 1952, p. 9. The immediately preceding paragraphs have also benefited from my having been permitted to read certain material in the GATT archives, that are not open for citation or quotation.

[50] Especially worrisome were various forms of what may be loosely called export subsidies resulting from preferential access to partners' markets.

[51] An analysis making these points by a then member of the EPU Managing Board, S. Posthuma, may be found in an article dated Dec. 15, 1952, appearing in a special edition of *The Journal of Finance and Credit*, Frankfurt-Main, 1952.

and external economic and financial situations greatly improved, and their international reserves mounting rapidly. Many Europeans believed, although cause-effect proof was not available, that this was due in part to the beneficial effects of the European regional arrangements on their production, productivity, and international competitive position. Whatever the cause, they consequently found less need for protected export markets in Europe; as they took a longer view of things, they developed a growing awareness and restiveness over the higher cost of imports resulting from the discrimination.[52]

Third, several EPU members, including not only Belgium, but by this time also West Germany and the Netherlands, were finding themselves persistent EPU creditors. They were thereby being "forced" by the operation of the system to extend rather large amounts of medium-term, and perhaps long-term, credits to the Union when they would have preferred to consume more goods and services from the rest of the world or to make other investments. That is, they were finding the economic costs of the EPU and regional trade liberalization arrangements higher than they had anticipated.[53]

---

[52] As discussed in Chapter II, this resulted in most individual members reducing their discrimination against dollar imports. This was done by gradually extending to the dollar area and, in important though not whole part, to the rest of the world, the trade liberalization measures which had first been taken for intra-European trade.

It can be argued, though apparently it was not much stressed, that these steps were more quickly taken because there had been the intervening intra-European relaxation. Such steps had often demonstrated that increased competition was less damaging to domestic producers than had been feared. Nations were thus encouraged to open their markets to still others—a risk they would not otherwise have been prepared to take so soon, had they had to do it for all in one fell swoop.

[53] The *Annual Report* of the EPU Managing Board shows that this problem was recognized as important from the beginning, but it took on special poignancy for those countries who found themselves so burdened month after month.

The original EPU agreement left open the question of how surpluses beyond the quota would be settled, but it was soon established policy to settle them 50 percent in gold and 50 percent in credit.

Fourth, the proximate, and perhaps most telling, force leading to decisions to end the arrangements was the conclusion by some members that the time was fast approaching when it was both feasible and desirable for them to make their currencies convertible and that this would be rendered much more difficult by their remaining in the EPU.

It was primarily because of the first three considerations that, beginning about mid-1952, those responsible for determining the intra-European trade and payments policies not only began more urgently to press members to extend their quantitative restriction liberalization measures to the dollar area but began to concentrate on ways of "hardening" the EPU, a process often called in the official Payments Union statements, "making improvements in the working of the Union." Movements in these two directions were, of course, steps toward convertibility and abandonment of discrimination. On the monetary side the most critical matter was the size of the quotas in the EPU and the ratio of gold and credit required for settlement of deficits and surpluses. Less important, but not negligible, were the rates of interest charged to debtors and paid to creditors, and the terms for amortizing outstanding debts and claims which would not be extinguished by a reversal in net positions.

Interest rates were raised in 1953 but it was some two years later before it was possible to reach agreement on increasing the gold percentage from 50 to 75 percent.[54] The long-drawn-out debate revolved around the familiar issues: quotas should be reduced and the gold-credit ratio increased, to (1) apply more pressure on debtors to take measures leading to a reduction in their balance of payments deficits, and (2) to make it easier for

[54] At the time the gold ratio was increased in 1955, the quotas were increased so as to keep unchanged the *absolute* amount of credit to which each member was entitled.

In 1952 the gold-credit scale for debtors had been altered in the direction of increasing the gold payment in the lower tranches of the quota and decreasing it in the higher, but leaving the total ratio unchanged if a nation used all of its quota. The purpose was not to facilitate a move toward convertibility but to strengthen the convertible assets of the Union itself. See OEEC, *European Payments Union, Second Annual Report of the Managing Board,* Paris, 1952, pp. 46ff.

creditors to liberalize their trade with the rest of the world and to make investments better suited to their own needs. But such harder terms, others argued, would induce debtors, actual or threatened, to seek relief via more stringent import restrictions on both European and non-European imports. In the end, the former considerations prevailed. The final decision to harden the terms of payment was, of course, facilitated by the continuation of various forms of United States extraordinary expenditures in Europe during these years.

At this same time much attention was also given to the problem of amortizing the large credits which certain members had extended to the Union. The details of the complicated arrangements and the negotiations leading up to them need not detain us,[55] but the trend here too was in the direction of stiffer terms for the debtors and larger hard currency receipts for the creditors. As immediate repayment of some of the debts in gold or dollars was agreed, and as specific schedules for repaying the balance were approved, the creditors were under less incentive than in the reverse case to discriminate against dollar imports and in favor of their debtors. The debtors were under more pressure to restore balance in their international accounts. Formal arrangements for amortizing debts also facilitated the debtors (including the United Kingdom) moving toward convertibility by removing one more uncertainty as to claims against its reserves after convertibility. Again, these were not easy to arrange, for, in addition to the reluctance of most debtors to pay their debts, some saw the major effect of these steps, too, as removing incentives for both debtors and creditors to liberalize more quickly *within* Europe and, by possibly reducing the already low gold and dollar reserves of debtors, delaying the day when they could risk liberalizing dollar imports.

These long discussions on "hardening" the system thus focused attention on the problem of conflict between measures that would jeopardize the growth of intra-European trade and

[55] The more important of them can be found in the OEEC, *European Payments Union, Fourth Annual Report of the Managing Board,* Paris, 1954.

those that would permit *some* to liberalize all intra- and extra-European trade even at the possible expense of delaying the return to full convertibility by the weaker partners. I cannot avoid the conclusion that the conflict was resolved in favor of a hardening of the system, and so a paving of the way toward multilateral trade and general convertibility, in large part because the inevitable EPU creditors and nonmember countries whose exports were suffering happened to be both economically and politically more powerful than those whose short-run interests at least lay in continuing the system as it was.

It was the fourth factor noted above—the decision of some members to make their currencies convertible—that sounded the death knell of the EPU, just as it had hastened the end of discrimination for balance of payments reasons. In March 1953 the British Chancellor of the Exchequer informed the OEEC officials in Paris that the Commonwealth Prime Ministers had concluded in recent discussions that their nations' interests would be best served by a return to the convertibility of sterling and freer trade *on a worldwide basis,* and that the time had come to start moving more quickly in that direction. He said they were anxious for this action to strengthen rather than damage the economies of the Europe and European cooperation.[56] But, he added, they did not see how a country making its currency convertible before the other members did so could remain in the European Payments Union. If it remained a member, others would be under an irresistible temptation to divert the proceeds of their exports to that member *outside* the EPU clearing and to convert them directly into an old, established hard currency. This would leave only their *payments* to the newly convertible country to be cleared through the European Payments Union. As a consequence, a convertible currency country would be paying for its imports from EPU members in its hard currency reserves and financing a part of its

---

[56] Britain was, in any event, at this time much less interested in seeing an "integrated Europe" emerge than were many of the Continental countries. An authoritative summary statement of the many reasons may be found in M. Camps, *Britain and the European Community, 1955–1963,* Princeton, 1964, pp. 45–53.

exports to Europe with credit—an intolerable situation, given the relatively low level of hard currency reserves.[57]

EPU Abandoned as Costs Mount, Benefits Decline

This decision forced a prolonged study at the policy level of the concrete problems of making currencies generally convertible and, more especially, of how and under what conditions the transition could best be made from a regional system to a worldwide system of trade and payments. The problem was no longer just one of making acceptable general statements of long-run intentions.[58] The technical analysis that was stimulated supported the British contention of the probable incompatibility in practice of convertibility of only some of the members with EPU membership. This led some—who valued highly the credit obtainable from the EPU, who treasured the regional arrangements for their noneconomic aspects, and who feared that, given the still severe dollar disequilibrium of several of the members, an abandonment of the Union would lead to much backsliding on intra-European trade liberalization—to argue that no EPU member should attempt convertibility until all could accompany it. Apparently, this extreme position did not find great support, but the majority of the EPU members did subscribe to the loose proposition that it would not be desirable for members to make their currencies convertible unless this could take place under conditions whereby the trade among EPU members, as well as trade between members and the rest of the world, could be maintained or increased.[59]

In the meantime, several EPU members, often following Britain's lead, found it in their national interests to gradually

[57] For a contemporary discussion of this, see A. C. L. Day, "Convertibility and the European Payments Union," *Bulletin,* Oxford University Institute of Statistics, May 1953, pp. 151–62; and *The Banker,* London, March 1953, pp. 130–33. For a more recent account of the 1952–1958 moves by Britain toward convertibility, see G. L. Rees, *Britain and the Postwar European Payments System,* Cardiff, Wales, 1963, Chap. 7.

[58] See OEEC, *European Payments Union, Fourth and Fifth Annual Reports of the Managing Board,* Paris, 1954 and 1956.

[59] See OEEC, *European Payments Union, Fourth Annual Report of the Managing Board,* p. 113.

increase the options open to the holders of their currencies. In this process they were removing much of the original *raison d'être* for the Payments Union. The resumption among several of them in mid-1953 of intra-EPU area foreign exchange arbitrage operations handled by private banks, was a return to traditional mechanisms and displaced much of the multilateral compensations previously performed by the Union.[60] More important were: the reopening of various international commodity markets in which goods bought for hard currency could be sold for soft; the gradual enlargement after early 1954 of the so-called transferable account areas, especially for sterling and the deutsch mark; the intervention in the major markets to maintain the price of such transferable currencies close to the official exchange rates; the relaxation of restrictions on transactions in blocked sterling accounts and in foreign securities; and the creation, in 1955 and 1956, respectively, of the so-called Hague Club and Paris Club.[61] These national moves toward convertibility were made easier because of the past operations of the European Payments Union and the cooperation among central banks that the Union had facilitated. They nonetheless removed the justification for that central feature of the EPU system: automatic credit arrangements designed to be associated with net payments positions only within the EPU area. This was so because members could now alter their EPU surpluses or deficits by using EPU currencies in non-EPU transactions.[62]

By 1954–1955 it was widely acknowledged that the EPU had "hardened" itself into being of less value to several of its

[60] See Bank for International Settlements, *Twenty-Fourth Annual Report,* Basle, 1954, pp. 121ff., for details on this development. This and the other *Annual Reports* of the BIS for these years provide much detail on the so-called "backdoor" convertibility.

[61] These last were arrangements whereby Brazil and Argentina, respectively, were permitted to spend their earnings from any of their European partners in the Club in any of the other partner countries. As a consequence of the other steps noted in the text, they were in fact able to spend them in many other countries as well.

[62] The EPU Managing Board appears to hold that these steps toward convertibility stemmed from the Union mechanism itself, but Triffin, a

members, that it was being undermined by the "backdoor" convertibility moves of its members,[63] and that it could not survive in its existing form the full and formal convertibility of the currencies which some of its members had now adopted as national objectives. To many, this was a measure of the system's success, and it was agreed in July 1955 that the Union would come to an end on the demand of members who accounted for at least 50 percent of the EPU quotas, it being understood such a request would be made in connection with the final step to formal convertibility.

The Search for a Place of Retreat

Many governments also believed, however, that a substitute organization was needed. Some had political objectives in the continuation and expansion of regional efforts. Some saw a need for a haven of quick retreat in the form of other arrangements for intra-European clearing in the event the multilateral world proved too severe and convertibility faltered or failed. Some feared that when the EPU was abolished the high level of trade within Europe would be placed in jeopardy unless there were some sort of special credit arrangements to permit members to withstand temporary balance of payments difficulties without resort to trade restrictions.

After many months of tortuous negotiations it was agreed, in mid-1955, that on the termination of the Payments Union a new European Monetary Agreement would come into force. Among other things, this called for establishing a European Fund to provide modest, nonautomatic short-term credits to members. A new multilateral system of settlements was also provided. This was designed both to facilitate multilateral

---

most knowledgeable student of the EPU, has stated that they were primarily "national measures . . . adopted by individual countries outside the EPU framework." See OEEC, *European Payments Union, Final Report of the Managing Board,* Paris, 1959; and Triffin, *Europe and the Money Muddle,* p. 212.

[63] The process of extending the transferability of national currencies was made easier by the fact that the central banks of the countries concerned knew they could obtain settlement from the Union at fixed parities for their holdings in other member countries' currencies.

compensation among members' currencies which were not convertible and to meet some of the problems that others holding sterling would face as a result of the fluctuating exchange rates which it was then thought the United Kingdom would introduce when sterling was made convertible.[64] As it turned out, the resurgence of inflation in 1956 and the effects of the Suez Crisis worked to postpone the British move toward formal convertibility until late December 1958. By that time, the other major EPU members were ready to take the same step, so there has been no need to use the new multilateral compensation arrangements. Other much more ambitious institutional frameworks for European economic cooperation were then in the process of being created and there has so far proved to be no need for a place to retreat from convertibility. The cumbersome European Monetary Agreement has, therefore, played no important role.[65]

The reluctance of many to see the regional European monetary arrangements disappear had its counterpart on the trade side. We saw in Chapter II that most nations by the mid-1950's were finding it in their national interest, narrowly conceived, to reduce their discriminatory trade practices. For the European countries this meant extending to others the measures they had already taken vis-à-vis each other in the OEEC Trade Liberalization Program. In a late 1954 meeting of the Contracting Parties of the GATT, however, the Benelux delegation formally proposed that the General Agreement nondiscriminatory rule be amended so as to permit the OEEC countries to continue to discriminate in favor of each other, so long as they were endeavoring to bring about a "closer

---

[64] Many of the problems faced in the complex and long negotiations involved in establishing the European Monetary Agreement are outlined in the OEEC, *European Payments Union, Annual Report of the Managing Board,* 1955 through 1958, and need not detain us here.

[65] Its chief function has been to provide some exchange guarantees which facilitated some bilateral credit arrangements between central banks. It has also made some loans to its less-developed members. Turkey has been the major recipient, but credits have also been provided to Greece, Iceland, and Spain.

integration of their economies." [66] Although their statements were not unambiguous, the main concern of the Benelux spokesmen seems to have been the fear that after convertibility some OEEC members might still have—or develop—balance of payments problems justifying quantitative restrictions on imports and that if these had now to be applied on a nondiscriminatory basis it would require that country to go back on the degree of liberalization achieved within the OEEC area. OEEC exporters would therefore suffer and their balance of payments problems would increase.[67] In other words, worldwide liberalization would be at the expense of regional deliberalization.

The proposal was, to put it mildly, coolly received by several of the non-European countries, especially the United States and Canada. They stated that they did not wish the price of nondiscrimination after convertibility to be a *decrease* in the volume of European trade and that if this seemed to be happening—which they thought unlikely—they would examine the situation with "sympathetic consideration." [68] But the

[66] The formal proposal was not limited to European countries. It provided that the rule of nondiscrimination "should not be applicable to contracting parties which endeavor to secure by means of freely concluded agreements a closer integration of their economies and which, by the application of special regulations, promote to the greatest possible measure the maximum development of multilateral trade." (GATT, *Doc. L/271*, 9 Nov. 1954.) It was accepted by all the discussants, however, that it was the OEEC Code of Trade Liberalization that was being considered and the proposal became known as the "European Clause."

[67] Elements of this same concern (when the balance of payments problems arose because of the emergence of a persistent and large surplus country) were also present (see Chapter II) in the British attempt at this same time to have the General Agreement amended so as to permit discrimination against nations whose currencies were "scarce." Theoretical foundations for a case with some important similarities had, of course, been set by Marcus Fleming in his March 1951 article in the *Economic Journal,* and by James Meade in his 1951 *The Balance of Payments.*

[68] See GATT, *Basic Instruments and Selected Documents, Third Supplement,* p. 178. See also, GATT, *Press Release 265,* 15 Nov. 1954, for a statement by the spokesman for the United States, expressing "particular regret" at the proposal.

proposal did not limit discrimination to cases where there were transitional and temporary problems associated with balance of payments deficits; it would permit discrimination for the purpose of perpetuating regional blocs. The proposal was therefore "unacceptable" to them, not only because it would be prejudicial to their exports, but—implicitly ruling out all second-best analysis—also because such discrimination would reduce world economic welfare.

The Canadian Minister of Trade and Commerce had the support of several governments when he asserted that while the OEEC–EPU arrangements had in the past helped their members improve their economic welfare they now threatened "to make further progress difficult," that regional groups of countries provide "a notoriously weak and unstable basis for trade," and that except for "brief periods" and "in exceptional circumstances," regional solutions to economic problems are not optimal ones.[69]

Some OEEC members, led by France, took strong exception to this. They argued [70] that the case for a universal nondiscriminatory system, which was so favored by the United States, Canada, and others, and which was back of the opposition to the Benelux proposal, was strong *if* conditions were "normal"— that is, if they were as they had been assumed to be in the 19th century, when the nondiscriminatory doctrines were formulated. But, they insisted, the mid-20th-century conditions were often a far cry from this. Prices were much more rigid than was assumed. As a consequence of differences in wages policy, social charges, and tax structures, the differences in "conditions of production" as among countries were much greater than the classicists had assumed. The result was that relative market prices had much less relation to relative real costs than some thought and assumed. The great value, they went on, now placed on full and stable employment and on strong and active labor unions, operated to vitiate many assumptions of the free trade nondiscrimination doctrine. Monopolistic elements, their

[69] GATT, *Press Release 208,* 6 December 1954.
[70] See GATT, *Press Release 175*, 10 Nov. 1954, for a statement by a French minister.

listeners were reminded, were present in most economies, thus further distorting the relations between real costs and prices.[71] These facts, continued the French spokesmen, meant that liberalizing trade might still be desirable but it would require much state intervention—presumably, although this was not clear, to offset the disparities between monetary and real social costs. This, they insisted, could best be done by *regional* authorities where close personal relations could be developed and where the problems of each nation had much in common and so could be better understood, with mutually satisfactory solutions reached. It was also argued that the distortions and disparities which needed correction and offsetting were likely to be smaller, and so more manageable, among neighboring countries. Moreover, it was asserted, though not demonstrated, that the regional arrangements in Western Europe deserved much of the credit for the economic and financial recovery of the area. It had been within the framework of regional, not multilateral, organizations that the most progress had so far been made in liberalizing trade and payments; therefore, these achievements must not be destroyed. (It is noteworthy that no one chose to argue that perhaps the regional progress had been at the expense of universal liberalization.) They warned that any precipitous rushing into a "universal" system might well lead again to a resurgence of national autarchic policies.

While not denying the fragility of the foundations of the classical nondiscrimination doctrine, many non-European spokesmen asserted that it was still a better guide to policy, from the point of view of improving general welfare, than resort to discriminatory regional arrangements. The spokesmen knew of no theory which provided a confident guide to policy in the ruling economic conditions, but they believed the "general drift" of the conclusions of classical doctrine for policy were more convincing than anything else they had heard.

[71] Although often expressed in imprecise terms, these statements clearly were driving at the same "disparities" that Meade was to formalize in his *Trade and Welfare,* Chap. 2.

It is not surprising that the discussion was inconclusive. These were, after all, the very years when the theoretical economists were wrestling with the theory of the second-best as it applied to regional economic groups, and were concluding that if it were impossible to reach at the same time all conditions for maximum welfare, then fulfilling any one of them might or might not improve welfare. All depends on the particular conditions of the particular case.[72] The analysis was further, and immensely, complicated because frequently cropping up in these policy-level discussions was the view that the major issue before the house was the creation of a "new Europe," that giving each other preferences contributed to this. Even if such preferences were costly to economic welfare, many believed this was a cheap price to pay for the political results.

It was, in any event, clearly evident to all that the matter of regionalism, as a feature of the international landscape, was only in its infancy and that many of these problems would come up again. It was also clear at this time, however, that no agreement could then be reached on amending the General Agreement so as to permit the European countries—short of forming a customs union or free trade area—permanently to discriminate in favor of each other in the application of quantitative import restrictions. The Benelux officials therefore withdrew their proposal, but with no implications that they might not sometime reintroduce it should their balance of payments position worsen.[73]

Thereafter, for the reasons discussed in Chapter II, individual European countries continued to reduce the discriminatory aspects of their quantitative restrictions to the point of near-extinction, except as they applied to Japan and some of the less-developed countries. The whole OEEC trade liberalization program was of course overtaken in the next few years by the

[72] For a citation of some of the relevant literature see the following chapter, footnote 2.

[73] See GATT, *Basic Instruments and Selected Documents, Third Supplement,* pp. 178–79, for a brief official description of this discussion.

division of its members into the "Six" and the "Seven." [74] It made no sense to keep a Code which called for nondiscrimination among all OEEC countries when a major characteristic of the area was that two discriminatory arrangements had been established and efforts to meld them into one were being resisted by the "Six," and frequently by many non-European nations which often saw such a union increasing the discrimination against them. But this is the subject of the next chapter. The Code formally went out of force when the Organization for European Economic Cooperation (OEEC) was replaced by the Organization for Economic Cooperation and Development (OECD) in 1960.

CONCLUSIONS

Three major conclusions may be drawn from this experience. First, the fears that the EPU and the Associated Intra-European Trade Liberalization measures would create a more or less permanent, protected, high-cost, soft-currency area were proven unjustified. But this result was not inherent in the arrangements, nor was it inevitable. The various crises, some of which were inherent in such a regional system, could have been resolved, and there was considerable pressure each time to do so, in ways which would have prolonged and perhaps perpetuated discrimination. That they were not was not due to the nature of the scheme but to the facts: (a) that the participants had committed themselves to phasing it out; (b) that powerful third countries, especially the United States, exercised considerable pressure toward liberalization at critical times; (c) that the members had reasons apart from these arrangements for avoiding inflationary policies; and (d) that those members who were,

[74] See Isaiah Frank, *The European Common Market,* New York, 1961, Chaps. V, VI, for an account of some of the difficulties presented for the Code of Trade Liberalization by the division of Europe into the European Economic Community and the European Free Trade Association. A fuller account may be found in Camps, *Britain and the European Community, 1955–1963,* Chaps. VI–VIII. See also, Curzon, *Multilateral Commercial Diplomacy,* pp. 269–72, for an account of the relations between the GATT and the OEEC on the question of the Code of Liberalization.

as it turned out, called upon to pay the highest prices for continuing the scheme—the United Kingdom, Germany, and the Benelux—were among the more economically and politically powerful. It follows that any such scheme at another time could easily prove to be more permanent.

Second, the arrangements probably did facilitate the movement toward convertibility and nondiscrimination in trade. Certainly during this period, Europe rapidly increased its production, productivity, and competitive ability in world markets; which in turn made it easier to pursue policies of general nondiscrimination. These basic improvements were the net result of an immense range of actions and policies, high on the list in most observers' eyes being the 1949 devaluations and the subsequent policies by governments to avoid inflation while pursuing fiscal and monetary policies leading to high and growing levels of demand and investment. It is not possible to quantify the role played in all this by these regional arrangements. Though long skeptical, I have been unable to find evidence disproving the widely-held belief in Europe among those who watched the developments with care, that the EPU and the associated trade measures made significant, if nonquantifiable, contributions. Compared with the previous arrangements, they both permitted and encouraged an expansion in total trade and production. The increased competition resulting from these regional arrangements, most believed, probably forced very little if any shifting in the locus of production from high-cost to lower-cost areas, but the regional arrangements did, nonetheless, often reduce costs and so increase competitive ability. This came about both by a squeezing of previously protected profit margins and by making it necessary and/or worthwhile for existing producers to adopt technological innovations, exploit existing potential economies of scale, and otherwise pursue more efficient production methods. Investment also probably increased because of the larger markets potentially made available to European producers by the trade and payments measures.[75] The most comprehensive recent study of growth in

[75] It can, of course, be argued that these benefits could have been achieved in even fuller measure had the European countries reduced

Western Europe concludes that during the 1950's the integration efforts played a modest—but only a modest—role. Such impact as they had was less on the invigorating effects of competition or economies of scale than on the effects the reduction of trade and payments barriers had on fostering new investments, and so growth, by reducing the risks and uncertainties of an important portion of their foreign trade.[76]

No evidence has been found that the effects of these arrangements was in any important respect to encourage new investments which could not stand "foreign" competition, thus creating barriers to a subsequent widening of the liberalization moves. These latter effects were, of course, small or nonexistent, in part, because the Payments Union and the trade liberalization schemes had only relatively short lives.

The third, and perhaps most interesting, general conclusion that can be drawn from all this is that, as with the discrimination for balance of payments reasons discussed in the preceding chapter, there were clear short-run advantages to the members of discriminatory policies, but these benefits tended over a fairly

---

their barriers against everyone, not just each other. The answer seems to be that, apart from the highly valued political objective of regionalism, in the early 1950's the European governments simply were unwilling to assume the risks involved in a general cut in import restrictions. In part, this was because the consequences seemed so uncertain after so many years of isolation from world markets; and partly it was because they believed it would necessitate a politically disastrous amount of internal change and adjustment and that much of this would not be necessary once their producers had the time and the incentive provided by increased European competition to increase their production and productivity. As we have just noted, they were also unwilling to move quickly on a worldwide basis because, given the extent of government intervention in economic affairs, they believed any freeing of trade required not only credit commitments but also agreements as to other policies directly related to trade. This, many believed, was only feasible among nations sharing several major problems in common. Finally, in a world where it has become accepted practice for reductions in trade barriers to take place only on a reciprocal basis, there was no reason to believe in these years that the rest of the world, and the United States in particular, was willing to move as fast as Western Europe.

[76] Angus Maddison, *Economic Growth in the West,* New York, 1964, pp. 66–75.

short period of years to level out, while the costs gradually became more obvious, more diverse, and greater. The time thus came when for most participants the costs exceeded the benefits. When this situation arrived for a sufficient number the arrangements were abandoned.

NOTE ON INTERNATIONAL MONETARY FUND— EUROPEAN PAYMENTS UNION RELATIONS

It has often been said that the International Monetary Fund was hostile to the EPU, that it was scathingly critical because it did not immediately restore full convertibility and worldwide nondiscriminatory trade. This is an oversimplification. In mid-1948 the Executive Board of the Fund took a decision welcoming the plan then being made for multilateralizing the intra-European payments scheme and stated that it would not object to moderate drawing by European countries of the currencies of other European countries held by the Fund to help in this multilateral process, *provided* the conditions and purposes of the Fund were met. The Board also said that the Fund would be prepared to have its advisory and technical facilities used for these purposes.[77]

This "offer" to become involved in the European regional monetary arrangements came to nothing. Part of the reason for this was that the Fund took little initiative on the matter. This, in turn, was due to differences of view within the organization as to whether the Fund should at that time become deeply involved in operations or concentrate on thinking and planning for the future, and, in part, to the fact that the world was developing so differently than had been assumed when the Articles of Agreement was signed.

In late 1949–early 1950 the EPU proposals came to the Fund's attention, and it was critical of them. The criticism

[77] The International Monetary Fund, *Annual Report of the Executive Directors, 1948,* Washington, D.C., 1948, pp. 32–35, 75, reproduces this decision. The *Report* also speaks in sympathetic terms of regional European trade and payments arrangements, provided they were gradually adapted to universal multilateral patterns. This theme reappeared in the *Annual Report, 1949,* pp. 30–32.

stemmed from both analytical and institutional considerations, for the Fund, in contrast to the EPU, had to take a worldwide and relatively long-run point of view. This meant that the question of the impact of the EPU on its members' progress toward convertibility was of primary, not secondary, concern. And in the Fund's early analysis, the inflationary and dollar export-diverting possibilities outlined in pages 84–90 above bulked large. In addition, many of those whose job it was to breathe life into the Fund saw their institution threatened. The proposed arrangements were designed to continue indefinitely and dealt with matters clearly within the scope and authority of the Fund. The Fund let it be known that it wished to participate in the discussions.

Several transatlantic trips were made, but it soon became clear that those, both Europeans and Americans, who were drafting and negotiating the Union's proposals did not want the Fund to become involved. In their view, the Fund could be of no help. The April 1948 decision: that so long as ECA aid was being received members should not draw dollars from the Fund, meant little financial assistance could be expected. The EPU architects saw little evidence that the Fund had given serious study to finding solutions to the *immediate* problems of Europe. The British were to become particularly disenchanted with the Fund because, as we have seen, in late 1950 it recommended that some members of the Sterling Area should liberalize their import restrictions while others need not; this was regarded as equivalent to denying the principle of pooled reserves, and on this largely hinged the Sterling Area at that time. All the EPU members-to-be feared that the Fund's emphasis would be on ensuring that the long-run results of the EPU would be consistent with the Fund's objectives. This, many of them reasoned, could lead to interminable delays in finding a solution to the immediate pressing problems. Not to be forgotten was that there were many in Paris to whom the political aspects of the EPU were extremely important. They wanted a European system, worked out in Europe and centered on the Continent.

The consequence was that the Fund played almost no direct

role in the negotiations. They did, nonetheless, exercise some influence. First, their analytical work, pointing out some of the possible adverse effects of the scheme on the avowed long-term goals, was some help to the EPU's authors. Second, and more important, Fund officials helped persuade the senior level of United States Government to formally state midway in the negotiations that the Union should be regarded as a temporary arrangement and should not conflict with the individual member's obligation under the Articles of Agreement to move as rapidly as that member could toward full convertibility of his currency.[78] This move greatly irritated many of those who were quite literally working day and night to devise a scheme that would be an improvement over the wholly inadequate, existing arrangement, but it presumably had some effects on the results.

Quite early, the majority of those concerned with these matters in the Fund accepted the EPU as a fact, recognized it as an improvement over the preceding arrangements, and concluded that the power of the EPU Managing Board was so weak as to preclude its becoming a long-term institutional threat. They thereupon bent their efforts neither to trying to destroy the EPU nor to helping it solve its immediate problems, but to ensuring that it did in face serve as a stepping-stone to general convertibility. To this end they used whatever influence they had to secure a "hardening" in the settlement terms—chiefly an increase in the ratio of gold to credit settlement for net positions.[79]

---

[78] National Advisory Council on International Monetary and Financial Problems, *Semi-Annual Report to the President and to the Congress for the Period Oct. 1, 1949–March 31, 1950,* Washington, D.C., 1950, p. 13, gives a brief summary statement of the decision.

[79] International Monetary Fund, *Annual Report, 1950,* Washington, D.C., 1950, p. 66.

It was a widely held view in the Fund at this time that a much more effective way to move to convertibility would be for the United States to give special assistance to the United Kingdom, permitting it to reduce the sterling balances, and for the Economic Cooperation Administration to give its aid to the EPU members in the form of "free" dollars, conditioned on recipients making settlements among each other in gold

The Fund stood aside during the German crisis in the first months of the EPU. This solidified the convictions in EPU circles that the Fund was hostile and that there was no point in trying to work together. By late 1950, however, there was within the Fund a growing determination that the institution should no longer be allowed to slumber. This was associated with a wholesale reorganization of the Fund staff and the creation of several "operating" divisions, including one on European affairs. This conviction was accompanied, on the analytical side, by more attention to the possible beneficial effects of the European arrangements. It was strengthened by the conclusion that, however valid the objections to creating the EPU may have been, for it to fail now that it was in being would almost certainly lead to a resurgence of bilateralism in Western Europe. Such a situation was not in the long-term interests of the Fund as an institution, nor was it likely to hasten the day when the assumptions on which the Fund was built would be realized.

By mid-1951 the prevailing mood in the Fund was that it should stand ready to assist *individual* countries—not the EPU itself, which was, after all, not a Fund member—who were members of the Payments Union meet their Union, and other, problems, *provided* in each individual case that the assistance would help the country move toward the Fund's long-term goal of convertibility. Much study was given again to the possibility, foreseen in the 1948 decision noted above, of the Fund's permitting individual EPU debtors to borrow the currency of extreme EPU creditors to pay off part of their Union debt. It was thought that by so providing a sort of second line of reserves the Fund might help resolve the EPU difficulties stemming from the emergence of extreme creditors. Subse-

---

or dollars, rather than making dollar aid dependent on a dollar deficit. This position was not pressed, for it was believed within the Fund that Congress would not agree to it.

It should also be recorded that the skepticism of those in Europe as to the help the Fund could give was strengthened by the fact that during this early period tentative inquiries by those working on the EPU in Paris often received no, or long delayed, replies from the Fund in Washington.

quently, the possibility was also explored of permitting extreme creditors to borrow dollars, if the alternative were likely to be that the creditor would resort to bilateral balancing in Europe, or debtors to deliberalization in Europe.

All this seemed timid and inadequate to the EPU officials and governments.[80] The EPU debtors hoped for easier credit terms from the EPU. The EPU creditors saw little advantage in taking on a hard loan to offset a softer EPU credit.[81] No such arrangements were then evolved.

In February 1952 the Executive Directors of the Fund took what they regarded as an important decision, designed to be a "practical" basis for unfreezing the Fund's resources.[82] The "gold tranche" decision provided that drawings up to the amount of gold or dollars each member had contributed to the Fund would be virtually automatic, but additional drawings were to be considered on a case by case basis and must not be outstanding beyond a "reasonable" period—three to five years were regarded as the outside range. The decision also specified that the drawers take measures to overcome the payments problem which had necessitated the drawings. One of the objects of this decision was to permit the Fund to help EPU countries in payments difficulties, but again the latter regarded it as modest and timid in the extreme.

Later in the year the Fund introduced its standby arrangements and shortly thereafter extended a $50 million standby

[80] Statements strongly criticizing the inactivity of the Fund and charging it with being out of touch with reality, while heaping praise on the EPU, were made by ministers of finance and central bank governors from the EPU countries at the 1951 meetings of the Board of Governors. The texts were often distributed as press releases, but the International Monetary Fund, *Summary Proceedings, Sixth Annual Meeting*, Washington, D.C., 1951, gives scarcely a hint of all this.

[81] Seven years after the above arrangements were discussed, when the EPU had but a little over a year to live, arrangements were worked out whereby, if all parties agreed, a debtor could draw a creditor's currency from the Fund and use it to settle an EPU deficit, with the EPU using these funds to settle a gold obligation to the creditor. This arrangement was used by France drawing deutsch marks in 1958.

[82] The International Monetary Fund, *Annual Report, 1952*, Washington, D.C., 1952, Appendix I, pp. 87–90.

credit to Belgium. This matched a seven-year funding of an equivalent amount of Belgium–EPU extra-quota surpluses which had been arranged at the same time and so assured Belgium of being able to obtain the $50 million funding in advance. It made the Belgian credit to the EPU "bankable." This seems to have been the first direct financial tie-in between the two organizations, but it was not to set a pattern.[83]

Shortly after, the question of United Kingdom and possibly other EPU countries making their currencies convertible began to move toward the center of the international financial stage; both the OEEC (EPU) and the Monetary Fund saw that this would bring with it great changes in their relationships. Convertibility was almost certain to increase the need for Fund help, because the removal of restrictions that would be required, all agreed, might well create at least short-term reserve difficulties for the EPU members who so moved. Moreover, that convertibility could be seriously considered also meant the emergence of the sort of world in which the Fund was supposed to operate, so Fund assistance and involvement was much more feasible under its rules than it had been before. Ever-closer working relationships developed between the Monetary Fund representatives in Paris and the OEEC–EPU officials; more and more documents were exchanged, and high-level EPU–Fund missions again made trips across the Atlantic to discuss common problems and possible joint efforts at solutions. The position of each became better understood by the other.

The Fund continued to insist that it must work with individual EPU members on a case by case basis and not with the regional group. No agreement was ever reached on any special financial arrangements for EPU members just because they

[83] In 1958, shortly before the EPU was terminated, the Fund joined with the Union, the United States Government, and several European nations in extending credits of one kind or another, totalling $359 million, to Turkey. The Union and the Fund each "contributed" $25 million. The Fund earlier that year also joined the Union and the United States Government in making available $655 million worth of assistance of various kinds to France, of which the EPU contributed $250 million and the Fund $131 million in the form of a standby credit. Both of these were associated with extensive stabilization programs in the countries receiving the assistance.

were EPU members. The Fund did gradually liberalize access to its resources for all members, but, apart from the 1952 Belgium standby credit, little if anything was ever done specifically to help EPU. In addition to the other reasons already noted, there developed considerable concern within the Fund that trouble would be created within the Executive Board if the Fund did anything that looked like giving preferential treatment to the European members.

Once the decision had actually been taken that individual EPU members would move toward convertibility the Fund came into its own. Now it was the EPU which spoke often of the need for closer cooperation between the two institutions.[84] But with convertibility the question was to become academic, for, as we have seen, the EPU was then to end.

To the end the Fund remained skeptical that the EPU was more effective than a gradual worldwide approach would have been for hastening the return of general convertibility. Some in the Fund regarded the thesis that it would serve as a stepping-stone as a phony, holding that this argument was intended only to divert the attention of others from the real purpose: to prepare for a permanent regional bloc whose objectives were primarily political. Be that as it may, the Fund did help in a minor way to ensure that the EPU serve as a stepping-stone. It did this, in part by the analysis within the Fund staff which pointed out most of the dangers to convertibility and long-term nondiscrimination that were possible in such a regional arrangement. By constantly harping on these dangers the Fund probably helped prevent the EPU drifting in that direction. More important, though still of minor influence, was the other work of the Fund. In its annual Article XIV consultations with European members and in its lending policy in general, the Fund probably did contribute a little to the adoption by the European countries of internal policies leading to financial stability and the simplification and relaxation of exchange restrictions. These helped create conditions where convertibility could be undertaken by individual countries without what they regarded as too great risks.

[84] See OEEC, *European Payments Union, Annual Report of Managing Board,* 1954 on.

CHAPTER IV

Discrimination and Permanent Regional Organizations, 1

INTRODUCTION

THE architects of the post-World War II international economic institutions and policies enshrined nondiscrimination as a guiding principle. But, as we saw in Chapter I, they blessed customs unions and free trade areas, classic discriminatory arrangements. At the time, this approval was founded less on rigorous systematic analysis than on the tradition that customs unions were a "good thing," this in turn being based on the conviction that the political implications of customs unions might often override the demands of economic consistency, and on the largely intuitive sense that policies which increased trade between some areas and were not accompanied by an increase in absolute levels of barriers to trade with other areas should, by creating some new trade, improve the economic welfare of the participants and probably would do little if any harm to others, and might even benefit them.[1]

[1] At war's end it was not anticipated that customs unions and free trade areas would be a major feature of the international scene. It was believed that if relatively full employment could be maintained and if progress could be made in reducing barriers to trade on a worldwide basis—assumptions underlying all the international post-war planning—then, except for special political, ethnic, historic, or geographic ties (such as went far to justify the four European Customs Unions which survived World War II: France–Monaco; Italy–San Marino; Switzerland–Lichtenstein; Belgium–Luxembourg; and those among some of the British and some of the Belgian colonies in Africa), regional preferential arrangements would have little appeal. See League of Nations, *Commercial Policy in the Post-War World,* Geneva, 1945, pp. 52–55, for a short statement of why regional arrangements had appeared in the 1930's.

Although the Benelux Customs Union tariff arrangements were not consummated until Jan. 1, 1948, they had been anticipated for some time and there had been an understanding during the ITO negotiations that other nations approved of it and would raise no objections. Its actual formation was not therefore a matter for extensive international discussions with nonmembers.

120

There was some uneasiness over these comfortable and easy conclusions, but it was not until the decade of the 1950's that a systematic theory of the effects of regional economic groupings was developed. This work [2] showed that the problem was a very complicated one because the customs union (and the analysis is largely applicable to free trade areas and to economic unions) combined elements of both freer trade and greater protection—freer trade as among members and greater protection for producers within the area in the markets of the other members against producers from outside the area. A customs union can therefore *both create* trade by shifting demand for some goods from domestic producers to imports from the partner countries, since the import restrictions on such trade are now lowered, and *divert* trade in some products from a foreign to a partner source, since the former now has higher barriers to overcome than the latter. The union will also have an effect on the level of income of the members; this, too, is clearly a matter of concern to the rest of the world. In these circumstances of a mixture of free trade and more protection, that is, something less than the conditions for maximizing welfare, the net effect on the economic welfare of third countries, as well as on the members, depends on the particular circumstances of the case. It might be either an increase or a decrease.[3]

[2] The literature is now extensive, but the classics are: Jacob Viner, *The Customs Union Issue*, 1950; James Meade, *The Theory of International Economic Policy*, Vol. I, *The Balance of Payments*, 1951, and Vol. II, *Trade and Welfare*, 1955, and *The Theory of Customs Unions*, 1956; R. G. Lipsey and Kelvin Lancaster, "The General Theory of Second Best," *Review of Economic Studies*, 1956–1957, No. 63, pp. 11–32; R. G. Lipsey, "The Theory of Customs Unions: A General Survey," *Economic Journal*, September 1960; J. M. Fleming, "On Making the Best of Balance of Payments Restrictions on Imports," *Economic Journal*, March 1951, pp. 48–71; Tibor Scitovsky, *Economic Theory and Western European Integration*, 1958; and Bela Balassa, *The Theory of Economic Integration*, 1961. Harry G. Johnson, in his *Money, Trade, and Economic Growth*, 1962, pp. 46–74, gives an excellent short synthesis and extension of this literature. For a highly abstract, theoretical treatment, see J. Vanek, *General Equilibrium of International Discrimination*, 1965.

[3] The analysis in the cited sources shows that in most circumstances likely to prevail a union will increase economic welfare *for the partners*

With regard *only* to the effects of a union on the efficiency of specialization and division of labor within the customs union, and between it and the outside world (the so-called "static production effects"), it is virtually certain that there will be some trade diversion. Assuming that the relevant demand and supply curves have their usually-assumed shapes, this will further adversely affect third countries by its effects on their terms of trade for that commerce which remains.[4] Moreover, it has also been shown recently [5] that if the partners seek, as they often have, objectives other than just maximizing the goods and services available for private consumption—for example, economic diversification—then trade diversion may become something to be valued, to be searched out by the union members, entirely apart from any terms of trade effects it may have.

The formation of the customs union will also have "static

---

as compared with a previous situation of high trade barriers by each member against all other countries.

[4] The question of whether, so far as these static production effects are concerned, the world *as a whole* gains or loses in terms of the usual real product considerations depends primarily on whether trade creation is greater or less than trade diversion and as the cost differences are greater among producers for commodities on which trade is created and smaller on goods for which trade is diverted. Trade-creation is more likely, as the various members of the union were "competitive" when the union was formed; that is, they produced goods of the same kind as a consequence of national import restrictions prior to the formation of the union; as the economic size of the union increased; as costs of transportation among the members was small; and as the initial tariffs of the members were high. Trade diversion will be less the lower the "average" tariff level on imports from nonmembers as compared with the pre-union tariff level. Johnson, in the above cited source, also points out that trade diversion will be less as foreign supply is more price-inelastic on the downward side. But since the less elastic foreign supply is to falling prices the greater the movement of the terms of trade against the foreign country, it follows that, with respect to this aspect of the problem, the world as a whole is more likely to gain the greater the damage inflicted on nonmembers.

[5] H. G. Johnson, "An Economic Theory of Protectionism, Tariff Bargaining, and the Formation of Customs Unions," *The Journal of Political Economy*, June 1965, pp. 256–83. See especially, pp. 279–81.

consumption effects" in the form of inter-commodity substitution in favor of goods whose prices have fallen to the consumer. These are also likely to be adverse to nonmembers because the duty-component of prices charged the consumer on intra-area produced and traded goods is now less than that on extra-area goods. Inasmuch as third countries do not, so far as static effects are concerned, benefit from any trade-creating consequences of a union, they are almost certain to suffer in the short-run from the formation of regional economic groups.

Most economists have concluded that these unhappy, direct static effects on foreign countries may be in part, in whole, or more than, indirectly offset by the so-called "dynamic effects" of an increase in demand for their output—and possibly subsequent improvement in their terms of trade—generated by an increase in incomes within the union attributable to the formation of the union.[6] A union, a larger market, may stimulate higher incomes among its members in four, sometimes overlapping, major ways. It may result in more effective competition between industries and firms. By so restraining monopolistic practices,[7] and by otherwise providing incentives for firms to take fuller advantage of known methods of reducing costs and improving quality, including economies of scale already technically possible, increases in productivity and levels of production may be achieved. This is in addition to any lowering of costs resulting from the possible trade-creating effects of a customs union in shifting the locus of production from one member country to another. Second, associated with the first, it may result in

[6] M. E. Kreinin, "On the Dynamic Effects of a Customs Union," *The Journal of Political Economy*, April 1964, pp. 193–95, is less optimistic than most writers as to the beneficial dynamic effects on nonparticipants. He points out that the increase in growth among the union members is due in part to the "static" terms of trade and trade diversion effects, that these two effects not only have the generally acknowledged, direct, "static," unfavorable effect on nonmembers but also directly adversely affect nonmembers' *growth* rates and so must be an offset to any favorable indirect "dynamic" effects on them of the higher incomes generated in the union.

[7] Some observers, of course, have feared that economic unions would in practice operate to increase the power of monopolies and cartels.

important external economies, including better use of the area's technical and organizational skills and the faster spreading of existing knowledge. Third, the creation of a larger market may permit fuller exploitation of economies of scale, particularly those internal to the plant.[8] Finally, for all of the above reasons, as well as by eliminating some of the risks and uncertainties of selling in important foreign markets, it may buoy entrepreneurial expectations and so encourage additional investment, both domestic and foreign, thus accelerating the rate of growth and changing its composition. With respect to any given regional grouping, opinions may differ greatly as to the magnitude of these phenomena, depending on what one assumes to be the facts.

Most of this theoretical analysis was not available to those who drafted the relevant articles of the General Agreement. *From the viewpoint of third countries,* the recent theoretical analysis does bear witness, however, to the wisdom and intuition of the GATT drafters in providing (Article XXIV) first, that if the customs union or free trade areas were to be blessed they should not involve barriers against nonmembers that on the whole were higher or more restrictive than the general incidence of members' pre-union restraints. This is so because the lower the common duties, as compared with the pre-union situation, the less the trade diversion. Second, that such a union include "substantially all the trade" in products originating in the areas making up the new union—because the larger the number of goods included the less likely trade-creating changes will in practice be excluded, and trade-creation increases real incomes of the members, and thus the beneficial, indirect "dynamic" effects on third countries. Third, that the union be consummated within a "reasonable" period of time, because the shorter the transitional period the sooner competition and other so-called dynamic effects will make themselves

[8] Scitovsky, in his *Economic Theory and Western European Integration,* first stressed several of these dynamic aspects. A more recent development of them may be found in Balassa, *Theory of Economic Integration,* Chaps. 5–8.

felt on members' incomes and so on third countries' exports.[9]

In view of this theoretical analysis it is not surprising that as concrete proposals for permanent regional groups were made the question of their discriminatory impact on others should have generated much debate, and that this debate should often have been inconclusive. Some of the more important variables were just being identified and systematically related after actual policy formulation had gone forward. Moreover, the analysis showed that this is an area where even the direction of net change is often uncertain and depends on the quantification of the variables in each instance; and such quantification was often virtually impossible. Policy makers were, more than usual, on their own and without confident theoretical guidelines.

THE EUROPEAN COAL AND STEEL COMMUNITY

The first such major, new, permanent regional arrangement to be subjected to extensive critical examination by nonmembers was the European Coal and Steel Community.[10] It was

[9] The General Agreement also requires that trade restriction removal within the union be complete and not partial. Recent theoretical work suggests, however, that, with tariffs vis-à-vis nonmembers fixed, a partial reduction of duties on imports from partners may well increase welfare of members more than a complete removal. This is because each successive reduction within the union will contribute less to the gains from the greater trade creation that results because the disparity between internal cost and price of imports is progressively less. But the loss in welfare (represented by the disparity between price of imports and cost of local substitutes) from any trade diversion resulting from additional lowering of barriers within the bloc will continue at the old level per unit of trade diverted. See Meade, *Theory of Customs Unions,* pp. 110–11; and Lipsey, "The Theory of Customs Unions: Trade Diversion and Welfare," *Economica,* Feb. 1957, pp. 40–46.

[10] In July 1947 the Committee on European Economic Cooperation, meeting in Paris and helping to prepare the first European Recovery Program, discussed the question of whether the formation of a large customs union was indicated. A Customs Union Study Group (later replaced by the Customs Cooperation Council) was set up and worked on technical aspects of the problem for several years, but it was not the father of any concrete arrangements. This was partly because of British

rumored that the signatories were going to ask the Contracting Parties to the General Agreement to treat the proposed new institution as a separate and distinct contracting party, so that the question of discrimination would not legally arise.[11] This was not done, however. Instead, in 1952, after the Treaty establishing the Community had been signed by the Six—but before it was ratified—the text was submitted to the GATT with the request that the signatories be authorized to do what they had just done. Such formal authorization was necessary because the Treaty was in clear conflict with the most-favored-nation obligations of the members. They did not intend to extend to other countries the exceptions from duties and other barriers to trade in coal and steel products which under the Treaty they agreed to grant each other. It was clearly discriminatory in intent and was therefore in conflict with several articles of the General Agreement. Nor did it come within the Customs Union provisions, since it concerned only two groups of products and not "substantially all the trade" among the members.

At the outset, the Community spokesmen took the position that little discussion of their proposal was needed because the

---

opposition. Britain wanted to be neither in it nor excluded from it. It was also because other problems were more pressing. Several abortive and short-lived attempts at customs unions and free trade areas were made in the years immediately after the war: France–Italy; France–Italy–Benelux; France–Tunisia; the proposed Nordic market of the Scandinavian countries; the United Kingdom–Netherlands–Denmark–Sweden; and some bilateral arrangements in Latin America, including Nicaragua–El Salvador; Panama–Venezuela; and Argentina–Chile. These are not discussed in this book, either because they came to nothing, or the countries involved became parties to larger arrangements, or they seem not to have raised any issues of interest and importance other than those treated here.

For summaries of the various cooperative efforts in Europe which helped lay the groundwork for the Coal and Steel Community, see OEEC, *A Decade of Cooperation*, Paris, 1948; R. Hinshaw, *The European Community and American Trade*, New York, 1964, Chap. 2; and W. Diebold, Jr., *Trade and Payments in Western Europe*, New York, 1952.

[11] See *The New York Times*, Oct. 4, 1950, p. 16.

Community was obviously a "courageous experiment," well designed to increase production and productivity in the affected sectors and to serve the major political purpose of making impossible war between Germany and France. All that was required, they said, was for the Contracting Parties to define the waivers necessary to reconcile the legal conflicts.[12]

Conditions Imposed for Agreeing to Discrimination

To some nonmembers it did not seem quite that simple. They viewed the arrangements with considerable apprehension. Spokesmen from the countries who had export interests in high-quality steel products, notably Austria and Sweden, were much concerned lest their industries not be able to survive the discrimination they would now be subjected to in some of their previously important and traditional export markets among the Six. Others, notably Denmark, Sweden and Norway, who relied heavily on the Six for imports of coke, iron, and scrap iron, feared that the Community might pursue cartel-like policies and, especially in times of short supply, both reduce the amounts available and increase the prices to outsiders. This, they feared, would not only increase the costs of goods for internal consumption but would reduce their international competitive ability, a matter of great importance to them, given their heavy dependence on foreign trade. There was also concern in the minds of many third countries over the precedent of approving such an outright breach of the General Agreement and the threat that carried to the authority of the only institution then taking a worldwide view of trade problems.[13]

The Community spokesmen replied that these worries were exaggerated. The European Coal and Steel Community had every intention of not drifting into cartel policies and of paying due regard to the interests of third countries. Without analyz-

[12] See GATT, *Doc. L/17,* 8 Sept. 1952; and GATT, *Press Release 77,* 7 Oct. 1952. Perhaps the reader should be reminded that these two kinds of GATT documents are in mimeographed form and can be found in the Geneva archives of the Contracting Parties to the GATT.

[13] E. Wyndham White, *Europe in the GATT* (Secretariat of the GATT), Geneva, 1960, pp. 8–10.

ing just how this was to happen, they said the elimination of barriers within the Six on coal and steel products would lead to a more "rational distribution of production," that this would result in lower costs, increased production, and more employment. This, in turn, would both increase the supply of products available to the rest of the world at "reasonable prices," and, via income effects, increase the opportunities of others to sell in the Community. They warned that a too rigid interpretation of the General Agreement was not advisable, that it would prevent "adjustments of principles" to the changing conditions of the world which were necessary if the GATT were to survive and be useful. More than passing attention was given to the consideration that the Six had assumed major risks in launching such an unprecedented experiment and therefore others "owed" it their support. But the clinching argument was a more brutal one. The Six had, in fact, already created the European Coal and Steel Community; and it was supported in GATT councils with uncritical enthusiasm by the United States Government. An intolerable situation would have been created if the Contracting Parties had refused the necessary waivers. There was, indeed, doubt in the minds of many as to whether the GATT could survive such a decision.[14]

On November 10, 1952, the needed waivers of their GATT commitments were formally granted the Six. They were authorized to discriminate in favor of each other in their trade in listed coal and steel products. In matters coming fully under the Community High Authority's control, the Community, in the person of the High Authority, would be treated as if it were a single contracting party with the same rights and obligations as others. But this was not the simple unconditional waiver they had requested and assumed would be granted. The noted apprehensions of others were reflected by incorporating in the waiver decision a set of statements, principles, stipulations, and assumptions which the Contracting Parties, though not the High Authority, came to regard as conditions.[15] The waiver turned

[14] For an official report on these early discussions, see General Agreement on Tariffs and Trade, *Basic Instruments and Selected Documents, First Supplement,* Geneva, 1953, pp. 85ff.

[15] For text of the waiver, see *ibid.,* pp. 17–22.

some of the Community's general statements of purpose into international commitments and thus in effect virtually modified the Treaty.

In particular, the formal decision found that the Community, if it pursued "appropriate trade policies" *could* contribute to the aims of the General Agreement and could benefit third countries "by increasing supplies of coal and steel products, and by providing increased markets for commodities used by the coal and steel industry and for other products. . . ." It then specifically noted that the Community had "undertaken to take account of the interests of third countries both as consumers and as suppliers of coal and steel products, to further the development of international trade, and to ensure that equitable prices are charged by its producers in markets outside the Community." [16] The waiver went on to specify that it "will be necessary" for the Community to avoid placing "unreasonable barriers" upon exports to third countries, and that the proposed harmonization of their tariffs and other trade regulations on coal and steel products originating outside the Community would be on a basis which "shall be lower and less restrictive than the general incidence of the duties and regulations" then applicable. Finally, during the five years of the transitional period foreseen in the Treaty, the Community was required to submit annual reports to the Contracting Parties, the purpose being to help ensure during the all-important formative period that the new market was operating consistently with the conditions of the waiver.

From the start, the annual reports were the occasions for discussions, often heated and lasting for weeks, during which third countries, especially the Scandinavian nations and Austria, asked for a detailed accounting of what the Community had been up to and for evidence that it was living up to all the conditions of the waiver.[17] The discussions centered on the

[16] Similarly worded statements are included in Art. III of the Treaty.
[17] The High Authority and the Coal and Steel Community governments were often distressed and sometimes alarmed over the "awkward" and "difficult" questions asked in the GATT reviews. They had not regarded the various statements in what they looked at as the preamble to the waiver as the binding commitments which many of the third

question of the effect of the Community on enlarging the market to outsiders and on increasing supplies of coal and steel products to nonmembers at equitable prices. Loosely speaking, the central issue was whether the Community was diverting trade—in either exports or imports.[18]

Impact on Exports

It was soon found that Coal and Steel Community producers sometimes charged different prices for some products as *among* export markets, with the United States and Canadian importers often paying less than European customers. The latter regarded this as evidence of "concerted," or "cartel-like," actions and asked that it cease.[19] They asserted it was contrary to the spirit of the Community and of the GATT waiver. They found it harmful to those being charged the higher prices because of its adverse effects on both their real incomes and, indirectly, on

---

countries did. (See European Coal and Steel Community. The High Authority, *Third General Report on the Activities of the Community*, Luxembourg, April 1955, pp. 33–34.)

In the end, the Contracting Parties always formally found that the Community was honoring the terms of the waiver or, at least, was not dishonoring them. But the skepticism of many was evident in the wording of the findings and in the accompanying reports.

[18] The account in the following pages, unless otherwise noted, is based on the long annual reports which were submitted to the Contracting Parties by the Coal and Steel Community and the GATT Working Party reports on them. On many of the issues between the Community and third countries bilateral discussions were also held, but records of these were not available. The Community's annual reports may be found in GATT, *Docs. L/120*, 13 Sept., 1953; *L/240*, 7 Oct. 1954; *L/419*, 12 Oct. 1955; *L/526*, 20 Sept. 1956; *L/526, Add. 1*, 24 Sept. 1956; *L/686*, 30 Sept. 1957; *L/686, Add. 1*, 14 Oct. 1957; and *L/804*, 3 April 1958. The GATT Working Party Reports are reproduced in the GATT, *Basic Instruments and Selected Documents, Second Supplement*, 1954, pp. 101ff.; *Third Supplement*, 1955, pp. 146ff.; *Fourth Supplement*, 1956, pp. 84ff.; *Fifth Supplement*, 1957, pp. 125ff.; and *Sixth Supplement*, 1958, pp. 139ff.

[19] An extensive bibliography on the question of cartels in the ECSC and the EEC may be found in Appendix D of *Economic Policies and Practices*, Paper No. 4, "Private Trade Barriers and the Atlantic Community," Joint Economic Committee, U.S. Congress, 1964.

their international competitive positions vis-à-vis the favored purchasers. Community spokesmen insisted that these price structures were fully consistent with conditions of competition. They said the price structures were the result of the Community producers' need to meet competition in the United States and Canada, and that they also reflected the fact that North American buyers often placed orders well in advance of desired delivery dates, so costs of production were less. The non-ECSC Europeans were not completely convinced by this but the divergencies were subsequently reduced and the matter dropped from the agenda.

A more prolonged dispute arose over whether the export prices being charged were "equitable." The position of some buyers, led by the Danes, was that large discrepancies had developed, leaving export prices well above internal Community market prices for certain products, especially steel. This inequality, they said, placed the processing industries of nonmembers at a serious competitive disadvantage in third markets vis-à-vis Community producers, and it followed that the Community was not charging the "equitable" prices to outsiders required in the waiver.[20] Community spokesmen replied that, first, the differences were not "substantial" and there were some Community products whose prices were lower for export than for domestic buyers. Second, the obligation to charge equitable prices required not that prices be equal to or even close to those charged *within* the Community but rather that they be similar to those charged on world markets by competing sellers, which, they insisted, they were. The issue was never formally resolved. It often proved impossible to reach agreement, both as to what were comparable products and on what were the relevant prices for comparison. When there was at least tacit agreement on these matters and the prices for comparable products inside the Community were below those charged for exports, there remained the question of whether the Community

[20] It was not denied that double pricing of steel had been common before the ECSC was formed; but before that there had been no comparable international commitment to charge "equitable" prices for exports.

producers taken together were such big suppliers to the world market that they could exert great influence on world prices if they acted in concert.[21] Many outside the Community believed that they could, and did, and that the result was higher prices than if Community producers had competed for export markets. In their view it followed that prices charged by the Community were not "equitable" ones and were in violation of the waiver. The High Authority spokesmen asserted that the Community producers were not large enough to exercise the degree of price leadership attributed to them. Since a detailed analysis of the current conditions determining world prices for these products was lacking, this question, too, ended in something of a standoff. But some of those who have studied the problem closely believe the complaints probably resulted in some moderation of export prices.[22]

In 1955 export prices of several steel products increased, some third countries thereupon argued that one of the main reasons for giving the waiver was that the creation of the Community would set in train forces increasing production and

[21] There was no doubt that the Community steel producers had gotten together in Brussels and established a cartel. Several third countries expressed much concern over this, but the High Authority said at the time that it could intervene in such arrangements only if the agreements had "disturbing" effects *within* the Common Market. To this, some nonmembers replied that when granting the waiver they had expected the High Authority to intervene if producers were making arrangements in restraint of trade which had the effect of their charging "inequitable" export prices or otherwise depriving third countries of the advantages which they had a right to expect under the waiver. In effect, they then told the High Authority that if the latter did not have the authority to intervene when agreements among producers were having such undesirable effects on nonmembers they had better get such authority. Whatever the legal position of the High Authority may have been, the GATT working party reports indicate that the former did in fact subsequently concern itself with "reminding" the producers that they had an obligation to charge "equitable prices" for exports.

[22] See William Diebold, Jr., *The Schuman Plan*, New York, 1959, Chap. 17, for a detailed analysis and account of this problem. See also, Louis Lister, *Europe's Coal and Steel Community*, New York, 1960, Chaps. 6–8, for a careful treatment of ECSC steel producers cartel-like actions toward third countries.

132

productivity, bringing about lower prices, and so benefiting all importing countries. The Community therefore had a particular responsibility to see to it that any benefits resulting from improved conditions of production were passed on to non-member countries, but this did not seem to be happening. That year the Community spokesmen provided much fuller explanations of their problems and activities. Their GATT questioners were satisfied with the reply that these particular increases were due to higher transportation rates and wages, plus the fact that 1955 had been a year of high internal demands, as well, and that it was normal for export prices to fluctuate more than internal prices and to be higher in times of high demand and lower in times of slack demand. Subsequently, and apparently for this last reason, these export prices fell below internal Community prices, Community exports showed an upward trend, and complaints by third countries tapered off.[23]

More complicated were the issues surrounding the increase in coke prices in the mid-1950's, which some countries claimed violated the Community's obligation to charge equitable prices for its exports. In this instance internal prices had also gone up, although some said not so much as export prices, because the increasing domestic demand had made it necessary to buy more United States coke and coal, more expensive than domestic supplies. Some third countries argued, however, that the reason for the need to use more costly U.S. coke and coal was the increase in Community demands, not the increase in export demands, and so higher export prices were not equitable. Apart from the obvious disagreements as to what was "fair" in such circumstances, there was again much disagreement as to the facts and once more the issue was left suspended. The High Authority, however, did undertake to see

[23] For a recent study finding the ECSC steel-pricing policies "superior" to those of the U.S. and U.K. systems, see A. Forsyth, *Steel Pricing Policies, Political and Economic Planning*, London, 1965. He found the great merits of the ECSC system to be that "it promotes competition," "it provides for a measure of outside supervision," and "it has brought the steel industry into the open." (Quotations come from review in European Community Information Service, *European Community*, Feb. 1965, pp. 8–9.)

to it that in these circumstances coke and coal export prices did not go up by an "unreasonable" amount. They seem to have been successful, for soon thereafter the spread between internal and export prices declined as internal prices rose, while export prices did not, and this item, too, disappeared from the agenda.

Many complaints were also lodged, especially in 1953 and 1954, over the inability of third countries to get what they regarded as "fair" supplies of scrap from the Community, their main supplier. Although acknowledging that scrap had been scarce before the ECSC was formed, and recognizing that each of the Six had a "right" to relieve its internal shortages before exporting, it was nonetheless argued that the fact that the Six had formed a regional organization meant that unreasonable barriers were being placed on exports. This was so because before the Six had joined together third countries presumably stood an even chance with any other country in obtaining any exports one of the Six might have. But once the Community was formed the partner countries had first call on any exports available from any one of its members and third countries became eligible only for what remained. While acknowledging that this was inherent in a regional arrangement, several third countries insisted that it had been their understanding when they voted for the waiver that they would not be "unreasonably" penalized. There being no objective criteria as to what was "reasonable," this point also remained unresolved; but it is to be noted that the Community was made to feel on the defensive on this issue, and a wish to maintain the flow of scrap to other countries that had traditionally relied on Community producers for their supplies was a contributing factor—though a minor one—to the many efforts made by the Community to relieve its demands for scrap.[24] In any event, after 1955 complaints on this score, too, became much more muted as the scarcity of scrap within the Community became more acute (and so the difficulty increased of making a case that their restrictions on exports were "unreasonable"), and as hopes rose

[24] See Diebold, *The Schuman Plan,* Chap. 12, for a full account of the scrap problem up to 1959.

that the large investment of the Community in pig iron production would soon relieve the scrap market. In recent years the European scrap market has been much more amply supplied and no further complaints on this score seem to have been filed against the Community by third countries.

Impact on Imports

Community members applied no tariffs on imports of coal, scrap, or iron ore (except for coke into Italy), but all had duties on imports of most steel products. The Six were not, traditionally, large importers of steel from the rest of the world, but they were an important market for certain special steels produced by some of the smaller European countries, especially Austria and Sweden. Moreover, since the pre-ECSC duties varied widely among the Six, "harmonization" was believed necessary to prevent trade deflection rendering ineffective the higher rates. The Six had stated that they were, with certain exceptions for Italy, going to adopt the low Benelux tariffs (if necessary, increased by two percentage points) as the basis for the "harmonized" tariff. The decision to set the new rates low, rather than high, came because of strong Dutch pressure for no increase in duties (the Netherlands was a large importer), together with the wish to demonstrate to third countries that the coal and steel community was an "outward looking enterprise." [25]

Beginning with the Community's first report to the Contracting Parties, several third countries expressed disappointment over the slowness with which the Six were "harmonizing" their tariffs on steel products, urged more speed in this process, and made it clear that they had not forgotten that the GATT waiver had specified that "harmonizing" meant "reducing." Their complaints became more insistent as the duties on intra-Six trade were quickly reduced and the margin of preferences

[25] H. H. Liesner reports that the granting of the GATT waiver might have been endangered had the ECSC chosen to align their tariffs at a high level. J. E. Meade, H. H. Liesner, and S. J. Wells, *Case Studies in European Economic Union,* London, 1962, p. 408. Pages 406–16 have been heavily drawn upon in this section.

thereby increased against outside suppliers. Austria, in particular, feared that during this interim period of especially heavy discrimination it would lose markets which it could not later recover, even assuming the final harmonized tariffs were as low as the Benelux ones. Austria therefore requested early negotiations looking toward a reduction right away in some of the rates that would not otherwise be fully aligned downward until the end of the transition period; that is, she wished to anticipate some of the reductions and, hopefully, even to negotiate them below what they might be under the anticipated aligning. Such negotiations were actually started in 1954 but differences quickly developed as to the "quid pro quo." Austria argued that in agreeing to the waiver, in renouncing its most-favored-nation rights, it had already made a concession in return for which its interests in terms of access to markets of the Six must not be worsened. In Austria's view, this called for immediate lower Community duties on products of interest to Austria. It did not, it said, want to pay twice. The High Authority disagreed, taking the position that if "special" tariff concessions were now to be made to such a nonmember, that nonmember must make some reciprocal concessions to the Community. The bilateral discussions came to nothing, but in the 1955–1956, regular GATT tariff negotiating conference French, German, and Italian duties on steel were substantially reduced. In the event, Austria, and some other countries as well, made tariff concessions on a number of goods, both steel and others, that it normally imported from Community countries. The available data do not make it possible to say whether account was taken of the Austrian contention, making its concessions lighter than they might otherwise have been.[26]

[26] Although there were difficulties over the years between Belgium and Germany, on one hand, and the United States and the United Kingdom, on the other, over restrictions applied by the two former nations on coal imports from the U.K., these early restraints were not a consequence peculiar to the formation of the Community. Indeed, it was precisely because each of the other ECSC members was virtually free to determine its own import policy and so was not obliged to give preference to Belgian and German coal that forced the latter two countries to restrict their imports so severely when stocks began to soar.

Although these 1955–1956 reductions helped third countries, large differences in tariffs among the Community members still remained, so Austria, Sweden, and others continued to press for harmonization. When harmonization actually began in 1957, however, there was further criticism of the Community. At first, it was alleged that in the process of aligning rates, the adverse effects on third countries of those rates that were aligned upward (the Benelux ones) was greater than the beneficial effects of those aligned downward. The Community spokesmen denied this, and pointed out that legally they were well within the permitted margin. Again there was not enough information or analysis to settle the substance of the point. A much more serious—but unavailing—complaint was voiced when, in response to French and Italian fears, the High Authority announced that these countries would be permitted under the harmonized tariff to apply duties that *exceeded* the Benelux tariff by more than two points, but not by so much more as to encourage imports via the low tariff members. The new rates went into effect in early 1958. The low-tariff Benelux raised most of its duties by two percentage points, Germany reduced its to this level, while French rates were cut to one percentage point higher than this, and the Italian to only two to four points higher, depending on the product. Some slight reductions were also negotiated for some products in the 1961–1962 Dillon round. Although this was not as favorable to foreign suppliers as had been hoped, third countries seem to have concluded that the new semi-harmonized tariff was low (it averaged some 6–7 percent for *all* steel products), and probably was less of an obstacle to their exports than the preceding national tariffs had been. Although the Benelux rate went up a bit, it had never been a large market for nonmember exports, in any case, and the rates in other countries had been substantially reduced.[27] In prepara-

---

This situation, however, forced the issue of the ECSC pursuing an agreed and common commercial policy vis-à-vis third countries that later probably resulted in a reduction of coal imports. See I. Kravis, *Domestic Interests and International Obligations,* Philadelphia, 1963, p. 263.

[27] According to Liesner, *Case Studies in European Economic Union,* p. 407, at the time the Coal and Steel Community was formed, legal duties

tion for the Kennedy Round of tariff negotiations, however, the Community in effect fixed a common external tariff of 14 percent "to be negotiated downward." [28] This was possible because no formal common external tariff had been set, and the pre-ECSC national tariffs, which were said to have averaged 14 percent, had not been bound. In light of the general commitment in the Kennedy Round to cut tariffs by 50 percent, the intent was to leave ECSC steel tariffs virtually unchanged.

By the time the period of compulsory annual reviews by the Contracting Parties of the European Coal and Steel Community activities ended in 1958, there had been, as we have seen, a great decline in the fears of third countries that their interests would be adversely affected by the Community.[29] The obligation of the Community to live up to the terms of the waiver continued and the fact that the Community has not appeared on the agenda of the Contracting Parties in recent years suggests that at least others have not found themselves greatly damaged by its operation. It may also be that the issue has not appeared because those concerned with the effects of regional arrangements on third countries have been preoccupied with the more ambitious schemes of the Six countries: the European Economic Community.

Before turning to that, what can be said about the role of the General Agreement in the development of the Coal and Steel Community? It may be argued that by granting the waiver the Contracting Parties capitulated before the fact of that Community. But what seems more interesting and more important is that the existence of the General Agreement permitted third

---

on finished steel products, for example, were 6–8 percent in Benelux, 16–20 in France, 15–28 in Germany, and 15–23 in Italy. Some of these had been temporarily suspended. The rates after the harmonization on these goods were therefore: Benelux, 8–10 percent; Germany, 8–10; France, 9–11; and Italy, 8–12. Duties on such common steel products as sheet and bars were less than these.

[28] European Community Information Service, *European Community,* Nov.–Dec. 1964, p. 3.

[29] See the report of the Contracting Parties to the GATT, made at the last of the compulsory reviews, reproduced in GATT, *Basic Instruments and Selected Documents, Seventh Supplement,* pp. 122–24.

countries, especially small ones, to express views at the outset on the impact of the Community on nonmembers, and that this led to a more critical examination of the whole scheme and of its effects on others than could otherwise have been expected. This, in turn, resulted in a decision which forced the Coal and Steel Community to seriously concern itself during its formative years with external relations, to give a detailed accounting of itself to those who were nonmembers but who were still affected by it, and strengthened the hands of those within the Community who wished that it be "outward" rather than "inward" looking.[30] Because of the action of the Contracting Parties, the Coal and Steel Community probably had less trade diverting effects than it otherwise would.[31]

COMMON MARKETS AND FREE TRADE AREAS

By 1955 the drive within Europe toward regionalism had carried the Six to the famous conference at Messina, which was to lead to another in Vienna in May 1956, and in March 1957, to the Treaty of Rome, creating the European Economic Community.[32] This was commonly regarded as one of the most important developments in Europe since the War, and one which would require far-reaching changes in the trade relations of the entire free world. To many, it also carried the risk of "a disintegration of the world-wide multilateral trading system which has been so painfully reestablished in the years since the War."[33]

And it was only the beginning of a worldwide movement that was to have reached by the time of this writing (mid-1965) such dimensions that just over half of the 79 contracting parties to the GATT would be linked to a regional economic bloc in

[30] Diebold, in an extensive and careful analysis of the Community in his *The Schuman Plan*, pp. 523–32, comes to the same general conclusion.

[31] For a similar view, see Raymond Vernon, "Economic Aspects of the Atlantic Community," in H. F. Haviland, ed., *The United States and the Western Community*, Haverford, Pa., 1957, pp. 58–59.

[32] An excellent, recent account of the complex political forces back of this "relaunching of Europe" is given in M. Camps, *Britain and the European Community, 1955–1963*, Princeton, 1964, Chaps. 1, 2.

[33] GATT, *International Trade, 1956*, Geneva, 1957, p. 247.

some stage of development. The Convention establishing the European Free Trade Association was signed in January 1960, following the breakdown of the efforts to create a Europe-Wide Free Trade Area. The Treaty of Montevideo, creating the Latin American Free Trade Association (LAFTA), was signed the following month, after several years of discussions, and by 1965 included Argentina, Brazil, Chile, Mexico, Paraguay, Peru, Uruguay, Colombia, and Ecuador, but envisages others entering.[34] The arrangements in Central America have a somewhat longer history.[35] For some time there had been bilateral, free trade arrangements among some of the countries on some

[34] Argentina, Brazil, Chile, and Uruguay had since the 1930's been granting preferences to each other via the way they administered their non-tariff trade and payments restrictions. As these types of controls were reduced these countries were sometimes interested in finding other measures for preserving existing preferential channels of trade.

[35] For an official United Nations study in 1960 of the various attempts up to that time to promote a Common Market in Latin America, see *The Significance of Recent Common Market Developments in Latin America*, UN, *Doc. E/CN.14/64*. A compilation of many of the official instruments in connection with these various Latin American arrangements is available in United Nations, *Multilateral Economic Cooperation in Latin America*, New York, 1962, UN Sales No. 62, II, G.3, Vol. 1. For an official review of activity in Central America up to the beginning of 1963, see the Economic Commission for Latin America, *Economic Bulletin for Latin America*, Vol. VIII, No. 1, pp. 9–24. The annual reports of the Economic Commission for Latin America to the United Nations Economic and Social Council from 1958 on also provide much detail on these regional arrangements. For an early statement of the rationale for Latin America-wide Common Market, see Economic Commission for Latin America, *The Latin American Common Market*, UN Sales No. 59, II, G.4, July 1959. See, too, the Commission's *Towards a Dynamic Development Policy for Latin America*, 1963, UN Sales No. 64, II, G.4.

Raymond F. Mikesell, in his "The Movement Toward Regional Trading Groups in Latin America," pp. 125–51, of A. O. Hirschman, ed., *Latin American Issues, Essays and Comments*, 1961, provides a useful account of the background of the movement, as well as a critical analysis of the Montevideo Treaty in particular. A fuller, more recent, and generally pessimistic appraisal of LAFTA's future is M. S. Wionczek's *"Latin American Free Trade Association,"* International Conciliation, Carnegie Endowment for International Peace, New York, Jan. 1965.

goods; beginning in 1950, with help from the U.N. Economic Commission for Latin America, interim arrangements were worked out for the establishment of a free trade area for some goods among several of the countries. A Multilateral Treaty on Free Trade and Central American Economic Integration was signed in June 1958. It was accompanied by an Agreement on the Régime for Central American Integration Industries. This was followed by a treaty of Economic Association and, finally in 1961, a General Treaty of Central American Economic Integration entered into force among Nicaragua, El Salvador, Costa Rica, Guatemala, and Honduras, creating a Central American Common Market. This was not likely to be the end, for at the time of this writing there is a revival of interest in establishing a continent-wide Latin American Common Market.

In Africa, so many regional groups have been formed, or are being planned, and changes are so frequent, that even a listing is soon out of date. Many of these, of course, are relics of earlier colonial arrangements: efforts to retain after independence certain trading arrangements built up earlier. Thus, the governments of the Central African Republic, the Congo (Brazzaville), Gabon, and Chad entered into an Equatorial Customs Union arrangement in 1959 and extended it to the Cameroons in 1962; in late 1964 this was converted into the Central African Economic and Customs Union. This is also true of the West African Customs Union (Dahomey, the Ivory Coast, Mali, Mauretania, Niger, Senegal, and Upper Volta). The members of both of these blocs are also associated with the EEC and each of the blocs, in effect, constitutes something resembling a free trade area with the Six. The East African Common Market (Kenya, Tanganyika [now Tanzania], and Uganda), which has been functioning since the early 1920's, still exists but is under considerable stress in the mid-1960's because, in addition to their political difficulties, the others believe Kenya has been getting the lion's share of the benefits. Since the early 1960's moves have been underway to create a so-called African Common Market (Algeria, the United Arab Republic, Ghana, Guinea, Mali, and Morocco), but political antipathies, if nothing else, have made implementation very

141

slow. Ghana–Upper Volta and Ghana–Niger Free Trade Associations were legally inaugurated in 1961 and 1963, respectively.[36] There are also many partial, preferential arrangements among pairs of countries on the African Continent. In this chaotic situation the African heads of state, in May 1963 at a meeting in Addis Ababa, established an all-embracing "Organization of African Unity," which, it was hoped, someday would result, among other things, in an African Common Market which would supersede the groupings listed above. But in 1965 its future lines of development are not at all clear,[37] and

[36] Some information on the Equatorial Customs Union (whose common external tariff probably violates the GATT requirements) may be found in GATT, *Docs. L/2061*, 13 Sept. 1963; *L/2061, Add. 1*, 24 Oct. 1963; and *L/2354*, 1965. For the African Common Market, see GATT, *Doc. L/1835*, 25 September 1962; and for the Ghana–Upper Volta arrangements, GATT, *Doc. L/2010*, 31 May, 1963.

Arrangements for re-establishing a customs union between the Union of South Africa and Southern Rhodesia had been made in the late 1940's. (South Africa had given duty-free entry to most imports from Northern Rhodesia since the turn of the century.) This was terminated in 1955 following the creation of the Federation of the Rhodesias and Nyasaland, which in turn became one customs area, but a good many of the old preferences were retained—sometimes in modified form—and some new ones were created in subsequent trade agreements signed by the Federation with South Africa. The Federation, in turn, broke up in early 1964 and customs barriers were re-erected among the three territories. In late 1964 a new trade agreement establishing preferences among them was signed by Rhodesia and South Africa. For an account of these extremely complicated arrangements, which received the qualified approval of the GATT, and the changes within them over the time, see GATT, *Basic Instruments and Selected Documents, Fourth Supplement*, pp. 17–20, 72–74; *Fifth Supplement*, p. 39; *Seventh Supplement*, pp. 40–41; *Ninth Supplement*, pp. 51–53, 231–36; and GATT, *Doc. L/2376*, 1965. See also, Kravis, *Domestic Industries and International Obligations*, pp. 87–89.

[37] See UN, *Doc. E/CN/14 STC 20*, 13 Oct. 1963, for a background paper on the establishment of an African Common Market. This is a preliminary attempt to explore some of the major problems. The difficulties are tremendous. The continent is riddled with disparate trade and payment systems and ties to Western Europe; reconciliation of them is a Herculean task. Primitive transportation, political frictions, large numbers of very small states, the political need to share any benefits "equitably," weak governmental administrative machinery; all constitute obstacles. But the drive to "unite" is also powerful.

subsequent to its formation an agreement to form a Maghreb Economic Community—Algeria, Libya, Morocco, and Tunisia —was signed.[38]

Regionalism has so far been less popular in Asia. Japan, concentrating on reducing the discrimination to which it has been subjected in the West,[39] has shown little interest in various proposals for a Pacific Common Market and others in the area, fearful of the competition, have shown no desire to open their markets to free trade with Japan. The Association of Southeast Asia recommended in 1963 that its members—Malaya, Thailand and the Philippines, explore the possibility of establishing among themselves a free trade area in certain products. The organizational work of the latter scheme came to a halt (not yet resumed) a few months later when diplomatic relations were broken between the Philippines and the new Federation of Malaysia. The latter was attempting to create a common market among its four component areas (Malaya, Singapore, and the Borneo states of Sarawak and Sabah), but this, too, came to at least a temporary halt in mid-1965 when Singapore decided to leave the Federation.[40] In 1963, too, at a ministerial meeting of the Economic Commission for Asia and the Far East it was agreed that one of their eventual objectives should be sub-regional customs unions or free trade areas. All of this is still most tentative and the obstacles to the consummation of anything approaching a genuine customs union or free trade area remain immense; differences in race, religion, culture, historical background are important; so too are the diverse economic institutions, widely different political systems, historic enmities, and new national jealousies.[41] In early 1965 an Arab Common Market looking toward internal free trade, common external tariffs, and common foreign economic policy, came into legal being.[42] Open to all Arab league states, the original

---

[38] *The New York Times,* Nov. 29, 1964, p. 7.

[39] See Chapter VI below.

[40] *The New York Times,* Aug. 15, 1965, pp. 8, 11.

[41] See Clair Wilcox, "Regional Cooperation in Southeast Asia," *Malayan Economic Review,* Oct. 1964.

[42] GATT, *Doc. L/2366,* March 1965, and GATT, *Doc. L/2518,* Nov. 1965.

members were to be limited to Egypt, Iraq, Jordan, Kuwait, and Syria. It is too early for this to have come to anything but the obstacles just mentioned for Southeast Asia, except differences in race and religion, are also present; Kuwait apparently has already decided to back out, at least for the time being.

In late August 1965, it was announced that Australia and New Zealand had signed an accord to create a New Zealand–Australian Free Trade Area. In forming such a regional grouping, these countries do not labor under the same obstacles as those just mentioned for the Asian states and African states, and it can be assumed that this one quickly will come into being. But it may face some of the same problems, noted below, in reaching full fruition that have beset the Latin American Free Trade Association and that can be expected to characterize regional blocs involving countries placing a high value on industrialization. Thus, although the details are not available at the time of this writing, initially the accord apparently covered only about 60 percent of the trade between the two countries, much of which was already free of import restrictions. This limitation was reportedly prompted by New Zealand's fears that otherwise it would not be able to reach the level of industrialization to which it aspired, given Australia's greater industrial development.

The core of all the new regional arrangements was that the members of each would extend to their partners favors and privileges not available to others. In each of them some—and sometimes all—the partners had signed the General Agreement on Tariffs and Trade and so committed themselves to policies of nondiscrimination. Unlike the Coal and Steel Community, those forming these new institutions did not ask for a waiver of their nondiscriminatory obligations under the GATT, but rather asked that the new arrangements be recognized as qualifying as customs unions or free trade areas under Article XXIV. As we have noted earlier, Article XXIV permitted customs unions and free trade areas under the conditions that they be formed within a reasonably short period of time, that they cover "substantially all of the trade" among members, and that the tariffs against third countries after their formation not be, in general, "more restrictive of trade" or have a "higher incidence" than were the prior tariffs of the constituent members.

In all cases, the practice has been for group spokesmen to outline to the assembled third countries what the group proposed to do and why.[43] Following a preliminary discussion, the proposed group was asked to submit written answers to a long series of written questions. This material was used as the raw material for a detailed study by a GATT Working Party, whose report was in turn discussed in a Plenary Session of the Contracting Parties. It has also been the practice for each regional arrangement which has gone through this process to report periodically to the Contracting Parties on their activities; this has often been the occasion for further discussion. These arrangements thus gave ample opportunity for third countries to express their views, hopes, and fears as to the effects of the regional arrangements on third countries, and so to have some influence on them.

Rationale

The essence of the proposals was that over a specified period —10 to 12 years was common for most of these schemes— duties and quantitative restrictions were to be removed on most trade among the partners. In the European arrangements, this removal, in general, was to be across the board, automatic, and on a predetermined time schedule, while those in the LAFTA were to be the result of a series of annual negotiations on

---

[43] See GATT, *Docs. L/582*, 10 Nov. 1956 and *L/656*, 2 Aug. 1957, and *Basic Instruments and Selected Documents, Sixth Supplement*, pp. 68–109, for the original statements and answers to questions submitted by the Contracting Parties concerning the European Economic Community and a GATT Working Party report largely based on these data. For the same type of information on the European Free Trade Association, see GATT, *Docs. L/1167, Add. 1, Add. 2*, and *Add. 3*, 14 April 1960, and *Basic Instruments and Selected Documents, Ninth Supplement*, pp. 70–86. For the Latin American Free Trade Area, see GATT, *Docs. L/1201*, 26 May 1960, *L/1311*, 14 Oct. 1960, and *Basic Instruments and Selected Documents, Ninth Supplement*, pp. 87–94. These documents are the source of much of the material in the following section.

individual products, with generous provisions for exceptions.[44] Special provisions were frequently made for certain products, particularly agricultural goods, but sometimes selected industrial commodities were subject to special rules as well. The European Common Market, as a formal customs union, provided for the gradual aligning of the individual member's tariffs toward a common external tariff. The Central American arrangements also provide for negotiating "equalized" barriers against third country exports, envisaging a full customs union at some unspecified time. The European Economic Community also differed in a major way from the others, in that it was extended to the trade with the overseas territories of the members.

In all of the schemes, except the European Free Trade Association, it was repeatedly emphasized that the political aspects were as important, or much more important, than the economic. It was only the Six which emphasized that one reason for their forming the Union was worry over their ability to otherwise "maintain their position" vis-à-vis the United States and Russia; but a wish to strengthen their bargaining positions in many forums was an important factor in all of the groups.[45] For all of them, except the Six, an important consideration seems to have been the belief that by forming a

[44] By the end of the rather unsuccessful fourth annual round of such negotiations in late 1964, many of the LAFTA members had about concluded that further progress would demand a change to the automatic, across-the-board techniques used by the European Economic Community and EFTA. See GATT, *Doc. L/2399,* 17 March 1965.

[45] The South American countries felt a particular bargaining need to create a "common front." Only nine of the twenty nations were members of the General Agreement. This meant in practice that the concessions other countries gave to products of particular interest to several of the Latin American countries were likely to be small. This was so because the noncontracting parties among them did not sit at the bargaining table and offer concessions in return, yet in practice would receive them from most contracting parties via most-favored-nation treatment. It was believed that if they formed an association they might thereby increase their bargaining power in the GATT negotiations, even though not all were members. See Gerard Curzon, *Multilateral Commercial Diplomacy,* London, 1965, p. 286.

bloc they could better defend themselves against the discriminatory effects of *other* regional groups. Thus, too, does discrimination spread. For the African states the desire to "consolidate"
or protect their newly-won independence by creating new
alliances was important. In the case of the European Common
Market the wish to institutionalize the rapprochement between
Germany and the others was also a powerful incentive for
forming the Community.

Many of the groups also argued that economic union,
although frequently only implicitly noted in the relevant treaty,
and not just a customs union or free trade area, was in mind.
This meant that their grouping involved many economic questions beyond the commercial policy matters which, they said,
were the proper concern of third countries. It therefore
followed, the proponents insisted, that commercial policy considerations must not be the determining factor in passing
judgment on their proposals.

In their "economic" justifications for forming their Community, the members of the EEC set forth a thesis which touched
on most of the "dynamic" or growth-inducing forces that are
now familiar in the theoretical literature on customs unions, and
which were drastically summarized at the beginning of this
chapter. In abbreviated from the rationale was to be para-
phrased by all who followed.

Thus, the heart of their case for forming a preferential
regional group, as set forth originally before third countries in
sessions of the GATT by the spokesmen for the European
Economic Community, was that no one of the parties was large
enough to command the immense amount of research and
investment needed "to launch the economic revolution heralded
by the advance of the atomic age." [46] This particular formula-

[46] The classic official statement of the motivation and rationale for the
EEC was the so-called "Spaak Report" (Comité Intergouvernemental créé
par la Conférence de Messine, *Rapport des Chefs de Délégation aux
Ministres des Affaires Etrangères,* Brussels, 21 April 1956). Formally,
this was a final report from the heads of delegations to the foreign
ministers of the Six, representing the results of the work that had been
done following the Messina Conference in developing plans for the
Common Market and for Euratom.

tion reflected the French preoccupation at that time with the development of atomic energy, but in elaboration of their case attention was placed on more prosaic considerations. Without supplying any detailed supporting data (and in this they were slavishly followed by all others), it was argued that separate national markets were too small to permit the optimum use of the new production techniques that were becoming available. A merging of markets, it was said, would tend to shift production within the area from the higher cost to the lower cost places. Perhaps more important, it would also bring about a more extensive division of labor, would give greater play to the efficiency of management, would permit the taking advantage of other internal economies of scale, and would both permit and force the use of up-to-date production techniques and the more energetic pursuit of opportunities to expand the level of plant and firm operations. It was also alleged that merger would encourage more standardization of product and specialization of plant. All this, in turn, would stimulate more investment and further economic growth.[47] It was stressed that the existing domestic markets often offered only to entrepreneurs with a virtual monopoly the opportunities to reach the size necessary for the adoption of most recent techniques of production. Therefore, one of the great advantages of the larger market would be that it would make possible mass production without this leading to the creation of monopolies. The

[47] There has been disagreement in the "academic" literature on the probable actual importance of such larger markets on economic growth in Western Europe and the United Kingdom. For example, Sydney Dell, *Trade Blocs and Common Markets,* Chaps. 2–4; and H. G. Johnson, "The Gains from Freer Trade with Europe: An Estimate," in *Manchester School of Economics and Social Studies,* Sept. 1958, are generally bearish. Balassa, *Theory of Economic Integration,* Chaps. 5–8; and The International Labor Office (B. Ohlin), *Social Aspects of European Economic Cooperation,* 1956, are bullish. Balassa, Dell, and the UN Department of Economic and Social Affairs (Secretariat of the Economic Commission for Latin America), in its *The Latin American Common Market,* are quite optimistic with respect to Latin American regional groupings, although actual data or relevant studies are even more scarce for Latin America than for Europe.

argument then went on that, with the national economies already subject to many governmental controls, a single market among several states calling for many adjustments could be achieved only with close cooperation at the government level. This meant that in practice a common market could have only a *regional,* not a worldwide, basis. It could be established only between states with a sufficiently common range of experience, problems, and outlook to understand each other's situation and to agree on and pursue joint and common policies. Not stressed, but present, in these forums was the belief that the dimensions of the inevitable structural adjustments calling for retrenchment in some sectors as a consequence of trade-creation would be smaller if membership were restricted, and might even, on balance, be more than offset by diverting demands to each other from nonmembers.

But, it was also always asserted, these regional efforts were not directed against the rest of the world, nor were they prejudicial to any increase in the international division of labor. On the contrary, the cited consequences of the regional groupings would be to strengthen the members' competitive position so as to permit them, in due course, to reduce their present protection against nonmembers. This was but slight comfort to those who thought that reduced barriers under these circumstances would be of little help to their exports. Much more important was the recurrent theme that, while accepting that some particular foreign producers might be hurt, the increase in the rate of economic growth which integration was expected to bring about in its members "cannot fail" to increase imports from the rest of the world.

In defending their plans before nonmembers, spokesmen for the regional groupings in the less-developed areas put forward these same economic considerations. But the differences in emphasis were often so great as to approach differences in kind.[48] Those forming regional blocs in Latin America, Africa

[48] For an analysis of the ways in which accepted customs union theory needs to be modified for application to the problems of the less-developed countries (mostly, he concludes by taking more fully into account the likely, long-term changes in production patterns), see

149

and Asia looked at the arrangements primarily as a tool for furthering their economic development plans and especially their goal of increasing their levels of industrialization and changing their patterns of production.[49]

The fact that their development programs often were being frustrated by shortages of foreign exchange frequently led governments in these areas, encouraged by the economists of the regional United Nations Economic Commissions, to favor regional groupings because the governments believed the hoped-for effects of larger-scale operations on productivity might permit both an expansion of exports and a good bit of import substitution for the region as a whole. But they frequently spoke of the major problem as being one of increasing production and employment possibilities, rather than productivity.[50] They emphasized that they desired to establish larger markets for each other because they believed this would encourage more domestic investment in productive enterprises and would entice more foreign investment. This would lead to the creation of *new* industries and expansion of existing ones, both having a

---

Mikesell, "The Theory of Common Markets as Applied to Regional Arrangements Among Developing Countries," in R. F. Harrod and D. Hague, eds., *International Trade Theory in a Developing World,* London, 1963, Chap. 9.

For a pioneering effort to incorporate into the theory community preferences for particular types of economic activity, see C. A. Cooper and B. F. Massell, "Toward a General Theory of Customs Unions for Developing Countries," *The Journal of Political Economy,* Oct. 1965, pp. 461–76. This important work was published after my manuscript had gone to press and so has not been considered here. It must at least be recorded, however, that it provides formal theoretical support to some of the arguments noted below which have been used by the less-developed countries to defend partial or incomplete customs unions.

[49] See S. Dell, *Trade Blocs and Common Markets,* Chaps. 5–7, for a sympathetic treatment of the case for regional blocs in the less-developed areas.

[50] The available evidence, which is scanty, suggests that modernization, in fact, tends for some time at least to increase unemployment. See Sir W. Arthur Lewis, "Unemployment in the Developing Areas," in *Proceedings of the Third Biennial Mid-west Research Conference on Underdeveloped Areas,* Chicago, 1965.

much higher priority than any efficiency benefits that might come from more intense competition amongst existing enterprises.[51]

But if increased industrialization was a goal for these regions it was also a goal for each member.[52] This meant, although it was played down in their public statements, that a regional and limited preferential arrangement was an especially attractive way of enlarging markets precisely because it would have trade diverting effects. That is, to the extent that there was trade diversion *each* member could increase its exports more than its imports (and so its level of production, employment, and industrialization)—assuming, of course, that there was no retaliation by nonmembers.[53] Therefore, much emphasis has also been placed in many of these areas on "planned integration," designed not only to achieve optimal economic development [54] but, perhaps more important, to help ensure that all members share "equitably" in the hoped-for industrialization.[55] Only if

[51] I have come across no careful analysis demonstrating how high the costs to new investments might be to the participants, of foregoing such competition. Orthodox analysis suggests that the increase in real incomes associated with more competition among existing enterprises could be an important factor in bringing about both cost and demand forces facilitating the creation of new industries.

[52] The importance of this matter is indicated by the fact that at the time of this writing the 40-odd-year-old East African Customs Union is threatened with being broken up because Kenya has become the site of most of the industrial clustering.

[53] Back of this preoccupation with establishing new industries was not only the political and sentimental attraction of smoking chimneys but a widely held, often expressed, view that if these countries did not drastically alter their economic structure their economic betterment would continue to be held back by secular deterioration in their terms of trade, and an otherwise slow growth in export proceeds because of unfavorable elasticities of demand and oligopolistic and protectionist policies in the advanced countries.

[54] For the economic case for such planning in the heavy industry field, see Jan Tinbergen, "Heavy Industry in the Latin American Common Market," UN Economic Commission for Latin America, *Economic Bulletin for Latin America,* March 1960, pp. 1–5.

[55] This concern over increases in disparities in growth was also present, in much less acute form, in the EEC. Thus, the Rome Treaty

specific provisions for the latter were made were the least developed among each proposed bloc willing to meet the acknowledged real economic costs of substituting bloc imports for outside ones. This policy has taken many forms. The most important and relevant for our concern are the various "complementary" agreements and "integration industries" plans incorporated in some of the less-developed area regional schemes. The former provide for the planned apportionment among the members of the production of various parts of a final manufactured product. The Montevideo Treaty makes specific provision for such agreements,[56] and the idea has appeared in the plans of other less-developed areas as well. The latter are industries or firms established by agreement of all members of a union and provide that they should have more or less of a monopoly in the others' markets for a certain period of time. These play an important role in the Latin American schemes; the principle is formalized in the General Treaty on Central American Integration, but they are foreseen in Africa, too.[57] This "planned integration," when combined with import restrictions against nonmembers, was often also defended on the grounds that it was an effective method of achieving sufficient economies of scale to make possible import substitution. This

---

(Arts. 93 and 80) has provisions for subsidies and special transportation rates in favor of the underdeveloped regions of members, especially southern Italy and southwestern France. And the associated states are permitted to levy imports when justified for revenue or economic development reasons. For a recent study of the former, see Sergio Barzanti, *The Underdeveloped Areas Within the Common Market,* Princeton, 1965.

[56] The difficulty in negotiating such accord for products *already* being produced in more than one nation was, not surprisingly, proving great. As of mid-1965 complementary agreements had been reached only on statistical machinery and electronic tubes—new industries with heavy foreign investment.

[57] UN Economic Commission for Africa, *Industrial Growth in Africa,* New York, 1963.

See, too, UN Economic Commission for Latin America, *Possibilities of Integrated Industrial Development in Central America,* UN Sales No. 63, II, G.10, 1964.

argument recognized the high cost of import substitution on a national scale, but found it tolerable on a regional scale. More generally, it was believed that the real cost of import substitution (protecting a domestic industry), in terms of income lost through production inefficiencies, would probably be lower to each member within an integrated region than it would have been within a single nation; and this lower cost would, it was assumed, be more than offset by the value placed by each member of the union on the increased level of industrialization being achieved in each country. I have seen no studies showing that the complex set of conditions necessary to bring about these happy results were, in fact, frequently present or could be established; but it was often believed by those who were working on the problems of the less developed countries that they were, or could be.

Generally-worded homage was often paid to the benefits of more internal competition, and, it was said, in principle, any resulting trade creation would be welcomed. But, in fact, competition was almost anathema to most of them and certainly the fear was great that "unbridled competition" within the area would not only create harsh problems of bankruptcies for particular firms but any uncontrolled trade-creation probably would be spread unevenly among the members resulting in adverse affects on levels of employment and industrialization in some. This not only was in conflict with the "equality of benefits" objective, but it could even result, they feared, in the less advanced among them becoming "economic colonies" of the others.[58]

For these complex and interrelated reasons these groups therefore insisted that their arrangements often could not include "substantially all the trade" of the members or envisage

[58] This is reflected, and an effort is made to dampen fears, in UN, Department of Economic and Social Affairs, *The Latin American Common Market*, 1959, pp. 18–21, 87–89.

A. O. Hirschman, *The Strategy of Economic Development*, New Haven, 1958, pp. 187–90, treats of the possibility of this "polarization" effect. So does G. Myrdal, *Economic Theory and Underdeveloped Regions*, London, 1957, pp. 27–29, with his "backwash" effects.

the abandonment of all duties on intra-area trade. Nor, given the importance of the goal of creating new industries, could they agree not to increase some tariffs against nonmembers even if they were free trade areas and so had no technical need to do this because of the necessity to align their tariffs. Little public acknowledgment was given that these limitations would be costly to the members in term of long-run economic efficiency. Moreover, like the spokesmen for the Western European groups, those presenting the case for regionalism in the less-developed area insisted that, *on balance,* nonmembers would not suffer from these trade-diverting policies because the projected integration would produce such an increase in members' national income as would increase imports from the rest of the world.

This was not obvious to many nonmembers as they examined the proposals in detail. But most of the keen concern of third countries over the discriminatory effects on them of regional arrangements has been focused on the European Common Market, and so it is here. In part, this is because the economic importance of that area is so large and because to date the extent of the economic integration has been greater there than elsewhere. It is also because many of the relevant issues were first raised in the case of the Common Market and therefore less discussion was felt needed for the others. The European Free Trade Association has been subject to less critical attention, in part because it has been, and at the time of this writing continues to be, regarded as a transitional arrangement by both its members and others, despite the new lease on life given it by the breakdown in early 1963 of negotiations looking toward Britain and the others joining the Six.

Most government observers from the developed nations believed that for both physical and cost reasons there was but little scope for trade diversion in the near future by the Latin American and Central American groups; moreover, many believed that the desire to industrialize was so strong that the real alternative to the regional arrangements was greater *national* self-sufficiency, and so total trade with nonmembers was not going to be hurt by the regional efforts. It was also assumed

154

by some of the nonmember governments that if these arrangements succeeded in their major objective of creating *new* industries, and if these displaced markets of third countries, this would be associated with such increases in the income of the regional group that third countries as a whole would benefit, though particular producers might suffer. It was also thought that these blocs would be economically too small in the world market for any discrimination to seriously affect nonmembers' terms of trade. The new arrangements in Afro-Asia are still so tentative, and run such great risks of being stillborn, if for no other reason than immensely complicated political tensions among the members, that most third countries apparently have not yet given much serious attention to them. In addition, the tendency in recent years has been for other nations, especially highly developed ones, to be gentle and uncritical of any effort by groups of less-developed countries to help themselves.[59] But most third countries have been neither gentle with nor uncritical of the European Economic Community.

Major Areas of Nonmembers' Concern

The fathers of the European Economic Community had the experience of the Coal and Steel Community and the provisions of the GATT very much in mind when they drafted the Rome Treaty. They believed that it did qualify as an approved customs union. Those who followed with other regional proposals also believed they were legally within the provisions of the GATT. But all of them, particularly the European Economic Community, underestimated the concern of the rest of the world over the discriminatory aspects of their schemes. In their defense of this misjudgment, it must be recalled that this was the first time in history that a large number of third countries, those most likely to suffer, had been given the joint

---

[59] It should nonetheless be recorded that often the governments of the developed countries did little or nothing to help the integration efforts of the developing nations. Some uneasiness over the discriminatory aspects of these schemes has from time to time been expressed in the GATT by other less-developed countries, especially India and Jamaica, who were not members of any regional group.

opportunity to examine in detail the regional plans of others. There were, it is true, some who saw little to criticize, at least in public. Included were not only those who hoped to become associated in one way or another with the group under discussion, or who were trying to create their own regional blocs,[60] but also the United States government, which for years seemed able to see only the favorable aspects of regional arrangements, especially the European Economic Community.[61]

[60] Thus, the Scandinavians, who had led the critics of the Coal and Steel Community, apparently raised but few objections to the EEC proposals. From the outset they thought they would sooner or later get inside the preferential walls, first as part of the original European-wide free trade area scheme, and, later, in the melding of the European Free Trade Association with the Common Market. The Scandinavians also saw a European regional arrangement as an effective way of reducing European tariff disparities, for years a major policy objective of these low tariff countries. Indeed, the five-year search from 1951 to 1956 within the GATT for a new policy to deal with the problem faced by the European low tariff countries in a world where trade restrictions were cut on a reciprocal basis, not only fostered European regionalism, but made it clear that any arrangements, to be generally satisfactory, would have to go beyond selected preferences and approach a customs union or a free trade area. See Curzon, *Multilateral and Commercial Diplomacy*, pp. 87–97; and Camps, *Britain and the European Community, 1955–1963*, pp. 97–99.

[61] The strongly favorable United States attitude toward the EEC during the early years was based on the belief that the Common Market, for reasons noted at the beginning of this chapter, would increase the economic well-being of its members, which would enhance the area's political cohesion, sense of responsibility, and military strength. It was further assumed that a stronger Europe's policies in these fields would in the important instances be aligned with those of the United States, or if not aligned, at least be consonant. For officials who had been wrestling for years with dollar shortage problems, the question of discrimination inherent in this scheme was given relatively little weight. The gradual shifting of the United States policy position toward one of worry and concern over the possibly adverse effects of the Common Market on third countries, including itself, was a response to several developments. The acceptance of a nuclear stalemate and subsequent easing of East-West tensions, together with the conclusion that Eastern Europe was perhaps less monolithic and so less dangerous to U.S. security than had been thought, played a part. The increasing "independence" of Western

Once the general statements were over and nations began to examine in detail the various proposals, many saw their interests threatened. The very nature of the problem determined that these examinations should be frustrating. In regional blocs, being "second-best" solutions, everything depends on the particulars of each case. Yet all recognized that the necessary facts to reach a confident conclusion were not available and that there were severe limits to what could usefully be discussed among governments on the basis of hypothetical cases. At the same time, it was acknowledged that once a treaty creating a regional economic arrangement had been negotiated, there were stringent limits on the changes that others could expect to have introduced into it. Certainly it was too late to stop the operation.[62]

Nonetheless, in their concern over the possible adverse effects on them, third countries raised so many questions to which answers satisfying a majority could not be found that in the end the Contracting Parties have not been able to say that the major schemes qualified as customs unions or free trade areas under the GATT rules. The formal action in the case of the European Economic Community was to lay aside "for the time being" questions of law and the compatibility of the Treaty with the General Agreements and to concentrate instead on specific and "practical" problems.[63] In the case of the European Free Trade Association and the Latin American Free

---

Europe's political and military policies, facilitated by the military standoff between Russia and the United States, and given direction by the leadership of General de Gaulle, was also a factor. The accumulating evidence that Europe had been able greatly to strengthen its economies without benefit of full integration contributed. So, too, did the emergence of the persistent balance of payments deficits and the resulting increasing importance of the discriminatory effects of the Common Market.

[62] The European Common Market members made their position on this clear and set the precedent for the others when they said: "There can . . . be no question either of a readjustment of the Treaty or of any of its provisions, or of waivers or of subjecting the Six to special controls." GATT, *Press Release 357,* 30 Oct. 1957.

[63] See GATT, *Basic Instruments and Selected Documents, Seventh Supplement,* Geneva, 1959, pp. 24, 69–71, for details on this position.

Trade Area it was concluded that the legal question could not be "fruitfully discussed further at this stage" and that "at this juncture" it would not be "appropriate to make any formal legal findings." [64] Certain new procedures for consultations for those who felt their interests likely to be damaged were approved.[65] It was also specified that the normal procedures of the General Agreement would be available to help resolve any specific or particular issues that might result from measures taken in application of the schemes.

Although much of the discussion at the policy level surrounding the regional arrangements has been concerned with the legal questions as to their compatibility with the commitments members have undertaken in international agreements, especially the General Agreement, the real concern of the non-members has been the substantive question of whether they were, *on balance,* going to be adversely affected by these discriminatory arrangements and what policies would best ensure that they would not. As the accepted, conventional theoretical analysis indicated it should, this concern has focused on four substantive issues: the level of the tariff against nonmembers; the policy with respect to quantitative restrictions by members finding themselves in balance of payments difficulties; exceptions to free trade within the new areas; and the size of the group and the handling of existing preferential arrangements.

[64] See GATT, *Basic Instruments and Selected Documents, Ninth Supplement,* pp. 20–22, 70–94.

For complex, legal reasons the GATT has not yet had to take a comparable "decision" on the Central American arrangements but it did in 1956 decide that Nicaragua, as a Contracting Party, was entitled to claim the benefits of the GATT customs union article. GATT found little objectionable in the Equatorial Customs Union, in the Ghana-Upper Volta scheme, or in the South Africa-Rhodesia one. No formal conclusions have yet been reached on the other proposals by developing countries, but precedents have of course been set.

[65] See GATT, *Basic Instruments and Selected Documents, Seventh Supplement,* p. 24, for the text.

THE LEVEL OF TARIFF BARRIERS AGAINST NONMEMBERS

Introduction

In the formation of regional economic groups the level of tariffs against outsiders is a matter of great concern. Within the group itself, this is one of the most difficult problems to resolve, for it is here that conflicts arise between those who wish more protection against imports of those goods they produce and those who consume such goods directly or use them in the further production, and whose competitive position is thereby "protected" by a low, common tariff.[66] This was one of the many reasons for Europe dividing itself into the EEC and the EFTA; several members of the latter group had industrial structures based on tariffs which would have had to be aligned upward were they to join the former.

To third countries the tariff levels have an obvious and direct influence on their future exports via the "static production effect" of trade diversion. In addition, the lower the common tariff—or the tariffs of individual nations in a free trade area—vis-à-vis the intra-area tariffs the less trade diversion induced economic inefficiencies there will be to offset beneficial "dynamic effects" of the trade-creating tendencies of the economic grouping in increasing the levels of real income inside the group and so tending to increase the level of imports from third countries. It should also be noted that there are institutional factors leading to stickiness, which give third countries a particular interest in the *initial* level of the external tariffs in a customs union. The external tariff is a common one and has, therefore, been negotiated; any change in it becomes very difficult because it represents a complex balancing of concessions among the members. Such a balancing is implicit in the external tariffs of each member of a free trade area, but since these have not been

[66] For a brief account of the particular forms this basic issue took in the early discussions of the Common Market, see Camps, *Britain and the European Community, 1955–1963,* pp. 37–38.

specifically negotiated changes in them are easier to make in practice.

The General Agreement requires that barriers to imports by a customs union or a free trade area must not "on the whole be higher or more restrictive" than those applicable in the constituent territories prior to the formation of such a union or area; the requirement is intended to set an upper limit, but since these words are not further defined and since most students have long since agreed that there is no satisfactory statistical basis for comparing the restrictive effect on imports of different tariffs,[67] there were bound to be many disputes when the new regional organizations asked that their plans be approved under the GATT.[68]

---

[67] Viner's "The Measurement of the 'Height' of Tariff Levels," reprinted in his *International Economics,* Glencoe, Ill., 1951, pp. 161–75, remains the classic statement on the difficulties of measuring the heights of tariffs. By the mid-1960's it was becoming increasingly recognized that the traditional methods of measuring the heights of tariffs were for most purposes virtually meaningless since they assumed all goods were final goods. Once it is recognized that many goods have input components that are imported and that the duties on these intermediate goods vary from the final product, the "real" duties on the final goods have no systematic relationship to the apparent ones. Although it has apparently not received much attention, this fact also makes virtually meaningless the discussions that have taken place on tariff disparities.

[68] The Benelux Common Tariff arrangements generated virtually no disputes with third countries. Although the customs union came into existence only on Jan. 1, 1948, it was anticipated for several years, and it had been generally understood that it had the approval of other nations. It was, therefore, accepted as a customs union from the outset and its formation was not debated in the GATT. As it happened, the Benelux common tariff, in general an averaging of the previous national duties, was being formed just at the time of the first GATT tariff negotiating conference in 1947 and the changes were incorporated in those negotiations. The problem of "compensating" for those previously bound tariffs which were increased in the aligning process and of satisfying others that they were not suffering net damage by being deprived of their most-favored-nation rights as regards intra-union trade, was rendered relatively easy of solution by the fact that the Benelux countries were small and in 1947 tariffs had relatively little importance in determining trade flows. For additional details, see Meade, Leisner, Wells, *Case Studies in European Economic Union,* pp. 75–84.

Minor Issues for Free Trade Areas

In practice, the problem of initial tariff levels has proved to be less a cause of dispute with third countries in connection with free trade areas than with customs unions, primarily because in the former case no tariffs need actually be raised, while, in the customs union, the common external tariff must be established, and this aligning process results in some increases which draws attention to the problem.

There have been other reasons, as well, why so relatively little concern has been expressed to date over the tariff policies of free trade areas. Involving no arithmetical increase in barriers against nonmembers, the matter of reducing the increased actual restrictiveness resulting from merely maintaining the previous barriers against third countries while they are reduced within the group, must, under well-established procedures, await regular GATT trade negotiations. But such sessions can usefully be held only when the giants—the United States and the Common Market—are ready to participate. Moreover, the European Free Trade Association, the most advanced of the new, free trade areas, has been regarded by most observers as merely a waiting room for entry in the European Economic Community; therefore, most did not find it worthwhile to make a major issue of the members' national tariff policies. The real issue, as regards them too, was thought to be the EEC's common external tariff. Worry in third countries over the tariff discrimination against them by the free trade areas was also tempered by the hope that because each member of a free trade area had different tariffs trans-shipments (deflection of trade) would create an incentive for the high tariff members to adjust their tariffs downward.[69] The fact that

[69] I have found no evidence that trade deflection has actually happened on any important scale. Indeed, the interesting development has been that in the EFTA, at least, trade deflection has been an insignificant problem. This suggests that in the prosperous environment of rapid economic growth moderate customs duty differentials are not very important in determining the direction of trade—or at least they are not important enough to compensate for the risks of lawbreaking. See P.

legally the members of a free trade area have no authority over the tariffs of their partners vis-à-vis third countries gives some additional reason for less fears that those tariffs may remain higher rather than lower. More important has been the well-founded general belief that the EFTA countries could at least be relied upon to pursue liberal policies in relation to nonmembers because it was in the tradition of several of them to do so and because all of them were too dependent on trade with others—for both imports and exports—to follow other than a liberal policy. There was always the risk that some vested interests might be created in the continuation of sheltered markets in other members, but for each of these nations the greater need, so far as their export industries were concerned, was clearly to obtain a reduction of import barriers in the rest of the world, and especially those of the Common Market.[70] This was reflected in the aggressive approach taken by them during the 1964–1966 GATT tariff negotiations.

Several specific factors have contributed to the relaxed attitude of most third countries toward the tariff levels of the members of the South American and Central American groups. The arrangements in the former have not proceeded very far to date,[71] their future remains uncertain, and tariffs in these areas are in any case often defended on revenue and economic development grounds and so in practice are less subject to reductions because of their alleged discriminatory effects. Most third countries have so far not regarded the discrimination in the Central American group as likely to be of great quantitative importance, given the relatively small size of

---

Gerosa, "The EFTA Origin System," *EFTA Bulletin,* May 1963; B. Nyren, "EFTA at Work, Problems of Origin," *EFTA Bulletin,* April–May 1965; and S. A. Green and K. W. B. Gabriel, *The Rules of Origin, European Free Trade Association,* Geneva, 1965.

[70] In 1962–1964, for example, EFTA members' combined exports to each other accounted for some 22 percent of their total and imports only about 20 percent of their total. Only in the Scandinavian countries did the figure reach into the 35–45 percent range. Details may be found in the periodic Organization for Economic Cooperation and Development, *Bulletin of Statistics, Series A,* Paris.

[71] See pages 220, 221 below.

the markets and the limited range of products the countries produce—although one of the major purposes of the arrangements is to widen this range. There has been, as already noted, great reluctance in recent years to be critical or to raise problems for any effort (well conceived or not) by the less-developed countries to help themselves. A final, and not unimportant, factor contributing to the lack of attention paid to the level of tariffs on foreign imports into the free trade areas has been that for many the concern with the common external tariff of the European Economic Community has absorbed all the time and energy available in many governments.

There has been, however, a good bit of interest by nonmembers in the "rules of origin" for intra-area commerce in the free trade areas.[72] Most of this has centered on the European Free Trade Association, but it has also been noted in connection with the Latin American Free Trade Area, though the rules there for such matters have not yet been fully determined. Nonmembers in general want these rules to be liberal: the percentage be high of goods imported from third countries that can be incorporated into domestic products and still have that product eligible for free trade treatment *within* the area.[73] The basic EFTA provision was that goods were eligible for free trade treatment within the area if 50 percent or more of the value (including any

[72] The trade, production, and investment deflection problems *among* the members of a free trade area have been much discussed, but our concern here is with nonmembers. For the former, see Camps, *Britain and the European Community, 1955–1963*, Chaps. 4–6. The origin problem was a major issue in the ill-fated OEEC–Free Trade Area negotiations, as Mrs. Camps makes clear.

[73] The members of free trade areas themselves are torn as to what is in their best interests. If there were *no* origin restrictions for intra-area treatment there would be an incentive for imports to come into the area via the country with the lowest tariffs (trade deflection), and this might undermine the actual freedom of members to set their own tariffs. But, as the restrictions become more severe (the percentage of value added required to qualify for area treatment goes up), the possible trade-creating effects of the area are reduced. See Organization for European Economic Cooperation, *Report on the Possibility of Creating a Free Trade Area in Europe,* Paris, 1958, for a discussion of various ways of handling origin problems.

duty paid on imports) were added by members. This rule was further liberalized by the provision that for a wide range of raw materials (Basic Materials List) origin would be considered EFTA even if in fact they were imported. Most third countries were satisfied that these provisions assured that area treatment would be accorded virtually all goods produced in the area from imported raw materials. Under these rules, area treatment became less likely, however, as the raw materials were processed abroad. Moreover, since EFTA producers wanted area treatment for their own share of the final products, spokesmen for some nonmember states feared there would now be a new incentive for the European countries to process raw materials themselves. This posed a potentially serious problem for underdeveloped areas who saw the processing of their own raw materials as an especially attractive part of their industrialization plans. The danger was reduced, but not eliminated, by the so-called "process criteria," under which lists of goods were established and against each was described a process of production which, if performed in the EFTA area, entitled the goods to be treated as EFTA origin. Many of the processes started with processed goods or semi-manufactures.[74] Up to the time of this writing there seem to have been but few complaints that the processing industries of third countries in fact have been damaged for these reasons.

Initial Attack on EEC's Proposed Common External Tariff

As expected, the architects of the EEC wrestled for a long time with the external tariff issue.[75] Standing out against the

[74] See General Agreement on Tariffs and Trade, *Basic Instruments and Selected Documents, Ninth Supplement,* pp. 71–75. Origin rules of less than 100 percent EFTA content do, of course, tend to discriminate as among third country suppliers in favor of those enjoying preferential access to one of the members. For reasons why this is not likely to be of great practical importance in connection with the Commonwealth preference system and Portugal's preferential system, see UN, *Doc. E/Conf. 46/31,* 3 Feb. 1964, Chap. 2, Sec. 3. (This document has been reproduced in *Proceedings of the United Nations Conference on Trade and Development, Vol. VI,* United Nations, New York, 1964, pp. 238–404.)

[75] See Isaiah Frank, *The European Common Market,* New York, 1961, pp. 102–107, for an account of some of the internal issues.

wishes of the low-tariff members, especially Benelux, to have a very low common tariff so as to protect their import-using consumers and producers was the desire of those like France and Italy that it be high so as to protect their producers of import-type goods. Also arguing for a higher, rather than a lower, rate was the consideration that to set a low common external tariff would be to throw away bargaining power for future reciprocal tariff-cutting sessions with nonmembers. In the end, they decided that, after making several important exceptions to take account of highly valued national interests, the rule should be that for each product it would be the simple, unweighted arithmetic average of the rate of the members as of Jan. 1, 1957, with the Benelux counting as one area.[76] Simplicity in calculation was a major consideration in this decision, but the Common Market authorities also believed the results met the criteria they thought the authors of the GATT had in mind.

At the first quick reading, the proposal sounded reasonable enough to most third countries. Very soon, however, it was sensed that there was no simple economic rationale to an arithmetical averaging of duties, and that you could not assume such a procedure meant nothing had happened to the ability of individual countries, or to that of the rest of the world as a

---

[76] A special regime is applicable for most agricultural products produced in the community and is discussed in the next section of this chapter. Ceilings *below* this average were set for some 300 raw and semi-processed materials. (See Annex 1, Lists B, C, D, and E of the Treaty.) For some 87 other commodities found to be of particular interest to some members, often involving the exports of the members' overseas territories, the rates were negotiated before the Treaty went into effect (List F of Annex 1), and for another 70 "sensitive" products on which the members had often followed quite different import policies the common tariff was left for future negotiations. This was the famous List G. It was assumed these rates would be higher than the arithmetic average. Not until May 1964 had agreement been reached within the EEC as to the initial common external tariff on all the List G items.

The common external tariff of Benelux, established in 1947, was also, with exceptions, a simple averaging of the national rates. Here it was the 1939 ad valorem or equivalent rates that were averaged and, as a general rule, where there had previously been free entry into one of the partners, free entry was provided in the final Benelux tariff.

whole, to export to the nations whose rates had been so averaged. Basic were two related phenomena, although the actual discussions were usually not on them since the desirability of customs unions as such was not up for debate. First, the fact that members would now face no restrictions in trade with each other meant that for some goods any external tariff represented an increase in the effective protection against nonmembers. Second, the extent to which a common tariff will keep out foreign imports depends on the relationship of that new tariff to the cost of the lowest cost dominant supplier in the entire community. To the extent that these suppliers are ones who previously operated behind a relatively low national rate (this is often to be expected), the creation of a common tariff that is somewhere between the highest and the lowest national rates raises hurdles others have to surmount throughout the *entire* Community.[77]

As foreign countries examined the possible effects of this proposed tariff on their own particular products, they usually concluded that it constituted for them an effective and substantial increase in barriers. They took no comfort from the fact that their "loss" might be offset by some other nonmember country's "gain," although the Six believed such an offset fulfilled their obligation not to raise the *general* level of tariffs. In practice, each third country focused its attention on those of its exports which had previously gone predominantly to the former low-tariff countries—those whose tariffs were to be actually raised in the aligning process—and was impressed with the difficulties of developing a demand for their goods in countries where the tariffs would fall, even ignoring the *new* competition it would now face from intra-EEC producers because the latter had no tariff to hurdle. Each also often seemed to believe that the demand for his exports was price elastic on the upward side and inelastic on the downward side. The Community's pro-

[77] The ability of former low-cost producers to "take over" will depend, of course, on their ability to increase output without large increases in unit costs. The increasing tightness of the European labor market after 1960 probably put severe limits on this. See Krause and Cooper, in *American Economic Review,* May 1963, pp. 187–91, 201–202.

posal was therefore subject to prolonged attack. Although necessarily couched in terms of whether the proposal met the legal requirements of the General Agreement, the real objective of the exercise was to achieve a lowering of the common tariff.

Part of the discussion centered on an inconclusive argument as to whether the GATT rules required that the common tariffs be weighted by the amount of each commodity imported, rather than a simple arithmetic average. Many third countries argued that the GATT rules demanded the former and did so not because of any conviction on the legal point but because they believed that a weighted average would be lower.[78] (A tariff weighted by the value of imports gives smaller weights to tariffs so high that they keep out most imports and creates some presumption that a weighted average would produce a lower figure than a simple arithmetic one.) Further, they argued, the simple unweighted arithmetical average would tend to have an upward bias because the high rates of France and Italy would be given as much weight as the low ones of Benelux and Germany, even though the volume of trade of the latter was greater than of the former. The Six, on the other hand, insisted that the arithmetic average was within the legal terms of the GATT; it also said that a sample they had run had shown that a weighted one did not yield a lower tariff than the one proposed.[79]

Some third countries noted that even if their trade in a given product were evenly distributed over the Six, a, say ten percent, increase in the duties of some might very well decrease imports more than a 10 percent decrease in others would increase them. This could happen because the decrease might be simply

[78] See, for example, the statement by the South African delegate in GATT, *Press Release 354,* 30 Oct. 1957.

[79] Frank, on the basis of incomplete data, tentatively concluded that in this instance a weighted index probably would yield a lower Common Tariff. See his *European Common Market,* pp. 175–181. Balassa, in his *Theory of Economic Integration,* p. 48, concluded that there was no significant difference, while Hinshaw, in his *European Community and American Trade,* pp. 70–86, using different years for comparison, found the weighted level substantially lower if all goods were included, but only slightly lower for manufactured goods.

removing excess protection, or because there was no established market in that country, or because the demand was price inelastic, while the increase might add effective protection in the other. These considerations led many to conclude that before a judgment could be passed as to whether the proposed tariffs were more or less restrictive than the prior tariffs of the individual countries, it would be necessary to make a country-by-country, commodity-by-commodity examination of the probable effects of the proposed tariff. This was seen as necessary to provide assurance that their exports would not suffer.[80] Members of the Common Market wanted no part of this. A product-by-product, country-by-country study, they said, would be laborious in the extreme, would be endless, and would give rise to insoluble problems of compensation. Beyond this, they insisted, was the fact that their responsibilities under the General Agreement were with respect to the *general* incidence of the new common tariff, not to prevent any increase in the incidence on each product and for each country separately. They too were aware that such a procedure would yield a lower common tariff than that proposed.

A further occasion for bitter dispute arose when it was realized that in calculating the arithmetic averages the Six intended to use the duties which, on the base date of Jan. 1, 1957, they had a *legal* right to use. These rates were in many cases appreciably above the rates *actually* being applied at that time.[81] Several third countries sharply attacked this procedure. The reaction of the Six was so strong that they refused even to provide data on the rates actually used at the base date. Later, a GATT Working Party, giving full recognition to the difficulties in making any reliable comparison of the heights of

[80] GATT, *Doc. L/778*, 20 Dec. 1957. Again, little attention seems to have been given at this time to the *structure* of rates, although it is this that determines effective rates for particular activities. Thus, low rates on imported intermediate goods and high rates on finished goods yield very high rates on the value-added process.

[81] This was largely because the calculations did not take into account the 25 percent "business cycle" reductions by Germany in 1957 or the 1951 cuts of about 10 percent in the Italian tariff.

tariffs, tentatively concluded that the general incidence of the common tariff on imports into the Common Market probably was lower (by about 10 percent, Common Market spokesmen said) than the general incidence of legal or bound rates in member states on the base date. But, they added, on the basis of very scrappy data it seemed to be higher (and for some countries it was said to work out to as much as 30 to 40 percent higher) than the general incidence of rates actually encountered by exporters to the Common Market countries on Jan. 1, 1957.[82] On all these aspects the discussions ended in an impasse. This was one important reason why the question of the legality of the EEC under the GATT was put aside.

Community Makes Modest Concessions

Failing to bring about a general lowering of the proposed external tariffs, an increasing number of governments which saw their export markets threatened, spent more and more time in bilateral discussions at EEC headquarters in Brussels, as well as Geneva and elsewhere. They urged the Community authorities to depart from the arithmetical average and to set especially low rates on items of particular interest to them. The representatives of the Six listened politely to these requests and promised to take note of the views expressed. But from the available evidence it appears that these representations had little

---

[82] See GATT, *Doc. L/1479,* 16 May 1961.

The unhappiness of some third countries with the common tariff was reflected further in the request that the Executive Secretary of the Contracting Parties look into the legal aspects of the question of whether applied or legal rates were appropriate. He found (see GATT, *Doc. L/1919,* 14 Nov. 1962) very little recorded history on this, but went on to offer as his personal opinion that in considering the matter it would be reasonable to disallow in the calculations of the common tariff certain *temporary* applied rates that were lower than legal rates and also to disallow certain legal tariffs for which there was in fact little reasonable prospect of their being applied. If this were done, he suggested, the gap between the two interpretations narrowed and he left the strong implication that if such calculations were actually made it was likely they would yield a result close to the one being proposed by the Common Market.

if any effect on the final decisions of the Common Market authorities.[83]

Rebuffed again, many third countries then placed their hopes for a reduction in two tariff negotiation sessions then on the agenda. In late 1958 the United States Congress having extended the Trade Agreements Act for four more years, Undersecretary of State for Economic Affairs Dillon proposed a new two-session round of tariff negotiations, which became known as the "Dillon Round." The first of these was a "renegotiating" session made necessary by the fact that in aligning their tariffs the Six altered many previously negotiated agreements with third countries (changed bound rates) and so created a need to restore a balance in concessions. The second were negotiations on the level of the common tariff itself.

The Common Market spokesmen formally welcomed this proposal. This reflected not only the influence of such traditionally liberal trade members as Benelux but also the sensitivity of many in the Community to the criticism that they were harming others, and reflected the wish to demonstrate that any problems the union might be creating for third countries could be met satisfactorily by mutual tariff reductions on a most-favored-nation basis. It also mirrored the very important policy of the Six on the great issue of their relations with the Seven: the approach of the former as a group was to be global, not European.[84]

Further evidence at this time of the Community's wish to

[83] See, for example, the minutes on some of the consultations in GATT, *Docs. L/1128* and *L/1129,* 11 Dec. 1959.

[84] In this they were much encouraged by the United States, to the considerable distress of the EFTA members, especially the British, who were then hoping for a single trading area in Europe. On this, see Camps, *Britain and the European Community, 1952–1963,* Chaps. 6–8.

The view of the EEC Commission at this time, that the Common Market should pursue liberal trade policies vis-à-vis all third countries and not just OEEC nations, was spelled out in the European Economic Community, *First Memorandum from the Commission of the European Economic Community to the Council of Ministers of the Community,* Brussels, 26 Feb. 1959.

moderate any adverse effect of internal tariff reductions on third countries, their spokesman said, was their decision to extend to all other countries enjoying most-favored-nation treatment the initial *internal* 10 percent tariff cut made on Jan. 1, 1959, and, for about three-fourths of the commodities, the second 10 percent cut made six months later, provided these did not reduce the rates of the national tariffs below the foreseen common tariff.[85] Most third countries, while welcoming this, recognized that it was, after all, only a speeding up of the process of aligning national tariffs to the common external tariff. This decision was also designed to soften the criticism resulting from the breakdown in late 1958 of the negotiations for an OEEC–free trade area in which the EEC would be one element and which had led many to charge that the Six were "inward" looking and were "dividing Europe." To have extended the new rates *only* to other OEEC members would have been a clear violation of the GATT rules, and this the Six did not want to do.[86] They could, under their action, still be charged with "dividing Europe," but the "inward looking" charge lost some of its sting.

On January 1, 1961 and on July 1, 1963, well ahead of schedule, and apparently in an easily reached decision, the Common Market took the first two steps (30 percent of the way each time for most nonfarm goods, but only about half this for agricultural products subject to regular duties) in aligning the national tariffs to the common tariff. For this purpose it took

[85] GATT, *Doc. L/1099*, 13 Nov. 1959. The extension to third countries did not, of course, apply to goods on List G, for which common rates had not been established. Nor did it apply to most agricultural products.

[86] In early 1959 the EEC did extend to some of the OEEC members a liberalization of quotas which were not extended to others. That is, the EEC discriminated against all ·third countries but more against non-European states than against the OEEC countries. But, as we saw in Chapter II, this form of discrimination was rapidly declining. The fact that the Six were discriminating against the other OEEC countries, not permitted under the OEEC Code of Trade Liberalization, did, however, create something of a storm in the OEEC. See Camp's *Britain and the European Community, 1955–1963,* pp. 176–83.

as a basis of calculations, except for a few "sensitive" goods on List G, the proposed initial common external tariff *reduced* by 20 percent.[87] This meant that where alignment called for a decrease the cut was more, and where it called for an increase the rise was less, than if this policy had not been adopted. The EFTA countries regarded the speeding up of the alignment process as a hostile act. It helped solidify the EEC and, specifically, it started the process of its becoming a customs union and not a free-trade area, thus limiting the range of choice for a Europe-wide trading arrangement which might remove all discrimination by the Six against the EFTA nations.[88] Others generally welcomed this move, in part precisely because it did reduce the chances of a Europe-wide bloc and the increased discrimination against nonmembers that would have resulted.

But any effect these various measures had in allaying their worries about the effects on them of the EEC itself was largely dissipated by what most countries regarded as an extremely tough attitude in late 1961 by the Community in the first sub-

---

[87] On each occasion the Community stated that its action was provisional. The first was said to hinge on receiving equivalent reciprocal concessions in the so-called Dillon Round. It was not rescinded in the many cases where the Dillon Round failed to result in agreement to permanently reduce the common tariff up to 20 percent, but the Community later emphasized that the second alignment so calculated would not apply after December 31, 1965, unless adequate reciprocity was obtained in the Kennedy Round. If this Round fails and the initial common external tariff is restored, a substantial *increase* will be called for in the low national duties as the EEC moves into the last stages of its customs union.

[88] See Camps, *Britain and the European Community, 1955–1963,* p. 257.

For a statement by the Six, citing this as evidence of their outward-looking policy, see GATT, *Doc. L/1372, Rev. 1,* 23 Nov. 1960. A formal "Declaration of Intention on External Relations," reaffirming the Community's intention to pursue a liberal trade policy, was issued by the EEC ministers on May 12, 1960. See also, European Economic Community, *Bulletin of the EEC,* No. 4, Brussels, May 1960, pp. 19–24.

round of tariff discussions—the negotiations to make compensation and adjustment for changes in the previously bound rates resulting from their being aligned to the common tariff.[89]

After several months almost no agreement had been reached. In general, each third country not only demanded that *its* losses be balanced by *its* gains, but, as earlier, focused its attention on the cases where the national tariffs had been increased in the aligning process and asked for compensating concessions elsewhere. The Six took the position that in most instances compensation for increases in some members' tariffs on each good were compensated in whole or in large part by the corresponding reduction in the duties on the same goods by other members of the Community. In the end, as measured by the value of commodity imports in 1958, only about 20 percent of the renegotiations led to reductions in the common tariff and these were often small.[90] Many third countries believed that previously negotiated concessions on balance had been nullified or impaired by the adjustments to the common tariff and the failure to have this accepted more fully and more concessions made by the Common Market led some to threaten retaliation. But once again it was decided to leave the matter in abeyance for the time being, this time with the hope that the second sub-round of tariff negotiations—those concerned with the level of the common tariff—would yield "practical results" which would go some way to meeting the problems which third countries saw being created for them by the Common Market. In the event, these negotiations also yielded only very modest results. The dimensions defy precise quantification, but it has been estimated that "very approximately" the "overall incidence of the common external tariff" on manufactured goods may have been reduced by some six to seven percent, about one third of the

---

[89] These were known in the trade as "Article 24, Para. 6, negotiations."

[90] See European Economic Community, *Fifth General Report*, Brussels, 1962, p. 235. Curzon, *Multilateral Commercial Diplomacy*, p. 99, reports that this was more than the Six had intended when the negotiations began.

original across-the-board offer.[91] Stated otherwise, the un-weighted average tariff on manufactures may have been cut by about one percentage point.

Several factors contributed to this disappointing result. For all practical purposes agricultural goods were not even consid-ered. The negotiating techniques for industrial goods, except for the EEC–U.K. negotiations, were the old product-by-product ones, a procedure which had earlier been shown to have yielded about all the results that could be expected and which had already been abandoned in favor of linear reductions by the EEC and the EFTA in their internal tariff cuts. The authority of the United States to negotiate reductions was limited to the gradual reduction of duties by no more than 20 percent on any one product. Such reductions were further limited to those that survived the Peril Point examination. Perhaps equally impor-tant was that at this time (1961–1962) the Administration in Washington had just been changed and new international economic policies were still being established. Some countries —Canada, Australia, and the Union of South Africa were perhaps the most important—also were not prepared to offer much in the way of concessions on manufactured goods because agricultural products were excluded from the negotiations; but others, most notably the EEC, took the position that these countries also produced a good many manufactured goods and that they could not extend to the latter access to their markets via a most-favored-nation treatment without some concessions in return. The result was fewer exchanges of concessions among them all. But the disappointing results were also attributable in part to the fact that the Common Market countries were not as anxious as some third countries had hoped, and, as the Community's earlier statements had implied, to move quickly or far in the field of lowering the common

---

[91] UN Economic Commission for Europe, *Economic Bulletin for Europe,* Vol. 14, No. 1, Geneva, Sept. 1962, p. 57, Table 26. The United States concessions were seen as a bit less than this, the EEC not in fact having demanded immediate full reciprocity. For a statement of the U.S. reductions, see U.S. Department of State, *Department of State Bulletin,* April 2, 1962, pp. 561–65.

tariff. There were many in the Community who wished first to see how some of the other effects of the formation of the union had worked themselves out before introducing, or reintroducing, competition from outsiders. This was also a time when the question of other nations, particularly the United Kingdom and some of the other members of EFTA, joining the Six was under active consideration and many wished to postpone major decisions on the common tariff until the interests of these nations could be properly represented in the negotiations.[92] The major test of the Community's position on reducing the common tariff was yet to come.

Major Assault Mounted: Kennedy Round

As the Six proceeded, in an accelerated manner and apparently without internal difficulties or important costs to themselves, to reduce the duties on intra-area trade (by early 1965 duties on intra-area trade in most manufactured goods had been cut to only 30 percent of the 1957 level, and those for agricultural products not coming under the common agricultural policy to about 55 percent), the margins of preference in favor of the members increased.[93] This had not reflected itself in an absolute decrease in imports from nonmembers as a group; indeed, as we shall see below, for all major regions exports to the Six had

[92] An OEEC Study Group had spent a lot of time in 1960 examining the possibilities of mitigating the adverse discriminatory effects on each other of the Six and the Seven by reducing tariffs on a most-favored-nation basis on goods of particular importance to each. The results showed that it was difficult to build up a list of "European" commodities such that most-favored-nation treatment would redound predominantly to the benefit of the European nations.

[93] The plans call for a further 10 percent cut in early 1966 and all remaining duties to be abolished on July 1, 1967. The third, and final, adjustment of national tariffs to the common external one is also scheduled for mid-1967.

The Treaty does permit the authorities of the Common Market to temporarily suspend duties or to grant tariff quotas for certain products when adequate supplies are not available from within the Community, but to date, such action has been taken sparingly and probably has involved no more than one to two percent of EEC imports from third countries.

been rising, although not as fast as intra-area exports. Most third countries believed they might have done even better had there been no Common Market and feared they might be adversely affected, given time for old habits to change, new Community investments to be reflected in the cost of and variety of goods produced, and new intra-Commuity commercial channels to be created. Most of them therefore continued to hope for a substantial reduction of the common tariff.[94]

In a world where it had become tradition that tariffs are lowered only by negotiation involving the exchange of equivalent concessions and that, because of the most-favored-nation clause, such negotiations must include the principal supplier, it was on the United States that others had to wait for a broad assault on the common external tariff of the Six. One of the early decisions of the Kennedy Administration was that a major effort should be made to reduce world trade barriers. The record [95] leaves no doubt that a compelling factor in the decision of the Administration to seek, and Congress to pass, legislation permitting a 50 percent linear cut in tariffs, and to make the authority more usable by provisions to meet injury problems by adjustment assistance, rather than by curtailing imports, was the belief that the Common Market posed a potentially serious threat to the growth, and perhaps even maintenance, of American exports and so the ability of the United States not only to take increasing advantage of international specialization opportunities but to maintain important foreign aid and military

---

[94] Several of the less-developed countries were beginning to believe what the EFTA members had long believed: they might best protect themselves by coming within the terms of the Common Market. Some therefore asked for associate status with the EEC or at least for bilateral negotiations looking toward a reduction in duties on goods of particular interest to them. Since most of these discussions were also related to the problem of discrimination resulting from the association of the members' overseas territories, this aspect is discussed in the next chapter.

[95] See the voluminous *Trade Expansion Act of 1962, Hearings,* U.S. Senate, Committee on Finance, 87th Cong., 2nd Sess., and *Hearings,* House of Representatives, Committee on Ways and Means, 87th Cong., 2nd Sess. Vols. 1 and 2 of the House *Hearings,* and Vol. 4 of the Senate *Hearings* are especially informative.

commitments.[96] It was, therefore, in the words of the House Ways and Means Committee, of "critical importance" that the United States be armed with sufficient authority to open up its own markets so that it could negotiate a substantial reduction in the common external tariff and a more liberal Community common agricultural policy. It was also seen as a general move to strengthen the forces within the Community seeking to liberalize its foreign trade policies, and as a part of the broad, ill-defined Kennedy goal of increasing the "interdependence of the Atlantic Community."

Although the potentially adverse short-run effects of the Common Market were seen as stemming primarily from the discrimination and resulting trade diversion American exporters would suffer directly, not forgotten were the reduced markets in those third countries which normally spend in the United States an appreciable portion of their export earnings from the Common Market and which would also suffer from a high, common external tariff.[97] The enticing effect of a high common external tariff on U.S. capital, and so to a further short-run deterioration in the U.S. balance of payments, was also seen by the Administration as another reason for being able to mount a heavy assault.[98]

Following the passage of this legislation, ministers represent-

[96] The Administration also argued, though not very convincingly, that a reciprocal lowering of trade barriers would, in the conditions of the 1960's, expand U.S. exports more than its imports and so have desirable effects on the nation's employment and balance of payments.

[97] For the results of an attempt in 1963 to quantify the effects of the EEC on United States exports, see Walter Salant and Associates, *The United States Balance of Payments in 1968*, Washington, D.C., 1963, Chap. 4.

[98] Beyond these immediate effects, there was concern in some quarters, though not much in the Congress, lest the Common Market, by its favorable effects on the supply of capital (both indigenous and imported) and on the supply of vigorous and imaginative entrepreneurs, etc., reduce the already narrowing margin of American technological superiority in many areas, further worsening the balance of payments. This has been set forth by Kravis, in "The United States Trade Position and the Common Market," L. B. Krause, ed., *The Common Market Progress and Controversy*, Englewood Cliffs, N.J., 1964, pp. 136–59.

ing countries accounting for a large share of the world's trade met in Geneva, and in May 1963 approved a resolution that comprehensive trade negotiations should be held, conducted on a most-favored-nation basis, and that the goal should be a "substantial linear reduction" with no more than a "bare minimum of exceptions." [99]

The following 20 months were spent in the all-important task of attempting to negotiate detailed rules for the actual negotiations, which formally got underway only in early 1965. The Community's position during this period created considerable uneasiness among those who had hoped the exercise would be a great success. Prominent in this group were the EFTA countries who might be discriminating against others but who, nonetheless, were much worried over the discrimination they faced in the Six. Most countries wanted to accept as a *goal* a 50 percent linear cut, but the Six insisted that this be accepted only as a "working hypothesis." Through 1965, third countries had been unable even to reach an agreement with the Six on what was to be negotiated so far as trade in most farm goods were concerned, a topic we will return to later. It had been agreed that the exceptions to an across-the-board cut should be "necessitated only by reasons of overriding national interest," but when the Community tabled its exceptions list in late 1964 it was found that about 10 percent of the area's total dutiable nonagricultural imports were to be completely excluded and another 20 percent were to be subject to

[99] GATT, *Basic Instruments and Selected Documents, Twelfth Supplement,* Geneva, June 1964, p. 47. This document gives a full account of the conclusions and resolutions adopted by the ministers at this important meeting. The decision also provided, *interalia,* that the negotiations should cover both agricultural and industrial products and should deal with both tariff and non-tariff barriers; that some countries with "special economic or trade structures" would not be expected to participate on the basis of linear reductions (Canada, Australia, New Zealand, and South Africa were later put on this list); that reciprocity would not be expected of the less-developed countries, while every effort would be made to reduce barriers to their exports; and that the negotiations should provide for "acceptable conditions of access to world markets for agricultural products."

less than the assumed 50 percent cuts.[100] Details of these lists have not been made public, they are subject to "confrontation and justification," and meaningful inter-country comparisons are extremely difficult. Nonetheless, most third countries believed the exceptions list of the Six was the largest submitted, except for the Japanese, and unless it could be modified threatened to result in a serious unravelling of the others' offers of tariff cuts. The Community was also responsible for the adoption of the general principle for the negotiations that "in those cases where there are significant disparities in tariff levels, the tariff reductions" may depart from the general rule of equal linear reductions.[101] Since, by and large, the United States could

[100] European Information Service, *European Community*, Nov.–Dec. 1964, p. 3. And, as we noted earlier, it was decided in effect, to fix a common steel tariff, which, after a 50 percent reduction, would be just about where it had in fact previously been.

This EEC exception list was a good bit shorter than the sum of the original proposals of each member government, thanks to forceful negotiations by the Commission; but the list was still long, precisely because the easiest way to reach agreement on it was to include items of great interest to any one member.

[101] The initial specific EEC proposal—known as "écrêtement"—was for a leveling of tariff peaks; tariffs should be reduced not by 50 percent of their existing level but by 50 percent of the *difference* between the existing levels and the following targets: 10 percent for manufactured goods, 5 percent for semi-processed goods and zero for raw materials. This was quickly found unacceptable by others, on the grounds that it would drastically limit the total tariff reductions possible under the Kennedy Round. The EEC then proposed, and this was accepted as a basis for negotiation by the others, that the disparity issue be tackled in terms of the differences in tariff rates on the *same* good. Here, for example, one of the formulas actively discussed was that a country could invoke a disparity rule and cut its tariff on a given good by only 25 percent, rather than 50 percent if the tariff on that good in a "key country" (the United States, the Common Market, the United Kingdom, or Japan) was at least twice as high and 10 percentage points above that of the invoking country. At the time of this writing the search for an acceptable formula seems to have been at least temporarily abandoned, but the "right" to invoke a disparity has been reserved.

The whole issue had its origin in the fact that, as these things are usually measured, while the overall U.S. tariff rates averaged about the same as those in the Community, there was a larger spread or dispersion

reduce duties only up to 50 percent on any good, an upper limit was set and so invoking this rule would mean that barriers by

---

in the U.S. structure. The Community spokesmen argued that large dispersions created a justification for departure from the rule of equal percentage tariff cuts. Their primary thesis was that a given percentage reduction in a high tariff would encourage imports to a lesser extent than the same percentage cut in a low tariff—and so reciprocity required larger percentage cuts by high tariff countries. This would seem likely to be true as a general proposition only if the value of imports is less sensitive to price cuts in high tariff situations than in low tariff ones; this in turn is likely to be true only if high tariffs are associated with low price elasticities of demands for imports (typically this would mean that higher tariffs have more water in them than lower ones) and/or if a system of high tariffs is inversely correlated with the initial value of imports. It is not obvious that either of these holds between the United States and the EEC today. (See R. N. Cooper, "Tariff Dispersion and Trade Negotiations," *The Journal of Political Economy*, Dec. 1964.)

The Six also injected this issue because they believed it would permit them to maintain more bargaining power for the future, fearing that 50 percent reductions now could leave them with little of value to offer in some future round while many U.S. tariffs would still be substantial. Again, as Cooper shows, it is not obvious that this is true. Introducing this consideration into the Kennedy Round, and getting it accepted, did provide the Community with a "justification" for adding items to its exceptions list (and this may yet prove to be the way in which the disparity issue is handled), as well as with a second line of negotiating strength in case the United States placed on its exceptions list goods of great interest to the Six. (One of the most lucid, publicly available accounts of the disparity issue may be found in the Committee for Economic Development, *Trade Negotiations for a Better Free World Economy*, New York, May 1964. See also, *Eighth Annual Report of the President of the United States on the Trade Agreements Program for 1963*, Washington, D.C., 1964, pp. 10–11.)

It should be remembered that the high tariff–low tariff country problem, especially within Europe, has been for years a major concern of the GATT, had led the low tariff countries to drag their heels in reducing quantitative restrictions under the OEEC trade liberalization plan, and had been a major factor leading to the adoption of the linear approach to tariff reductions. Several GATT working party reports on this issue during the 1950's may be found in GATT, *Basic Instruments and Selected Documents*, Vol. 2, pp. 211–17; *First Supplement*, pp. 69–85; *Second Supplement*, pp. 68–92; *Third Supplement*, pp. 218–221; and *Fourth Supplement*, pp. 74–82.

the invoking country, no matter which it was, would be cut less than 50 percent. It was, in other words, a device that would operate to limit the level of import barrier disarmament and so was of great interest not only to the United States and the Six but to third countries as well. Indeed, it appeared that, in many cases, invoking the disparity rule between the United States and the Six would frequently bear most heavily on exports of third countries to the country invoking the rule.

At the time of this writing, the negotiations are still in full swing and it is too early to forecast their outcome. If it turns out that the exceptions lists can in the end be cut down (and many believed the 20 percent portion of the EEC list was negotiable), if the disparity rule can be severely defined and rarely invoked, and if agricultural goods can somehow be brought into the system in a way that is meaningful in terms of increasing the access of other countries to domestic markets, the 1964–1966 negotiations will lead to a very substantial reduction in import barriers, not only in the Common Market and the United States, but also in the EFTA members. Restrictions in the less-developed countries will be cut much less, if at all, because this time it has been agreed that full reciprocity will not be expected from them. If this happens, a considerable part of any benefit to general welfare resulting therefrom can be attributed to the discriminatory aspects of the Common Market —via its role in generating the new United States policy—and so can be offset against whatever cost to welfare the remaining discrimination may cause.

Some Preliminary Conclusions

The interesting issue for us is not whether in these negotiations the Community engages in hard bargaining. The individual member states could be expected to do that. And since the Six runs a large trade deficit with the United States it will demand reciprocity, severely defined. The issue is rather whether the joining of six nations into the Six (which act increased the effective height of previous barriers) has, on balance, created new reasons for the group's not lowering import barriers on manufactured goods; as we will see below, it has probably created new reasons for a more protective policy on farm goods. There is little documentary evidence available on this at the time of this writing, but some of the forces at work, frequently in opposite directions, can be identified and preliminary judgments made as to their importance.

Not insignificant here was the fact that the Six were under considerable pressure from nonmembers to *prove* that they were "outward looking." Over and beyond this, the question of Britain's relations with the Community seemed to be a force for larger rather than smaller cuts. France, which did not want Britain to join, was reported to believe that it could better withstand the pressure of other members for British entry if the common external tariffs were reduced. The Dutch, on the other hand, favored British entry, believing the path would be smoothed by a lowered common tariff.

Although proof is still lacking, many in Europe believe that creation of the Common Market has contributed significantly to the area's increased productivity, and so competitive ability, and that this means there is less resistance to lower import barriers. Apart from this, a fact often stressed by observers in Europe is that many producers have now successfully faced greater competition within the Community and, finding it less trouble-some than had been feared, have a confidence in their ability to compete with outsiders, which they would not otherwise have had. They are therefore less inclined to urge their governments to maintain import restrictions.[102] The export industries also have new confidence and they see the desired larger markets abroad depending in part on a reduction of Community import restrictions. The need for a growing volume of Community exports, to finance the increase in imports associated with the

[102] Even where this increased confidence of European industrialists in their ability to compete in home markets is strong, there often remains reluctance to give up duties on the grounds they permit the charging of higher internal prices and so increase the profits and amount of internal (to the firm) financing available for the expansion of productive facilities being planned. Some continue to urge tariffs from the fear that American companies are so big and well financed that they could and would sell at the loss necessary to destroy at least some of their competitors if access were eased by lower tariffs.

confidently expected continued rate of growth of income in the Community, constitutes for the Community's authorities another powerful reason for liberalizing trade. Moreover, although the contributions to this of the formation of the Community are debatable, the Six, by and large, are enjoying full employment and great internal prosperity and are under some inflationary pressures—conditions conducive to more liberal trade policies.

On the other hand, it would be surprising if the removal of intra-area barriers has not created some new vested interests in the maintenance of the resultant level of discriminatory shelter in partners' markets. I have found no evidence that this is as yet important, however; what there is must be at least partially offset by the disappearance of some old vested interests in protection, as a consequence of the greater intra-European competition. Both of these are thought to be small at this time, but the former could become stronger the longer the common external tariff remains unchanged; so this adds to the importance to third countries of a successful "Kennedy Round." A closely related issue arises from the fact that the common external tariff represents for each good an increase in duties by some members and a decrease by others. It is not yet clear whether the considerations that prompted those nations with low tariffs to have low tariffs still are strong and operating or whether they have been offset by new activities for the Community market encouraged by the higher tariffs. And do those which had to lower their tariffs in the aligning still wish to see them restored or, having made at least part of the adjustment to the lower tariff, are they no longer interested in the old high rates? Lack of discussion or concern with these questions leads one to conclude that probably there is not much in these considerations one way or the other.

The European Economic Community is first and foremost a political institution and there are political cohesion advantages to maintaining preferential tariff arrangements. It is often said that they are a political necessity. These considerations do preclude a policy of cutting many of the existing common tariffs to zero. In the mid-1960's, however, I have the strong impression that while tariff preferences do have some political value as a symbol, very small preferences will now suffice for this purpose, given all the other "common" activities of the Six. Probably a more important new force against reducing tariffs is the fact that the initial common external tariff represents a complex balancing of concessions among the various members and any lowering of it will upset that balance. Observers within the secretariat of the Community recognize this possibility but report seeing little or no evidence that it has so far constituted an important obstacle to cuts.[103]

Finally, the formation of the Community has meant that the bargaining power of the group vis-à-vis the rest of the world probably is greater than the combined bargaining power of the Six when they acted individually. This tends to follow from the fact that, in tariff negotiations, they now have more to give (a cut in the increased protection that results from no internal barriers and an arithmetic-average common external tariff) and, perhaps, less to gain (as a group, they are more self-sufficient and less dependent on "foreign" trade than they were as individual states). In any event, other nations *think* the Community now has more bargaining power and this may be enough to give them that power. But the consequence of this, too, is uncertain.[104] Nothing can be said with confidence as to whether this increases or decreases the likelihood that any negotiations would result in large tariff reductions. What is certain is that, since the formation of the Community made it the principal supplier for a large number of goods to many countries, no vigorous most-favored-nation negotiations can be carried out unless the Six are prepared to participate. Moreover, given the general rule of reciprocity in tariff negotiations, the overall percentage cuts among negotiators cannot vary much

[103] In private conversations that I held on the understanding there would be no attribution.

[104] It is usually said that the larger the trading area negotiating as a unit, the better the terms of trade it can exact in negotiations, but even this is not certain. (See Meade, *Theory of Customs Unions,* Amsterdam, 1956, p. 96.)

from those that the least enthusiastic bargainer is prepared to give.

It may well be that the Six will prove to be the most reluctant negotiator and will be blamed for any failure of the Kennedy Round to come closer to the potential 50 percent reduction. If so, this will not be because of the effects of the formation of the union, discussed in the preceding few pages. They *seem* to add up to the Community's having perhaps fewer reasons for maintaining tariffs on manufactured goods than would its members have had, had they not formed themselves into the Common Market. Rather, it will reflect other things, often having to do with the unfortunate timing of the negotiations. The Community is currently enjoying a comfortable balance of payments position even though the area's trade balance was deteriorating during the period of the negotiations. The pressure on it to "do something" about other people's restrictions on their exports was therefore not great, especially when they had lots of other problems that seemed more pressing.[105]

The problems of the common agricultural policy and changing relations with the associated overseas countries, discussed in the next chapter, are occupying much of their time. Moreover, in 1964–1966 the Community had not yet fashioned a good negotiating instrument. The Commission, which is carrying out the negotiations, has to operate on the basis of a mandate given by the Council of Ministers.[106] Such a mandate is often part of an extremely complex set of agreements and concessions involving many matters of importance, political as

[105] This is not to deny that some members, West Germany in particular, were most anxious to see their access to the rest of the world, especially EFTA, made easier.

[106] The requirement that this be by unanimous vote expires in favor of majority vote in January 1966. Up to the mid-1965 crisis on the financing of the common agricultural policy, it had been generally assumed that this was not likely to make much difference in practice, and that "escape from the unanimity rule would remain in the realm of theory." At the time of this writing, however, it appears that France may now insist that explicit arrangements be made, giving veto rights to each member on matters regarded by it as important.

well as economic, to the member states. As a result, it not only takes a long time to get such a mandate but it is extremely difficult to change it. This constitutes a serious restraint on the process of give-and-take in negotiations.

Important, too, was the fact that these were years when the Commission was preoccupied with trying to *create* a genuine Community and to this end exerted considerable pressure on the member governments to agree on common policies—just getting such a decision tended to become an end in itself. But decisions so forced often tend to veer toward more rather than less protectionism. Moreover, the fact that the EEC was not yet a single Community meant that the exceptions list to across-the-board cuts would be long (as we saw it was) because of the tendency to include for all six what would otherwise have been exceptions only for one. Dominating all at this time of writing, late summer 1965, were the difficulties created by revived French reservations over the whole concept of a truly united Community, with a powerful Commission; these were, for the moment at least, sapping some of the Six's enthusiasm for, and virtually all of its ability to carry out, arduous tariff negotiations.

The possibility that the Six will stand in the way of a vigorous multilateral program of trade barrier reductions has led some (senators, business leaders, and academics) in the United States at least to suggest that if this should come to pass the United States should take the lead, abandon unconditional-most-favored-nation treatment, and, via one method or another, reduce trade barriers among "like-minded countries," [107] This has some genuine appeal, but would it be wise? The usually stated purpose of this policy was to apply pressure on the EEC to cooperate in lowering trade barriers on a multilateral basis. Presumably, therefore, some form of

---

[107] See Hinshaw, *European Community and American Trade*, pp. 174–77; Committee for Economic Development, *Trade Negotiations for a Better Free World Economy*, p. 41; *United States Balance of Payments, Hearings*, Joint Economic Committee, U.S. Congress, 88th Cong., 1st Sess., Part 2, July 29–30, 1963, pp. 318–19; and *Trade Expansion Act of 1962, Hearings Before the Committee on Finance*, U.S. Senate, 87th Cong., 2nd Sess., Part 4, pp. 2,277–84.

conditional-most-favored-nation policy is envisaged. This would have the disadvantage of adversely affecting not only the Common Market, but also any others which might for any reason not find it possible fully to participate, including probably many less-developed countries, as well as others who were already seeking "special relations" with the Six. Further, as the experience of the EFTA in discriminating against the EEC has shown, it is not obvious that the EEC would capitulate. This is made more doubtful by the fact that for many of those that might be involved with the U.S., notably the EFTA countries, trade with the EEC is more important than their trade with the United States. They might therefore be expected to try and work out similar conditional MFN arrangements with the Six.[108] This would not only reduce pressure on the latter to join in a worldwide effort but would be to the clear disadvantage of the United States. This, as well as a raised common external tariff, could constitute a very effective reprisal. Beyond this, the major finding of this study is that discrimination in recent years seems always to have a great many costly side effects, economic and political.

Before going very far in support of such a policy it would be well to examine some American history, which records that after a century and a half of experience in following conditional-most-favored-nation treatment, the United States abandoned it in 1923 for the very good reasons that, despite some benefits, on balance it had been found to be impractical (because of the complexities and costs of implementation), ineffective (because others retaliated), and imprudent (because it led to higher trade barriers all around the world).[109] A preferable policy, in the unhappy event that, despite continued ne-

[108] Indeed, this may be just what British Prime Minister Wilson had in mind in mid-1965 when he urged that ways be found to "build bridges and dig tunnels" between the EFTA and the EEC, *The New York Times*, May 21, 1965, p. 47.

[109] See United States Tariff Commission, *Report on Reciprocity and Commercial Treaties*, Washington, D.C., 1919; and Viner, "The Most Favored Nation Clause in American Commercial Treaties," 1924, reproduced in his *International Economics*, pp. 17–39.

gotiations in the face of setbacks and delays, an acceptable agreement under the Kennedy Round is in the end frustrated by the EEC, might therefore be to accept failure, making it quite clear to the entire world that the responsibility rested on the European Economic Community.[110] This, too, is a way of applying very considerable pressure on the Community. While not forgetting the tremendous difficulties in mounting a new round of trade negotiations at some later date, such a policy seems to me to hold better *long run* prospects for a freer trading world than a settlement now which excluded the Six and introduced a massive amount of new discrimination.

[110] If a failure of the Kennedy Round were associated with events leading to a break-up of the Common Market itself, then problems of commercial policy between the countries in that area and the rest of the world would for some time move far into the background.

CHAPTER V

Discrimination and Permanent Regional Organizations, 2

INTRODUCTION

THE level of a regional bloc's tariffs against nonmembers is a major determinant of the amount and direction of discrimination third countries may suffer. But it is not the only discriminatory aspect that has preoccupied the policy makers in the years since World War II. Much time has been given, and many disputes have arisen, as to the effects on others of the differential use of quantitative restrictions when a member of a regional group finds itself in balance of payments difficulties; to exceptions from intra-area free trade, notably the special arrangements made for trade in farm goods; and, finally, to the related problems of the admission of new members to a bloc and the treatment to be accorded prior preferential arrangements of some of the group's members. It is to these three major problems that we turn in this chapter.

BALANCE OF PAYMENTS DIFFICULTIES AND THE DISCRIMINATORY USE OF QUANTITATIVE RESTRICTIONS

We saw in Chapter II that even before World War II ended it had become accepted doctrine and practice that a nation might impose quantitative restrictions in a discriminatory fashion if it had severe balance of payments difficulties *and* if its earnings included large amounts of inconvertible currencies. We saw too that by the time the Treaty of Rome was signed such discrimination was being rapidly removed and that, despite the theoretical case that had been made for it, efforts had failed in 1955 to obtain general acceptance at the government policy level of the doctrine that the discriminatory application of quantitative restrictions was justified even under conditions of convertibility if there were severe international disequilibrium. The growth of permanent regional organizations presented the issue again, this time as one facet of that central economic union problem, most aspects of which are beyond the scope of this study: what to do if, even though all currencies are convertible, one member of a union runs into serious and prolonged overall balance of payments difficulties.[1]

The Problem Foreseen

In the early post-war years one of the most serious problems the Benelux members faced in consummating their union was that the Netherlands, traditionally running a deficit with Belgium–Luxembourg, was at that time also running a deficit with the rest of the world. The major response to this from 1946 to 1949 was to delay the planned liberalization by Holland of both intra- and extra-Benelux trade. The 1949 devaluations, involving the depreciation of the guilder vis-à-vis the Belgian franc, helped close the gap. After that, increasing reliance was put on the adoption within each of the Benelux countries of monetary, fiscal, and wage policies appropriate to their balance of payments positions. These, together with external factors and increased Benelux output, resulted in all members avoiding serious and prolonged overall deficits; and permitted them, with only temporary setbacks, to reduce barriers amongst themselves and between them and the rest of the world as well, although the latter were cut somewhat less rapidly than the former. Third countries did not, as it turned out, have much reason to complain about Benelux behavior on this score.[2]

Mindful of the Benelux problems, however, those creating the European Coal and Steel Community explicitly warned third countries of the possibility that one of their members might get into severe overall balance of payments difficulties and find it "necessary" to impose quantitative restrictions on imports.

---

[1] We saw in Chapter III that aid from some members to debtors can be a temporary answer and that, if major currencies are inconvertible, even overall balance, if combined with regional imbalances, can create great pressures for additional discrimination.

[2] For a detailed account of the Benelux experience from 1944 to 1950, see J. E. Meade, H. H. Liesner, and S. J. Wells, *Case Studies in European Economic Union*, London, 1962, pp. 135–73.

Since, in general, it would be forbidden to place restrictions on imports from its partners, the result would be that the restrictions would be discriminatory—even if its earnings were convertible. But, they warned, the difficulties would not end here. If, in these circumstances, the other members of the regional arrangement, although not in balance of payments difficulties themselves, did not also restrict imports from third countries of the items the first country was restricting, these items might enter the first country via its partners. If so, the first country's quantitative import restrictions would not be effective in meeting its balance of payments problems—or could be made so only by intra-area restrictions which would violate the terms of the regional agreement. But, if others applied comparable restrictions they would be taking action which, under their GATT obligations could be taken only if they themselves suffered severe balance of payments problems. Although posed, the dilemma was not pursued at the time, largely because those were days when discriminatory application of quantitative restrictions was widespread and this particular manifestation did not seem very important, or at least its resolution urgent. Moreover, it was assumed that the problem would not in fact arise because the Coal and Steel Community was concerned with only a few items; so even if one member got into balance of payments difficulties it would not find a "solution" in discriminatory import restrictions on just coal and steel products.[3] The members of the Community have not so far found it necessary to take such measures.

Issue Left "en suspense"

The Rome Treaty, the Stockholm Convention, and the Montevideo Treaty, however, raised the issue again. These times there was much discussion, for they were creating blocs covering a lot of trade and so the problem was a potentially major one. The international climate was quite different too, for by then the discriminatory aspects of quantitative restrictions were being abandoned by most. The Rome Treaty clearly au-

[3] For this early concern, see GATT, *Doc. L/17,* 8 Sept. 1952.

thorizes a member, even though currencies are convertible, to apply quantitative restrictions against trade with third countries, but not against each other.[4] It also provides that members should pursue a common commercial policy vis-à-vis third countries, and in reply to specific questions from nonmembers, EEC spokesmen acknowledged that this permitted an individual member state to apply quantitative restrictions against third countries, even when such member was not itself in balance of payments difficulties, provided some other member was.[5]

In defending their wish to keep both prongs of this policy in their arsenal, the spokesmen for the Common Market relied heavily on the argument that it was essential for the success of the Community that competition within the area be increased, that this meant quantitative restrictions must be quickly removed on intra-area trade and not reimposed. At the same time, for some countries it might not be possible, for balance of payments reasons, to remove as quickly such controls against everyone, or in future emergencies, to refrain from resorting to them. Furthermore, they argued, as had the Coal and Steel Community several years before, that these controls might very well not be effective unless the country in balance of payments difficulties was supported by its partners. Comparable policies by them would both reduce the flow (via them) of third countries' exports to the country in difficulty and might also help the latter's payments position by diverting their imports to it. Common Market spokesmen emphasized repeatedly that it is inherent in a customs union that distinctions are made in the treatment accorded imports from members and nonmembers, that this is so whether duties or quantitative restrictions are the device chosen to make the distinction.[6]

[4] Treaty Establishing the European Economic Community (Rome Treaty), Arts. 30–37, 108–16. Art. 109 allows a member for a short period to impose quantitative restrictions on imports from other members if a "sudden crisis in the balance of payments occurs."

[5] GATT, *Doc. L/656*, 2 Aug. 1957.

[6] When the EEC spokesmen said that just such discrimination had happened under the OEEC trade liberalization program and that no one had created a fuss, the critics replied that they had not objected to that because of "their feeling that as a practical matter [that] programme was,

Several third countries found all this very bothersome, particularly the idea of a common policy. Led by the United States and Canada, they took the position that if and when the time came that members of the Common Market were so thoroughly integrated that they could be regarded as a single economic unit, holding their reserves in common, then they might quite properly have a common policy on quantitative restrictions against outsiders. Until such time arrived a member should not be permitted to apply quantitative restrictions unless his own balance of payments position justified it. And then, they insisted, if currencies were convertible, the quantitative restrictions should be applied to all countries equally.

Worry, lest the discrimination be detrimental to their particular exports, was back of much of this attack. There was also concern that its practice by members of the Common Market might revive the use of discriminatory restrictions by others, with all the attendant costs, which we discussed in Chapter II. The third countries believed their strongest argument against a common policy, when members of the Common Market still held their reserves separately, was that it would be "contrary to fundamental economic reasoning." It could mean that those in balance of payments difficulties would be unable to apply restrictions as severe as their conditions dictated, while others would be applying restrictions not required or justified by their position. Under such a system, unless intra-group restraints were put on, imports would tend to flow to members not in a position to finance them, at the expense of the reserves of other members who had no such problems.[7]

This thesis, of course, reflected a profound difference in view as to the responsibilities—or at least the freedom—of individual countries which had joined the Community to make sacrifices, if

---

on the whole, moving in the right direction" [i.e., toward extinction]. (GATT, *Basic Instruments and Selected Documents, Sixth Supplement,* March 1958, p. 80.)

[7] See GATT, *ibid.,* p. 79. It was also argued that if members of the Six were no longer bound individually by the GATT rules against imposing discriminatory quantitative restrictions, then the balance of rights and obligations under the General Agreement would be impaired.

necessary, for its partners. Because of this and because once again the legal issue was not clear, the question was left "en suspense." It was agreed not to try to reach a formal judgment or conclusion but to leave it thus: if a member of the Community, whether in disequilibrium itself or not, should resort to the discriminatory application of quantitative restrictions, any nonmember which believed its interests had suffered could bring its specific case before the Contracting Parties under the relevant complaint provisions of the General Agreement. No such cases have yet been presented.

The Convention creating the European Free Trade Association also permitted its members to apply quantitative restrictions in a discriminatory fashion.[8] When this was examined by the Contracting Parties the same legal and substantive issues were reworked. The Seven held to the same legal position the Six had taken: the customs union provisions of the GATT legally permitted them to apply quantitative restrictions against others which they were forbidden by terms of the Stockholm Convention to apply against each other. They insisted that they intended to follow a liberal trade policy and hoped not to use quantitative restrictions in a discriminatory fashion, but they were not willing to forego this "right."[9] Nonetheless, the record shows that the Seven came close to committing themselves to the position that a member would apply restrictions against third countries only in light of the problems of the member concerned, and not as a means of helping another member which was having balance of payments difficulties. There was also something of a consensus that if currencies were convertible the discriminatory application of quantitative restrictions would usually make "little economic sense" for members of a free trade area. This was so because, not having

---

[8] Convention Establishing the European Free Trade Association, (Stockholm Convention), Art. X. Although the general rule is that members shall not apply quantitative restrictions on trade with each other, Art. XIX permits them, under certain stipulations, if necessary to "safeguard" the balance of payments.

[9] See GATT, *Basic Instruments and Selected Documents, Ninth Supplement,* Geneva, 1961. pp. 75–78, for a report on these discussions.

a common commercial policy, an attempt to apply quantitative restrictions only against nonmember countries usually would not be an effective way of reducing imports. Situations were foreseen by the Seven, however, when it might not be prudent for a member with balance of payments difficulties to *relax* restrictions against third countries as fast as it might be *required* to relax them against members. The matter again was not pressed to a formal conclusion or decision.

The Montevideo Treaty has provisions comparable to those of the Stockholm Convention. The discussions on these in the GATT were a mild and abbreviated version of the earlier ones and again the issue was not pressed to a formal conclusion.[10] The Latin Americans refused, however, to commit themselves as the EFTA members virtually had in their various statements, though not in the Treaty itself, to nondiscrimination, except in transitional or most exceptional circumstances.

No Great Conflicts—Yet

As we noted in Chapter II, most countries after 1955 proceeded with the dismantling of the great bulk of their discriminatory, quantitative restrictive systems. When the Common Market finally abolished quantitative restrictions on most intra-area trade in non-agricultural goods, as of early 1962, they were also, with several important exceptions, removed on trade with the rest of the world. EFTA members also proceeded to remove their quantitative restrictions against both each other and third countries more or less at an equal rate.[11] Those that remained were often directed against "low cost" imports from Japan and the less-developed countries and are discussed in Chapter VI below. These were retained, however, for protective, not balance of payments, reasons. As of mid-1965 no complaints had been filed by third countries under the GATT procedures charging damage from the discriminatory application of quantitative restrictions by any of the regional blocs. None of the European nations, in turn, had up to the time of this writing found themselves in balance of payments

[10] This is apparent from the summary in GATT, *ibid.,* p. 91.
[11] See GATT, *Doc. L/1893,* 5 Nov. 1962.

difficulties such that they felt obliged to reimpose quantitative restrictions. In late October 1964, in the face of a very serious depletion of reserves, the United Kingdom did impose "strictly temporary" 15 percent import surcharges (cut to 10 percent six months later) on all goods except foodstuffs, tobacco, and basic raw materials, as a device to curtail imports. The U.K. did not distinguish between imports from EFTA members and others, so the question of discrimination as it had been foreseen did not arise.

But discrimination was, nonetheless, an issue. Several of the less-developed countries requested that Britain exclude from the surcharges goods for which they were substantial suppliers. These requests were turned down by Britain, supported by the United States, on the grounds that they would be discriminatory and difficult to administer.[12] More bothersome to Britain were the charges by its EFTA partners that it had violated the spirit of the Stockholm Convention and had "struck at the roots" of the new economic order by this action which in effect more than cancelled the previous tariff reductions in intra-trade,[13] although it did not wipe out the margin of preferences given members. In the face of this criticism Britain for a time considered some changes which would effectively discriminate in the surcharges in favor of imports from the EFTA nations; but third countries, especially members of the Six, objected so strongly that it desisted. These objections were especially meaningful because Britain was trying to borrow large amounts from them at the time.[14]

Some members of the Latin American Free Trade Association have reimposed quantitative restrictions and done so in a discriminatory fashion.[15] No great issue seems to be made of this. Indeed, in the international organizations most concerned

[12] GATT, *Press Release 913,* 21 Dec. 1964.

[13] European Free Trade Association, *EFTA Reporter,* 11 Dec. 1964, p. 2.

[14] European Community Information Service, *European Community,* Nov.–Dec. 1964, p. 18. See also, *The New York Times,* Nov. 19, 1964, p. 57.

[15] See GATT, *Doc. L/1861,* 15 Oct. 1962, in which the Latin American Free Trade Association, in reporting to others on its activities, strongly implies this, although it is not made explicit.

—the International Monetary Fund and the GATT—there are now so many countries that are members of regional organizations where they have reserved to themselves the right so to discriminate that anything like large-scale protests of the practice seem unlikely, despite the noted warnings issued to the British by members of the Common Market in late 1964. As regional blocs become more an accepted part of the landscape there is little if any basis for a distinction in principle between granting preferences by means of tariffs or by means of quantitative restrictions, although one method may be preferred to another on grounds of effectiveness, side effects, speed, etc. The United Kingdom, which had technically violated Article XII of the GATT, as well as the Stockholm Convention, by resort in late 1964 to surcharges rather than quantitative restrictions to "safeguard its external financial position," was on solid ground in saying that the two devices were opposite sides of the same coin, even though in Britain's particular circumstances the surcharges were preferable because they could be made effective more quickly and were less likely to freeze the patterns of trade.

The objections raised by the United States, Canada, and others in the mid- and latter 1950's reflected consistent adherence to a general doctrine of nondiscrimination, but they were largely irrelevant in a world which had accepted, and often glorified, regionalism. If members of a union are likely from time to time to get into overall balance of payments problems; if aid or exchange rate changes or "harmonized" fiscal and monetary policies are not always available or considered desirable; and if, as seems likely, one of the greatest beneficial effects regionalism has on the rates of economic growth of its members is that it encourages investment because it removes some of the uncertainties of foreign markets as among members—if all of these conditions are sometimes present, then more occasions when quantitative restrictions are applied in a discriminatory fashion can be expected.

EXCEPTIONS TO INTRA-AREA FREE TRADE

Third countries, as well as members, have a great interest in any rules of the regional groups permitting some commodities to

197

be exempted from free trade within the area or subjected to special regulations. Exceptions invite a decrease in the trade-creating possibilities of the regional arrangements and so tend to act as a restraint on the growth of real income within the area, thus also limiting the increase in demand for imports. If special arrangements for some commodities are made there is also always the danger that they will be directed toward a reduction in competition from nonregion sources. Each of the post-war regional arrangements has provided special treatment for some goods, the most important, by far, being agricultural products although some of the less-developed countries' plans for regional arrangements, in which "equality" of industrialization among members is a goal, exempt quite a few industrial goods as well from the intra-area free trade rule.

EEC Common Agricultural Policy

MAJOR PROVISIONS AND EARLY WORRIES. The Rome Treaty provides that the Common Market shall extend to trade in farm goods but that this shall be accompanied by the establishment of a "common agricultural policy" among its members. The political objective of identifying national goals with Community goals was of great importance in this decision to have a common farm policy, but the Treaty stressed that its objectives would be to increase productivity, to ensure thereby "fair" standards of living for farmers, to stabilize markets and to ensure "reasonable" prices to consumers. In only thinly concealed acknowledgment that the authors had gotten no further than to agree that there was a problem to be solved, the details were left to be worked out in subsequent negotiations. The Treaty did anticipate that there would be need, both in the transitional and the later period, for extensive management and regulations of agricultural trade, both internal and external, including price controls and subsidies for both production and marketing.[16]

Many third countries feared from their first reading of the document that the arrangements finally worked out under this

---

[16] See Title II of the Treaty.

broad and intentionally vague authority would have the effect of encouraging self-sufficiency in agricultural and so of raising still higher the barriers against their agricultural exports.[17] It was recognized that the governments of each of the Six were already, and could be expected to continue, providing all sorts of encouragement to domestic producers of farm products and would continue protecting them from imports.[18] But it was feared that once the Six joined as a group and had a common policy, much more protection would be provided. Would there not be irresistible political pressures to set the level of support and protection high enough for each good to provide a "fair standard of living" to the least efficient producers *in the whole area?*[19] Believing that the income and price elasticities of demand were low for most foodstuffs in such affluent societies as those of Western Europe, would not even a small increase in domestic output so encouraged have a large percentage effect on imports and, indeed, even produce surpluses for export?

[17] GATT, *Basic Instruments and Selected Documents, Sixth Supplement,* pp. 81–89. See, too, the statement by the Australians in GATT, *Press Release 349,* 30 Oct. 1957; the South Africans, GATT, *Press Release 354,* 30 Oct. 1957; and New Zealand, GATT, *Press Release 363,* 30 Oct. 1957. Efforts to protect Australia's and New Zealand's agricultural export industries constituted one of the more difficult problems in the ill-fated negotiations for British entry into the Common Market.

Since the agricultural policy primarily affected temperate zone agricultural products, it concerned not only the producers in the so-called developed parts of the world but also was the source of much apprehension in Latin America. See UN Economic Commission for Latin America, *Economic Bulletin for Latin America,* Oct. 1962, pp. 127–66.

[18] For an account of the many agricultural support schemes already in operation in the European Common Market and in the European Free Trade Area, as well as in North America, see the OEEC, *Fifth Report on Agricultural Policies in Europe and North America, Trends in Agricultural Policies Since 1955,* Paris, 1961.

[19] The marginal producer in the EEC area would, for many agricultural products, be a sub-marginal producer in the world's economy, in the sense that his production would not be needed to clear the markets at prices he was receiving.

Spokesmen for the Six replied that it would not in fact be possible to remove existing barriers on trade and agricultural products within the Common Market—as was required of customs unions under the GATT rules—unless measures, including the setting of minimum prices, were taken to ease the adjustment problem of the higher cost producers. They acknowledged [20] that internal price supports could be set at levels which would encourage domestic production to displace imports. But these results were not necessary, they said. In reply to the worry that political pressure would exist to set levels of protection in each country high enough to provide shelter to the least efficient producer in the whole area, thus raising barriers higher than they would otherwise have been, the Six spokesmen said this would not happen, that it would be an inefficient use of resources and would make more difficult the Community's reaching its general objectives of increasing real growth. They reminded their critics that the Treaty specifically provided that in working out the agricultural policy, account had to be taken of the fact that agriculture was only one sector of the economy. They further tried to allay apprehensions by stating that the to-be-expected increase in the level of economic activity within the member countries as a consequence of the formation of the union would lead to increases in imports of most goods, including agricultural ones. Moreover, they said, they had no intentions of harming others and if they should in fact do so, that was the time to consider remedial action.

Spokesmen for countries exporting farm goods did not regard this as a satisfactory reply, but the debate was inevitably restrained by the facts that the Treaty permitted a wide range of policies, and that few if any nations had "clean hands" when it came to pursuing agricultural policies that were all square with the policy of nondiscriminatory multilateral freer trade to which most had committed themselves. These were years, too, when there was a growing recognition that existing practices made a mockery of most of the rules in international agreements on

---

[20] As had the "Spaak Report" (Comité Intergouvernmental créé par la Conférence de Messine, *Rapport des Chefs de Délégation aux Ministres des Affaires Etrangères,* Brussels, 21 April 1956), p. 5.

foreign trade in agricultural products and that new attempts would have to be made to define new rules.[21]

Still, a deep sense of uneasiness continued and nonmembers took frequent occasion in the GATT sessions and elsewhere to restate their worries. It was even proposed that arrangements be made for the Contracting Parties and the Community jointly to work out details of the Common Market's agricultural policy. The latter would have none of this. Formidable enough difficulties were being encountered within the Six in developing a common agricultural policy, for, as the Benelux experience had shown, political and social attitudes toward agriculture are such that government officials are extremely reluctant to agree to arrangements allowing lower cost farming in one country, whether a "partner" or not, to seriously undermine higher cost farming at home.[22] Almost every major decision on Community agricultural policy was reached in an atmosphere of crisis and amid predictions in the press that the Community would collapse. It was not until January 1962 that an accord was finally reached on the major principles and concepts. Even this date probably would not have been met had it not been that the Six were very anxious to reach agreement amongst themselves before the negotiations for British accession were very far along.

This policy, they said, in explaining it later to third countries,[23] was designed to ensure for their agricultural population a

---

[21] The so-called Haberler Committee was requested by the Contracting Parties in 1958 to examine certain aspects of trade in agricultural products, particularly as they affected the underdeveloped countries. Subsequently, the Contracting Parties developed a new "Program of Action" for expanding international trade and in this connection created a major new standing group—Committee II—to concern itself with the problem of trade in agricultural products.

See Gerard Curzon, *Multilateral Commercial Diplomacy,* London, 1965, Chap. 7, for an account of action by the Contracting Parties in the field of farm goods from 1948 through 1964.

[22] For an account of the Benelux experience, see Meade, Liesner, and Wells, *Case Studies in European Economic Union,* pp. 34–41, 114–28.

[23] At a meeting of the Contracting Parties to the GATT. See GATT, *Doc. L/1887,* 31 Oct. 1962.

"fair" level of income, one commensurate with that of the other sectors of the economy, while "taking account" of the desirability of foreign trade.[24] There were to be variations in techniques and goals from product to product, but the core of the policy for most major farm goods which are produced in significant volume in the Community was the setting of a minimum ("target" or "indicative") price in each country for each of the goods coming under the system and replacing the existing import restrictions of all kinds by a variable levy.[25] The latter was designed to offset the difference between the lowest world market price and this minimum price, after it had been adjusted to take account of transport and marketing costs and after the addition of a *montant forfaitaire*—then called the "threshold price." The effect would be that the markets of each member would first be cleared of domestic production available for sale at the indicative price. Any unsatisfied demand would then be available to other Common Market producers.[26] Further demands if any, could be met by third countries. The plan required that the difference in domestic prices among members

[24] It was later specified that in determining what was meant by "fair" income, "comparisons will be made with the incomes of other occupational groups living in proximity to the farming population." (European Economic Community Commission, *Sixth General Report*, Brussels, June 1963, p. 149.) The European Parliament defined it as "comparable à celui obtenu par les diverses catégories de personnes travaillant à des conditions équivalentes dans les autres groupes professionels." *Bulletin de la Communauté Economique Europeene*, Mars 1963. p. 53.

[25] For many goods there is also an "intervention" price—the price, somewhat below the target price, at which the government intervenes in order to make the minimum price effective. For some goods there are no "indicative" or "intervention" prices, but rather "sluice gate" prices, also in effect minimum prices below which imports cannot enter. Farm goods such as cotton, soybeans, tallow, tobacco, hides and skins, some fruits and vegetables, etc., which are produced in only very small amounts in the Community, are subject to a fixed common external tariff, sometimes zero. About 65–70 percent of U.S. farm goods exports to the Common Market in 1960 fell into this category.

[26] This is assured by deducting the *montant forfaitaire* from the calculations in their case and so reducing the import levy by that amount.

be gradually reduced until a one-price system emerged, hopefully by 1970 for most goods, at which time, of course, the variable levy would no longer apply to intra-area trade. Provisions were also made for a European Agriculture Guidance and Guarantee Fund, which, among such other things as purchasing farm goods offered at or below the support price and promoting structural changes in agriculture, could finance export subsidies to permit members with exportable surpluses to sell in other markets with lower prices, indefinitely in third markets and to partner's markets until the price levels were unified. These subsidies could cover even more than the full difference between the internal price and the world market price.[27]

The immediate reaction of most third countries was that the Community had concocted about as watertight a system of protection as could be devised and that their worst fears as to the adverse effects on their exports would be realized.[28] It was

[27] Perhaps the most readable detailed exposition of this complex scheme was that prepared by the GATT Secretariat, and published in GATT, *GATT Programme for Expansion of International Trade, Trade in Agricultural Products: Report of Committee II on the Consultations with the European Economic Community,* Geneva, 1962, pp. 7–65 (hereafter cited as *Report of Committee II on Consultations with European Economic Community*).

The noted fund was initially, and provisionally, fed primarily by budgetary contributions from member states. The question of the permanent arrangements for financing the common agricultural policy remains, at the time of this writing, a major unresolved issue. The Commission proposed in the spring of 1965 that the Community soon take over financial responsibility and for that purpose receive in its own right the proceeds of all the agricultural levies, as well as customs duties on nonfarm goods imports into the Community. Huge sums were involved (potentially, some estimated, $2.4 billion per year); the Commission therefore proposed that the European Parliament also participate in the decision as to the use of this revenue. All this supra-nationalism was a cost that General de Gaulle has been unwilling to pay up to now, and new proposals are likely to be forthcoming. See European Community Information Service, *European Community,* July 1965, pp. 3ff., and Aug. 1965, pp. 4–7.

[28] GATT, *Report of Committee II on Consultations with European Economic Community,* pp. 66–113. It was noted that since the variable

recognized that the system itself did not demand this result. The criticial question would be the policy with respect to the common minimum (indicative) prices. The higher they are, the more local production would be expanded and, given the variable levy system, the smaller the market for foreigners. The more likely too that resources, especially labor, would remain in agriculture rather than transfer to more efficient sectors; this in turn would impede the rate of growth in the Community and so third countries' exports of all kinds. But the matter of the common prices was left for future determination. Others saw in this fact many reasons to fear that there would be powerful forces pushing them up. There would be political pressures from producers in each country, who could be expected to join in efforts to level the price upward toward that needed by the highest cost producer in the entire Community. Logrolling techniques at the government level were foreseen: countries producing goods for which the consumer interest in other members was dispersed might well agree to higher prices for each other's goods than could be sustained in the consuming markets in the absence of the variable levy system.[29] It was also anticipated that since the existing ratio of farm labor to land and capital for many crops in Europe was much higher than in many other areas (notably North America and Australia) and sectors, and since one of the general aims of the policy was to achieve something approaching equivalent incomes as between farm laborers and others, that farm prices would be under great upward pressure from this source, too.[30]

---

levy was calculated on the basis of the lowest world market price this meant that if one exporter cut his price below the ruling one, the levy would go up against all other exporters.

[29] This seems to have taken place in the late 1964 negotiations for the common wheat price, with Italy obtaining some additional protection for its fruits and vegetables in return for agreeing to what the majority wanted on cereal prices. *The New York Times,* December 14, 1964, p. 57 and December 16, 1964, p. 63; and European Community Information Service, *European Community,* March 1965, p. 2.

[30] The desire of the manufacturing sectors, especially in West Germany, to cut farm production in order to increase urban labor supplies was not thought by most observers to be a very potent force.

Therefore, third countries expressed again the belief they had stated several years earlier when the Rome Treaty was first under consideration: the influence of the policy on increasing production "would be greater than in the past as the combined effect of the Common Policy of the whole Community was greater than the sum of previous individual national measures." [31]

It was not just access to the Common Market that was at stake. There was also worry lest the encouraged domestic production yield exportable surpluses, which, with the help of the Common Market's refunding or subsidy system, would create fiercer competition for other producers in the rest of the world, many of whom, it was asserted, could not afford to protect themselves by subsidies against the subsidized exports from the Common Market.[32] The available records do not indicate that the further point was made that the prospect of surpluses in one country would not deter production as much as before the Community was formed, for two reasons: First, each now has prior rights over third countries to any deficiency in any of the other partners. Second, since any export subsidies would be jointly financed there would be less restraint by national governments on national producers going beyond self-sufficiency than if such surpluses had to be financed solely by the country concerned.[33]

Common Market spokesmen again did not deny that the cited

[31] GATT, *Report of Committee II on Consultations with European Economic Community*, p. 103.

At that time, 1962, the British were in the midst of their unsuccessful negotiations to join the EEC and one of the important and difficult issues was their wish to assure some access by Commonwealth producers of farm goods to the Common Market. In this they failed. Had they succeeded, the effect could have been greater discrimination against other suppliers, unless the British were also able to bring about much lower internal target prices.

[32] Curzon, *Multilateral Commercial Diplomacy*, pp. 203–204, points out that the arrangements technically would allow Community producers to sell abroad at *below* world prices.

[33] These last two points have been made by Walter Salant and Associates, *The United States Balance of Payments in 1968*, Washington, D.C., 1963, pp. 108–109.

forces might be at work, but said the Community was aware of its responsibilities, did not aim at self-sufficiency as a general policy, and would operate a "reasonable" price and export subsidy policy. They asserted that the mechanism of the Common Market—with a central Commission and Council and with a Rome Treaty behind it which had several provisions charging the Community to be "outward" looking—could be expected to take a broader view and to give more weight than national governments sometimes do to the effects of agricultural policies on the other sectors of the economy and on the nation's international economic position, including its need to import agricultural goods, so as to be able to export. The Commission especially could occasionally be used as a new scapegoat, taking pressure off national governments that wanted to do the "right thing" on agricultural price policy but could not afford to do so for internal political reasons.[34] They also argued that by replacing a host of protective devices with a simple variable levy–minimum price scheme it would be easier for all to negotiate on the relevant issues. They sometimes held that if the effect of the system were to raise world prices somewhat, this might permit some countries (the United States in particular) to reduce its subsidies and other agricultural exporters to improve their terms of trade a bit. Others often permitted themselves to doubt that a scheme increasing production was likely to raise world market prices. As for the export subsidies, Community spokesmen said they did not like them, would limit their use, and would prevent "abuses," but that in view of the resort to subsidies by some other countries—the United States was most in mind—the subsidies were indispensable if the Common Market countries were to have the possibility of exporting.

THIRD COUNTRY FEARS RECEIVE SUPPORT. At the time of this writing, mid-1965, it is still too early to reach definite conclusions as to the actual effects of the policy on third countries, but the noted and oft-repeated fears had been

---

[34] This last point has been emphasized by Community officials in conversation with me.

receiving some support.[35] In the 1962–1963 discussions of general criteria for fixing target prices, the Common Market Parliamentarians and the Commission agreed that "The Community's price policy must first enable those working on well-managed and economically viable farms to earn a fair income over the average of several years." Many of the Parliamentarians recognized that "well-managed and economically viable" were terms subject to interpretation and made it perfectly clear that they would give the fair income consideration much the highest priority and would assign lower emphasis than the Commission to such "secondary" criteria as "the need for balance between production and consumption" and the need to encourage a division of labor corresponding to the "economic structures and the natural conditions prevailing in the Community." In both the Commission's and the European Parliament's scheme of things the criteria should also include such items as not impairing "the Community's contribution to the harmonious expansion of world trade," but this was well down on everyone's list, although the Commission itself resisted any formal "hierarchisation" of the criteria.[36] And General de Gaulle's famous statement on January 3, 1963, vetoing U.K.

[35] The Economic Commission for Europe reported that the *anticipation of the policy,* "indubitably stimulated production toward the end of the 1950's in the low-cost countries of the EEC," which saw the prospect of disposing easily of future surpluses at remunerative prices in the EEC partners' markets. UN, *Doc. E/Conf. 46/31,* 3 Feb. 1964, p. 130.

As of mid-1965 it had been agreed that the following products (accounting for about 90 percent of the Community's farm production) would be included in the system: cereals, pork, beef, veal, eggs, poultry, meat, many fruits and vegetables, wine, olive oil, sugar, dairy products, and rice. For a brief and clear statement of the various regulations and organizations of markets up to mid-1964, see M. Butterwick, "Before and After December 23, 1963," *Journal of Common Market Studies,* Oct. 1964, pp. 62–73. Details of the regulations are given in G. L. Weil, *A Handbook on the European Economic Community,* New York, 1965, Chap. 9.

[36] European Economic Community Commission, *Sixth General Report,* Brussels, 1963, pp. 148–50.

admission to the Community left no doubt that he envisaged a highly protectionist agricultural policy.

More detailed cause for concern was given in the prolonged discussions of the common target prices for cereals, the prices of which were critical. There is much foreign trade in cereals. Cereal prices not only affect bread, and thus the cost of living and wages, but also the prices for meats, poultry, and dairy products. Moreover, it was generally accepted within and without the Community that the cereal prices would set the "spirit" or "pattern" for other goods, even where, unlike meat, there might be little direct relationship between them.

Intently watched by third countries, this proved most difficult for the Commission to resolve. This was not only because of its significance to the world as a bellwether of Community policy and its inherent importance in the economies of the Six, but also because there were particularly serious conflicts of interest within the Community. Germany, a high-cost producer, and a heavy importer, wanted to keep prices high for its domestic producers but would have liked to import from the cheapest source and so wanted no encouragement given to French production. (These objectives could best be met if no common prices were set.) France, a low-cost producer in Europe but high by world standards, wanted the German import market for its producers. France was quite willing to see a common price somewhat above its own, but feared a price close to the German level would "unduly" encourage West German and other European producers and would result in France's farmers producing larger surpluses than could easily be disposed of. They were even more concerned over its effect on adding to the inflationary pressures in France. Other partners, being net importers, also favored prices well below the German level.

The Commission first urged, in late 1962, that the aligning process toward a common price include both increases in the lower national prices and declines in the upper ones. The German authorities said flatly that they could make no reductions in their support prices for the crop years 1963–1964 and 1964–1965. In the face of this it was decided to make the first approximation to the common price by raising the lower prices for the feed grains and, in effect, to leave untouched the others for the crop years 1963–1964.

Late in the following year the Commission put forward new proposals for establishing a common level of cereal prices—recommending that it take full effect in the 1964–1965 crop year. It was complicated in its details, but for our purposes it is enough to note that it would involve for soft wheat and barley, respectively, and as compared with the 1963–1964 crop year, an 11–15 percent lowering of prices in Germany and an 8–16 percent increase in France.[37] The proposal also provided for compensation to farmers of countries whose prices were to be lowered in the form of cash grants, higher social security benefits, increased productivity aids, etc.[38] Although the other member governments thought the prices, especially for feed grains, were still too high, the German Government again refused to accept this proposal, asserting they could not agree to any lower prices for the time being. In June 1964 the Commission made another major effort to get agreement by the Six governments on its grain price policy, this time suggesting that the implementation date be made mid-1966—after the then-scheduled German national elections.[39] Again they failed.

Taking advantage of the facts that Germany, as a major exporter of industrial goods to non-EEC countries, was most

[37] In Italy and Luxembourg wheat prices would fall and barley rise; in the Netherlands and Belgium both would rise. Most third countries were particularly interested in the feed grain prices because a low price here, it was hoped, would greatly encourage the feeding and consumption of livestock, huge consumers of grains.

[38] The problem of how to finance all this remains unresolved at the time of this writing, and, as we noted in footnote 27 above, was creating still another internal crisis, involving as it does matters of both economic burden and national sovereignty.

[39] Official running accounts of the problems met in working out the common agricultural policy may be found in the European Economic Community's periodic *Bulletin of the EEC*. Somewhat livelier accounts are to be found in the periodic European Community Information Service, *European Community*, a joint publication of the Common Market, Euratom, and the Coal and Steel Community. A useful collection of many of the relevant official documents may be found in Weil, *Handbook on the European Economic Community*.

anxious that the Kennedy Round succeed in sharply reducing tariffs on those items, and that there earlier had been at least a tacit understanding between France and Germany that the former would make concessions on the Kennedy Round if the latter made them on grain prices,[40] the EEC Commission pressed its case. It took the position in many forums that unless agreement was soon reached on grain prices the whole Kennedy Round negotiations were threatened with failure. They argued that it would not be possible to do much on industrial goods until the parties were ready to start talking about farm goods and that it would not be possible to negotiate on agricultural products unless the common grain prices had been set.[41] The other EEC governments embraced this position. In the autumn of 1964 General de Gaulle stated that unless the grain price matter were settled soon France might not find it possible to continue to actively participate in the various other aspects of European economic and political unification.[42]

Under all these pressures, the German government agreed in December to the late-1963 proposals of the EEC Commission, except that the prices for some feed grains were slightly below those first proposed, and it was specified that the new common prices would not go into effect until July 1967.[43]

[40] *The New York Times,* Jan. 15, 1965, p. 50.

[41] The United States had insisted that before the Kennedy Round was *completed,* and in calculating whether reciprocity had been achieved, import barrier cuts on both industrial and agricultural products would have to be considered. But they had not said that they would refuse to *begin* negotiation on industrial goods until the EEC was also ready to start negotiation on farm products. The EEC Commission's intense pressure on the member governments reflected, in part, the former's great desire to create a genuine Community, and to that end it was willing to force common decisions even if their substance was somewhat less to their liking than ones more leisurely arrived at might have been.

[42] The negotiations on the grain price were further complicated by the fact that at this time the question of the Multilateral Nuclear Force—which Germany liked and France did not—was also under active discussion. But this is not part of our story.

[43] This delay was important, not only because it meant Germany would not have to lower its prices until long after the approaching

Although many aspects of the Community's common agricultural policy remained to be worked out (most notably the long-term arrangements for financing it), the pattern and spirit was now thought to be set.

Most third countries' response to the agreement was that it "could have been worse," but most also expected that the effect would be to considerably expand production in the Common Market and to reduce third countries' exports. It was feared that higher prices in the low-cost areas, primarily France, would attract more resources into production than would be withdrawn in the higher-cost areas, where the pressure to "get off the land" might well be reduced by sharply increased productivity that continues to characterize agricultural production. Moreover, given the EEC policy of trying to achieve "parity of incomes" between persons in agriculture and in other sectors, it was expected that the governments of those countries where prices would be reduced would be under great pressure to increase productivity, and so yield larger outputs and fewer imports.

Rough, and independent, quantitative projections and estimates by the Commission of the Common Market and the United States Department of Agriculture lent support to these fears. These estimates indicated that a continuation of the *national* policies of the EEC states through the 1960's would probably result in increases in production about equal to the projected increases in consumption, leaving imports from the rest of the world almost stable. The EEC common farm policy, with prices for cereals equal to the average of the German and French levels—which is about where they were left in the

---

elections, but also because it was anticipated that well before mid-1967 the Kennedy Round of tariff negotiations would be concluded and so Germany would know whether or not it had received its "quo" or "quid" from its EEC partners in the matter of negotiated reductions in tariffs on industrial goods. *The New York Times* reported from Brussels on the occasion that "if there is no successful Kennedy Round, then most assuredly there will be no lowering of German grain prices on July 1, 1967, despite the preliminary agreements reached today." *The New York Times,* Dec. 16, 1964, p. 69.

December 1964 accord—were estimated to result in production increases sufficient to cut imports by 1970 to approximately half their 1957–1959 level.[44] Most nonmembers concluded that the creation of this particular regional group, the EEC, was working to their disadvantage so far as trade in farm goods was concerned.

ISSUES IN NEGOTIATING FOR GREATER ACCESS. Many third governments, therefore, were counting on the Kennedy Round of tariff negotiations to provide the occasion for a concerted attack on the Community's barriers to trade in farm goods.[45] For many of the products to come under the common agricultural policy third countries had received tariff bindings in past tariff negotiations.[46] These would be incompatible with the

[44] For a summary and references to these studies, see Committee for Economic Development, *Trade Negotiations for a Better Free World Economy*, May 1964, pp. 29–32. The Secretariat of the UN Economic Commission for Europe in early 1964 also concluded that, apart from the effects of regional groupings, imports of temperate zone agricultural products into the EEC and EFTA countries would, in the medium term and on balance, have remained stable or perhaps declined a bit. See UN, *Doc. E/Conf. 46/31*, pp. 102–21.

[45] Some countries, including the United States, had engaged in more or less constant discussions with Community officials from 1961 on, trying to influence the latter's decisions on farm policy. Early efforts by the United States to get some kind of "assured access" failed, but with respect to hard wheat there was some sort of understanding reached that if United States and Canadian exports fell during the period pending agreement and implementation of the common agricultural policy in wheat, "remedial adjustments" would be made. *Trade Expansion Act of 1962, Hearings,* Committee on Finance, U.S. Senate, 87th Cong., 2nd Sess., 1962, pp. 2,135–98, *passim,* gives some information on United States activity during this period.

[46] In the 1961–1962 Dillion Round, the Six had each withdrawn all the tariff bindings on farm goods to which they were then committed and, following renegotiations with the earlier beneficiaries, had replaced many of them with new bindings of a common external tariff. (For a comparison of the original proposed common external tariffs on many farm goods and those finally negotiated and bound, see *Trade Expansion Act of 1962, Hearings,* Committee on Finance, U.S. Senate, 87th Cong., 2nd Sess., pp. 2,155–57.) However, for reasons stated in the text, for those goods to which it was then planned to apply a common agricultural policy with variable levies, no new rates were bound, or renegotiated.

variable levy system and most countries refused to engage in the necessary renegotiations on these except in the context of the Kennedy Round and the entire Common Market agricultural policy. The Ministerial decision to hold the Kennedy Round had specified that farm goods were to be included and that the negotiations "shall provide for acceptable conditions of access to world markets for agricultural products."

For those goods subject to fixed duties—cotton, tobacco, etc.—it was initially assumed by many that the pattern under the Kennedy Round would be the traditional one of tariff bargaining, and since these goods were not produced in large quantities in the Community and were important in the exports of others, it was hoped that bargains might be struck here which would offset at least some of the losses that might arise on items subject to the variable levy system. With respect to those goods subject to the variable levy system, the problems were seen to be much more difficult. This was not just because substantial quantities of these goods were already produced in the Community and, as we have seen, some members wished to produce even more. There was also the problem of what one was to negotiate on, the Community having made it clear that the question of what the final common prices were to be under their system was not negotiable.

In early 1964 the EEC proposed a negotiating plan to cover almost *all* farm goods, its central feature being the freezing or binding of maximum margins of support for each affected good in each country. Each country, with the EEC acting as one, would determine the level of its own domestic price supports for each product. World "reference prices" would be negotiated with other countries for each product. Each country would then offer to freeze the margin between the domestic price that had been set and these world reference prices which had been negotiated. Levies equal to the margin would be placed on any imports. If the actual world price fell below this negotiated reference price, a "supplemental levy" would be collected equal to the difference. This meant that it was really the internal prices received by the domestic producers, and not the *"montant de soutien,"* that was being bound. ·

Community spokesmen asserted that this plan was a major

concession by those responsible for the welfare of Europe's farmers (it was assumed in the argument that the level of price support would not be changed even though it was bound only for a few years at a time), because it would mean that a farmer's real income could increase only as his productivity increased and that this restraint would encourage an acceleration in the movement of farmers off the land—the best assurance the rest of the world could have that they would continue to enjoy markets in the Six. They also said it had the great virtue of introducing some form of international control over that sensitive part of domestic agricultural policies: subsidies of all kinds.

From the outset most other countries that exported farm goods found this proposal unsatisfactory. In the first place, it was implicit that there could be no negotiations until the Community had agreed on its common policies for all farm goods, and this seemed a long time in the future. In the second place, it would have effectively terminated those fixed bindings which had been agreed to in earlier negotiations, thus clearing the way for a wider use of variable levies and so making possible an increase in duties previously bound, sometimes at zero duties. Third, it not only had no provision for reducing existing trade barriers, but, as we noted above, nonmember countries feared that for goods under the Common Agricultural Policy at least the initial level of support—that which was to be bound and was not to be negotiated—might be so high that production within the Community would expand to such an extent that it would deprive nonmembers of their existing markets. They found little attraction in binding this situation. There were other worries, too. Although recognizing that total demand for agricultural goods in the Common Market *might* increase in the future more than productivity rose and so lead to greater demand for imports, they were not sanguine that even in this event bindings of support levels, which were subject to periodic review, would not be "unbound." They also noted that the system would mean that increased productivity abroad, reflected in lower world prices, would not by itself permit the rest of the world greater access to the Common Market as ordinary tariffs do, because of the "supplementary levy" device. This was particularly bothersome because the proposed system was to replace the existing system of tariff bindings for many goods, bindings which would become more valuable as third countries' productivity increased and bindings for which they had "paid" in earlier negotiations. There was also some concern lest, given the political role played by farmers in most countries, a scheme that permitted the farmers to increase their real income only as productivity increased might lead to all sorts of subsidized efforts to increase productivity; which efforts would not in fact be reflected in the margin of support statistics, yet would increase output and so limit markets for others.[47] Moreover, even if the scheme did operate to move the less efficient farmers off the land, as claimed, might not this operate to aggravate, rather than relieve, the problem for foreign suppliers, by resulting in the land moving into the hands of more efficient farmers? From the foreign producer's point of view there was both excess people and land in the agricultural sector of the EEC.

In early 1965, after a year of often bitter and still fruitless negotiations on trying to develop an overall negotiating plan, Mr. Wyndham White, the Director General of the General Agreement, with strong support from the U.S. and several other non-EEC nations, proposed, in the GATT conciliation tradition, that negotiation of the general rules be suspended in favor of a "pragmatic" approach involving negotiations on specific products, one by one, beginning with cereals and aiming at a reduction of barriers in whatever form they existed. The non-EEC countries still hoped that under this approach the procedure for goods subject only to fixed duties and not under the Community's variable levy system would be the traditional one

---

[47] For a brief statement of the Common Market's proposals on agricultural negotiations (the details seem not to have been published), see European Community Information Service, *European Community*, March 1965, pp. 4–5. For a critical appraisal of the proposals by United States official Irwin Hedges, see his Feb. 11, 1965 address in Des Moines, Iowa, released in mimeographed form by the Office of the Special Representative for Trade Negotiations, Washington, D.C.

of negotiating tariff cuts and binding the results. For those goods subject to the Community's variable levy system, the aim would be to work out arrangements—product by product— looking toward a reduction in barriers, taking into account all the "relevant" issues in maintaining a "fair balance between domestic production and imports," and which, it was understood, would include, in the case of grains for example, domestic support policies, production controls, access agreements, assurances of supply, tariffs and quotas, noncommercial transactions, and international prices. In sum, the approach was to explore the possibility of commodity agreements touching on all aspects of trade in the goods.

The Community had earlier said it would not negotiate on guaranteed access, a position it also had taken when Britain asked for it for some Commonwealth goods during the ill-fated negotiations looking toward possible accession. In the meantime, however, various GATT Committees, notably the one on grains that had been set up in 1961, had been moving toward the conclusion that future policy for many agricultural products should be in the direction of international arrangements providing for some kind of access assurances and a sharing between importing and exporting countries of the responsibility for adjusting supply to the available outlets.[48] After reserving its position for a time, the Community did agree to commence negotiations on cereals in the spring of 1965 and on the other farm goods in the autumn. At the time of this writing a general procedure for negotiating has finally been agreed upon. But even apart from the grave differences remaining among the Six on many aspects of the common agricultural policy—including its financing—which make serious trade negotiations on matters of substance virtually impossible, the Six and the other negotiators are still at loggerheads.

It did seem almost certain, however, that the formation of the EEC was going to operate to increase the barriers to others'

[48] These principles had been included in the 1964 United States– United Kingdom market-sharing cereals agreement. See GATT, *Doc. L/2388,* 13 March 1965.

exports of farm goods to the member states, to increase the real costs to the Six of many foodstuffs, and to be for some time at least a continuing source of friction within the Community and between it and the rest of the world.

EFTA Arrangements Create Few Issues

The European Free Trade Association Agreement handles the problem of agricultural products differently. It simply excludes most of them from the general commitments of the members to remove all barriers to trade amongst themselves.[49] The signatories acknowledged that in most of their countries the agricultural sectors were subject to extensive government intervention, that farmers were given much protection from imports, and that it was not "practicable" to contemplate free trade in most farm goods. At the same time, one of their members—Denmark—relied very heavily on agricultural exports. "The most difficult aspect of the negotiation [of the Stockholm Convention] was that of finding a way of making the plan attractive to the Danes." [50] It was finally agreed that trade among themselves with respect to most agricultural products would be on the basis of bilateral agreements, the purpose of which would be to "facilitate an expansion of trade which will provide reasonable reciprocity to Member States whose economies depend to a great extent on exports of agricultural goods." [51] These terms were not limited to Denmark; the Treaty did require that any *tariff* changes incorporated in such agreements would be applied to all members. But it was anticipated that these bilateral agreements would be chiefly aimed at using more direct methods of giving Danish (and, to a much more limited degree, Portuguese and Norwegian) exports

[49] Stockholm Convention, Arts. XXI–XXVIII, Annexes D and E. The procedure is to have the free trade rules apply to "industrial" goods and to define these as everything except the goods listed in the Annexes.

[50] M. Camps, *Britain and the European Community, 1955–1963*, Princeton, 1964, p. 220.

[51] Stockholm Convention, Art. XXII, Para. 2. Special arrangements are also provided for trade in certain marine products.

an assured market, resulting in an expansion of Danish sales sufficient to provide the quid for the pro provided by Denmark in committing itself to free trade in the industrial products of the members.

In principle, this aspect of the EFTA Agreement was particularly discriminatory against third parties *with respect to the affected commodities* because it was expected that specific quotas would be allocated to the favored members. Moreover, since bilateral agreements which had been signed, and were in prospect, did not completely remove the restrictions on trade among the members in many of the affected farm goods, the advantages to nonmembers' exports via the income effects of the trade-creating possibilities of the area were reduced. Many of the contracting parties found this sufficient reason for denying formal GATT blessing to the European Free Trade Association,[52] but no third country believed its interests were going to be greatly damaged. This is not surprising, since for all practical purposes the preferences given were limited both in range and amount to those produced by Denmark and included chiefly pork and dairy products exported to the United Kingdom and Switzerland, markets in which Denmark already had a prominent position. The absence of any complaints under the normal procedures of the GATT indicate that at least up to the time of this writing this has proven to be the case. Still, although the time is far too short to permit any confident conclusions, the most recently available statistics do show that the preferences may be having some effect. The Danish share of EFTA food imports grew from 6 to nearly 7 percent from 1959 to 1963; this reflected a 12 percent increase in total EFTA imports of these goods and a 25 percent increase in the value of imports from Denmark.[53]

[52] See GATT, *Basic Instruments and Selected Documents, Ninth Supplement,* pp. 80–87. The legal argument was that by excluding agricultural products the EFTA did not meet "substantially all the trade" criteria of GATT Art. XXIV.

[53] European Free Trade Association, *EFTA Trade,* Geneva, 1964, Appendix Tables 19, 41, 42, 63, and 64.

Exceptions Extensive but Tolerated in LAFTA

The Montevideo Treaty, creating the Latin American Free Trade Association,[54] is much less precise and definite on the question of what is to be included in intra-area free trade than are the instruments creating the European Common Market and the European Free Trade Association. Often only very general statements or commitments are made, leaving a great part of the detailed arrangements to be worked out in the future. Although members undertook a general commitment to remove, over a 12-year period, restrictions on trade amongst themselves, it was clear that for some time at least nothing like free trade in farm goods was contemplated among the members, thus limiting the possibilities of trade creation. It was also planned that efforts would be made—via long-term agreements of one kind or another—to give partners preferential access to other partners' markets *whenever there was a short fall in domestic production,* thus increasing the possibilities of trade diversion.[55]

The exceptions to free trade treatment, however, extend well beyond agricultural goods, reflecting (as we noted earlier, this has been typical in the less-developed areas), not only a distaste for competition but a conviction held by many of those responsible for determining the policies that it is economically desirable and politically necessary that the industrial development of the area be "harmonious" and "balanced" and that action be taken to avoid "any repetition within the Area of the world division of countries exporting manufactures and countries exporting raw materials, . . ."[56] Thus, the Treaty has

[54] GATT, *Doc. L/921*, 21 Nov. 1958; *L/921, Add. 1,* 1 Dec. 1958; *L/991,* 27 May 1959; *L/1092,* 5 Nov. 1959; and especially, *L/1201,* 26 May 1960 and *L/1311,* 14 Oct. 1960, provide much background information on this association and the defense of it offered by its officials.

[55] See Montevideo Treaty, Art. 29.

[56] GATT, *Doc. L/2189,* 19 March 1964.

Raymond F. Mikesell, in his "The Movement Toward Regional Trading Groups in Latin America," pp. 125–51, in A. O. Hirschman, ed., *Latin American Issues, Essays and Comments,* was an early skeptic of

an escape clause which permits members to retain barriers on intra-trade in order to protect "newly established industries" or those whose "competitive positions [are] weak." [57] And, as we saw on pages 151–53, the various "complementary" agreements and proposed "integration industries" serve to limit competition among the participants. Moreover, the procedures in the Treaty for moving toward intra-area free trade work in the same direction. The reduction in existing restrictions on intra-area trade are not made on an automatic linear basis as in the EEC and the EFTA, but are the result of annual negotiations on a product-by-product basis. This both permits and encourages postponement until toward the end of the transitional period (and perhaps forever?) those reductions that might hurt some members the most by creating trade.

The extent to which all this permissive authority and these procedures will be used to prevent trade-creating effects, or to put obstacles in the way of placing new investments in the most economically efficient places, remains to be fully demonstrated. But through mid-1965 the reduction of barriers on intra-LAFTA trade have been limited largely to removing excess protection. Great difficulties were encountered in the late 1964 annual negotiations when an unsuccessful attempt was made to agree on the first "common schedule"—a list of goods which would cover 25 percent of zonal trade and on which the members collectively would agree gradually to eliminate all duties. The "national" reductions in 1964 were also well below the 8 percent scheduled in the Treaty. The basic problem seems to have been that for most goods, especially manufactured ones, there were several partners that, on the one hand, were

---

the assertions by LAFTA supporters that "harmonious" and "balanced" growth was compatible with the most efficient use of the available resources.

But see C. A. Cooper and B. F. Massell, "Toward a General Theory of Customs Unions for Developing Countries," *The Journal of Political Economy*, Oct. 1965, pp. 461–76, for a theoretical justification of such policies *once value is given to industrialization per se.*

[57] GATT, *Basic Instruments and Selected Documents, Ninth Supplement*, Geneva, 1961, p. 91.

conscious of the real cost to them of substituting imports from the region for those from the outside, and, on the other hand, simply did not believe that intra-area tariff cuts would—taking account of both trade-creation and trade diversion effects—lead, on balance, to an increase in *their* levels of industrial production: a high-priority goal. These problems were intensified by the product-by-product approach. They were exacerbated by the low priority assigned regional integration on the operating governmental level in most of these countries and the tendency of each member to demand an immediate quid pro quo for any trade concessions.

There was in mid-1965, therefore, a general sense of malaise in the Latin American Free Trade Association. Proposals were being made by senior officials of the Economic Commission for Latin America, the Intra-American Bank, and others that the LAFTA and the Central American arrangements be replaced by a new continent-wide Latin American Common Market. This should be patterned, it was said, somewhat more closely after the European Economic Community than the existing schemes.[58] But the record to date encourages the conclusion that in any such new arrangements the probability is great, first, that considerable restrictions on intra-area trade will remain, and second, that measures leading to trade diversion will be sought out. The first, because of the fears of competition and the high value put on the social benefits of "equality" among themselves. The second, because if properly selected and if there is no retaliation by nonmembers, trade diversion can permit each member to increase its exports more than its imports and so facilitate the economic diversification and industrialization that is often more highly valued than the economic costs of the inefficiency that results.

---

[58] See M. S. Wionczek, *Latin American Free Trade Association,* International Conciliation, Carnegie Endowment for International Peace, New York, Jan. 1965, pp. 32–35, 52–62, for an account of some of the difficulties that organization faced in 1964 and earlier years.

See, too, United Nations Economic Commission for Latin America, *Towards A Dynamic Development Policy for Latin America,* 1964 (Sales No. 64, II, G.4).

Developments in this direction would, of course, increase the discrimination faced by nonmembers. It remains to be seen whether, as they have up to now, such countries will refrain from raising serious objections, content to hope that the adverse effects on them would be offset by the regional economic arrangements' stimulating effect on investments and economic growth, and so on demands for imports.

SIZE OF REGION AND PRIOR PREFERENTIAL ARRANGEMENTS

Other things remaining the same, the greater the size of an economic union the greater the potential gains to its members and to the world as a whole. But, at least in the short-run, the larger the union the greater the adverse discriminatory effects on nonmembers and so the larger the incentive offered to others to join. The question of size is immensely complicated if some members of the union were previously parties to other preferential arrangements. To abandon them is to take away established favors and to demand of others and yourself many structural adjustments. To incorporate old preferential arrangements in the new ones can be costly in several ways to the new partners and can constitute a particularly bothersome form of new discrimination against third countries. The policy issues involved here played an important role in the abortive efforts to date in Europe to enlarge the Common Market beyond the original six members. They were a minor problem for the EFTA, but associating the former preference-receiving overseas territories with the EEC has proven to be one of that group's most difficult problems.

Existing Preferences a Major Obstacle to Formation of Europe-Wide Bloc

The 1956–1958 efforts in Europe to create a free trade area encompassing all the OEEC countries, with the European Economic Community as one element, reflected not only the wish of several states to reap the "positive" advantages of joining any regional organization (outlined at the beginning of Chapter IV), but also the desire of the United Kingdom and others which had previously been enjoying full membership in the preferential arrangements of the OEEC trade and payments schemes, to avoid now being discriminated against in the Common Market. The reasons for the failure of this effort were many. Consideration of most of them, including the reasons for the United Kingdom and others not being determined to join the Six in the beginning, would divert us from our main concern. Fortunately, the whole long and complicated episode has been admirably chronicled elsewhere and so only a brief sketch need be given here.[59]

High on the list, probably at the very top, was the political concern among the "Europeans" in the Six, that, whether Britain wished it so or not (and many believed it did), this device would weaken the Common Market and perhaps even destroy the whole effort to create a European Economic Community, and ultimately a political union, by offering an alternative to, or at least reasons for delaying the implementation of, the Treaty of Rome. Beyond this, there were the extremely difficult problems of meeting the desires of many that a marriage of a customs union and a free trade area result in a "balance of advantages" and "disadvantages" among each group and, indeed, each member. The French negotiators in particular argued that a free trade area scheme was not "workable." They held that free trade was tolerable only when accompanied by all the other "common" policies and institutions which were foreseen in the Common Market. Many of

---

[59] An excellent and detailed account, much relied on here, may be found in M. Camps, *Britain and the European Commuity, 1955–1963*, Chaps. 1–8. See also, R. Hinshaw, *The European Community and American Trade*, New York, 1964, Chap. III. An earlier and briefer account was given by I. Frank, *The European Common Market*, New York, 1961, Chap. V. For a European account of these free trade discussions see Baron Snoy de Oppuers, "Les Etapes de la Cooperation Europenne et les Negociationes Relatives à Une Zone de Libre Exchange," *Chronique de Politique Etrangers*, Vol. XII, Nos. 5–6, Sept.–Nov. 1959. An official working-party-type study of many of the problems inherent in creating a free trade area may be found in OEEC, *Report on the Possibility of Creating a Free Trade Area in Europe*, Paris, Jan. 1957.

these, it was argued, would tend to offset what might otherwise be "unfair" economic advantages of one member over another in a free trade environment. For example, why should other nations be permitted to enjoy free trade with the Six if they were not prepared to assume the obligations of a common external tariff and commercial policy? Otherwise, would not the low tariff countries have an unfair competitive advantage in lower-cost import inputs? And if others were not prepared to join in a common agricultural policy, which would, among other things, enlarge the markets for French farm goods, why should they enjoy duty-free treatment in the French market for their manufactured goods? In the absence of commitments to such "common" policies, many considered it appropriate that there be some form of discrimination—euphemistically called "differences"—in trade arrangements between the Six and the others. But to avoid being discriminated against was one of the major reasons why the non-Common Market nations were interested in a Europe-wide free trade area.

This general concern for "equating advantages" involved a host of problems, most of which are outside our central concern, but especially nettlesome was the question of "coordinating" each member's commercial policies, and here the matter of Commonwealth preferences loomed large. Sentiment was strong in Britain then that to give up the preferences, to say nothing of establishing "reverse" preferences and treating Commonwealth goods less favorably than European ones, would be an intolerable cost in the weakening of the political-economic fabric of the Commonwealth. But it was not evident to the continental countries why Britain should maintain a preferential position over them in the Commonwealth markets. And, as just noted, many felt that the cost advantages of duty-free imports of food and raw materials from the Commonwealth would give the U.K. an "unfair" cost advantage in the free trade area over producers in the Six who had to cope with a common external tariff, and who were committed to buying relatively high-priced, temperate zone farm goods from each other. Underlying all of this, too, was a good bit of sheer protectionism on the part of some members of the Six, especially France.

Following the breakdown of these negotiations, in late 1958, in an atmosphere of great bitterness, the EFTA was quickly formed. As a permanent arrangement its rationale was similar to that of the other regional groupings. But originally it was not seen as a permanent arrangement. Rather, it was regarded as a time-buying expedient and an effort by the members to create a stronger bargaining position vis-à-vis the Common Market, looking toward some future accommodation between the two groups. As barriers were reduced on intra-EFTA trade, discrimination against imports from the EEC countries increased, thus, many hoped, the case would be strengthened among the EEC members for a joining of the two groups.[60]

[60] Finland, which had important political and economic ties to several members of the European Free Trade Association, was from the outset particularly concerned about being excluded from that preferential arrangement, and so signed with them an "Agreement of Association" on March 27, 1961. In most respects, the rights and obligations ran parallel to those of the other members of the EFTA. Indeed, many say Finland became the eighth member of EFTA. Third countries have given little attention to the association and saw no reason for raising new objections, that is, objections other than those which they had already raised to the original Stockholm Convention. In one important respect, however, the Finnish case presented a serious new issue of discrimination. Finland had found it possible to sign the Association Agreement only after concluding a trade agreement with Russia in late 1960, which provided for the gradual removal of Finnish import duties on most imports from the Soviet Union, this treatment not to be extended to third countries other than the EFTA members. Some of the latter were uneasy about this because they feared that "Finland would become a back door entrance to the EFTA for Russian goods." (Camps, *Britain and the European Community, 1955–1963*, pp. 351–52.) More serious was the fact that this was a flagrant violation of the most-favored-nations obligations of Finland and was presumably tolerated by the non-EFTA parties to the General Agreement only because of what Curzon calls the "political wisdom of having Finland in EFTA and GATT," even at the price of violating the most-favored-nation clause and because enough of a fuss was made in the GATT to discourage other contracting parties from making similar arrangements. (Curzon, *Multilateral Commercial Diplomacy*, pp. 65, 285–86.) The publicly available GATT documents are silent on this aspect of the Finnish association with EFTA.

In December 1965, after this book was in the hands of the printer, it was reported that Britain and Ireland had agreed to establish between

Early attempts at "bridge building," creating some modified Europe-wide free trade area, in 1960 failed. Pretty much the same considerations as before were responsible, but a new contributing factor this time was the growing concern of third countries (the United States was often their spokesman) lest the coming together of these two groups increase the discriminations against nonmembers.[61] These countries, therefore, in GATT and elsewhere urged and encouraged the EEC to adopt a global, rather than European, approach to their external relations. As we have seen in Chapter IV, this was in fact done.

As the EEC moved forward, ahead of its original time schedule, EFTA members became increasingly worried about the economic discrimination they were suffering and impressed with the advantages they might reap from a freer access to the markets of the Six. Included in the benefits was an expected boost to their production and productivity, growing out of increased exposure to competition and by becoming a more attractive place for foreigners to invest their funds, thus facilitating a large retooling of industry. More important, for United Kingdom officials at least, was concern over the political division within Europe that might result from a permanent Six and Seven arrangement and the effects on Britain's relative political power position in Europe and elsewhere should the Six prosper, as then seemed likely.

Britain, along with Denmark and Norway, concluded in early 1961 that its most attractive alternative, after all, was to join the Common Market as a full member.[62] Political consid-

---

themselves, over a 10-year period, a free-trade area, thus returning to a situation which had existed before Irish independence. The press speculated that a next step would be for Ireland also to join the European Free Trade Association. *The New York Times,* December 19, 1965.

[61] Without—as the United States saw it—the compensating advantages of European political unification.

[62] See Camps, *Britain and the European Community, 1955–1963,* Chaps. 9 and 10; and Hinshaw, *European Community and American Trade,* Chap. VI, for details. The neutrals, Switzerland, Sweden, and Austria, were most dubious as to the wisdom of formally joining the EEC and continued to hope for some time that some form of free trade area arrangement with the Six could be worked out. Later they modified

erations having to do with preventing a political division of Europe and the growth of a powerful six-nation Common Market whose political and military policies it was by then believed might not always coincide with its own, led a new United States Administration in 1961 and 1962 to encourage Britain and the other EFTA members in this.[63] The United

this position and were prepared to go some distance toward pursuing "common" agricultural, tariff, and other policies, provided they did so "independently" and not because of Community decisions. The 1961–1962 negotiations for some kind of association status for them, in which freedom to bargain on commercial matters with Eastern Europe was a requisite for their political neutrality, never got off the ground before the whole movement was stopped by General de Gaulle's January 1963 veto of British entry.

In 1964, however, Austria again started "exploratory" conversations with the EEC commission on "possible arrangements" with the Community, and these are still underway. The Danish Government, on the other hand, declared in early 1965 that it was not then interested in reopening formal discussions but made it clear that when and if British membership again became a realistic possibility, Denmark would be ready to reconsider. (*EFTA Reporter*, Washington, D.C., 8 March 1965, p. 2.)

[63] One of the more concrete manifestations of this new policy was the "dominant supplier authority" in the 1962 Trade Expansion Act. This authorized the elimination (not just a 50 percent cut) of tariffs on categories of goods for which the United States and the Common Market together accounted for at least 80 percent of free world trade. This provision would cover only jet aircraft, vegetable oils, and perfume if the EEC included just the Six. But it would include 26 categories of commodities accounting for over $1.2 billion of U.S. imports and $2.1 billion of exports in 1960 from an EEC expanded to include the U.K., Denmark, Norway, Ireland, and Greece. A major purpose of this provision for making possible larger access to the U.S. market for goods which the EEC and the U.K. were especially interested in exporting to the United States, was to fashion a "carrot" (or a "club") to get Britain into the Community. (I, however, have found no evidence that the EEC was at all attracted by the prospect of a reciprocal *elimination* of tariffs.) The provision was also justified on the grounds that it would make it more likely that the United Kingdom would be willing to phase out the Commonwealth preferences (an old grievance of the United States) when it joined the EEC. This was so because if the common external tariff on goods of interest to the Commonwealth was zero, the U.K.'s joining the Common Market would be less costly to the exports of the

States not only hoped that having Britain a full member of the Community would result in political and military policies more consonant with her own but also believed that Britain would be a trade liberalizing influence within the Common Market, especially on agricultural policy where the British interest was clearly in low-priced imports.[64] These benefits, it was believed, would more than offset the increase in discrimination against the rest of the world attendant on the enlargement of the Community, especially if, under the new Trade Expansion Act, a large cut in the common external tariff could be negotiated.

On the economic side, the most difficult problem for Britain to resolve was how to protect the preferences that had been given, and repeatedly promised would remain, to imports from the Commonwealth; or how to compensate if they had to be given up, or if "reverse preferences" proved necessary because Britain was required to grant duty-free treatment to EEC exports while charging the common external tariff, or the variable levy, on those of the Commonwealth. Related—because Britain imported many farm goods from the Commonwealth, but also going beyond—was the problem of reconciling Britain's method of supporting farm incomes—deficiency income payments—with

---

Commonwealth; no reverse preferences would be created and there would hopefully be larger compensating markets on the Continent. The 80 percent provision was also defended by the U.S. Administration on the grounds that for those goods where the United States and a *single* other bargaining area constituted such a large part of the market, it would be easier to negotiate larger cuts in barriers because neither would have to worry about obtaining compensation for benefits third countries might get via most-favored-nation treatment. (See *Trade Expansion Act of 1962, Hearings Before the Committee on Ways and Means,* House of Rep., 87th Cong., 2nd Sess., *Part 1,* pp. 7–8, 97; and *Hearings Before the Committee on Finance,* U.S. Senate, 87th Cong., 2nd Sess., *Part 4,* pp. 2,199–2,278 *passim.*

It should be noted that this 80 percent provision was also discriminatory, in that under it there is no area except the EEC expanded, where tariffs can be reduced so much even if trade reaches this percentage.

[64] This support for British entry backfired. What the United States saw as advantages were just what General de Gaulle saw as disadvantages, as he made clear in his famous January 14, 1963 press conference.

the continental methods of price support.[65] Underlying this was the more important problem of the real cost to Britain of entering an arrangement which would involve some shifting of purchases of foodstuffs from low-cost Commonwealth and other sources to higher-cost European sources.

Following a new examination of the Commonwealth preferences, the United Kingdom finally concluded that there were sufficient doubts about their economic and political value, currently and in the future, so that abandoning them was not too high a price to pay, *provided* this was absolutely necessary to assure the United Kingdom's entry into the Common Market and provided, too, that "comparable" outlets could be arranged elsewhere or it was otherwise ensured that their "essential interests" were safeguarded.[66]

After months of difficult and tension-creating negotiations on this, and largely for reasons already encountered in the earlier Europe-wide free trade area discussions, it proved impossible to negotiate very much in the way of special favorable arrangements of one kind or another for Commonwealth exports.[67]

[65] Britain was also under the obligation not to abandon EFTA and join the EEC until satisfactory arrangements had been worked out between the Common Market and other EFTA members. See *EFTA Bulletin,* Geneva, July 1961, p. 8.

[66] The main questions asked in the re-examination were: How important in fact were the preferences to the political cohesion of the Commonwealth? Given the erosions in the margins of preference over the previous two decades and all the other changes in costs and demands that had taken place, were the preferences of much genuine economic advantage? Was not Western Europe becoming relatively more important and the Commonwealth relatively less so, in any case? Would a United Kingdom that stayed out of the EEC be able and willing to maintain the preferential arrangements much longer? Were the outer members of the Commonwealth interested in keeping the arrangements much longer? These were not, of course, the sort of questions to which firm and precise answers could be given. (See Camps, *Britain and the European Community, 1955–1963,* pp. 338–51.)

[67] The Six turned down British proposals for "guaranteed access," zero common external tariffs on relevant goods, limiting Britain's Community commitments to industrial goods, tariff-free quotas for some foods, etc. It was agreed by the Six that some of the African countries would be

But the British government by this time, the summer of 1962, had become convinced that, unfortunate as it was that more could not be done to preserve the old preferences, the economic interests of the Commonwealth could still be safeguarded by the buoyant effects on the British economy, and so on its demand for Commonwealth exports, of Britain's joining the Common Market. The other Commonwealth governments, some of them angry with the British, were much less sure, but the final decision was not theirs. In any event, the whole complex episode further whittled away the institution of imperial preferences.

On agricultural policy it was soon clear that reconciling U.K. agricultural policy with the common agricultural policy of the Community would have to take the form of the United Kingdom making most of the adjustments. This meant shifting the burden of supporting the farmer in Britain from the Treasury—via income deficiency payments—to the consumer directly, by way of higher prices. The Six also wanted a much more rapid adaptation by the British to the new system than the latter thought reasonable. Especially resisted by the British was the demand by the Six that the domestic target wheat price in the U.K. be quickly raised to a figure between the French and German ones. This would call for a substantial rise in Britain and would, it was feared, adversely affect United Kingdom costs, and thus, exports. Commonwealth wheat producers would also be harmed, both by the increased production in the U.K. that would be encouraged and by the larger imports from France, whose prices would now be lower than those of other sellers to Britain after paying the variable levy. The matter was still a

eligible for "association" status after the fashion of the former French territories, that the Community would later negotiate trade agreements with India, Ceylon, and Pakistan, looking toward an increase and diversification in their exports, and that the Six would lend their support to helping work out worldwide commodity agreements for some goods of a special interest to the Commonwealth. The British white paper reporting all this is reproduced in *Trade Expansion Act of 1962, Hearings Before the Committee on Finance,* U.S. Senate, 87th Cong., 2nd Sess., 1962, pp. 2,241–44.

subject of controversy on January 14, 1963, when General de Gaulle vetoed the British application.[68]

Difficult as the matter of preferences and agricultural policy was, most observers believed they could have been resolved. The decisive reason for General de Gaulle's unwillingness to continue the negotiations was his belief that British entry was a challenge to the political influence of France in the Community. Beyond this, British entry threatened to make the Community more "Atlantic"- or possibly global-oriented—and so less of an independent "new Europe" or "third force" which could deal with the United States and Russia as an equal: a goal much prized by de Gaulle. But that is not a part of our story; the problems that each of the two regional European groups have confronted in accommodating the preferential arrangements of some of their members, is.

Existing Preferences Small Problem for EFTA

The Stockholm Convention provided that the overseas members of the Commonwealth preference area would no longer enjoy preferential treatment in the British market over the other EFTA members, but they would continue to enjoy them in the British market over other third countries.[69] The fears that the latter provision—via shipments to other EFTA members through the United Kingdom—would be important enough to cause any significant increase in the discrimination against nonmember countries were largely allayed by two considerations. First, for a great many raw materials several EFTA members already gave duty-free treatment, so there was no reason to import such goods from the preferential areas of members unless they were already doing so; and, since there was to be no aligning of national tariffs as in the European

[68] For an official statement on the state of the negotiations on all the issues at the time the negotiations were broken off, see European Economic Community Commission, *Report to the European Parliament on the State of the Negotiations with the United Kingdom,* Brussels, 26 Feb. 1963.

[69] Comparable provisions were made for the quantitatively less important Portuguese colonies.

Common Market, the EFTA arrangements created no reason for those without duties to impose them because others had them. Second, if a member of EFTA found reason for levying a protective duty on a product produced by a nonmember it would be reluctant to let the product be imported free of duty via another member, and could be counted on to find ways of preventing it.

On the other hand, those that had been enjoying preferences in the United Kingdom were deprived of these with respect to goods produced by other members of the Free Trade Association. Although this had little or no significance for most raw materials, the arrangements also applied to manufactured goods, which was a matter of some immediate concern to those Commonwealth countries (India, Pakistan, and Ceylon, especially) which had developed export markets in Britain for a few manufactures. No great issue appears to have been made of this, however, reflecting the considerable erosion that had taken place in recent years in preferential margins [70] and the fact that India, Pakistan, and Ceylon assumed Britain would join the Six; so the important issues were those discussed in the preceding section. Those countries enjoying Commonwealth preferences believed that their products were also often not close substitutes for those available in the EFTA area and that tradition, established commercial ties, British investments, etc., would continue to provide effective preferences. Beyond this, the overseas countries had in fact no choice but to accept. And, several reasoned, the full effect was not likely to be felt for at least a decade, so could be heavily discounted.[71]

[70] See D. MacDougall and R. Hitt, "Imperial Preferences: Quantitative Analysis," *Economic Journal,* June 1954. See also, Political and Economic Planning, *Commonwealth Preferences in the United Kingdom,* London, 1960. Tariff cuts and the effects of inflation on the ad valorem incidence of specific duties had reduced the average percentage margin of preference on goods enjoying preferences (about half of the British imports from the Commonwealth) from 17–20 percent in 1937 to 11–13 percent in 1949, to 9 percent in 1957.

[71] The appraisal in this paragraph is based largely on conversations I held in Geneva in the spring of 1964 with officials of various Commonwealth countries.

Major Problems Flow from Associating Overseas Territories with European Common Market

No such easy solutions were found in the case of the European Common Market. Indeed, the most difficult aspects of the Rome Treaty for many third countries to accept were the arrangements for associating with the Community the overseas territories of its members. The Treaty (Part IV) provided that each of the Six would treat the trade with non-European territories which already had "special relations" with members as they treated trade among themselves. That is, each would permit duty-free entry to the products of the overseas territories and together they would impose a common tariff on competing imports from third countries.[72] In addition, the Treaty provided that the Six would jointly contribute to new investments in these overseas territories via the planned European Development Fund. The overseas areas, for their part, would treat imports from each of the Six essentially the same. That is, the Overseas Territories were not committed to freeing all imports from the Six from all restrictions but only to progressively reducing any *differences* in treatment between that given to the mother country and that accorded to the others.[73]

[72] Although the legal situation is not clear to me, the French overseas "Departments" are, with some special provisions, in effect incorporated into the European Economic Community. Morocco, Tunisia, Viet Nam, Cambodia, and Laos have, generally by special protocols, been permitted to retain their old special customs treatment in France but have *not* yet been accorded special treatment by the other EEC countries. Both Tunisia and Morocco, however, have been discussing possible association with the Community. Algeria, at the moment, is some place in between, having been a Department for a time after the Treaty of Rome was signed; but it too has been holding discussions "on future relations." Similar arrangements to those with Morocco, Tunisia, etc., have been made for Libya and Somali exports to Italy, and for Suranim and Dutch West Indian exports to Benelux. That is, none of these areas are associated with the Economic Community in a formal sense but all continue to enjoy some preferential arrangements with at least one of the European Common Market members; talks looking toward some form of association with the Community are held periodically.

[73] There was a complex legal question as to whether under the General Agreement, to which all the Six were participants, one could combine

When first presenting the proposal to third countries, spokesmen for the Six alleged that the main reason for these arrangements was to comply with the provisions of the United Nations Charter calling on the richer and more fortunate countries to help the less fortunate countries prosper. These arrangements did this, they said, both by enlarging markets for the underdeveloped countries' products and by increasing investments in these areas. But it was soon evident that a more compelling reason was that France, whose African dependent territories were much the most important beneficiaries, held that it would be "unthinkable" that France should pay the price of severing its existing special trade relations with its Overseas Territories [74] as the price of entering the European Economic Community, and that France believed it would be "wholly impracticable" for it to extend duty-free treatment and for the other five to levy duties when all the trading among them was to be free of restrictions.[75] The French were also anxious to have

---

features of a customs union and a free trade area in the fashion envisaged. The British, supported by others, argued that the proposed treatment of the Overseas Territories was a clear legal case of increasing margins of preference (not creating either a customs union or free trade area) and so was in conflict with Art. I of the GATT. Those interested in the legal aspects of the question should read Appendix Z to the Contracting Parties Working Party Report on the European Economic Community, reproduced in GATT, *Basic Instruments and Selected Documents, Sixth Supplement,* especially pp. 104–107.

[74] The preferential arrangements of the Franc Zone go back to 1928. The French tariff laws granting preferences were subsequently reinforced by quantitative restrictions and various subsidies. After World War II, currency arrangements contributed to the preferences. Elaborate marketing schemes for several of the older territories' most important products were also introduced, supplementing or replacing tariff preferences. For details, see UN, *Doc. E/Conf. 46/31,* 3 Feb., 1964, Paras. 53–61, and Annex 1. This document has been reproduced in *Proceedings of the United Nations Conferences on Trade and Development,* Vol. VI, United Nations, New York, 1964, pp. 328–404.

[75] As noted earlier, the European Free Trade Association has found, at least to date, that the trade deflecting problem was not so serious as the French assumed. During prosperous times it takes more than modest tariff differentials to overcome the additional expense of circuitous rout-

the territories associated with the Common Market in the manner described because they believed this would help ensure that France would continue to keep its favored position in the territories for its exports, it being assumed that even though the Overseas Territories granted similar treatment to all other members of the Common Market, past traditions, habits, established trade channels, and tastes would continue to assure French exporters a favored position.[76] Moreover, France was, through her various managed marketing arrangements for many of the goods produced in the Territories, paying substantially higher prices than its EEC partners for a good bit of its raw materials and food supplies. France hoped that the association arrangements would result in its Common Market partners giving it some relief by contributing to the subsidies involved. This was, however, not specified in the Convention and, as had been indicated during the negotiations, proved unacceptable to her Common Market partners. In broader terms, France, in

---

ing and the other costs of violating regulations. The fact that EFTA countries are often not contiguous has also, no doubt, served to limit trade deflection.

[76] There was growing concern among the former Associated Territories themselves as they became independent, lest these preferential arrangements perpetuate their economic dependency on the former Metropole or on the EEC countries. The Secretariat of the United Nations Economic Commission for Africa has emphasized this dependency aspect in its work. (See, for example, the Commission's, *The Impact of Western European Integration on African Trade and Development,* UN, *Doc. E/CN14/72, Corr. 1* and *2,* and *Add. 1,* Dec. 7, 1960.) The short-run benefits, including financial aid, however, often loomed large to these poor countries; they believed that with the benefits provided by the preferences and aid they could more quickly diversify their economies, and become more competitive in non-EEC markets. Only Guinea, on becoming independent, refused to continue association status with the Common Market (it left the Franc Area altogether). This seems to have been prompted for lots of other reasons as well.

Relevant here is the fact that the present convention *does* permit the overseas states to restrict imports from the Six if this can be justified on economic development grounds or the need for revenue. Still, the consultations with the Six requirements before advantage can be taken of these provisions, may in fact restrict their freedom. To date, the Six seem to have been tolerant on this.

contrast with its rather cavalier approach to permissible relations between Britain and the rest of the Commonwealth should Britain join the Six, sought in these arrangements to create conditions which would help ensure that as the areas moved to independence, as it was then clear they were doing, they would continue to be closely linked to France. From the outset, all this was not particularly attractive to the other five, but the arrangements were seen, in important respects, as a price they had to pay to ensure France's participation.[77]

THIRD COUNTRIES FEAR EFFECTS ON TRADE AND INVESTMENT. As soon as some of the details of the Convention of Association were made public, spokesmen for many of the underdeveloped nations expressed great apprehension lest they have serious adverse effects on underdeveloped nations. The Associated Territories produced—especially in the field of tropical products—goods similar to those produced in many of the other less-developed countries; the latter saw the proposed arrangements as immediately and directly depriving them of existing markets in the Six. They also feared they would have serious long-run effects because they would divert European investment funds to the Overseas Territories and so retard the future development of other regions which might otherwise have received such capital. Entirely apart from the special investment funds to be provided via the Community's new European Development Fund, private capital, they feared, would also now have a new incentive to move more heavily to the Associated Territories because production there would have a larger and more protected market.

Relatively little attention has been given so far to the fact that the exchange of preferential treatment between the Overseas Territories and the Common Market members also applied in general to manufactured goods and so might prejudice third country exports of such products to both the members and the

[77] It should be recalled that during the period of negotiating the Treaty of Rome the French government was often less enthusiastic than the other five and there was much opposition in the French public to France joining the Common Market.

associates.[78] Since the Associated States export almost no manufactured goods at this time there was no problem of immediate trade diversion involving their exports. But this could, of course, become important in the future, although that future at the moment seems a long way off. Similarly, it seems to have been generally accepted that France already had such an overwhelmingly dominant position in the markets of the Associated States that there was little scope there for any diversion of third countries' exports.

Early in the discussion some spokesmen for nonmember governments were also working toward the idea, soon to be made explicit and precise in the Haberler Report,[79] that since the Six themselves, by and large, did not produce the same internationally traded goods as the Overseas Territories, giving preferences in the Common Market to the former's goods could be only trade-*diverting* and never trade-creating, for there were no higher-cost producers to be displaced in the Six. The scheme thus lacked one of the major economic justifications for discriminatory arrangements. Moreover, there seemed to be little in the planned association that would contribute to a more rapid rate of economic growth in the Six, and so to the higher incomes—which, the Six kept repeating the future would show —would offset any trade diverting effects of the Community.[80]

Britain, then responsible for some 40 colonial territories, spoke for many in the early debates when it said it fully

[78] This problem was raised, but not emphasized, in the 1964 discussions among the Contracting Parties to the GATT of the Equatorial Customs Union which is formally associated with the European Economic Community. It was also involved in the discussion of preferences on manufactured goods from all developed countries to all the less-developed ones, which is the subject of Chapter VII below.

[79] General Trade Agreement on Tariffs and Trade, *Trends in International Trade,* Geneva, 1958, pp. 119–22.

[80] All this was hinted at, for example, in the statements by the Indonesian representatives, reproduced in GATT, *Press Release 367,* 30 Oct. 1957. It was more explicit in the plenary session debates, but the records of these are not available for citation.

sympathized with the desire of the Six to assist the development of their own overseas territories, "but we cannot welcome any plan which seeks to achieve such ends at the expense of the trade of other under-developed countries. . . ."[81] Over the years, many picked up this theme, noting that one of the major costs of this policy was that it exacerbated relations *among* the less-developed nations.

The EEC spokesmen acknowledged at once that the policy involved some discrimination, but they defended it originally on two major grounds. First, the question of discrimination against nonmembers, whether underdeveloped or not, was settled in 1947 when customs unions and free trade areas were authorized under the General Agreement. It was, they once again pointed out, inherent in customs unions and free trade areas that they accord different treatment to members and

[81] GATT, *Press Release 345,* 30 Oct. 1957.

According to available records, the United States, despite its great concern with the welfare of the underdeveloped areas, did nothing to champion their cause in this instance or to urge that this aspect of the Rome Treaty be changed. It was common gossip at the time that the United States went further than simply doing nothing, and let it be known that it supported these Community arrangements. (See Curzon, *Multilateral Commercial Diplomacy,* p. 280.) Be that as it may, with the advent of the Kennedy Administration and the beginning of the Alliance for Progress program, American officials were put under considerable pressure by the Latin American countries to "do something" about the discrimination against them in the EEC arrangements for the Overseas Territories. At least two major efforts were made to apply pressure on the EEC. The 1962 Trade Expansion Act authorized the President to eliminate duties and other import restrictions on many tropical agricultural and forestry products, *provided* the EEC took comparable action on a nondiscriminatory basis.

The United States also took the initiative within the GATT after 1960 in trying to work out arrangements for improving world markets for tropical products along the lines of favoring a worldwide elimination of import duties against them, the reducton of internal taxes on such products, etc. It also relaxed considerably its traditional policy against international commodity agreements designed to increase and stabilize the earnings from the export of tropical products. It has, however, up to now given little encouragement to some Latin Americans who have urged the United States to give preferences to Latin American exports comparable to those given by the EEC to the Associated States.

nonmembers, so why all the surprise now? Second, the apprehensions were not justified, they said, because the direct damage was likely to be small, maybe even nonexistent, and the effect of the Common Market on the member countries would be such as to increase their income so that total imports would increase, which would more than offset any adverse direct trade diversion effects on others. As to the question of investment diversion, EEC spokesmen asserted that the total funds available for foreign investment were not fixed, that as incomes in the Six went up so too would the funds available for investment abroad, including those in the other underdeveloped countries.[82]

These assertions, often repeated, and in many variations, did not satisfy those who saw their export markets immediately threatened. The fact that something had been agreed to more than a decade before gave no comfort to those who now were faced with what they believed would be concrete and important damage. Moreover, they asserted, it had not been contemplated that customs unions would take the form of such huge regional groupings as the European Economic Community, nor that they would have such special relations with their Overseas Territories. Although no proof was at hand, there was no expression of doubt that incomes within the Community would increase as a consequence of the union, but the expected effects on imports into the Community were to many relatively long-run phenomena and so were heavily discounted. In any case, it was not obvious to all that this would lead to increases in the

---

[82] See statements by the French and Dutch officials in GATT, *Press Release 357*, 30 Oct. 1957, and *360*, 30 Oct. 1957. I have also benefited from reading the records of the discussions on these questions in various meetings of the Contracting Parties, but present regulations forbid the citation of such sources.

No serious effort was made at the time to explore the possibility that the Common Market might attract to itself investment funds from third countries that might otherwise have gone to some of the less-developed countries discriminated against. It should be noted that through 1964 nearly all of the investments of the European Development Fund in the Associated States had been for infra-structure rather than for particular industries. See the periodic *Bulletin* of the EEC for many details on the financing by the Development Fund.

total value of imports by the Community of the products of interest to the underdeveloped countries, or, even if this happened, that *their* exports would share in the increase.[83] It was noted that the former was more likely to happen for any commodity as the income elasticity of demand for it was high in Europe (and as the price elasticity of demand was high in countries whose tariffs went down in the aligning process and low for those where they went up) and the less elastic was supply in the Overseas Territories. Virtually nothing was known about these elasticities, but most of the third countries were pessimistic and feared they would work against their exports. These early discussions were therefore often heated and always inconclusive.

STUDIES OF EFFECTS INCONCLUSIVE: INTERNATIONAL FRIC-TION MOUNTS. Immediately after this first encounter, the Secretariat of the GATT quickly prepared a short study on the possible impact of the European Economic Community upon world trade. While carefully acknowledging that they did not have adequate information to reach firm conclusions, the tenor of their report was that trade diversion, as a consequence of the European Economic Community's formation, probably would not be very great. Beyond this, if, as hoped, the Common Market served significantly to speed up the annual rate of economic growth in the Six then, it was found, on balance, ". . . it would clearly make an important contribution to the well-being of the other parts of the world as well." [84] These optimistic conclusions were not shared by many of the spokesmen for the less-developed countries. They noted that in its income-effect calculations the report had assumed that integration would increase the annual rate of growth by some 33–50 percent over what would be achieved in the absence of

[83] See UN Economic Commission for Latin America, *Economic Bulletin for Latin America,* March 1958, pp. 9–50. See also a statement by the New Zealand representative in GATT, *Press Release* (*Spec*) (*59*) *233,* 28 Oct. 1959.

[84] GATT, *The Possible Impact of the European Economic Community, in Particular the Common Market, on World Trade,* Geneva, 1957, p. 8.

integration. To many, this seemed optimistic. They also noted that the empirical evidence used as the basis for concluding that there would probably not be much trade diversion even in the short run was largely that of the estimated effects of the OEEC Trade Liberalization Program. Since this was regarded as temporary, was limited to quantitative restrictions, and was among highly industrialized countries, they concluded that it had little obvious predictive value for the effects of a permanent granting of preferential treatment on all import restrictions and between very differently structured and dissimilar economies.

In the early months of 1958 a special GATT Working Party was asked to examine the possible effects of the proposed association on 12 commodities. These were chosen because they bulked large at that time in the exports of both the Associated Territories and of many of the other underdeveloped countries.[85] Voluminous commodity studies were quickly prepared on each of these goods by the interested underdeveloped countries, with the help of the GATT Secretariat. The general conclusion of the majority—apparently all the members except representatives of the Six—was that the Common Market differential tariffs, ranging from nine percent for cocoa up to 80 percent for sugar, were "substantial" and would seriously divert Community imports from third countries to the associated territories. The majority also concluded that the arrangements would lead to increased investment and production in these favored areas. This, they thought, would decrease the other traditional suppliers' share of the markets in the Six and would force them to compete more severely amongst themselves in other markets. It was even foreseen that the associated territories might develop exportable surpluses beyond the Community, bringing down world prices even more, and so worsening the others' terms of trade.

Representatives of the Common Market flatly refused to accept these conclusions. Part of their reasons were legal ones,

[85] The commodities then accounting for about 80 percent of the exports of the Associated Territories were: cocoa, coffee, tea, bananas, sugar, tobacco, oil seed, cotton, hard fibers, wool, aluminum, and lead.

but on substantive grounds they charged, among other things, that the studies were often based on "hypothetical" and unreliable data. They stressed that the analysis failed to take account of the effects of increased economic activity which the Common Market would engender. They believed the majority consistently underestimated the physical and financial problems of increasing production in the overseas territories and that the supply elasticities were much less than others had assumed. They insisted that the group had paid far too little attention to the powerful force of consumer habits, qualitative differences, and established commercial ties in maintaining markets for traditional suppliers despite the price advantages that might accrue to the Associated Territories because of the preferential arrangements.[86]

The result was that the final report was correctly characterized as a "collection of conflicting evidence and conclusions." [87] Nonetheless, a strong presumption had been established outside the Community that the EEC plans would prejudice the export interests of many underdeveloped countries and that efforts should be made to minimize the likely damage. The action most frequently urged at the time was simply to extend the margins of preference to everyone: to set a zero, or very low, common tariff on these products.

The Six were not receptive to this or to the suggestion that they work out the specific and detailed arrangements between the EEC and the associated territories jointly with other countries whose exports might be involved. This was a head-on clash. An impasse had been reached, on this, as well as on the question of the Common Market common tariff, agricultural

---

[86] They did not point out that the managed market arrangements France had with several of the Associated States were probably much more important than tariff preferences in determining trade flows at that time.

[87] The report was originally produced as GATT, *Doc. L/805/Rev. 1*, 17 April 1958, and various addenda. In late 1958 it was published by the GATT in mimeographed form under the title, *Report of the Working Party on the Association of Overseas Territories with the European Economic Community, Including Commodity Trade Studies.*

policies, and the use of quantitative restrictions. It was therefore agreed to put aside for the time being the issues of legality and of general principles and to concentrate on specific "practical problems arising out of the application . . . of the Treaty." [88] Shortly thereafter several countries requested "consultations" with the Community on a few commodities important to them: sugar, cocoa, coffee, tea, bananas, and tobacco. But these not only settled nothing, they exacerbated relations still further between the Six and others. The Community spokesmen stated at the outset that there was no reason why any third country should keep the same percentage of trade with the Six as before the Common Market was created. This, they asserted, would be an uneconomic crystallization of trade channels. The only obligation of the Common Market, in their view, was to try and ensure the third country that no one suffered an absolute decline in exports to the Six because of the preferences given members of the overseas territories. This position was a keen disappointment to third countries which insisted that to keep only the same absolute level of trade in the face of economic growth was contrary to the spirit of the General Agreement. They charged that this was not the position the Six had taken earlier when the Contracting Parties were discussing the broad principles of the Common Market. They made no great effort, however, to get agreement on their "right" to no reduction in their percentage shares of the Six's market.

When the discussion turned to particular commodities the Six said again and again that they had every interest in and intention of being "outward" looking in their policies, but that they could not consult very far, or be expected to commit

[88] GATT, *Press Release 413*, 18 Oct. 1958. This proposal seems to have originated with Eric Wyndham White, the Executive Secretary of the GATT. Although widely accepted as the best thing to do in the circumstances, many feared that by concentrating on specific and concrete problems the Contracting Parties might be led into a whittling away of important rights because no one country's interests might be great enough to warrant its making a major issue of any infringement.

themselves to take specific action on specific products, purely on the basis of apprehension, or "theoretical possibilities." [89] Before they could commit themselves to any concrete "remedial" action they insisted that they needed firm evidence— actual trade figures showing trade diversion—that others had suffered as a consequence of the creation of the Common Market. The Six were relying heavily on their belief that any trade-diverting effects of their union would be hidden or offset by increased imports resulting from the expected growth in their national incomes. Third countries, of course, wanted action to *prevent* damage, not just efforts to remedy or offset it. They held, with some vehemence, that if they waited until damage could be proved by actual trade figures it would in fact be too late for feasible remedial steps to be taken. By that time new investments would have been made in the overseas territories and new vested interests would have been created, which would make it economically costly and politically difficult, if not impossible, to change.

Before this round of discussions was over some of the less-developed countries were beginning to question the good faith of the Community. The latter was not insensitive to this and made occasion a few months later to point out that part of the differences arose because others concentrated on the fact that the Common Market would necessarily result in some trade diversion, while the Six believed such effects would be small. In addition, they believed that the "income effects" of the unions would substantially benefit others.[90] The Six therefore asked if it were reasonable to expect them to take action to meet a problem they did not believe would arise unless there was concrete evidence that it in fact had. Since it was not possible to "prove" in advance whose beliefs would be verified —the forces at work were much too complex for that—the most logical policy, they said, would be to "wait and see." If damage

---

[89] Among other things, the Six pointed out that they did not have enough qualified experts to properly examine every "theoretical" possibility.

[90] See GATT, *Doc. L/1006,* 4 June 1959.

were caused, the Common Market would then consider "practical measures which the situation might warrant."

This policy statement and approach did nothing to allay the apprehensions of others. It was relatively easy for them to see, and it was to be expected that they would search for, examples of possible trade diversion and to have few means of estimating either the trade-creating or the growth-creating effects of the union, for these involved primarily the economic relations among the members of the Six and not those with outsiders. When to this disappointment were added the failure of the Dillon Round of tariff negotiations to yield more than meager results, and when the Community gave no serious attention to a 1961 formal proposal by a group of less-developed countries that the Common Market extend on a multilateral basis to all less-developed countries any benefits being extended their overseas territories,[91] there was another upsurge of resentment against the Six. At this juncture, the cleavage that the issue had created *among the less-developed countries* came into the open when spokesmen for some of the former French territories, now associated with the Common Market, publicly spoke in favor of the arrangements. They asserted that while they sympathized with the problems of their sister, underdeveloped nations, the latter must not look for solutions that took away the preferences of the former, a major factor, they said, in their fight against poverty.[92]

[91] This was part of a "Program of Action" submitted by a group of less-developed countries to the 1961 Ministerial Meeting of the Contracting Parties to the GATT.

[92] See GATT, *Doc. L/1645*, 24 Nov. 1961. Differences among the associated and non-associated African states over the cost and benefits of the former's ties with the Common Market often emerged in the sessions of the Economic Commission for Africa. (For a recent summary of this, see UN *Doc. E/Conf. 46/31*, pp. 183–88.) The major concerns of the nonmembers were not only that the arrangements discriminated against their exports but also that they created another obstacle to pan-Africanism (for a time, a potent political concern) and tended to keep the Associated States in a "neo-colonial" relationship with their former metropoles, preventing "adequate" industrialization. Although the availa-

One major consequence of all this was a growing conviction among many less-developed nations that existing international arrangements, especially the General Agreement, were not adequate to protect and further their interests.[93] This contributed to the 1964 Amendments to the GATT in the form of the New Chapter, entitled "Trade and Development," in which the developed nations agreed "to the fullest extent possible," [94] and via a variety of devices, to help bring about an expansion in the export earnings of the less-developed countries. More important, it contributed to the many forces that led to the calling of the 1964 United Nations Conference on Trade and Development and to the proposals there approved by the majority (with the developed nations often abstaining or voting "no"), that a

---

ble record is not unambiguous, it appears that the EEC is prepared to see the Associated African States enter into regional arrangements with other African states provided this does not result in the Associated States discriminating against imports from the Six.

[93] See GATT, *Press Release 631,* 27 Nov. 1961, for a strong statement to this effect by the Brazilian representative, which was supported by many of the other spokesmen for less-developed countries. GATT, *Press Releases 629–668* (statements by ministers at the 19th Session of the Contracting Parties), issued 27 Nov.–30 Nov. 1961, give much of the material that was presented later in closed Plenary Session on this question.

For further evidence of the concern with which many of the less-developed countries' spokesmen regarded the trading policies of the more industrialized nations, see E. Ivovich, "Latin America's Position in Relation to World Changes in Trade Policy," in Economic Commission for Latin America, *Economic Bulletin for Latin America,* Feb. 1962, pp. 53–72.

[94] This qualification, plus the fact that the Chapter said nothing about the developed countries giving preferences to the less developed ones (see Chapter VII below), led many of the latter to say that the Chapter was not worth the months of effort it had taken to draft it. Many of them had not yet ratified it by mid-1965, but it seemed likely that most would; it had been agreed in February 1965 that it would enter into force de facto at that time.

It is worth noting, because the matter of escalated tariffs seems likely to become an important policy issue in the future, that among the "commitments" of the developed countries was to accord high priority to reducing duties which differentiated "unreasonably" between goods in their primary and in their processed form.

"new" international trade organization be created, that "new" trade principles be adopted, and that a "new" international division of labor somehow be brought about.[95] Among other things, this Conference also recommended that *all* the industrially advanced countries give preferences in their imports to the manufactured exports from *all* the less-developed countries—a problem which is the subject of Chapter VII below.

BILATERAL EFFORTS TO LIMIT ADVERSE EFFECTS. A more immediate result of this keen disappointment in their efforts to prevent the Common Market discriminating against their goods was that several of the less-developed countries decided that the best way to further their interests was to try in bilateral discussions with the Community to work out solutions to their particular problems. The Community apparently encouraged this approach. For several countries the center of discussions for trade barrier questions thus shifted in the early 1960's from Geneva and the GATT to Brussels and the EEC. Some of the less-developed countries sought formal association with the Six, while others sought only a low—preferably zero—common tariff on their major exports.

Greece and Turkey, which had benefited from their earlier association with the Six and other Western European countries in the European Payments Union and in the associated OEEC Trade Liberalization Program, wished, for both political and economic reasons, to continue to be treated as a part of Western Europe.[96] The maintenance and growth of markets in the Six for such products as tobacco, raisins, figs, and fresh fruits were important to them, and they now felt threatened on two counts. Some of the Associated States supplied the same commodities, and the common external tariff on these was to be higher than the German duties—by far the most important of the Commu-

[95] See United Nations Conference on Trade and Development, *Final Act*, Geneva, 1964.

[96] For an elaboration of these reasons, see S. J. Ettinger, "The Association of Greece and Turkey with the European Economic Community," *Public and International Affairs*, Vol. III, No. 1, Woodrow Wilson School of Public and International Affairs, Princeton University, Spring 1965, pp. 130–61.

nity buyers. The Greeks and, to a lesser extent, the Turks, also harbored hopes that free entry of their products to the markets of the Six would encourage investment in them from foreign countries and so facilitate their economic growth.

The Community was receptive to their overtures for formal association. Beyond the general wish to tie both countries closer to the West, and to the Six if Europe were to be at Sixes and Sevens, the Six wanted to give further evidence that they were "outward" looking. Arrangements here, hopefully, would remove some of the political pressures on them, stemming from the belief that they were "running roughshod" over the less-developed countries. Furthermore, the associations were not likely to create severe competition to producers in the Community (Italy having been given special safeguards against some agricultural imports), and preferred access by Community producers in those markets had some attractions, as did the prospect of a freer flow of Greek and Turkish workers to over-employed Germany and Benelux.

In July 1961 Greece, 40 percent of whose exports had been going to the EEC countries, and the Common Market signed the Athens Agreement, formally associating Greece with the Community. Most third countries found this had so many exceptions to intra-area free trade that it failed to meet the requirements of a customs union as it was defined in the General Agreement.[97] But since the agreement was a fact when

---

[97] The major difficulties on this score were that the transitional period before Greece was required to permit free trade was as long as 22 years for many goods, and a few industrial products were exempted altogether from the requirements that there be free trade into Greece from the Community partners. The complex agricultural provisions which, like much of the rest of the agreement, left lots of latitude for interpretation, not only permitted exceptions to the elimination of trade barriers but gave Greece the right to block EEC reductions in the common tariff on tobacco, raisins, olives, and a few other products of a special export interest to it. (The Convention of Association with the African States requires only "consultation" when the common external tariff is changed, but since changes require the unanimous vote of the European Economic Community Council strong objection by the former colonies may be effective.) These "exceptions" to the normal customs union arrange-

it was brought formally before the Contracting Parties, and since Greece was small and did not seriously threaten most countries' interests, it was agreed that the Contracting Parties would simply "not find it desirable to pursue [the question] at this time." It was also specified, however, that this was without prejudice to the rights of the other countries under the General Agreement to complain and seek redress if they found themselves suffering discrimination or other impairment of concessions previously granted by Greece in trade negotiations.[98] No one has yet done so.

This "approval," even if by way of the backdoor, was of general interest because Greece was regarded by many as something of a test case for arrangements associating with the Community less-developed countries not previously dependent territories of the Six; [99] the EEC, it should be noted, does not regard it as a precedent and the Commission has opposed the formation of any *general* policy on association.

It remains to be seen whether the Greek experience will add to the attractiveness of this approach to others. Perhaps inevitably, the *early* developments often were disappointing to the Greeks. They found their exports increasing less than they had hoped, and that what they regarded as unpleasantly severe

---

ments were defended primarily on the grounds that they were needed to take account of the marked differences in the state of the economic development of Greece and the members and to give the former a little more elbow room to make adjustments. That is, it was feared, many Greek manufacturing products could not survive free trade within Western Europe. (For the text of the GATT Working Party Report, see GATT, *Basic Instruments and Selected Documents, Eleventh Supplement,* Geneva, 1963, pp. 149–58.) By mid-1965 Greece had cut its duties on imports from its EEC partners by varying amounts ranging downward from 20 percent. It had made no progress in aligning its tariffs with the common external tariff.

[98] For the text of the decision, see GATT, *Basic Instruments and Selected Documents, Eleventh Supplement,* pp. 56–57.

[99] Spain applied in February 1962 for association status, but following the breakdown of the United Kingdom bid for membership in the Common Market, this request was left unattended until the middle of 1964, when discussions were once more resumed, apparently on a rather leisurely scale.

criteria were being applied by the European Investment Bank for loans to Greece. The Greeks were unhappy at what they regarded as "unfair" treatment accorded by the Six to some of their agriculture products which competed directly with those of Italy. Especially disappointing to the Greeks so far has been the unwillingness of the Six to permit them to participate fully in the Community's Agricultural Guidance and Guarantee Fund.[100] Nonetheless, the Greeks still found association preferable to no association; they valued the political implications, the loans that were received, and the preferences that were effective.

Turkey, whose economic interests would be adversely affected by Greece being given preferential treatment in the Common Market for such major export products as tobacco and figs, also applied for association status in 1959. The Six had the same reasons for welcoming Turkey as they had for Greece, plus the fact that, having accepted Greece, not accepting Turkey would be an extremely unfriendly act. But because of the political instability and the continued acute internal economic difficulties in Turkey it was not until September 1963 that the Ankara Agreement was signed, going into effect in December 1964. This provides that during a five-year "preparatory" stage Turkey, with help from the Community, will "strengthen its economy," with a view to taking on the obligations that will accrue during the proposed "transitional," and "final," stages of customs union. This initial help is to take the form primarily of loans from the European Investment Bank, plus the Six granting tariff quotas for imports of Turkish tobacco, raisins, dried figs, and hazelnuts. The tariff quota arrangement created a Greek–EEC dispute when the former alleged this violated the Athens Accord. It is also possible that the preparatory stage may be extended and many of the detailed arrangements for the proposed 12-year transitional period and the final stage are left to be worked out later. This lack of firm commitments as to

[100] For details on the developments in the Greek association during its first two and a half years, see Ettinger, "Association of Greece and Turkey with European Economic Community," *Public and International Affairs,* pp. 148–58.

when the "preparatory" and the "transitional" stages would end led to much concern by some third governments, lest the arrangements end in an old-fashioned preferential scheme, largely covering only those goods which would result in trade diversion. But, mindful of the earlier Greek decision, of the fact that the Ankara Agreement was already in effect, and of the fact that the Cyprus dispute was brewing and Turkey was flirting with Russia; mindful of all these things, the Contracting Parties in March 1965 decided merely to note the doubts about its compatibility with the General Agreement and to keep it on the agenda.[101] This was probably equivalent to approval, and, because the arrangements fell so far short of a customs union, it appeared likely that this would strengthen the claims of the less-developed countries for a generalized system of preferences in their favor.

Those less-developed countries not seeking formal association, but wishing to make other arrangements to safeguard their outlets in the Common Market, found at first that the Community spokesmen, while polite, and promising to take note of the views expressed, promised nothing and pointed out that as yet there has been no evidence of damage. By early 1963 the Community, sensitive to the fact that the Associated Territory problem had been politically costly, and mindful of the new charges, growing out of the breakdown of the discussions for British entry, that the Community was a self-centered and inward looking organization, softened its position.[102] Asking no

---

[101] For the text of the agreement and the protocol, see GATT, *Doc. L/2155, Add. 1,* 12 March 1964. See also, GATT, *Doc. L/2265,* March 1965, for some of the reasons why other countries found this was in violation of the General Agreement.

[102] Brief, running accounts of some of the many discussions are often reported in the monthly *Bulletin of the European Economic Community.* The Commission of the European Economic Community has also made efforts to explain its policies to many of the less-developed countries, has urged that internal taxes on tropical products be abolished by its members, and has joined with all the other developed nations in recommending that the Kennedy Round not make exceptions to the 50 percent linear cut for goods of special interest to the less-developed countries.

specific concessions in return, it reached a formal agreement with Iran in September 1963, which provided that the common external tariffs on carpets, dried apricots, raisins, and caviar be reduced or suspended for a three-year period. The reductions, 10 to 20 percent in most cases, were on a most-favored-nation basis. Later in the year, following prolonged discussions, the common tariff was also suspended, in whole or in part, again on a most-favored-nation basis and for some two years, on about 16 relatively minor items of special interest to India.[103] This arrangement was not in the form of a formal trade agreement, but such a formal three-year trade agreement was initialed in early 1964 with Israel, aligning at once to the common external tariff levels the duties of the members on 23 goods,[104] plus reductions of from 10 to 40 percent in the common tariff on most of them. No cut in the external tariff was made for the major Israeli export, oranges, also a major Italian export crop.[105]

The willingness of the Common Market to negotiate this type of limited bilateral accord was welcomed by the third countries involved, but it was generally recognized that the moves were important chiefly as symbols of attitudes. Substantively, they were not of great moment. The value of the imports of the products concerned was small,[106] the concessions were on a

[103] For details, see GATT, *Doc. Comm. III/130,* 18 Feb. 1964. The list includes such items as ginger, mango chutney, pimento, and certain sporting goods, etc. The total accounted for only about three percent of India's exports to the Common Market.

It will be recalled (footnote 67 above) that during the still-born negotiations for British accession to the EEC in 1962 it had been tentatively agreed that the Community would later negotiate comprehensive trade agreements with India, Pakistan and Ceylon, looking toward an expansion in their trade and a diversification of their economies.

[104] Some foods, a few chemicals, bathing suits, stockings, and window glass were the more important, in terms of Israel's trade.

[105] For some details on these bilateral accords, see G. L. Weil, *A Handbook on the European Economic Community,* pp. 130–33. Israel later said that it still hoped for something approaching association status with the Common Market.

[106] The EEC imports from *all* sources of *all* the goods covered in Iranian and Indian agreements were about $200 million in 1963. See GATT, *Doc. L/2394,* 15 March 1964.

most-favored-nation basis, and the commitments were for only a few years. If the Kennedy Round of tariff negotiations proves successful, and if, as expected, these particular commodities are included, then they will be incorporated in the results of these negotiations. The bilateral accords therefore probably represent only a sort of advance payment. This mild welcoming attitude on the part of the less-developed countries was further tempered by the fear of some that such bilateral arrangements might introduce differential treatment, if not formal discrimination, as among various less-developed countries.[107] This might mean helping some at the expense of others, and could do damage to the cohesiveness of the "third world." Another sobering note, so far as the developing countries were concerned, was introduced in May 1963 when the European Economic Community would not endorse the proposed GATT "Program of Action." [108] This called, among other things, for the duty-free entry into the industrialized countries of all tropical products and primary goods of importance to the less-developed countries. Community spokesmen argued that a system of "organized markets" was a better approach to the problem of increasing the export earnings of the poorer countries, but their position was widely regarded as also prompted by the determination to continue and protect preferential treatment to the associated overseas states.[109]

[107] See, for example, UN, Economic Commission for Asia and the Far East, *Annual Report* (1962–1963), Economic and Social Council, *Official Records*, 36th Sess., Supp. No. 2, New York, 1963, p. 8.

In 1962 the EEC approached the Latin American countries and suggested that it might be preferable for everyone if there were a greater exchange of information on each area's regional efforts and if the EEC were to adopt a "unified attitude towards Latin America." This was welcomed by the latter. There has since been an increase in the flow of information, but unified action by the Latin American nations vis-à-vis the Six and vice versa has been slow in developing. See UN Economic Commission for Latin America, *Economic Bulletin for Latin America*, Oct. 1962, pp. 127–66, and European Economic Community, *Bulletin of the EEC*, July 1963, p. 21.

[108] GATT, *Press Release 794*, 29 May 1963.

[109] Especially interesting were the negotiations in 1963 between the Community and the United Kingdom on tea and tropical timber. Each of these two industrial areas granted preferences with respect to these

DISCRIMINATION REDUCED IN NEW CONVENTION OF ASSO-
CIATION. Pending the outcome of the 1964–1966 tariff negotiations, the most important measure of the Community's policy in
relation to discrimination against the less-developed countries,
in particular, was to be found in the new Convention of
Association, the Yaoundé Convention, which entered into force
on January 1, 1964, and which had to be drawn up when the
former territories became independent states.[110] As far as the
question of preferences is concerned, the great difference with
the original arrangement was that for nine tropical goods of
considerable interest to less-developed third countries the Six
agreed to apply immediately the common external tariff and to
admit exports from the associated states, duty-free. This
represented an acceleration in the duty-free treatment, and so
immediately increased the preferences they enjoy. But the
Convention also significantly reduced the common external
tariff, which will reduce the level of ultimate preferences.[111]

goods in favor of its own overseas friends. The Community, in a move
designed both to meet some of the objections to their overseas territories'
policies and also to protect the interests of these territories in the British
market, took the initiative in proposing the negotiations which led to
agreement that each would suspend for a two-year period the duties on
these goods. (EEC imports of these goods from all sources totalled $165
million in 1963.) This seems to be a case where preferences were used
by each side as a bargaining device to get rid of preferences extended by
the other. It has been assumed by most observers that the result of this
agreement will also be incorporated into the results of the Kennedy
Round.

[110] The new accord was formally signed in July 1963. For an official
description of it, see European Economic Community, *Bulletin of the
EEC,* Brussels, Feb. 1963, pp. 21–25. The text may be found in Weil,
Handbook on the European Economic Community, pp. 395–433.

[111] The commodities, followed by the original common external tariff
and then the new common tariff calculated on an ad valorem basis are as
follows: coffee, 16 and 9.6; cocoa, 9 and 5.4; pineapples, 12 and 9;
cocoanut, 5 and 4; tea, 18 and 10.8 (this duty was subsequently
suspended altogether in the British–Common Market negotiations noted
above); pepper, 20 and 17; vanilla, 15 and 11.5; cloves, 20.6 and 15;
muscat nuts, 20 and 15. EEC imports of the goods totalled some $738
million in 1963, of which only $198 million came from the Associated
States.

The new Convention also provides that, gradually, world market prices shall be paid for Community imports from the Associated Countries. This is an important provision, because these are likely to be below the levels of the prices France had been paying for many products imported from its former territories under the various "managed market" schemes it employed.[112]

The Six agreed to broaden the uses and to increase by nearly 40 percent the amount of financial aid to be provided by the Development Fund to the overseas states during the five years of the second Convention, as compared with the same period of the first one. Part of this aid, which may take the form of loans, gifts, technical assistance, etc., will be used to facilitate the transition to the system of world market prices, including diminishing deficiency payments to producers of goods previously enjoying the benefits of the French managed markets. It may also be spent on infra-structure investments, and to help diversify and increase the productivity of the economies. Finally, at German and Dutch insistence, the new Convention provides that other states having an economic structure and production "comparable" to those of the Associated States may request association with the Common Market.[113] The possibilities foreseen included not only full accession to the Yaoundé Convention, with the same rights and obligations as the original members, but also *sui generis* association with more limited reciprocal rights and obligations, and, finally, commercial agreements aimed at increasing trade. Details of the last two possibilities were to be spelled out in such bilateral negotiations as might take place.

These changes in the EEC policy should reduce some of the apprehensions of third countries so far as their *traditional*

---

[112] For a recent description of these, prepared by the Secretariat of the United Nations Economic Commission for Europe, see UN, *Doc. E/Conf. 46/31, Annex 1.*

[113] Art. 58.

This particular Convention applies only to the 18 independent African nations and the Malagasy States. A separate but comparable Convention was signed with the Territories that were not yet independent.

exports are concerned, although they do not deal directly with the potentially much greater problem of the possibly adverse effects on others of the preferences for semi-processed and manufactured goods originating in the Associated States and enjoying preferential access to the Common Market. Not only are the ultimate preferences on some important goods reduced, but the changes in the price system noted, unless often breached, are likely to go some way toward meeting the concern that the arrangements would increase production in the Associated States and so deprive others of markets. If the increased aid that is being provided reduces production costs in the export sector, then, of course, even the reduced preferences may prove to have greater effectiveness in encouraging additional production. Although, to date, most of the financial assistance has gone for such infra-structure as roads, schools, irrigation facilities, and does not seem to be concentrated in its effects on exports, it is planned that under the new Convention more funds than in the past will be used to help increase agricultural productivity.

Finally, the increased possibility of other less-developed countries coming within the provisions of the arrangement is being seen by some of them as the best *available* answer to their problems. Such moves will increase even more the discrimination against those who still remain outside, and to a much greater degree than the bilateral trade agreements noted earlier. They were particularly resented by those who believed the interests of the less-developed countries would be better served by a system of generalized preferences from all developed to all developing countries—a matter discussed at length in Chapter VII below. Nigeria, despite earlier hostility to the EEC and to the original association arrangements, showed interest early (as did Kenya, Uganda, Tanganyika, and Sierra Leone), saying that it preferred a system of preferences from all developed to all less-developed countries but until that was agreed it felt obliged to do what it could to prevent damage to its exports. The Nigerian negotiations got seriously underway in early 1965 and were regarded as particularly important in the setting of precedents, especially since on the matter of Community relations with the less-developed countries the former were moving less from principle than from problem to problem. Agreement was reached in July, but at the time of this writing the details are not available. Press reports indicated that in the accord—to expire at the same time as the Yaoundé Convention —Nigeria would give only mild preferences to a small part (only four percent) of its imports from the Six but would be granted preferences similar to those enjoyed by the eighteen Associated States except for those Nigerian exports (cocoa beans, palm oil, peanut oil, and plywood) which were also important in the exports of the eighteen.[114] In other words, Nigeria would be given preferences vis-à-vis outsiders, but would not, in effect, be permitted seriously to dilute those of the original members. More important was the probability that, having given some preferential treatment to Nigeria to help offset the adverse effects on her exports from having previously given preferences to the Associated States, the European Economic Community would soon find it expedient to negotiate a comparable "special" arrangement with some other developing country whose exports had been adversely affected by the Nigerian accord. Thus does discrimination spread.

These changes incorporated in the Yaoundé Convention were the response to several forces.[115] The Community believed that it had paid a high political price in terms of its relations with all the other less-developed countries for the association policy and it was anxious to reduce this cost. The stilling of the constant criticism in international forums, which had gone on since 1958, had become in itself a goal of some value to each of

[114] International Monetary Fund, *International Financial News Survey*, July 30, 1965, p. 269. The possibility of the African members of the British Commonwealth joining the EEC in one way or another should make easier any future negotiations looking toward United Kingdom entry into the Common Market. It will be recalled (footnote 67) that something like this new clause had been more or less agreed to in the aborted U.K.–EEC 1962 negotiations.

[115] The following account is based on oral conversations I had in the summer of 1964 with many officials of the Community and with some of the members of the governments concerned. They took place on the understanding that there would be no attributions.

the Six. Some members, especially Germany and the Netherlands, had become increasingly unhappy with the existing arrangements, which they had not liked from the beginning. They found themselves paying the price—especially the political one—of extending preferences to a few less-developed countries but were receiving virtually no benefits in terms of larger exports to these markets because France kept its dominant supplier role in them. They were, therefore, prepared to increase their financial contribution to the Associated States if this was a necessary price of reduced preferences. France, anxious to maintain its special relation with its former overseas territories, was also anxious to reduce the criticism of other less-developed countries. Replacing some of the tariff preferences with more aid, some of which was to be used to "phase out" the high-price support arrangements that France had inaugurated, had triple advantages: continuing special ties; reducing the resentment of others; and having its Common Market partners in effect take over some of the financial burden on the French consumer of the high prices paid for imports from the Associated States. Moreover, France had found that it would be difficult to pursue the Community's common agricultural policy if it continued to pay especially high support prices for imports from its former territories and, as we have seen, France was most anxious that the Common Market agricultural policy be implemented.

The Associated States themselves had been keenly disappointed with the benefits, in terms of increased export earnings, that they had been able to reap from the tariff preferences in the non-French states of the Community. They had also been subjected to much criticism from other African states, who saw the arrangements as not only prejudicial to their exports but also as a divisive force in Africa and constituting an obstacle to pan-Africanism.[116] The latter concerns seem to have abated considerably after 1963, but they had by no means disappeared.[117] And, as the Associated States assumed greater

[116] See A. A. Mazrui, "African Attitudes to the European Economic Community," *International Affairs*, London, Jan. 1963, pp. 24–36.

[117] See A. Rivkin, "Africa and the European Common Market," *Monograph Series in World Affairs*, University of Denver, 1964.

responsibility for their own affairs, they developed a growing concern lest the special preferential relationships with only a few (in practice, largely limited to France), tend to freeze old colonial relationships. With independence, they began to put more and more value on diversifying their economies and, in particular, on expanding their investment in manufacturing and processing industries. They sometimes feared that, given the competition within the Common Market, not only would the value of preferences for their manufactured goods be negligible, but when this competition was combined with more beneficial preferences on *existing* exports industries the result would be an effective new barrier to their industrialization. Therefore, a new agreement in which more aid replaced some preferences was appealing to them, too.

SOME TENTATIVE CONCLUSIONS. Again, the time span has been too short to permit any confident conclusions, but the first few years of the Common Market's preferential arrangements with the Associated States provide no evidence that the *total* absolute effect has been prejudicial to other less-developed countries.

Professor Thorbecke, writing in 1962, had tentatively concluded that probably the initial "static" impact (adverse) of the EEC on the total exports of most less-developed countries would be small, primarily because his researches had shown that "on the whole, very few outside under-developed countries experience both a high degree of geographical concentration of exports to the EEC and a commodity concentration" on goods subject to a high external tariff.[118] He also found, however, that

[118] E. Thorbecke, "European Economic Integration and the Pattern of World Trade," *American Economic Review,* May 1963, pp. 147–74. The quote is from p. 155. On the assumption that the process of economic integration resulted in levels of GNP in the Community by 1975 some 30 percent higher than if there had been no integration, he made, "in the nature of an exercise" a series of projections which led him to conclude that the so-called "dynamic effects" of integration might well be favorable to the exports of some third countries—especially those who exported fuels, iron ore, copper, and natural rubber—but that they might also be negative on some nonmembers who exported foodstuffs, especially the tropical beverages. This adverse dynamic effect, if it happened, was likely to be the result of the increase in investment and

for several products the trade diverting effects might turn out to be important. This, he thought, was most likely to be the case for coffee, sugar, tobacco, bread and grains, fruits and vegetables. The Economic Commission for Europe Secretariat found in early 1964 that "there was hardly any important commodity subject to discrimination where developing third countries suffered an absolute or even a relative decline of their exports" because of increased intra-trade within the EEC or EFTA or larger EEC imports from the Associated Overseas States.[119]

Community officials have regularly reported in one forum or another that imports from less-developed areas having no preferential access to the Common Market were increasing a good bit more rapidly than those from the associated areas. Thus, as the following table shows, merchandise imports by the Six from the latter were almost stable from 1958 through 1962 and in 1964 were only about 25 percent greater than they had been in 1958, while those from the former increased more or less steadily and were nearly 50 percent greater in 1964 than they had been in 1958.

I have found no detailed empirical studies explaining these trends. The available evidence [120] suggests that on the demand side price differences represented by the tariff differentials often were not enough, at least in the short run, to offset habit and qualitative differences and the existence of established commercial and merchandizing channels by EEC nations with sources of supply in nonassociated areas.[121] The relative importance of

---

production in the Overseas Associated States that the EEC would encourage. All of this, of course, rested on a host of assumptions as to supply and demand elasticities, new technology, etc., and could easily prove wrong, as he carefully pointed out. It should also be remembered that these favorable or negative effects are as compared with non-integrated Western Europe and so even negative effects are compatible with an *absolute* increase in the area's imports from nonmembers.

[119] UN, *Doc. E/Conf. 46/31,* Chap. V, Para. 3.

[120] Largely conversations with European officials, whose views often were impressionistic and so not very reliable.

[121] See UN, *Doc. E/Conf. 46/31,* Chap. III, Paras. 66–81 for an early 1964 appraisal of the importance of some of these non-price factors with respect to several goods.

TABLE I

EUROPEAN ECONOMIC COMMUNITY:
MERCHANDISE IMPORTS
(IN MILLIONS OF DOLLARS: MONTHLY AVERAGES)

	From Associated Countries, Territories, and Departments [a]	From All Other Developing Countries [b]
1958	90	479
1959	84	472
1960	94	530
1961	93	538
1962	91	580
1963	104	631
1964	113	706

Sources: Organization for Economic Cooperation and Development, *Foreign Trade, Series A;* and Statistical Office of the European Communities, *General Statistical Bulletin.*

[a] The 18 Associated African and Malagasy States, plus Curacao, Aruba, Surinam, French Coast of Somali, Comoro, St. Pierre and Miquelon, New Caledonia, French Polynesia, Reunion, Guadeloupe, Martinique, and Guyane. Imports from Algeria are *not* included.

[b] All countries other than those listed in footnote a, and Europe, North America, Oceania, South Africa, Japan, Mainland China, North Viet Nam, North Korea, and Outer Mongolia.

the latter factors in determining sources becomes greater as the value of import inputs to the value of the final products produced by the importing country declines; it is typical of many of the present exports of the less-developed countries that these ratios are often small.

On the supply side, the fact that the Associated States' previous commercial relations had been almost exclusively with France meant that as a practical matter they were finding it difficult to develop markets in the other five members of the Common Market. Other less-developed countries, on the other hand, frequently could build on previous commercial relations with many of the Six. Given the long gestation period for some tropical goods, there simply has not yet been enough time for some trade-diverting effects to be felt. Some observers also believed that the preferences were to some extent self-defeating, for they encouraged those enjoying them to relax, and those discriminated against to intensify, their marketing and cost-reducing efforts. In the longer run, since even before the Common Market was formed the Associated States sent the bulk of their exports to the Six (France), an increase in their relative share of the growing market will largely depend on increasing output, which, in turn, depends mostly on the amount and kinds of new investments. Very little information seems to be available about recent internal capital formation or foreign private investments in these areas; the official capital inflows since 1959 have been largely for infra-structure, but the new Convention provides for more attention being given by the Development Fund to increasing productivity. It is too early to know what the effects will be on export costs and production. In any case, the level of tariff preferences foreseen in the new Convention would not seem to be enough to be a potent consideration in attracting capital to the favored sectors.

One can at least conclude that so far the discrimination involved in the arrangements for the overseas territories has been much less harmful to other developing countries than they feared; that the price of the discrimination in terms of exacerbating political relations was high—among the Six, as well as between the Six and the associated countries on one hand and the rest of the world on the other; that the benefits were disappointing to those enjoying the preferences; and that, after five years, powerful forces were working to reduce the level of preferences.

CONCLUSIONS

What may one say by way of conclusions with respect to this unfinished chapter in the use of regional discrimination as a major policy tool? First, preferences had become a highly respected, and respectable, instrument in policy formulation circles. Discrimination, especially when it was associated with that alluring word "integration," was no longer a bad word. Second, regional economic integration in the two European blocs, the only groups on which there is enough information to have even preliminary views, so far has brought to its members more economic benefits than economic costs; moreover, it has not yet inflicted absolute damage on nonmembers as a whole. But there does remain enough doubt as to the so-called "dynamic effects" to have warranted all the concern shown by nonmembers. We will shortly come back to this point. Third, regional discrimination tends to spread. Emulation, as well as efforts to protect themselves from the feared otherwise loss of bargaining power, contributed to the growing interest in regional organizations in other areas. Fourth, the discriminatory aspects of the regional economic groups have created many political tensions.[122] Fifth, the authority and prestige of the GATT were damaged by the emergence of the permanent regional groups, especially in the eyes of the less-developed countries. This added support to the movement to create a new forum, new rules, and new commitments in international trade. Nonetheless, given the drive which did exist toward regionalism in Europe, at least, had the Contracting Parties tried to stop it on the grounds that it did not meet the legal requirements of the General Agreement, the GATT itself probably would have been destroyed.[123] The European countries were going ahead with their regional arrangements and the only possibility for GATT survival was for it to recognize this fact; the only worthy role for it to play was to attempt to influence the regional groups in the direction of measures that would lead to more rather than less trade-creation, and less rather than more trade diversion. Sixth, badly damaged as the institution was, the existence of the General Agreement and the periodic meetings of the Contract-

---

[122] Mrs. Camps' excellent *Britain and the European Community, 1955–1963,* is, among other things, an impressive catalog of the political frictions that were created between the United Kingdom and virtually everyone else as a result of the various regional economic arrangements in which it was involved—or wished to be.

[123] The prestige of the GATT had already suffered greatly from the earlier United States quotas on dairy products.

ing Parties have made the regional groups more concerned with the effects of their action on the third countries and have resulted in their tempering some of their discriminatory policies, most notably on the EEC–Associated States arrangements and, hopefully, on the level of the common tariff.

Returning to the all-important second point: At the very least, regionalism in Western Europe, to date, has been accompanied by great economic vitality and real growth—and that has been most evident in the group (EEC) which has most fully integrated itself. Moreover, so far there is no evidence that, taking all things into account, the discrimination arising from regionalism has actually hurt third countries as a group.[124] But any firm conclusions on these matters must await more evidence. Preferences enjoyed by area producers have not yet reached their full stature; taking agriculture into account, they are probably little more than halfway, and both the supply and demand elasticities can be expected to be greater in the long-run than in the short. Moreover, the fact that all of the West European countries had enjoyed very high levels of employment since 1958 meant that trade diversion was probably not great in the aggregate simply because of the small amount of intra-block production capacity available to displace imports from nonmembers. Nonetheless, in early 1965, some observers, noting that in 1964 EFTA countries exports to the EEC increased by only about half as much as they had, on the average, in each of the previous four years, expressed fears that this might not be a temporary phenomenon but rather the first evidence of a trend—evidence that the EEC discrimination finally was beginning to "make its mark." [125]

So it may prove to be, but the following tables on the trade of the Six and the Seven with the rest of the world certainly belies the fears of those who saw the European blocs as an early and certain catastrophe for nonmember's exports. The fact that

[124] The LAFTA and other new regional groups in the less-developed countries seem so far to have had very little effect on the composition and direction of the trade of their members or their national incomes.

[125] See *The London Economist,* Jan. 30, 1965, p. 462; and European Free Trade Association, *EFTA Reporter,* June 14, 1965, p. 2.

TABLE II

EUROPEAN ECONOMIC COMMUNITY: MERCHANDISE IMPORTS
(IN MILLIONS OF DOLLARS: MONTHLY AVERAGES, C.I.F.)

	Total	Intra-EEC [a]	Extra-EEC					
			Total	EFTA Countries	All Non-associated Developing Countries [b]	United States and Canada	Eastern Europe Countries [c]	Other
1952	1281	302	979	n.a.	n.a.	n.a.	n.a.	n.a.
1958	1912	656	1256	301	479	270	56	150
1959	2023	757	1266	325	472	248	69	152
1960	2466	940	1526	372	530	357	81	186
1961	2681	1069	1612	410	538	378	90	198
1962	2981	1209	1772	459	580	409	100	224
1963	3367	1415	1952	514	631	459	114	234
1964	3738	1616	2122	549	706	495	113	259
Percentage Increase from 1952 to 1958								
	49	87 [d]	38 [e]					
Percentage Increase from 1958 to 1964								
	95	146	69	. 82	48	84	101	73

ources: Organization for Economic Cooperation and Development, *Foreign Trade*, *Series* ; and Statistical Office of the European Communities, *General Statistical Bulletin*.

[a] Includes only trade among the six principals in 1952. For the period 1958–1964 also clude imports by the six principals from the associated underdeveloped areas.

[b] See footnotes to Table I for composition.

[c] U.S.S.R., East Germany, Poland, Czechoslovakia, Hungary, Rumania, Bulgaria, nd Albania.

[d] Because the 1952 figure does not include imports by the Six from the associated over-as areas, in making this calculation the 1958 figure was reduced to $566 million to make comparable.

[e] Because the 1952 figure includes imports by the Six from the associated overseas areas, making this calculation, the 1958 figure has been increased to $1,346,000,000 to make it mparable.

intra-EEC (and intra-EFTA) imports increased at a faster rate than extra-bloc imports, no doubt, reflects both trade-creation and some trade-diversion. I have not attempted the very diffi-

TABLE III

EUROPEAN FREE TRADE ASSOCIATION: MERCHANDISE IMPORTS
(IN MILLIONS OF DOLLARS: MONTHLY AVERAGES, C.I.F.)

			Extra-EFTA					
	Total	Intra-EFTA [a]	Total	EEC Countries	All Developing Countries [b]	United States and Canada	Eastern Europe [c]	Oth
1952	1292	201	1091	n.a.	n.a.	n.a.	n.a.	n.a.
1958	1571	253	1318	434	381	232	53	21
1959	1668	270	1398	468	401	238	60	23
1960	1923	311	1612	547	424	320	71	25
1961	1962	338	1624	596	411	292	76	24
1962	2050	362	1688	635	424	291	79	25
1963	2199	402	1797	673	457	303	87	27
1964	2509	471	2038	759	480	371	94	33
			Percentage Increase from 1952 to 1958					
	22	26	21					
			Percentage Increase from 1958 to 1964					
	60	86	55	75	26	60	77	5

Source: OECD, *Foreign Trade, Series A.*

[a] Includes only trade among the seven principals.

[b] All countries other than Europe (East and West), North America, Oceania, Sou Africa, Japan, Mainland China, North Viet Nam and Outer Mongolia.

[c] U.S.S.R., East Germany, Poland, Czechoslovakia, Hungary, Rumania, Bulgaria, a Albania.

cult task of trying to determine the extent of each,[126] and, in any case, some of the change may be due to forces having nothing to do with the formation of regional blocs as is suggested, but not

[126] See Bela Balassa, "European Integration: Problems and Issues," *American Economic Review,* May 1963, pp. 178–80, for a possible way to approach this task. But see, too, M. June Flanders, "Measuring Protectionism and Predicting Trade Diversion," *The Journal of Political Economy,* April 1965, p. 169, who concludes that there is "no alternative to painstaking examination, commodity by commodity, of the relevant cost and demand conditions."

of course proved, by the fact that between 1952 and 1958 intra-EEC (and intra-EFTA) imports also increased more rapidly in percentage terms than the bloc's total imports.

But since one does not, and cannot, know what would have happened had there been no EEC or EFTA, these data do not provide a definitive answer to the question of whether the rest of the world, and the members, are better or worse off than they would have been had there been no Rome Treaty or Stockholm Convention. The experience to date does make evident what all observers had expected: a great many of the problems arising from discrimination become "manageable" in the context of rapid economic growth. If that growth is rapid enough, not only will the members find it easy to pay for any costs to them of the discrimination, but the adverse "static" and "direct dynamic" effects of the unions on nonmembers will be more than offset by the beneficial "indirect dynamic" ones. A critical question then is: how much of the impressive and prolonged rates of growth in the European blocs, especially the EEC, summarized in the table below, can be credited to the fact of regionalism?

Several writers have started off "assuming" that integration will increase the rate of growth of the union and then estimated the effects on others. Erdman and Rogge, for example, attempted in 1960 to estimate all this for the Common Market and concluded that the "growth" ("dynamic") effects on nonmembers would probably outweigh the "preference" ("static") effects over the next 20-year period *if* the national incomes of the EEC members increased at least 120 percent.[127] But

[127] This report is cited in Balassa, "European Integration," *American Economic Review,* pp. 185–87. There have been several other attempts to estimate some of the likely effects under various assumptions. Among the more interesting is the GATT study noted in footnote 84 above; and H. G. Johnson, "The Gains from Freer Trade with Europe: An Estimate," *The Manchester School of Economics and Social Studies,* Sept. 1958; Jan Tinbergen, "The Impact of the European Economic Community on Third Countries," in College D'Europe, *Sciences humaines et intégration européen,* Leiden, 1960, and Thorbecke, "European Economic Integration and Pattern of World Trade," *American Economic Review,* May 1963, pp. 147–74.

TABLE IV

INDEXES OF GROSS NATIONAL PRODUCT
1953 EQUALS 100
(CONSTANT PRICES)

	Common Market	EFTA	United States
1950	86	88	86
1951	91	92	93
1952	94	5.4% [a]	95	4.5%	96	3.3%
1953	100	100	100
1954	106	105	98
1955	114	109	106
1956	120	5.0%	112	2.8%	108	2.7%
1957	126	115	110
1958	129	117	109
1959	136	121	116
1960	145	127	119
1961	154	5.5%	132	3.8%	121	4.1%
1962	162	135	129
1963	169	139	133
1964	178	147	139

Sources: 1950–1963 data from J. M. Letiche, "European Integration: An American View," *Lloyds Bank Review*, Jan. 1965, p. 6; 1964 figures calculated from data in European Free Trade Association, *EFTA Reporter*, July 19, 1965, p. 3.

[a] Percentage figures are compounded annual rates of increase.

this does not answer the question posed. A. Lamfalussy, in a study completed in 1962,[128] wrestled with the immensely difficult problem of trying to determine why the Six had been doing better than the United Kingdom. He found little evidence that the creation of the Common Market had so far had much to do with the rapid economic growth of the EEC countries. He suggests that the explanation lies largely in the effects of the relatively large exports of the Six (sometimes helped along by undervalued exchange rates) which induced

[128] A. Lamfalussy, *The United Kingdom and the Six,* London, 1963, and "Europe's Progress Due to Common Market?," *Lloyds Bank Review*, Oct. 1961, pp. 1–16.

relatively large capital accumulations leading to rapid increases in production and productivity which, in turn, solidified and strengthened their export position. Since the EEC countries had settled in this happy orbit before the Common Market was formed, he thought that could not be the explanation.[129] He does, however, think that the EEC, especially if it were to include Britain, could help ensure the continuation of this virtuous circle. Others have noted that this analysis underestimates the beneficial effects of integration, because it assumes that the autonomous factors contributing to growth remained unchanged after integration got underway. At least three of the factors that contributed to growth in the countries prior to the formation of the Common Market—ample supplies of labor, large pent-up demands, and readily available technological innovations· not used during the war—were becoming less available by the late 1950's; so, in the absence of the EEC, one might have expected a slow-down in the rate of growth.[130]

A more recent study by Angus Maddison [131] also finds it impossible to quantify the effects of European integration on economic growth or to prove much yet one way or the other, empirically. He concludes that the major part of the explanation for the rapid rate of growth in the EEC countries, apart from pure luck, were the members' fiscal and monetary policies that contributed importantly to the high and stable levels of demand leading to high levels of investment and economic growth; less important were various government policies directly aimed at increasing investment. The relationship of European economic integration, including not only the EEC but the earlier EPU and OEEC arrangements, with those policies and the responsiveness of investment to them he finds have not been, and perhaps never can be, sorted out. Maddison believes, however, that the regionalism enthusiasts often have exaggerated the effects of the integration efforts on the members'

[129] He did not attempt to appraise the significance of the earlier integration efforts, the EPU and the OEEC Trade Liberalization measures.

[130] Balassa, "European Integration, Problems and Issues," *American Economic Review,* May 1963, p. 176.

[131] Angus Maddison, *Economic Growth in the West,* New York, 1964.

growth and that the various efforts since World War II to reduce the intra-European barriers to trade and payments have had only modest effects on members' growth rates. The contributions from the often-vaunted economies of scale and those resulting from greater competition, he thinks, have been minor. Much more important has been that integration reduced the entrepreneurial risks associated with important export markets—by reducing "external deflationary shocks and by the security induced by the feeling that export markets would steadily increase." [132] This strengthened the forces making for buoyant entrepreneurial expectations and so raised the level of investment with the expected effects on productivity and rates of economic growth. He notes that the reduction of trade barriers among the members will come to an end at some stage, so these beneficial effects on growth will have a once-and-for-all effect, but he expects that "integration," in the wider sense of "a new mode of international behavior," should continue to reduce the entrepreneurial risks and so continue to promote high levels of investment.

Accepting this is not to deny—indeed it is to strengthen—the conclusion that even more stimulus to growth might come from a worldwide "integration effort," which may be read "dismantlement of trade and payments barriers." This brings us to the question whether the present regional arrangements are facilitating movement in that direction. Here, too, the evidence today is too slim to warrant much of an answer. Probably the most important conclusion from what has so far happened is that the discriminatory aspects of the new permanent regional groups, especially the Common Market, have led the United States to take a much more energetic role in reducing trade barriers than it otherwise would. This may yet result in such a reduction of trade restrictions around the world as to offset, or more than offset, any adverse static effects of the discrimination on the economic welfare of others.

[132] *Ibid.*, p. 74. The results of tariff negotiations under the General Agreement, and the greatly reduced likelihood of retaliation that the General Agreement makes possible, also contributed to this confidence leading to additional investment.

CHAPTER VI

Discrimination as a Tool for Protection

INTRODUCTION

Any restrictions on trade and payments designed to protect domestic producers, or, for that matter, to bring in revenue, will bear more heavily on some third countries than on others. In recent years it has become commonplace in international economic forums to hear that for reasons of protection the industrialized countries "discriminate" heavily against the less-developed nations.[1] Frequently cited as evidence is the common practice in the former of levying import duties that increase with the degree of processing or transformation of raw materials. In such cases, the effective duty on the economic product actually being produced—the value added—may of course be very high, easily a multiple of the apparent duty. This practice does often bear with special severity on just those exports which many of the less-developed countries see as the most promising in their efforts to industrialize. They are, therefore, a matter of great concern and are relevant to the issues discussed in Chapter VII.[2] But the vast bulk of such "discrimination" (as we use the term) is incidental and does not concern us in this study. That is, those urging such import restrictions usually have as an objective the providing of a deceptive amount of protection to domestic processors against all comers. The restrictions do not have as a policy objective

---

[1] *The Final Act* of the 1964 United Nations Conference on Trade and Development, for example, is permeated with this belief.

[2] See UN *Doc. E/Conf. 46/6*, 14 Feb. 1964, pp. 24–38, prepared by the United Nations Bureau of General Economic Research and Policies for the 1964 United Nations Conference on Trade and Development, for an official report and analysis of several aspects of this problem. See also, UN Doc. *TD/B/AC.1/1*, 23 March 1965; and G. Basevi, "The U.S. Tariff Structure: Estimate of Effective Rates of Protection of U.S. Industries and Industrial Labor," *Review of Economics and Statistics,* (*in press*) 1965.

the making more difficult of imports *because* they come from one region of the world rather than another.

There has been in the post-war years, however, one major and continuing instance of clearcut protection-motivated discrimination by source: the treatment accorded by most countries to imports from Japan. Recently, this has been developing into a formal and generalized policy known as the "market disruption" case for discrimination; it has been extended to selected commodities from many of the less-developed countries. For several years the Japanese case involved complex political and emotional considerations, but underlying these, and dominating the emerging discrimination against the developing countries, has been a desire for protection based on sophisticated variations of the discredited but hardy "cheap" or "exploited" foreign labor arguments.

POLICY TOWARD JAPAN

Political and "Unfair Practices" Issues

The question of policy toward countries under occupation had been reserved for further study when the ITO Charter was being negotiated and when the General Agreement was signed in 1947. The following year, at United States initiative, most of the GATT signatories agreed to grant most-favored-nation treatment to Germany and that country participated in the 1950 round of tariff negotiations at Torquay. Germany formally acceded to the General Agreement soon thereafter. The only serious opposition to this, other than by some of the East European countries which objected to any such "recognition" of the existence of two Germanies, was the fear of many that it might constitute a precedent for Japan.[3]

Indeed, the United States did not hide the fact that it had just this in mind, and took the occasion early to urge other nations to cease the then pervasive discrimination against imports from Japan which had been carried over from the war and pre-war period. The arguments offered were essentially ·the same as

---

[3] This section relies heavily on material in the GATT archives which are not open for direct quotation or citation.

those used when the U.S. had urged them to extend most-favored-nation treatment to German ·exports: Japan was the particular responsibility of the United States and was not then self-supporting, and any discriminatory restrictions imposed by others on Japanese exports therefore meant heavier financial burdens on the United States. More important than this, it was argued, was that it was in the interest of all nations that Japan be self-supporting as soon as possible. If Japan were truly to embrace democratic institutions it must be able to sell enough of its manufactures to pay for the imports of food and raw materials needed not only for subsistence but for a relatively full employment policy. A continuation of the discrimination, for other than the balance of payments reason,[4] against Japanese exports would almost certainly in time result in new political frictions between Japan and those who discriminated against it. It was also said that it was psychologically of great importance to the Japanese, and so to their continued cooperation with the West, that they be treated as well as others. Although not much talked about in the official public discussions, there was also concern lest continued discrimination by others lead Japan, once the American occupation ended, to abandon the policy of sharply curtailing trade with Mainland China and North Korea, countries which had taken about 40 percent of its merchandise exports in the 1934–1936 period.[5] Finally, argued the United States spokesmen, the development of Japanese trade along the lines of comparative advantage could contribute to a general expansion of world trade and to an increase in the economic welfare of all. They reminded others that United States assistance to Japan would decline and that other countries would then pay for their discrimination by fewer exports to Japan.

---

[4] It was accepted that so long as Japan was, in effect, a member of the Dollar Area some nations would continue to apply discriminatory import restrictions on the balance of payments grounds, which were the subject of Chapter II above.

[5] Later events were to demonstrate that Mainland China itself erected many barriers to any great expansion of this trade, reflecting internal demands for the goods Japan was interested in buying, shortages of foreign exchange, strategic considerations, and its autarchic-bent policy.

In 1949 the United States Government formally proposed that the agenda of that year's session of the Contracting Parties include the question of the extension of most-favored-nation treatment to Japan, and in 1950 asked that the issue be discussed. These generated such quick and strong opposition that the proposal was withdrawn, and the issue was not pressed.[6] Several nations in Asia and in Oceania said that the anti-Japanese sentiment in their countries growing out of World War II was still so strong that they were embarrassed by the proposal, that it would be politically most unwise to pursue the question at that time, and that they might have to withdraw from the scheduled round of tariff negotiations if the matter were pressed. The anti-Japanese sentiment was to subside in later years, but the fact that most nations—except the United States—had little political interest in liberalizing trade with Japan, while many of them had great political interest in expanding trade with others, served to perpetuate discrimination.

The political arguments for discrimination were buttressed in 1949 and, increasingly, in the following several years, by reminders that Japan had in the past engaged in "unfair competition" and allegations that it would probably do so in the future. The most frequently cited transgressions were: dumping, exploiting labor, violating copyright laws and patent rights, using false marks of origin, and "sudden flooding" of markets for the purpose of destroying competition. If one accepted that these were to be a hallmark of future Japanese policy, then of course the theoretical and policy case for most-favored-nation treatment was not convincing. The United States and Japan, however, insisted that new laws and institutions had made most unlikely a revival of these practices. This convinced no one for many years.

Low-Wage Issue

It was soon clear, however, that the determination of most nations to discriminate against Japanese goods was not based

[6] See *Department of State Bulletin,* Nov. 21, 1949, p. 776, and July 24, 1950, p. 153, and *The New York Times,* June 17, 1949, p. 17, and Nov. 7, 1950, p. 10.

only on narrow sentimental and political considerations or fear of classic malpractices. Underlying these was the knowledge that Japan was a country with a large and talented population relative to its other factors of production (84 million people in 1950 living on a few mountainous islands with a total area about that of California), that mass emigration was most unlikely, and that Japan must import huge amounts of food and raw materials as well as many manufactured goods if it was to maintain domestic full employment. Japan was therefore seen as almost certain to be a particularly aggressive, international competitor in labor-intensive manufactured goods. The concern was heightened in Britain and Western Europe because many expected and had long believed, but so far as I can determine no one had actually demonstrated, that the known low absolute wage rates in Japan reflected not just low productivity but "exploitation" in the sense of wage payments below the value of labor's marginal output at *going world prices for the goods produced by that labor,* even if not below the value of the marginal product at the prices the Japanese were charging. There was, in sum, a widespread conviction among the policy makers and most of the public that Japan's low wages meant "unfair" competition and constituted a valid reason for restricting imports from her.[7]

Japanese competition was especially feared—even by those who saw no exploitation, who believed that low wages in almost all cases reflected low productivity, and who believed that the low wages were often offset by high capital costs—because it was anticipated it would be concentrated on a relatively few industries: textiles of all kinds, simple clothing, footwear, chinaware, and toys were the ones most often cited in the early years. But these were precisely the industries other nations

---

[7] Irving Kravis has reminded me that any advantage foreigners may have in producing certain goods—superior natural resources, unusually efficient capital markets, etc., etc.—often creates the conviction that foreign competition is unfair and justifies protection. It is, however, only the competitive advantages associated with low absolute wages that has led in recent years to widespread *discrimination*—excepting, of course, those associated with overall balance of payments problems.

were often especially anxious to protect. These were seen by many of the less-developed countries as among the most likely candidates for early growth in their economic development plans. In the already developed countries these were the industries that often were old, relatively inefficient, employing a good bit of labor, and facing relatively slow growing domestic markets. They were the sectors confronting unemployment problems even in the absence of Japanese competition.

Variations on Low-Wage Theme

The Japanese relationship to the GATT early became not only a symbol of Japan's place in the international trading world but also a testing ground of the devotion of others to the principle of nondiscrimination when its short-run costs might be high. It is therefore worthwhile to trace in some detail Japan's efforts to become a regular member of the GATT club.

In the autumn of 1951 many nations signed the peace treaty with Japan. This removed some possible legal complications to its participation in the General Agreement.[8] In addition, an Anglo-Japanese payments agreement had been signed in September 1951. The intention of the accord was that quantitative import controls should be so manipulated as to achieve a broad balance between Japan and the entire Sterling Area, then taking about a third of Japanese merchandise exports. Any balance that did accumulate, however, was to be settled in sterling. This arrangement thus greatly reduced the risk to Britain of dollar drains in its trade with Japan.

At this juncture, the Government of Japan decided to formally ask permission to send an "observer" to the next session of the Contracting Parties. Similar requests from other governments had been treated as routine matters and quickly granted, but many governments opposed this one. The *stated* reasons were that this was in fact the first step in a request for accession and that while all recognized the need for Japan to expand its exports and many were in fact granting it de facto

---

[8] Article 12 of the Peace Treaty obliged Japan to grant, for at least four years, most-favored-nation treatment, as regards customs duties, to any of the allies that granted the same treatment to it.

most-favored-nation treatment, *so far as tariffs were concerned,* they were not prepared formally to commit themselves to continuing this, or even to start doing so with respect to other restraints, until there was more evidence that Japan was not going to follow the same "unfair" commercial policies it had pursued before the war. Britain was the leader of the opposition to Japan's request. It apparently believed that formal Japanese accession would mean that the recent payments arrangement, being officially discriminatory, would have to be abolished; and, among other things, the British feared that if this happened and they were not free to discriminate against Japanese goods, and Japan to discriminate in favor of Sterling Area goods, it would not be possible for the U.K. to offset what it believed to be the tendency for Japan to run deficits with the dollar countries and surpluses with the Sterling Area, with the resulting threat to the latter's hard currency reserves.[9]

The GATT discussions [10] of this Japanese request were largely a rehash of what had been said before. But more specific fears were also just beginning to emerge—they were to

[9] See James E. Meade, *Japan and the General Agreement on Tariffs and Trade,* The University of Adelaide, 1956. (This was reproduced and brought up to date in *The Three Banks Review,* London, June, 1957.) This lecture details the British concern over freer trade with Japan in the decade after World War II.

Except in 1959, the United States has had a surplus on its trade account with Japan in every year since 1945, averaging in 1952–1964 almost $300 million per year. This has, over the same period, been more than offset by direct United States aid, various kinds of United States procurement and military expenditures, and some private long-term capital. Overall, in the period 1952–1964, it is estimated that Japanese receipts from transactions with the United States exceeded payments by an amount averaging about $275 million per year. See Committee for Economic Development, *Japan in the Free World Economy,* April 1963, p. 55, and U.S. Department of Commerce, *Survey of Current Business,* March 1965, p. 15.

[10] Again, the summary records of these were made available to me with the understanding that they would be neither quoted nor cited.

The points made in this paragraph have been elaborated recently by W. S. Hunsberger, in his *Japan and the United States in World Trade,* New York, 1964, pp. 165–69 and 247–50. His analysis has been drawn upon here.

grow stronger in the years to follow, and, apparently, justifiably so for quite a few commodities—that there were strong reasons why Japanese exporters might sometimes cut prices below those traditional economic analysis indicated should obtain. The Japanese were thought often to be more motivated by a desire to maintain or increase market shares than to achieve a short-run maximization of profits. And given all the fringes and the high element of fixed costs attached to wages in Japan, including high severance pay, Japanese firms often had very low average variable costs, so might it not be rational to sell at times at very low prices? And did not the "dual economy" aspect encourage disruptive pricing? [11] Wasn't it true, too, that Japanese exports often were handled by trading companies whose pay was a percentage of gross sales—encouraging what could only be regarded as "cutthroat" pricing? Furthermore, the government policy at times of linking foreign exchange to buy imports, on which high yen profits could be made, with amounts of exports sales could make price policies that seemingly cut into yen profits worthwhile. More generally, many believed that in foreign markets the Japanese, perhaps in response to adverse consumer attitudes to "Made in Japan" labels, had developed a stronger tradition than most other exporters of competing chiefly by price rather than by the many non-price devices others often used to effect the demand schedules for their goods.

[11] Japan had, *in the manufacturing sector,* and to an unusually high degree as compared with other industrialized countries, what was usually referred to as a "dual economy." Some large firms employed a relatively large amount of capital and advance techniques, enjoyed high labor productivity, and paid relatively high wages. Other firms in the same industry were often very small, had a low capital–labor ratio, used old traditional methods, suffered from low labor productivity but paid very low absolute wages, taking advantage of the absence of labor unions and the abundant labor supply from the farms, plus many women. It was commonly asserted by spokesmen for producers in third countries that these small firms could and did charge very low or "disruptive" prices, often concentrating their sales in the less-developed countries, and also exerted downward pressure on wages in the more modern and technically efficient firms.

But in 1951 these justifications for treating imports from Japan differently than imports from other areas were only beginning to be developed and very little was made of them. The opposition by most governments at the time of the Japanese request was still grounded in the simple conviction that Japanese competition—whether "unfair" or not—would be intolerably intense in sectors they wished for domestic reasons to nurture. In the end, the weakness of the case of those who were opposed, weak when measured against the spirit of their commitments under the GATT, and the flagrant discourtesy that refusal would constitute, led to a decision to invite Japan as an "observer." [12] In a move designed to discourage Japan from believing that future full accession would be easy, the invitation was also accompanied by a summary record of the discussions leading to this decision.

Undeterred, nine months later Japan formally asked to join the GATT.[13] In pleading its case Japan cited its great need to export, given its natural endowments and the structure of its economy. Japan noted that it was a member of other world economic organizations—The International Monetary Fund, The World Bank, The Food and Agricultural Organization, among others—and was cooperating with many of the contracting parties in restricting trade in strategic goods with the communist countries. Japan then tried to counter the general arguments against its accession, which had been openly advanced in the previous years. It said that profound changes had taken place since the war in Japanese political, economic, and social life which removed the basis for fears others had that Japan would compete "unfairly," as they believed it had done before the war. Thus, Japan emphasized, labor unions were flourishing, precluding labor "exploitation." Much new social legislation had been passed which substantially increased the

[12] See GATT, *Press Release 53,* 4 Oct. 1951. The strongest opposition came from spokesmen from Britain, France, Australia, New Zealand, South Africa, and the Benelux.

[13] More specifically, Japan asked the contracting parties to enter into tariff and related negotiations with it, with a view to its acceding to the General Agreement.

real wages which had to be paid industrial workers. New laws prohibited the export of articles with false marks of origin, or in violation of copyright or industrial property laws.[14]

There was little here that others could openly challenge, although deep-seated mistrust and suspicion of Japanese business methods remained, especially among the Europeans. Rather than debate the stark protectionist issues, which were actually leading them to discriminate, they now chose to concentrate on the "problems" that would first have to be satisfactorily resolved before Japan could accede to the GATT. Many seized on the fact that the tariff negotiations involved in full membership were immensely difficult and complicated. If Japan were to become a full-fledged contracting party it would be entitled under the most-favored-nation rule to all the reductions of import barriers which the existing contracting parties had already negotiated among themselves. But since these were negotiated when it had not been envisaged that Japan—a major producer of several commodities involved—would accede, there was not only the question of what would be "equivalent" concessions for Japan to give but some nations might find, it was said, that they could no longer tolerate the previously negotiated reductions, which would require renegotiations among the original partners as well. The conclusion of many was that all of this was just too difficult to contemplate managing in a short period of time, especially as no general round of tariff negotiations was then being planned. Since, so far as tariffs were concerned, most of the contracting parties were actually, although not contractually, extending most-favored-nation treatment to Japan, presumably the real worry was that Japan's accession would make more difficult the maintenance of the discriminatory quantitative restrictions against Japanese goods.

Some government spokesmen, mostly from Asia and Oceania, said that the anti-Japanese sentiment amongst their people was still so strong that if they were soon to assume the full obligations of the General Agreement vis-à-vis Japan,

[14] See GATT, *Press Release 82,* 13 Oct. 1952, for an excellent summary of these discussions.

public opinion might be so inflamed that the governments might find it difficult to remain in the GATT. More time was needed to prepare the public for a change in policy affecting something so visible to the public as imports from Japan. Others came closer to the nub of the difficulty when they said that they would need to examine with some care precisely what products it was Japan was likely to develop as future exports and what the present Japanese export prices were of goods that might compete. This, of course, could not be done quickly.

The Matter of "Safeguards"

As was so often done, when an impasse has been reached in the GATT, a working party was set up to make recommendations on the Japanese application. In recognition of the real problem, it was specifically charged with examining the "adequacy" of safeguards provided in the General Agreement against "injury" from imports. This group easily agreed that Japan should "take her rightful place" in the community of trading nations, but it, too, foundered on the critical question of the necessity and desirability of establishing special conditions to Japan's membership. A few members believed no "special" safeguards were needed, but many governments stated again that unless there were specific and adequate safeguards against the "flooding of markets" [15] such as they had suffered from Japan before the war they could not approve Japanese accession. It was agreed that the standard escape clause of the General Agreement (Article XIX) was not adequate to meet the "flooding of markets" problem—if it were indeed a real problem—precisely because it had to be applied in a nondiscriminatory fashion. This meant that if a case could be made for protecting an industry from "cheap" Japanese imports, the invoking nation would also have to restrict imports from all other countries, which she might not "need" or want to do, and which, if done, might lead to retaliation and a further unravelling of commitments to lower trade barriers. Proposals to amend this article and permit unilateral discriminatory action

[15] This was not defined in the available records.

281

were unacceptable to many, on the orthodox grounds used to defend the general policy of nondiscrimination.[16] The anti-dumping provisions of the General Agreement (Article VI) did not cover cases of simply very cheaply produced exports. Some argued that the "nullification and impairment" (Article XXIII) and the "special circumstances" (Article XXVIII) procedures were big enough escape hatches to permit members to defend themselves, but others held that action under these procedures was too slow and uncertain. In the end, the group could reach no agreement on the matter of the adequacy of existing safeguards or need for new ones and retreated to the conclusion that the question of accession should be linked to a new round of tariff negotiations.[17]

But such negotiations were not in early prospect. The United States had just changed to a Republican Administration and was trying to work out a new foreign economic policy; the United Kingdom was preoccupied with the problem of making sterling convertible; and many of the smaller, low-tariff countries wished to delay further tariff negotiations until a solution had been found to the low tariff–high tariff problem.[18] Faced with this, the Japanese, in the fall of 1953, pressed their case again.[19] This time they stressed that the Japanese people were becoming impatient and, in light of the failure to be admitted to the GATT, were beginning to question the Japanese Government's policies of collaborating with the free world in both the economic and political spheres. Inasmuch as a full round of tariff negotiations was not in sight, they specifically proposed that Japan be accorded "provisional accession," pending the next tariff negotiating round, in exchange for Japan's agreeing to bind the duties affecting most of its imports.

Again, a few countries, led by the United States, Germany

[16] As we shall note later, it was being proposed in the mid-1960's that a special escape clause for market disruption be introduced.
[17] See GATT, *Press Release 110*, 14 Feb. 1953, for a detailed summary of this report.
[18] See footnote 101 of Chapter IV.
[19] See GATT, *Press Release 129*, 23 Sept. 1953.

and Canada, strongly supported the Japanese request. All the old arguments were reassembled, particular emphasis being put this time on the general proposition that a satisfactory international trading system could be created only if all those who agreed to abide by the rules were permitted to join. Much more significant, however, was the increasingly explicit assertion that the real issue was that straightforward competition and the goals they had all ascribed to when they acceded to the GATT could not be achieved by ostracizing those who were good at it. But again, others, with the United Kingdom playing a major role, stood in opposition. They, too, repeated all their old arguments, but this time the major thrust of their case was that provisional accession differed little from permanent accession and that, *whether justified or not,* there were in many countries great fears of Japanese competition, fears increased because Mainland China and North Korea were closed to Japan as markets, and if nations committed themselves to granting most-favored-nation treatment they would be much more cautious in the future in lowering their tariffs. Indeed, some might feel obliged to raise them. The consequence of Japanese accession thus could be an appreciably higher level of tariff barriers over the world as a whole than if Japan stayed out of the GATT.[20]

Japan Gains Qualified Admission to GATT Club

Despite these continuing sharp differences, it was by this time tacitly agreed that "something has to be done about Japan." Its request could no longer be simply deferred for further consideration. But it was also clear that there was no routine solution acceptable to a large majority of the contracting parties. In the end, it was decided to separate the matter into two elements. One would deal with the problem of associating Japan with the work of the Contracting Parties, in the sense of participating in its councils and sharing in the administration of its trade rules. The other would be concerned with applying the provisions of

[20] GATT, *Press Releases 130, 131,* and *132,* dated Sept. 25, 24, and 24, 1953, respectively.

the General Agreement to the commercial relations between Japan and other countries.[21] The first was embodied in a "decision" inviting Japan to participate in the sessions of the Contracting Parties.[22] Japan was to have no vote, but this was not important, for formal votes were rarely taken. Although there were some abstentions, including the United Kingdom, Australia, New Zealand, and South Africa, no one voted against this proposal. The second was handled by a "declaration," open for the signature of anyone who wished to sign. This stated that in light of the facts that Japan "should" take its "rightful place in the community of trading nations," that Japan already was granting most-favored-nation tariff treatment to the other contracting parties whether or not it was reciprocated, that Japan wanted to accede to the GATT but that it had not yet been possible for the Contracting Parties to proceed with its application [23]—for all these reasons those who signed this declared that, pending formal accession by Japan and without prejudice to their freedom of action on the question of later full accession, their commercial relations with Japan would be based on the General Agreement.[24] No provision was included for "special safeguards" against Japanese imports, reflecting the continued inability of the Contracting Parties to agree on their need or form, but the report accompanying the "declaration"

[21] See General Agreement on Tariffs and Trade, *Basic Instruments and Selected Documents, Second Supplement,* Geneva, 1954, pp. 117–19.

[22] For text, see *ibid.,* p. 30.

[23] The formal statement implies that the only problem was the fact that no arrangements were in sight for a general round of tariff negotiations. For the text of the declaration, see *ibid.,* pp. 31–32.

[24] Annexed to the "declaration" was a Japanese tariff schedule binding against increase tariffs on items accounting for nearly 85 percent of its imports in 1952. A thoroughly revised tariff had been put into effect in 1951. Many raw materials were admitted duty free; of the dutiable imports, about half the items carried duties of 15 percent or less. Most of the remainder ranged between 15 percent and 50 percent, and were specifically designed to protect selected manufacturing industries. At the time, quantitative restrictions were providing much of the desired shelter and some of the tariffs were later raised when the quantitative barriers were removed. See Hunsberger, *Japan and United States in World Trade,* pp. 138–39.

specifically recognized the right of participants to request that this be reconsidered. Vis-à-vis the countries signing the declaration, Japan now had the same rights and same obligations as if it were a contracting party. In other words, this declaration gave Japan what it had requested in provisional accession except that it applied only to those who signed, not to all the contracting parties.

Less than a year later, in July 1954, Japan again pressed its case and formally asked that tariff negotiations be held with a view to its formally acceding to the GATT.[25] Again, and for the same reasons, the response was divided, but the position of Japan vis-à-vis the GATT was now different. A majority of the contracting parties had signed the "declaration"[26] applying the Agreement; most of them believed that such tariff negotiations should be held and no longer insisted that these would have to be part of a general round of tariff negotiations. Those who remained unwilling to participate said that they did not want to stand in the way of others doing so.[27] Finally, in the spring of 1955, Japan held tariff negotiations with 17 of the contracting parties. Relatively small mutual reductions in duties were agreed upon and Japan, with the approval of all the members, at long last, became a contracting party in September 1955.[28]

But contracting parties which accounted for about 40 percent

[25] GATT, *Doc. L/205,* 6 July 1954.

[26] Twenty-four of the 34 then contracting parties had signed by the summer of 1954. The nonsigners included the United Kingdom, France, the Netherlands, Belgium, Luxembourg, Austria, Australia, New Zealand, and South Africa.

[27] The United States took the position that it was so important that Japan accede that it, the United States, was prepared to consider compensating (via tariff cuts) third countries for concessions that they might grant Japan but for which Japan could not provide adequate compensation, provided: such action by the United States would widen the scope of the whole negotiations, and provided further—as United States law required—that an overall balance was struck between concessions granted and received so far as the United States was concerned. A few such concessions were made and were "paid for" by Japanese concessions to the United States.

[28] This arrangement then superseded that under the "declaration" noted above.

of Japan's exports to the whole group immediately invoked a provision of the General Agreement (Article XXXV), making it nonapplicable to their relations with Japan, including those of their dependent territories.[29] Although this could not have been a surprise, nothing like it had ever happened before.[30] A few of those invoking Article XXXV were discriminating against Japan in their tariffs and in their administration and most of them were discriminating in their application of their quantitative restrictions.[31] Even where the extent of such actual discrimination was relatively mild, those invoking Article XXXV defended their actions on the oft-stated precautionary

[29] The 14 countries taking this action were Australia, Austria, Belgium, Brazil, Cuba, France, Haiti, India, Luxembourg, the Netherlands, New Zealand, the Federation of Rhodesia and Nyasaland, the Union of South Africa, and the United Kingdom.

Since the European Economic Community countries were soon to be committed under the Treaty of Rome (Arts. 110–16) to evolve a common commercial policy, the fact that some EEC members evoked Article XXXV and some did not, was seen as creating an intolerable long-term situation. The Japanese feared the pull would be towards all members following the practices of those who invoked the Article, but others regarded the fact that Germany and Italy were now under international treaty obligations to accord Japan most-favored-nation treatment, although in practice often violated, was likely to work in the direction of making these members' treaty commitments binding on the rest of the Six in the development of a common policy. And so it did in fact turn out to be, with regard to disinvoking Article XXXV. But up to the time of this writing the Community has not been able to agree on other aspects of a common commercial policy towards Japan. As noted below, the proposals being discussed do provide for a "safeguard" clause and/or marketing arrangements which would permit continued discrimination.

[30] India and Pakistan had invoked the clause against South Africa, and Cuba at one time or another had invoked it against 15 countries. See GATT, *Analytical Index of the General Agreement* (revised), Geneva, 1959, pp. 125–26.

[31] Japan continued to grant most-favored-nation treatment to all contracting parties except that it did withhold the tariff concessions granted in the negotiations for accession from those who practiced *tariff* discrimination against it. Japan did continue to apply a good many quantitative restrictions, but I have found no evidence that these, as a matter of policy, were applied in a discriminatory fashion.

grounds that they still feared Japan might resort to "unfair practices" and they therefore wanted to keep their freedom to impose restrictions against it without going through the GATT procedures, which, it was often repeated, did not provide adequate safeguards. As they had done in the immediately preceding years, they often emphasized, in an effort to stimulate support for their position, that they could now protect themselves from Japan's exports if necessary without being required to raise restrictions against similar imports from all other sources, to the detriment of "innocent" third countries.

Japan now stepped up its efforts to get these nations to apply the General Agreement to their trade with it. The Japanese authorities were well aware that nations could and did discriminate against Japan even though they legally recognized the General Agreement as controlling relations between them, Italy being a major example. But the Japanese also believed that discrimination was more difficult and less likely to persist in these circumstances; if it became too serious, Japan could then challenge the practice under established GATT procedures. In the absence of the General Agreement being applicable, Japan had no legal "rights" to nondiscriminatory treatment and so no good platform from which to issue a challenge.[32] Also very important to the Japanese Government were considerations of "respectability" and the strong desire to be accepted as a regular member of the various international organizations. In its efforts to get other countries to disinvoke Article XXXV, Japan now enjoyed an additional measure of support from those countries which had committed themselves not to discriminate against Japan because the existing situation threatened to result in a concentration of Japanese imports in their home markets and in their traditional markets in third countries.[33] Indeed, several

---

[32] All this was to be verified later by a GATT Working Party. See GATT, *Basic Instruments and Selected Documents, Tenth Supplement,* Geneva, 1962, pp. 69–74.

[33] This effect would flow not only from those who actually discriminated but also from those who did not but had not *committed* themselves not to. In the latter case, Japanese exporters were thought likely to be deterred from making any great export efforts lest these prove to have been in vain.

countries said an important consideration in their decision to invoke Article XXXV was their fear that with so many others doing so they would otherwise be subjected to intensified competition.

These new Japanese efforts took two major forms. One was to argue the general merits of Japan's case on the level of both fact and broad principle. The other was to work out particular solutions with particular countries.

Facts Challenged; Principles Stressed and Costs Cited

From 1955 to the time of this writing Japan has placed this item on the agenda at every session of the Contracting Parties and used that occasion to remind everyone that some of them were discriminating against Japan, to reassert that the fears others had of Japan's commercial practices were unjustified and were nothing more than obsessions based on pre-war activities, and to ask for concrete evidence that they were well founded. The Japanese spokesmen regularly challenged others to state "frankly" and "explicitly" their reasons for not agreeing to accord Japan most-favored-nation treatment and to give fuller explanations than merely that there were "undefined political problems" or "psychological" difficulties or "certain aspects of Japanese competition" that were intolerable.[34] The Japanese also took these occasions to repeat to the other Contracting Parties that this situation was contrary to the whole spirit of the General Agreement and tended to discredit it. They seized every opportunity to say to the others that the very foundations of the General Agreement were that exports should originate in the place of lowest cost. It was pointed out that the situation raised difficult internal problems within the GATT. One could argue, for example, that it was not proper for Japan to vote on matters affecting those contracting parties which had invoked

---

[34] See, for example, GATT, *Doc. L/420,* 11 Oct. 1955; GATT, *Press Release 425,* 6 Nov. 1958; and GATT, *Press Release Spec. (59) 226,* 27 Oct. 1959.

Although I have seen no documentary evidence of this, presumably the Japanese have also similarly used every occasion provided by their membership since 1964 in the OECD.

Article XXXV, but that if Japan did not, it would be excluded from most GATT affairs, for at least one of the contracting parties was usually involved. In 1960, and again in 1964, the Japanese emphasized that since Japan could not negotiate on tariffs with those who had invoked Article XXXV the scope of the possible tariff cuts resulting from the Dillon Round and Kennedy Round, respectively, would be reduced. As the years went by they also reminded everyone that no complaints of unfair or illegal practices had been successfully lodged against them in the GATT.

In 1960 Japan varied its attack a bit and asked the Contracting Parties formally to review the situation, especially from the point of view of its harmful effects on the then approaching tariff negotiations (Dillon Round), on the administration of the General Agreement, and on the "spirit" of the GATT.[35] The subsequent report [36] found that in fact only a few countries were applying straightforward tariff discrimination against Japan, but that Japan's trade was being subjected to a vast variety of "special" (discriminatory) treatment involving both trade and financial quantitative restrictions, and a wide range of such administrative devices as health and market regulations, anti-dumping restrictions, customs delays, marking requirements. Although this was *not* limited to nations that had invoked Article XXXV, it was concluded that the Japanese were correct in believing that the fact of invoking Article XXXV was of importance, because when it was not invoked the restrictions were subject to the control and remedial provisions of the General Agreement, and this fact had some restraining influence.

The report noted that although Japanese trade had increased a great deal in recent years [37] the atmosphere of uncertainty

[35] GATT, *Doc. L/1391*, 29 Nov. 1960.

[36] GATT, *Basic Instruments and Selected Documents, Tenth Supplement*, pp. 69–74. See also, GATT, *Doc. L/1531*, 22 Aug. 1961, for a GATT Secretariat report on the treatment given Japan's exports by the contracting parties.

[37] The value of Japanese exports increased by an annual average of nearly 15 percent during the period 1950–1963.

created by the lack of contractional relations with many states did have an inhibitive effect on Japanese exports, and so on Japan's imports, and thus was of concern to all trading nations. They also found that the "situation" probably did serve to reduce the amount of tariff reduction in the world. First, Japan itself was less likely to negotiate reductions with such countries. Second, the tendency of Japanese exports to concentrate on the markets of countries with which Japan had contractual trade relations made it more difficult for the latter to reduce further their tariffs on these products. Although not spelled out in detail, the report made clear that the discriminatory restrictions applied by others against Japan were contrary to the spirit of the GATT and did increase the problems of administering it.

It was becoming embarrassingly clear that within the GATT principles there was little defense to be made of the discriminatory practices, even ignoring, as some governments were wont to do in these discussions, the drastic changes that had been taking place in Japan's economy and the great reshuffling of comparative advantages and so patterns of exports that had taken place as it had become a major financial and industrial power.[38] But late 1961 was judged too soon for any drastic changes in well-established policies, and the Contracting Parties' recommendations were weak, limited to asserting that it would be to the advantage of all if ways could be found to disinvoke Article XXXV and if new nations acceding to the GATT, and on whose behalf the article had formally been invoked by the metropolitan governments, considered the matter on its merits and did not simply "inherit" the discrimination policy.[39] When many of these new countries did examine the

---

[38] For a lengthy analysis of the changes in the pattern of Japan's foreign trade, see Hunsberger, *Japan and the United States in World Trade,* Chaps. 5–7.

[39] GATT, Art. XXVI, 5(c), provides that upon achieving autonomy a former territory has the *right* to become a contracting party, if this is requested by the former Metropole, under the terms and conditions previously accepted by the latter on behalf of the former. Consequently, if the mother country had invoked Article XXXV it would continue to apply to the new state *unless* it were expressly disinvoked by her.

question on its merits they found value in starting life with the right to discriminate against Japan. This might give them some bargaining counters in future tariff negotiations, or in negotiating contracts for sales of their raw materials, that they might not otherwise have had. Then, too, they often simply did not have the personnel to examine the problem with care and so took the easy way out and adopted the practices of their former mother governments. Furthermore, as noted earlier, the new nations were often particularly anxious not to face competition from Japan; they thought it would be especially severe on many of the new industries they wished to encourage. Their fears were often of the competition not of the large, relatively highly capitalized enterprises which had flourished after 1950 but of the many, small nonunionized firms in what was called the "dual economy" of Japan—firms employing many women workers, and men in transit from rural to urban areas, at very low wages. It was assumed that these workers were being exploited, although there seems to have been little systematic evidence accumulated to support this.

Following this major re-examination, the entire question, at Japanese request, continued to remain on the agenda of the Contracting Parties' periodic sessions. Each time, Japan restated its case. Increasingly, the others resorted to the defense that Japan, too, still imposed many import restrictions, though generally not *discriminatory* ones, against them and that until it liberalized its import policy they were not going to change theirs.[40]

---

[40] Although many of its important industries (textiles, shipbuilding, machinery, etc.) are heavily dependent on foreign markets, and the nation's merchandise exports have equalled about 10 percent of GNP since 1950, Japan has shown a marked reluctance to permit foreigners to compete in the Japanese manufacturing market. Japan's "average" tariff is not greatly out of line with those of Western Europe and the U.S. It has relatively low, or zero, duties on its large imports of noncompeting raw materials and food stuffs. But the tariffs on manufactured goods tend to run above those in Western Europe and the United States, reflecting not only the protective motives found in all countries but also the absence of a strong tradition of competition as a determinant of productive patterns and the belief, increasingly hard to defend in the

Although there is no way of measuring it, these periodic confrontations probably did have some effect on others' policies. At least the records of the sessions show that the discriminating governments found it increasingly difficult to

---

mid-1960's, that Japan was, at most, a "semi-developed" country with many legitimate infant industries. This was the reason Japan advanced for submitting in November 1964 one of the longest lists of "exceptions" to the across-the-board tariff cuts in connection with the Kennedy Round.

Like most nations, Japan emerged from World War II with a comprehensive and complex set of quantitative restrictions on trade and payments, and during the post-war years it lagged far behind the developed countries in relaxing them. It was not until February 1963 that Japan accepted the obligations of GATT Art. XI, prohibiting the use of quantitative restrictions for balance of payments purposes, and not until April 1964 did it accept the obligations of Art. VIII of the International Monetary Fund and agreed not to apply exchange restrictions to current transactions. It is still too early to tell whether some of Japan's impressive increases in domestic production in some of the new heavy industries can readily survive the removal of this shelter, but it did accompany a relaxation of quantitative restrictions in the early 1960's with tariff increases on competitive imports, leading, of course, to compensatory renegotiations.

Japan defended its long and continued reliance on quantitative controls primarily on the grounds that, being so dependent on imports, it had to have machinery to keep out "non-essentials," and on the further grounds that its payments position was particularly precarious, as indeed it was just after the war. Still, Japan had in fact had during the 1950's and early 1960's only three relatively minor payment crises (1954, 1957, and 1961), each growing out of its extremely rapid internal expansion. In the event, swift and sharp restrictive action by the monetary authorities quickly corrected these situations, primarily via the restraining effect on inventory accumulation, longer-term investments, prices and domestic consumption of exportables. (See Jerome B. Cohen, in *The New Japan: Prospects and Promise,* Princeton University Conference, 1963, p. 76; and Organization for Economic Cooperation and Development, *Economic Surveys by the OECD, Japan,* Paris, July 1964, p. 29.) Indeed, the distinctive feature of Japan's experience in the eyes of most observers was not that it had some payments problems in boom times, but that it was able to meet them by internal measures without seriously braking its long-term growth. This was possible chiefly because the growth was associated not only with generating a demand for more imports but with increased productivity, which was stimulating exports.

In 1959 the Japanese adopted a policy of removing their quantitative

justify their policies and took much pride and pleasure when they could announce some amelioration in them.

Some Pragmatic Solutions: "Sensitive" Goods and "Voluntary" Export Restraints

More effective than the GATT confrontation and justification technique was the second approach used by Japan: a continuing series of bilateral discussions aimed at convincing others that "intolerable" competition was likely in only a few cases, and then working out "solutions" to these cases. The emphasis here was not on matters of worldwide interest or general principles but rather on trying to isolate the *particular* problems as seen by *particular* countries, and then taking action to overcome them.[41]

The formula that was evolved over the next decade did lead to the disinvoking of Article XXXV by all the major free world trading countries, but it did not mean that discrimination for protective purposes had been effectively proscribed.[42] Indeed,

---

restrictions and, à la OEEC, calculated a "liberalization percentage." This had reached a 93 percent level by mid-1964 (items making up 93 percent of Japan's imports in 1959 were not subject to quantitative import restrictions) but it was not a very significant calculation for it was based on the goods Japan imported in 1959 and its industrial good imports in that year did not include many that were seriously competitive with domestic production. The Government of Japan has successfully resisted some pressure within itself for a policy of relaxing these quantitative restrictions on a discriminatory basis as a bargaining device to get others to remove their discrimination against Japanese goods. The controlling concern here seems to have been a wish not to emasculate Japan's moral and legal case, and doubts that it would be successful anyway.

[41] GATT, *Press Release 255*, 20 Nov. 1955.

This approach received new encouragement in the spring of 1955, when the United Kingdom Government issued a short white paper defending its policy of invoking Article XXXV. The essence of their case was that they did not want legally to commit themselves to nondiscrimination in the absence of greater assurances than they yet had that the Japanese competition in the future would be "fair." *The Economist*, London, April 23, 1955, pp. 315–16.

[42] Although in mid-1965 there were nearly 30 contracting parties invoking Art. XXXV, together they accounted for less than five percent of world trade. Except for Austria and Portugal, they were all less-developed countries and all but these two, and Haiti and South Africa,

it may have fathered what could prove to be an even more invidious form of discrimination.

Details on most of the bilateral agreements entered into by Japan are not available, but particular attention was given to the negotiations with the United Kingdom. The U.K.'s market was important; it was thought to have much influence on the trade policy of the other Commonwealth countries and former colonies that were becoming independent. Moreover, as we have seen, it had been the United Kingdom which over the years had been the most articulate leader of those holding that Japan had in the past and might easily again indulge in unfair commercial practices and therefore others must not deny themselves the right to discriminate against Japan. Finally, effective in the spring of 1963, and following seven years of negotiations, a six-year Anglo-Japanese Treaty of Commerce, Establishment, and Navigation was signed. Britain thereupon removed many of its previous import quota restrictions and disinvoked Article XXXV. Australia, with merchandise exports to Japan running well over double its imports, followed suit in July. At about the same time, the earlier commercial agreements with Benelux were amended and an agreement was signed with France, following which some import quotas were removed or relaxed and each also agreed that the General Agreement should control its commercial relations with Japan.

But the price for this was not cheap. The most-favored-

---

had "inherited" the policy. Known to be included in the countries still invoking Art. XXXV were the Cameroons, the Central African Republic, Chad, the Congo (Brazzaville), Cyprus, Dahomey, Gabon, the Ivory Coast, Jamaica, Kenya, Kuwait, Madagascar, Mauritania, Niger, Nigeria, Senegal, Sierra Leone, Tanganyika, Togo, Trinidad, Tobago, Uganda, and the Upper Volta.

Japan has continued its bilateral efforts with many of these nations and has warned that it would be difficult for it to extend to these countries any tariff cuts that it may make in the Kennedy Round. Japan also gave notice that it would not apply to any country invoking Art. XXXV against it the provisions of the new GATT chapter on "Trade and Development." This chapter was specifically designed in 1964 to increase the commitments of the more-developed nations to provide larger markets for the exports of the less-developed ones.

nation commitments which they undertook in disinvoking Article XXXV were qualified and the principle of "orderly marketing" was endorsed. Thus, the agreements included a general "safeguard clause" in the form of a blanket authorization permitting either party (normally after consultations) to restrict imports when its market was threatened with being disrupted, this condition not being defined in advance. Perhaps even more important were the protocols in which, in the British case, for example, were listed over 60 "sensitive" goods, with provisions for adding others. On some of these it was agreed that Britain would continue to impose quantitative restrictions, although these were to be made progressively more liberal and to disappear by 1968. On others, however, the Japanese agreed to impose "voluntary" export controls—with no specific commitments as to termination. The other treaties differed in detail but were comparable in their major substantive provisions.[43] That a pattern of continued discrimination for protective purposes was being set was indicated by the fact that, although the European Economic Community has made little progress to date in establishing a common commercial policy vis-à-vis Japan (in part because of the differing extent among the six of their discrimination against Japanese goods [44]), the proposals so

[43] United Kingdom Board of Trade, *Board of Trade Journal,* London, Nov. 23, 1962, pp. 1,050–51. *The Economist,* London, Aug. 18, 1962, p. 642; Nov. 10, 1962, p. 593; Nov. 17, 1962, p. 705, and April 27, 1963, p. 359; and International Monetary Fund, *International Financial News Survey,* May 24, 1963, p. 184.

[44] The members of the Common Market have been reducing their "negative list" (quantitative restrictions) on imports from Japan but they still remain substantial. The following number of items, entire or partial tariff headings, in 1962 and 1964, respectively, were on such negative lists: Germany, 105, 72; Benelux, 96, 71; France, 500, 176; Italy, 410, 152. (European Economic Community, *Bulletin of the EEC,* Sept.–Oct. 1964, p. 11.) Although not explicitly stated in this source, it is implied and it was made explicit in UN, *Doc. E/Conf. 46/6,* 14 Feb. 1964, pp. 40–45 (this document has been reproduced in *Proceedings of United Nations Conference on Trade and Development,* Vol. IV, United Nations, New York, 1964, pp. 15–18), that far fewer restrictions were applied by each on trade with other West European and North American countries.

far under serious discussion all include a "general safeguard clause," as well as provisions for an agreed list of "sensitive" goods to be subjected to special quantitative restrictions.[45]

The "voluntary" export restrictions, a device the Japanese had occasionally used in the late 1930's, had been rediscovered, with a hefty assist from the United States, in the mid-1950's and had quickly become widespread.[46] By the mid-1960's Japan reportedly had such agreements with at least 20 countries, including, among others, the United States, Benelux, Canada, Switzerland, Germany, Denmark, Australia, and New Zealand. The device, apart from the International Textiles Arrangement discussed below, had also been used by a few other countries: Pakistan, Hong Kong, and India at least had agreed to voluntarily restrict some of their exports to the United Kingdom. The most important commodities affected were various kinds of textiles and clothing, but other commodities were sometimes included. The latter were usually trivial items in terms of world trade: wood screws, clinical thermometers, stainless steel flatware, combs, china and glassware, some kinds of leather goods, plywood, plastic buttons, etc.[47]

The specific arrangements for such voluntary restrictions were complex and varied and an examination of their details, many of which have not been published, is beyond the scope of this study.[48] Sometimes, as we have just noted, they were incorporated in formal trade agreements between governments. Sometimes, in response to government representation, the Government of Japan worked out arrangements with its busi-

[45] European Economic Community, *Bulletin of the EEC,* Sept.–Oct. 1964, pp. 11–12.

[46] United States Tariff Commission, *Post-War Developments in Japan's Foreign Trade,* Washington, D.C., 1958, pp. 43–49; and U.S. Department of State, *Department of State Bulletin,* June 4, 1956, pp. 921–22.

[47] For the only extensive study of this which I have found, and one which covers the situation at the beginning of the decade, see GATT, *Doc. L/1164,* 17 May 1960.

[48] Hunsberger, *Japan and the United States in World Trade,* pp. 322–23, gives some details.

nessmen;[49] and sometimes they were understandings or agreements between businessmen in the different countries with little or no formal government participation.

The core of this "orderly marketing system," as it was often euphemistically called, was that the Japanese agreed, subject to frequent changes, to limit to agreed amounts, to minimum prices,[50] to minimum standards of quality, or to some combination of all these, their exports of specified goods to specified markets. In return, they asked that the importing countries desist from any other discriminatory practices against these exports and, in general, otherwise extend most-favored-nation treatment to Japan.[51]

[49] This was the case in the deals between Japan and the United States, where "in deference to the strong desires of the United States Government" the Japanese Government "urged the Japanese textile people to restrict their exports to the United States voluntarily." Statement of Japanese Ambassador Asakai, in *The New Japan: Prospects and Promise,* Princeton University Conference, Nov. 1962, p. 38. United States antitrust laws probably prohibited direct deals between American and Japanese businessmen.

[50] Although such minimum price agreements were usually designed to meet the complaint of "price cutting" in the importing countries, they were sometimes welcomed by the Japanese; if foreign demand was not met because of quantitative restrictions being enforced, limiting price competition among Japanese exporters permitted higher profits.

[51] In some cases, Japan was motivated less by a desire to stop existing discrimination against itself than in making a calculated move to prevent what it feared might be even more severe restrictions imposed unilaterally by the importing country, even on a nondiscriminatory basis. This seems to have been the main consideration in the 1955–1956 voluntary quotas imposed on certain cotton textile exports to the United States. Japan was reportedly only trying to recapture its pre-war, 2 percent share of the United States consumption of cotton textiles, but their export drive concentrated on a few lines—ginghams, velveteen fabrics, pillow cases, and blouses and skirts were among the more important. By 1955 they had captured half of the American velveteen market. This led to an escape clause application to the U.S. Tariff Commission to find that serious damage was being caused U.S. producers—which it later did. Voluntary quotas soon followed, limiting exports not only of velveteens but also of ginghams, cotton blouses, as well as certain cotton fabrics. Later, the system was extended to no less

The case for this intrinsically discriminatory commercial policy device was largely pragmatic. It worked, at least in the short-run. Arrangements could be agreed upon quite quickly and they did in fact quiet some of the fears in the importing countries, thus preventing what might well have been much greater increases in trade barriers. They were also defended on the grounds that their future removal would be easier than unilaterally imposed or retained import quotas—usually regarded as the only immediate actual alternative—because in the former case those imposing them had an ever-present incentive to remove them. It was also argued that the arrangements were less damaging to international comity and less likely to lead to retaliation than the latter because they were discussed and negotiated. Finally, the fact that these agreements did not legally violate GATT rules, while the likely alternative would, were also seen by many as a point in their favor.[52]

But the device had many shortcomings. The basic ones were that it grossly violated the general liberal trade commitments of all the parties involved and did this by reintroducing quantitative restrictions, and this at a time when, as we saw in Chapter II, efforts to remove the earlier ones were bearing fruit. Furthermore, the arrangements were bilateral, worked out behind the scenes, and so not subject to established international procedures of review, control, and complaint designed to protect the interest of third countries as well as participants.[53] There were also defects on less lofty grounds. Since they were "voluntary" they provided less assurances for the future than some of the importing countries wished if they were to bind themselves legally and formally to extend most-favored-nation

---

than 23 goods, accounting for about a fifth of U.S. imports from Japan and ranging from woolen fabrics to paper cups to canned tuna. See GATT, *Doc. L/1164, Annex C,* 17 May 1960.

[52] For more detailed discussion of the case for and against voluntary quotas, see Hunsberger, *Japan and the United States in World Trade,* pp. 354–60.

[53] Thus, Japan was not entitled to compensatory concessions as it often would have been under normal GATT procedures. Another defect of the device is its tendency to strengthen cartel-like organizations in exporting countries.

treatment to Japan. They were, often via trans-shipments, subject to widespread evasion. Much more serious was the fact that in the early years they were largely restricted to Japan, so not only did it therefore find them inequitable, but their effectiveness was cut because any drop in exports of the affected goods by Japan was often filled, or more than filled, by exports from other low-cost suppliers. Thus, the 1955 and later agreements by which Japan voluntarily agreed to restrict exports to the United States of many cotton textiles did result in a freeze in its exports, but those from India, Hong Kong, Pakistan, Portugal, and Spain in particular so increased that total cotton textile imports as a percentage of total United States consumption increased threefold between 1955 and 1960: from two percent to about six percent of domestic consumption.[54]

The United States Government—prompted by concern over these defects, by its continuing interest in an expansion of world trade and in having Japan a full member of the GATT; by its worry lest some countries (Germany was a major instance) find new reasons for retaining their so-called balance of payments quantitative import restrictions; and, by no means least, by the great upsurge in protectionist sentiment in the United States stimulated by the rapid increase in U.S. imports of Japanese goods [55]—in 1959 officially proposed that the Contracting Parties underwrite a study aimed at finding an acceptable multilateral solution to the problem of "sharp increases in imports, over a brief period of time and in a narrow range of commodities [which] can have serious economic, political and social repercussions in the importing countries. The problem is to find the means to ameliorate the adverse effects of an abrupt invasion of established markets while continuing to provide steadily enlarged opportunities for trade." [56] Thus was the

[54] Cohen, in *The New Japan: Prospects and Promise*, p. 75.

[55] The imports had increased from about $250 million per year in the early 1950's to over one billion dollars in 1959—a rate of increase faster than that of total imports, than growth in United States national income, and than growth in total world trade.

[56] Speech by Undersecretary of State Douglas Dillon, reproduced in GATT, *Press Release Spec.* (59) 222, 27 October 1959.

concept of "market disruption"—a handmaiden of discrimination—formally introduced.

AVOIDANCE OF MARKET DISRUPTION POLICY EMERGES

The reaction at the time was confused. Some governments favored the proposal to set up a panel of experts to examine the problem because they believed that some kind of internationally agreed upon safeguards would facilitate an expansion of trade, especially if they resulted in a decline in the bilateral voluntary export quota and import quota restrictions. Some developed countries liked the proposal because they believed it might provide a new international sanction for import restrictions against so-called low-wage imports. Some of the official spokesmen for less-developed countries disliked it for the same reasons, while others were attracted to it by the hope that it might focus on the ways to bring about the "steadily enlarged opportunities for trade" that Dillon had mentioned.

Part of the uncertainties seem, in retrospect, to have stemmed from the fact that many sensed the problem was, or soon was to be, different, and very likely, much more important than they had been assuming. Up to this time, concern over low-cost imports was largely centered on imports from Japan and on a relatively few, traditional, light manufactured goods: textiles, clothing, china, and similar items being much the most important, which were produced with labor-intensive methods and at hourly wages which were low compared with those in the industrially advanced countries. This permitted, it was alleged, the price cutting on exports and the resultant invasion of foreign markets, which was encouraged by Japanese traditions and Japan's particular institutional arrangements, sketched on pp. 277–78.

By 1959–1960, however, it was becoming apparent that phenomenal changes had been taking place in Japan, shortly to be epitomized by its joining that select "Western" industrial group, the Organization for Economic Cooperation and Development, and becoming a lender under the General Arrangement to Borrow. Japan's real gross national product had grown by some 125 percent during the 1950's and the annual rate in 1959 was the highest of the period. By the end of the 1950's it had become a major industrial power. Japan was by then the world's largest shipbuilder, its second largest producer of ball-bearings, cameras, radios and television sets, and the fourth largest producer of machine tools, pharmaceuticals, and iron and steel. Japan's rapid economic growth was resulting in shortages of many kinds of labor, wage rates were being pushed up rapidly and to the point where some of the traditional low-wage, low-productivity goods were less and less attractive to the Japanese entrepreneurs. The "dual economy" structure of Japan's economy was slowly disappearing in the face of this. Such industries as textiles, chinaware, paper products, toys, rubber and cork products—partly in response to these market forces and partly as a consequence of deliberate calculations by private entrepreneurs and the government—were expanding at a relatively slow rate, while many heavy and chemical industries, and industries producing high-quality and sophisticated light goods, were growing more rapidly. As a result, the composition of Japanese exports was becoming increasingly diverse and was beginning to shift away from the old worrisome light manufactures and toward high-quality sophisticated consumer goods, heavy machinery, transportation equipment, and chemical products. Thus, the share of textiles in Japanese total commodity exports fell from 34 percent in 1954 to 23 in 1960 and 19 in 1962, pottery and glassware fell from 2.7 percent to 2.3 to 1.8, while the category industrial machinery, transport and electrical equipment soared from 12 percent to 23 to 25.[57]

But if Japan was showing signs of developing in ways that would make it a more traditional or orthodox competitor and so less subject to discriminatory treatment for reasons of protec-

---

[57] For recent accounts of the Japanese economic "miracle," see Organization for Economic Cooperation and Development (Economic Surveys by the OECD), *Japan,* Paris, 1964; *The Economist,* London, Sept. 1, 8, 1962; and Hunsberger, *Japan and the United States in World Trade.* Chap. 6 of the last source gives much detailed data on the changing composition of Japanese exports. See also, W. W. Lockwood, "Japan's 'New Capitalism,'" in W. W. Lockwood, ed., *The State and Economic Enterprise in Modern Japan,* Princeton, 1965, Chap. 10.

tion, *for the present* it remained a most vigorous one in the so-called low-wage imports. After all, with the value of total merchandise exports increasing at an average of nearly 15 percent per year, compounded, between 1950 and 1963 the absolute level of Japan's exports of such goods as textiles, cutlery, pottery, footwear, and similar light industrial products was increasing even if the relative level was declining. Many governments therefore still believed that it was necessary to "do something."

From the point of view of our concern, much more important than the sense that the problem presented by Japan might become less serious was that the attempts in 1959–1960 to formalize the concept of market disruption brought into the open the growing belief, especially among the officials of the European Economic Community, that the problem could be a very big one in the future because it might involve several exports from most of the less-developed countries. The thesis was advanced that it was, and would continue to be, the typical case for countries undertaking economic development programs to tend to concentrate in the early years on a few selected sectors. In these sectors would be introduced the most advanced technologies and capital equipment. Local labor often could and would be trained to the point where its physical productivity approached or even equalled that of labor in the more advanced countries. But in the developing countries the wage rates and standards of living in the much larger traditional sectors (primarily agriculture and raw materials) would be very low, reflecting low productivity there. In this situation, the modernized manufacturing sectors would "inherit" low wages, *permitting,* for a more or less lengthy period, the charging of prices for goods produced in the very efficient modern sector which would be substantially below the cost in the already advanced countries.[58] It was feared that the less-developed countries would be encouraged to take advantage of this opportunity because of their great need to expand exports and their belief that as newcomers they would have to offer

[58] Those concerned with the problems of the less-developed countries were more often concerned about the opposite problem: the tendency of high productivity in the modern sectors to lead to wages which were

302

substantial price advantages if they were to establish themselves in foreign markets. This was precisely what most of the developed countries would regard as "unfair and disruptive."

The issues involved were clearly too complex to be resolved quickly, so in 1959 the matter was put on the agenda for the next year's GATT session and the Secretariat was asked to prepare a factual report on market disruption. Mr. Wyndham White asked all contracting parties to report on whether they had experienced "market disruption," if so what they had done about it, and if their exports had been treated as disruptive by others. He found [59] that many countries,[60] by a variety of devices—tariffs, import quotas, anti-dumping duties, internal taxes, exchange manipulations, voluntary export quotas, and a host of administrative measures—were taking measures to keep out imports which they feared might otherwise "disrupt" their markets. Textiles were much the most important of the goods

---

much higher than in the traditional sector, resulting in a movement of workers from rural areas to cities far in excess of employment possibilities at those wages, pulling up wages in other export sectors to the point where production had to be cut back, and of encouraging "excessive" capital-intensive production in the modern sector. (See Sir W. Arthur Lewis, "Unemployment in the Developing Areas," in *Proceedings of the Third Biennial Midwest Conference on Underdeveloped Areas,* Chicago, 1965, for recent development of this thesis.) It is, of course, quite possible for a less-developed country to find itself in the worst of all worlds. This would be when the wages in the modern sector are high enough to have the undesirable consequences noted in this footnote but low enough to permit export at prices sufficiently below those in the advanced countries to lead them to impose import barriers on market disruption grounds.

[59] GATT, *Doc. L/1164, Add. 1,* 17 May 1960.

[60] The United States, the United Kingdom, France, the Netherlands, Germany, Belgium, Luxembourg, Italy, Austria, Switzerland, Norway, Denmark, Sweden, Finland, Canada, Australia, South Africa, Haiti, Cuba, Rhodesia, and Nyasaland acknowledged they had taken restrictive action against what they regarded as disruptive imports. It was known that there were others. Several countries reported that they were applying GATT Art. XXXV to Japan and so did not feel "obligated" to report; others said they had no market disruption action to report because "safeguards" were being provided via import restrictions still being applied for balance of payments reasons.

affected, but restrictions had also been applied to a long list of industrial products, including various types of clothing, stainless steel flatware, china and glassware, clinical thermometers, aluminum foil, plywood, plastic buttons, leather goods, electric batteries, wood screws, iron pipe fittings, transistor radios, and umbrellas, among others. Japan was the exporter involved in the great majority of cited cases, with Hong Kong and some of the eastern European countries, especially Poland, Hungary, and East Germany occasionally listed as the villain by the importers. Of the free world less-developed countries, only India and Pakistan, and they only in connection with textiles and clothing, were singled out in this report as the occasional source of disruptive imports. It is important to record here that, except for some textiles and clothing items, very little concrete evidence was provided which showed that there had in fact been much in the way of massive invasion of markets by the low-wage countries. Rather, the report showed that most of the measures had been taken because of apprehensions, or simply because the governments of the importing countries wished to protect certain domestic producers from almost all severe foreign competition.

Nonetheless, most of the contracting parties agreed that the fact of apprehension was enought to create a problem and so another GATT Working Party was established to consider the issue and to suggest an acceptable multilateral solution which would reduce this discrimination. This group made no progress in reaching agreement on the substantive issues: how to distinguish between "normal" competition and "real market disruption"; was the latter likely to be important; and, if it occurred, how best to deal with it? The conflict of interest between Japan and the less-developed countries on the one hand and the advanced, Western industrial countries on the other, and indeed, increasingly between Japan and the less-developed countries, was acute. The Working Party reported [61] in November 1960 there was a problem known as "market disruption," that its existence should be recognized, that there

[61] GATT, *Basic Instruments and Selected Documents, Ninth Supplement,* Geneva, 1961, pp. 106–10.

were "political and psychological elements in it," and that unless some new "safeguards" were found, nations would not abandon the "exceptional" measures they were then taking. Their specific recommendations were limited merely to proposing that the search for solutions go on and that procedures be established to facilitate multilateral consultations when incidents of alleged market disruption arose and when bilateral settlements could not be reached or would raise difficulties for other countries.

In an effort to push the issue toward some fuller resolution, the Executive Secretary of the GATT, Mr. Wyndham White, then drafted a definition of market disruption and some proposals for beginning to deal with it. The Working Party itself was not able to agree on these, but it forwarded them on to the Contracting Parties. The latter, in plenary session, formally approved them. Many governments were not happy, believing a solution was still to be found, but one more step had been taken in the formalization of a new justification for a discriminatory commercial policy.

The significantly titled "Avoidance of Market Disruption" decision stated that market disruptions situations do occur, or threaten to occur, and they "generally contain the following elements in combination: (i) a sharp and substantial increase or potential increase of imports of particular products from particular sources; (ii) these products are offered at prices which are substantially below those prevailing for similar goods of comparable quality in the market of the importing country; (iii) there is serious damage to domestic producers or threat thereof; (iv) the price differentials referred to in (ii) above do not arise from governmental intervention in the fixing or formation of prices or from dumping practices." [62]

Inevitably left undefined were the critically important adjec-

---

[62] GATT, *Basic Instruments and Selected Documents, Ninth Supplement*, pp. 26–28. Point iv was intended to restrict the concept to goods sold at low prices because of cost factors alone; that is, disruption for which countervailing or anti-dumping duties were not generally applicable. This clause also was intended to exclude problems arising from imports from state-controlled economies.

tives: "sharp," "substantially below," and "serious damage."
Nor was it settled whether all the three elements must exist in
each case, or whether "generally" modifies "in combination."
Involved here, of course, was the central substantive issue: just
how severe must the competition from less-developed countries
be before special restrictions are to be internationally sanctioned, when such competition is based on comparative advantages stemming from low labor costs per unit of output because
of the circumstances outlined on page 302 above?

Although the real beginning of the answer was to be given
later in the practices followed under the cotton textile arrangements, discussed below, the governments did agree at this time
that the objective in market disruption situations was to find
solutions "consistent with the basic aims of the General Agreement." In support of this, a permanent Committee on the
Avoidance of Market Disruption was created, its function being
to continue to search for "constructive solutions" and to
facilitate future consultations when market disruption was
alleged to have occurred. It was recognized at the time that the
device of a committee for consultation was a weak one. Other
parts of the "decision," in effect, left the matter pretty much to
bilateral discussion and the Committee had no authority to force
changes in members' policies, or even to insist that multilateral
discussions be held. Moreover, it was foreseen that those who
maintained discrimination against low-wage imports would for
that very reason suffer no market disruption and would therefore have no occasion to bring a case to the Committee. Still, it
was hoped that the fact of a standing international committee to
consider cases of market disruption might encourage some to
relax their restrictions, simply because its existence might give
them some safeguards in the event they suffered as a consequence of their liberalizing action. Up to mid-1965 no one had
asked the Committee to do anything, except help plan a still
incompleted GATT–ILO study,[63] and it has taken no initiative

[63] The GATT Secretariat, in cooperation with the International Labor
Organization, was asked in the 1960 decision to prepare a report on "the
various economic, social and commercial factors underlying the problems" and, in particular, "the relevance to international trade of

in searching for solutions. It was bypassed in the first major internationally negotiated market disruption arrangements.

FIRST FORMALIZED MARKET DISRUPTION AGREEMENT: COTTON TEXTILES ARRANGEMENT

The willingness in the early 1960's of many governments to disinvoke Article XXXV of the General Agreement vis-à-vis Japan and to assume even the extensively modified nondiscriminatory obligations which we have discussed earlier in this chapter, followed the negotiation of an international arrangement on trade in cotton textiles which gave international blessing to countries keeping "disrupting" imports of these goods out of their markets. As we have seen, textiles, especially cotton textiles, had been by far the most important single apprehension-creator among Japanese exports. The problem was exacerbated for the industrialized countries because domestic demands were growing relatively slowly and textile

---

differences in the costs of various factors of production and marketing, including labor costs." The first such study was to be on the textile and clothing industry, but it ran into great difficulties because of the lack of enthusiasm of many governments for it and the failure, or inability, of many of them to supply the needed information. It seems to have been put permanently on the shelf. See GATT, *Docs. L/1500*, 2 June 1961; *L/1900*, 8 Nov. 1962; *L/2135*, 27 Feb. 1964.

Using the data that had been furnished, together with other material, the staff of the International Labor Organization did publish a study in early 1963, in *International Labor Review*, Geneva, Jan. 1963, entitled "Trade, Wages and Employment in Textiles." This study concluded that the problem of the textile industries in the advanced, high-wage countries have many sources and "cannot be primarily attributed to the alleged unfairness of competition from low-wage underdeveloped countries." (p. 28). They found that, except for the United States, textiles imports in the industrially advanced countries still come predominantly—usually over 80 percent—from other industrially advanced countries. They also concluded that in the less-developed countries (the evidence was less clear in the case of Japan) the wages of textile workers were not "unfairly" low as compared with other wages in those countries. In another study, Hunsberger concluded that costs of production of textiles in Japan was less favorable to it than most had assumed. See his *Japan and the United States in World Trade*, pp. 295–304.

production in the less-developed areas had not only increased rapidly but these countries often used the newest and most efficient machinery and methods.[64] This meant not only that in the latter were markets for foreign supplies decreasing, but also that competition facing the traditional producers in third markets and at home was increasing.[65] The voluntary bilateral export restrictions arrangements that had been negotiated with Japan could therefore easily be, and often were, nullified by increased imports from other sources. As we noted earlier, to help meet this problem the governments of a few industrialized countries had by the late 1950's negotiated bilateral agreements with several major cotton textile-producing countries, in addition to Japan, setting limits to exports by them. Thus, for example, in 1958–1959 the United Kingdom had negotiated such agreements with Hong Kong, India, and Pakistan, as well as with Japan. The United States had some kind of an accord with Hong Kong,[66] and Denmark was reported to have agreements with various East Asian and Eastern European Countries. Earlier, in 1956, the cotton textile producers, in what were to be European Economic Community member states, and Austria and Switzerland had formed the so-called Club of Noordwijk whose main purpose was to stop re-exportation to each other of finished goods processed from "abnormally low priced" gray fabrics imported from Asian sources.[67] A year later, a group of experts set up by the OEEC Council had recommended that negotiations be held between the European countries and the

[64] See Organization for Economic Cooperation and Development, *Modern Cotton Industry,* Part II, Paris, 1965.

[65] This was acutely reflected in the fact that the quantity of *Japanese* exports of cotton cloth to Africa and Latin America in 1962 were little more than half the 1934–1936 average and only a third the earlier average for exports to Asia, despite the great increases in the economic size of these markets. See Hunsberger, *Japan and the United States in World Trade,* p. 281.

[66] An exception to the general practice of restricting these agreements to Japan and the less-developed countries was the "undertaking" by Italy in 1957 to restrict its exports of velveteen to the United States. See U.S. Department of State, *Department of State Bulletin,* Feb. 11, 1957, p. 220.   [67] UN, *Doc. E/Conf. 46/6,* p. 51.

appropriate Asiatic countries, looking toward arrangements that would "make it possible to avoid grave perturbations being caused" by "unregulated" and "excessive" imports.[68]

In mid-1961, against the background of these moves and the market disruption decisions and discussions of the previous year, the United States Government formally proposed that the whole problem of trade in cotton textiles be considered in the GATT, "with a view to reaching agreement on arrangements for the orderly development of the trade in such products, so as progressively to increase the export possibilities of the less-developed countries and territories and of Japan, while at the same time avoiding disruptive conditions in import markets." [69] This American action reflected several concerns. One was the recognition of the "need" for growing markets for these goods in the less-developed countries, as well as Japan. Another was worry lest—in the absence of an agreement among both the major importers and exporters—the bilateral accords that had been negotiated prove ineffective and the burden of adjustment to larger exports be concentrated on only a few of the importing countries, notably, of course, the United States. A major force back of the move was that the newly-installed Kennedy Administration had decided to ask Congress for new and much more liberal foreign trade legislation; it was believed that unless arrangements could be made satisfying the domestic cotton industry, very active politically in favoring higher import barriers, that the new legislation would not increase their problems, the chances were poor of obtaining Congressional approval of it.[70]

[68] OEEC, *Report of a Group of Experts, The Future of the European Cotton Industry,* Paris, 1957, p. 24.

[69] GATT, *The Activities of GATT, 1961/1962,* Geneva, 1962, p. 29.

[70] The domestic cotton textile industry had a very potent argument for "special" import barriers stemming from the two-price U.S. cotton system, under which foreign mills could buy United States raw cotton at prices subsidized by the U.S. Government. This meant that their raw material costs at that time were often 8¢ a pound below those of the United States mills. At one stage, the Executive Branch proposed that relief be given to the American textile industry by putting an "equalization fee" of 8½¢ a pound on imports of cotton textiles, to offset or

There were several reasons why the exporting countries were willing to negotiate an agreement controlling .trade in cotton textiles. They hoped that one result might be an appreciable increase in their access to *European* markets. They wanted the United States to adopt new trade legislation. Most importantly, they feared that unless something was worked out in an international forum, the U.S. and others might unilaterally impose even more stringent import quotas on their exports. They also hoped that by insisting on provisions for periodic review under GATT auspices they could introduce a liberalizing influence.

In mid-1961 a short-term (one year) cotton textile agreement was quickly negotiated in Geneva.[71] A few months later a long-term (five years from October 1, 1962) accord was reached by 19 countries, and several others have since signed.[72] This "Long Term Arrangement Regarding International

---

eliminate the then price differential. This was strongly opposed by the Japanese and other purchasers of American cotton, who threatened that if it was imposed they would reconsider their practice of buying so much American raw cotton. This threat to U.S. exports was effective; the tax was not levied. Moreover, several countries had threatened in the 1961–1962 negotiations not to sign the cotton textiles arrangement if the U.S. were to apply some form of one-price cotton policy.

In April 1964, however, "one-price cotton" legislation was passed, under which American textile producers using American cotton were given a payment equal to the export subsidy ($5\frac{3}{4}¢$ per pound in 1965). This, of course, greatly strengthened their ability to compete with imports, and the *quantity* of cotton textile imports by the United States fell about seven percent in the second year of the cotton textile arrangement; the value of imports fell only slightly from the previous year because of price and qualitative changes. (GATT, *Doc. L/2360,* 26 Feb. 1965.)

For a record of the respectable, as well as nonrespectable, arguments for raising U.S. barriers to textile imports, see the testimony of industry representatives in U.S. Senate, Committee on Interstate and Foreign Commerce, *Problems of the Domestic Textile Industry, Hearings,* 58th Cong., 2nd Sess., 1958 (Pastore Subcommittee).

[71] For the text, see GATT, *Basic Instruments and Selected Documents, Tenth Supplement,* Geneva, 1962, pp. 18–23.

[72] See General Agreement on Tariffs and Trade, *Basic Instruments and Selected Documents, Eleventh Supplement,* Geneva, 1963, pp. 25–41. The signatories, as of mid-1965, having a substantial interest in

Trade in Cotton Textiles" specifically incorporated the concept and definition of market disruption discussed in the preceding section and embodied two major operating provisions. First, those importing participants who still maintained import restrictions other than duties undertook to progressively relax them and to expand the access to their markets. It was specified that for items then subjected to direct import controls, not less than the following percentage increases over 1962 would be reached by 1967 by the following countries: Austria, 95 percent; Denmark, 15; the European Economic Community, 88; Norway, 15; Sweden, 15. The high percentages for the EEC and Austria reflected such low levels of quotas in 1962 that some exporters regarded even the new commitment as bordering on fraud.[73] Second, in cases where a participating importing country was not imposing nontariff import restrictions, it was authorized (Article 3), after consultation, to limit imports of specified cotton textile goods which it found were disrupting or threatening to disrupt its markets. This may take the form of "export restraints" by the exporter or, if this cannot be agreed to, the importer may "decline to accept" imports above the level of the preceding year. However, this level is to be increased by five percent for each additional year the restrictions remain in force, except that the increase can be set aside for the first additional year. Although it was formally stated that resort to this provision should be "strictly limited" to cases where market disruption, as earlier defined by the Contracting Parties, existed

---

controlling imports were: Australia, Austria, Belgium, Canada, Denmark, Finland, France, Germany, Italy, Luxembourg, the Netherlands, Norway, Sweden, the United Kingdom, and the United States. Those signatories primarily interested in expanding their exports were: Nationalist China, Colombia, India, Israel, Jamaica, Japan, Mexico, Pakistan, Portugal, Spain, Hong Kong, Korea, the United Arab Republic, Yugoslavia, Greece, Turkey, and the Philippines.

[73] The United States did not itself apply quantitative restrictions and so did not come within these provisions. The United Kingdom and Canada were exempted from this requirement specifically to increase access to their markets on the grounds, that they had already experienced a "substantial contraction" in their domestic cotton textile industry and already were importing a "substantial volume" of cotton textiles from Japan and the less-developed countries.

or threatened, the determination of the existence of this state of affairs was left in fact entirely in the hands of the importing countries. Moreover, it did not even require the sort of due process that typically is required for invoking the standard escape clause.[74] The sting of this is lessened by the agreement (Article 4) also providing that this new machinery need not be used at all and that members can continue to work out on a bilateral basis "mutually acceptable arrangements on other terms" so long as they are consistent with the general objectives of the Arrangement.

This Arrangement, specifically condoning discrimination against selected low-cost producers of textiles, modified and extended in several ways the emerging policy of avoiding market disruption. On the one hand it specifically recognized that international action should be designed to enlarge the opportunities of the less-developed countries to export manufactured goods and that importing nations should be enjoined not to reduce trade below the level of a defined preceding period. It also provided for an annual review, under international (GATT) auspices, of activity under the accord. On the other hand, it gave the importing country the unilateral right to determine when disruption was taking place and to impose import restraints. It also accepted that a "market" or "goods" may be defined in very narrow, rather than broad, terms. These elaborations thus permitted almost anything; the extent of discrimination under the accord was to depend on how it was actually implemented.

The recorded experience during the first two and a half years —up to the time of this writing—proved most discouraging to those who had hoped that this would be a device leading to more liberal policies than a protectionist-sensitive world might otherwise manage, more liberal because market disruption would in practice be interpreted to mean a good bit more than just tough competition; because the importing nations would

[74] The Arrangement has provisions designed to avoid circumvention of the accord by trans-shipment and substitution of directly competitive textiles. Also, those importing participants who do restrain imports for market disruption reasons agree to take measures to insure that imports from nonparticipants do not frustrate the agreements.

take seriously and would honor their implicit and explicit obligations regularly and significantly to enlarge any quotas and to facilitate the movement of resources out of these areas in their own countries; and because effective international supervision would be exercised over the arrangements. After only a few months of operation spokesmen for the less-developed exporting countries, and to a lesser extent Japan, reported "very serious misgivings" about the way in which the whole thing was working out, and after two years some of the best-informed observers, whose frame of reference was the welfare of the entire trading community, believed that a serious "searching of conscience" by the importing countries was in order.[75]

Under one provision or another of the Arrangement, including bilateral agreements with countries which had not signed the pact, Germany had successfully "requested" restrictions on exports from Hong Kong; Canada from Greece, Japan, Hong Kong, Israel, Macao, Portugal, and Taiwan; Norway from Hong Kong; The United Kingdom on exports from Hong Kong, India, Pakistan, The Irish Republic, Japan, Malaysia, Portugal, Yugoslavia, Spain, and Taiwan, as well as under other arrangements limiting imports of cotton textiles from most of the East European countries; the United States, sometimes it was said by using "strong-arm tactics," from Japan, Taiwan, Jamaica, Spain, Argentina, Brazil, Poland, Trinidad, the U.S.S.R., India, Israel, Pakistan, Mexico, Colombia, Greece, Turkey, the Philippines, Portugal, Yugoslavia, the United Arab Republic, and Hong Kong. And there were no doubt others.[76] This does not, of course, give a full measure of the extent of the

[75] See GATT, *Docs. L/2135,* 27 Feb. 1964, and *L/2360,* 26 Feb. 1965.

[76] Looked at from another point of view, as of mid-1965, cotton textile exports from the following countries, and there may have been more, were being restrained under various kinds of agreements: Argentina, Brazil, Colombia, Formosa, Greece, Hong Kong, India, Israel, Italy, Japan, Jamaica, Korea, Malaysia, Macao, Mexico, Pakistan, the Philippines, Poland, Portugal, Spain, Trinidad and Togo, Turkey, the United Arab Republic, and Yugoslavia. Several of these were not parties to the long-term Arrangement, reflecting the efforts that were being made to prevent the accord being frustrated by shipments from nonmembers. GATT, *Docs. L/2135,* 27 Feb. 1964, and *L/2360,* 26 Feb. 1965.

restrictions being applied, since many nations—especially in Western Europe—were still applying earlier import quotas and so there had been no need for them to ask others to restrain their exports or to impose new import restraints under the Arrangement.

Spokesmen for the exporting countries often said that the accord had become a virtual charter of restrictions. They charged that in alleging market disruption the importing countries had often regarded as a cause for such a finding *any* adverse change in domestic production, not a sharp and substantial increase of imports *compared* to domestic production. They also alleged that the importing nations regarded even very small price differentials as "substantial" and had not adequately taken qualitative differences into account in comparing imports and domestic prices. It was charged that some, including the United States, seemed to have abandoned altogether the criteria of market disruption set out in the official decision and had substituted a simple statistical standard: any increase above the base year was "disruptive" and warranted action curtailing imports. The less-developed countries also found that the importing countries often had established so many categories of textiles, each subject to a base period quota, as to cut the total well below what the former had assumed when they had signed the agreement. Moreover, the exporting countries were increasingly distressed over the fact that there was no due process procedure for invoking the market disruption criteria. Beyond this, there was growing concern over the possible precedent-setting role of the arrangements, even though the text of the Arrangement had specified that the measures "are not to be considered as lending themselves to application in other fields." [77]

[77] In the United States the wool textile industry had been urging a similar arrangement for their products, but to date the Administration seems to have been unresponsive, in part probably because such an agreement was thought not likely to be negotiable. To satisfy the American wool textile industry, such an agreement would have to extend to imports of West European producers, as well as Japan and some of the less-developed countries, and preliminary "soundings" had indicated

The exporting countries tried in GATT meetings in late 1963 and early 1964 to amend the agreement by, among other things, establishing more objective and strict criteria for determining the fact of market disruption. Specified minimum price differentials, minimum ratios of imports to domestic production, minimum categorization, etc., were suggested. But these were successfully opposed by the importing countries which relied chiefly on the argument that it was too early to make changes because there was not yet enough experience on how the scheme was working out.[78]

A year later, these demands were repeated, but in somewhat more muted terms, because it had been agreed that a major review would take place at the end of the third year, and there were bits of evidence that some of the importing countries had taken to heart the noted criticisms and were making more sparing use of restraint actions.[79] Several of the spokesmen for

---

that the European countries probably would insist on compensating concessions, or the withdrawal of earlier tariff concessions in favor of United States exports, if the U.S. restricted imports of wool textiles.

[78] The importing countries have sometimes complained that the exporters have not always lived up to their export restraint commitments, but by and large, the importers have had little ground for complaint in the operations of the accord.

[79] See, for example, the United States statement in U.S. Department of State, *Department of State Bulletin,* Jan. 11, 1965, pp. 49–56.

Several countries have noted that the slightly more liberal policies in 1964 by the United States—the father of this cotton textiles arrangement—did not mean what they seemed to mean, because its position had greatly changed as a result of the 1964 one-price cotton legislation (see footnote 70 above). This latter move had quickly led to increased employment, profits, and investment in the American industry. (See *The New York Times,* May 5, 1965, p. 69, for glowing accounts by industry representatives on the benefits of the one-price cotton law.)

Official United States spokesmen did not accept the conclusion of others that merely permitting American textile producers to buy U.S.-grown cotton at the same prices as it was offered to foreign mills removed the need for market disruption safeguards—although two-price cotton had been their most effective argument for instituting the safeguards in the first place. Moreover, as we have noted, at the time the Long-Term Arrangement was being negotiated several had threatened not to sign if the U.S. applied a one-price cotton policy.

the less-developed countries, however, took some pains to point out that it most certainly could not be taken for granted that the Arrangement, as it then was, could be renewed and that they expected trade in textiles to benefit from cuts in import restrictions during the Kennedy Round.

Actual trade flows under the Arrangement up to the time of this writing were regarded as disappointing by the less-developed countries. They believed the accord had not, in its own words, adequately provided "larger opportunities [to the developing countries] for increasing their exchange earnings from the sale in world markets of products which they can efficiently manufacture." Far from complete data on actual trade are available but, measured in metric tons, the imports of cotton yarn and fabrics by OECD Europe, the United States, and Canada from the rest of the world in 1963 were only about four percent greater than they had averaged in 1960–1961. Substantially larger percentages were recorded, however, if 1959 was chosen as the base year; it may be that when value data are available they will show larger increases, reflecting the tendency of yardage quotas to upgrade the quality of goods traded.[80] Still, the experience has been too short to draw any firm conclusions from these scrappy data. In any event, as the exporting nations have acknowledged, it may well be that in the absence of the Arrangement, unilateral restrictive actions by the importing countries would have restrained trade even more.

Of particular interest to the exporting nations in the late 1964 and early 1965 GATT discussions was the extent to which the importing countries were making the structural adjustments which would make the Arrangement unnecessary.[81] There was a consensus that the Arrangement would have failed if it led to no structural changes, but it was quickly apparent that there were sharply conflicting views as to the nature of the desirable adjustments. To the less-developed countries adjustment in the developed importing countries meant transferring resources out

[80] OECD, *Modern Cotton Industry,* Paris, 1965, pp. 45, 51.

[81] GATT, *Doc. L/2360,* 26 Feb. 1965. Again, I have also benefited from reading the nonattributable records of the Plenary Sessions of the Contracting Parties in Geneva in March 1965.

of cotton textile production into other areas entirely. But to most of the developed countries adjustment did not mean getting out of the textile business so that the less-developed countries could move in. Instead, the importing countries believed the Arrangement could only be regarded as successful if it served to encourage and speed up such structural adjustments as were required to enable the domestic cotton textile industry in the developed countries to flourish.

The national policies and actions of the industry itself are at the time of this writing still being formed, and I have not attempted a careful study of the matter. Such information as was easily found indicates that in Western Europe and the United States the intense competition that had developed after the war, together with the medium-term security against it offered by the International Cotton Textile Arrangement and other national protective measures, has operated much more in the direction of stimulating efforts to increase productivity in the industry—largely through making it more capital-intensive—than in encouraging the transfer of resources to other sectors altogether.[82] If this results either in such low costs as to make the current special restraints unnecessary even from the producer's point of view, or so increases productive capacity as to strengthen the demands for continued protection, perhaps at levels somewhat below those now prevailing, the less-developed countries will conclude that the textile Arrangement has been a cruel hoax. If it is the latter, most observers would have to agree.

CONCLUSIONS

The practices and the policies of the rest of the world toward Japan in the two decades following the end of World War II built up a substantial amount of case law precedent and hazily qualified international approval for the use of discriminatory measures for sheer protectionist purposes when the competition was severe, was associated with low wages, and was concentrated on relatively slow growing, labor-intensive domestic

[82] See especially, OECD, *Modern Cotton Industry,* Part III.

industries. This was one of the more unsavory chapters in post-war international commercial policy.

By the mid-1960's Japan's economic structure had so changed that one could anticipate it would soon no longer be the important object of such discrimination. Before this happened, however, not only had such insidious discriminatory devices as "voluntary" export controls been added to the arsenals of many governments and the notion of "orderly marketing arrangements" been gaining much favor, but the many shortcomings of the bilateral arrangements that had been made with Japan to effect this discrimination had led to an attempt to deal with the problem on a multilateral basis. Unfortunately, from the point of view of those favoring freer trade, this coincided with the growing recognition that throughout the vast "third world," conditions might well be emerging which would duplicate some of those earlier found so bothersome by others in Japan: wage rates throughout the economy being held down by low productivity in the traditional sectors, combined with pockets of high productivity in the modern sectors, permitting the selling of large quantities of labor-intensive and relatively simple manufactures at prices well below those previously prevailing in foreign markets.

The upshot of the efforts to cope with a difficult current problem—but one that was receding—and an anticipated one, was to give formal international respectability to trade restraints designed to avoid unusually severe competition based on low costs. This was defended primarily on the grounds that it would be less restrictive to trade and less costly to economic efficiency than the next actual alternatives: maintaining or increasing the widespread unilateral or bilateral restrictions. This may well be so; one can only guess as to what otherwise would have been. But it is worth noting that this came at a time when other discrimination against Japan and the less-developed countries was decreasing, be it ever so slowly. More important is the fact that the spirit and the mood of the international community was that the then existing discrimination against low-wage imports was "wrong." The new concept tended to make it "right."

Some of the support at government levels for the avoidance of market disruption doctrine came from those who simply wished to protect their inefficient domestic industries. Charity demands that it be assumed that support of the policy by some rested on the argument that an exception to the policy of encouraging trade to flow from low-cost to high-cost areas was justified if the cost conditions in the low-cost areas (a) were likely to be importantly modified—in an upward direction—within a reasonably short period of time, and so, in the absence of trade intervention, the extent of adjustment called for in importing countries would be excessive; and/or (b) were such that unless restrained the increase in imports would be so great as to create intolerable domestic political problems, and possibly a degree of adjustment and relocation of resources that was more costly in terms of unemployment than a more gradual one would be.

Satisfying these defensible concerns while not abusing them depends on the specific definition given to such components of the market disruption concept as that the increase in imports must be "sharp and substantial," that the imports must be offered at the prices which are "substantially" below those prevailing, that "serious" damage be caused or threatened domestic producers. The only experience, to date, in defining these critical adjectives, and the equally critical noun "producer," has been in the measures actually taken under the long-term international textile Arrangement.

Despite many misgivings, this scheme was accepted by the governments of many of the less-developed countries, primarily because they were convinced that the alternative was likely to be extremely severe, unilaterally imposed restrictions on their exports. They were attracted, too, by the fact that this proposal did specifically recognize that international action taken under it should be designed to enlarge their opportunities to export manufactured goods. But the Arrangement also gave the importing countries the unilateral right to determine if their markets were being disrupted and, if so, to impose quantitative import restrictions or ask for export quotas by the exporter. To expect countries given this freedom to act in a restrained manner was asking too much; during the first year most of the importing countries so abused their rights and the less-developed countries were as a consequence so dissatisfied with the way the scheme was being implemented and the precedents being set, that the idea of sanctioned discrimination to avoid market disruption seemed on the way to being thoroughly discredited. The scanty evidence available at the time of this writing suggests that in the year and a half since then the importing countries have relaxed their restraints somewhat. This tempered, but by no means stilled, complaints by the developing nations.[83]

Is this the end or just the beginning of a major chapter in discriminatory commercial policy? Some believe that cotton textiles are likely to be the only products which will qualify for market disruption treatment at this time. This may be the case. One could be reasonably confident that it were so only after having made a detailed examination of costs, as well as demand conditions, for a wide range of goods, and made specific assumptions as to what would be regarded as sharp increases in imports and substantial differences in price. I cannot make such a study. It is possible, however, to identify the major characteristics of the factor inputs, the products, and the markets which could easily give rise to unusually sharp and rapid increases in imports from less-developed countries having the noted modern–traditional sector dichotomies.[84]

First of all, the labor costs must represent a substantial proportion of total costs even under modern production tech-

[83] Presumably in an effort to salvage the concept, some European governments in late 1963 and early 1964 tentatively and informally proposed that the GATT be amended by establishing a new "escape clause" which would be tied to the market disruption definition of the Contracting Parties, but which would at least require that a country invoking it would have to justify its action, genuinely consult with the affected countries, and progressively relax the restrictions and suspend them by a certain time. This would clearly be an improvement over the cotton textile arrangements from the less-developed countries' point of view, but up to mid-1965 the proposal has not been pressed.

[84] The following paragraphs have drawn on some unpublished work by Clifford Goldman and Henry Gassner.

niques; the greater the proportion the greater will be the advantage of the less-developed countries. Furthermore, the necessary skills must be easily and quickly acquired; otherwise, there is not likely to be a rapid increase in competition. The good must be one in the production of which external economies are relatively unimportant, for such economies are less widespread in the less-developed countries than in the developed ones. The product itself should also be one not subject to frequent style changes, for which quality variations are relatively small, and for which the price elasticity of demand in the importing country is high and the income elasticity of demand in the exporting country low. The good should, further, be one for which brand names are normally not important and one for which extensive servicing arrangements are not needed. It is probably also necessary that several of the developed countries already have a domestic industry, otherwise they could not move quickly and substantially into the export markets. Market disruption is most likely to occur in the industrialized importing country if demand for the good there is relatively stagnant, if the industry has a labor force which is immobile and a physical capital stock specific to the particular function. Finally, and perhaps the most critical aspect of all is whether, for policy purposes, the domestic industry is defined narrowly or broadly; the narrower it is, the greater the probability that any given increase in imports will create serious damage.

A cursory examination of the GATT 1963 "Comprehensive List of Products of Importance in the Export Trade of Less Developed Countries" [85] leads me to the tentative, and entirely intuitively derived, conclusion that there are no other goods on this list comparable to cotton textiles in the degree to which they possess the above characteristics. But that list will grow, especially in the area of less complex types of intermediate goods. Even now there are several on it—woolen textiles, leather and leather manufactures, cutlery, linoleum, many wood and cork manufactures, rugs and carpets, footwear, and various

[85] GATT, *Doc., Com. III/105,* 25 March 1963.

electrical appliances are the most important ones—which have already been the subject of pleas for protection in many developed countries. There is, therefore, a serious risk that the recent international sanctioning of measures to avoid market disruption from low-cost imports will trigger new restrictions as the less-developed countries move ahead in their industrialization plans unless action is taken soon to define the criteria more severely than they have so far been defined in practice under the cotton textile Arrangement.

The formal endorsement of the "avoidance of market disruption" concept—that it is proper to keep out imports from certain countries because they are low cost—may have prevented something worse. But that should not blind us to the fact that official international credibility has been given to that great and ancient enemy of freer trade: the idea that low wages abroad justify special restrictions on imports. Ironically, the efforts to create new safeguards against "market disrupting" imports from the less-developed countries probably will take on new urgency if the latter succeed in their efforts to incorporate into the world trading system a scheme of systematic discrimination by the developed countries in favor of the manufactured exports of the less-developed ones. It is to this nettlesome problem that we now turn.

CHAPTER VII

Discrimination to Facilitate Economic Development

INTRODUCTION

FAIRLY late in the negotiations for the ITO Charter, a serious effort was made by some of the less-developed countries to incorporate wide authority for all manner of discriminatory practices, if these were intended to foster economic development.[1] Led by the United States, and resting on their pre-war orthodox arguments against discrimination, many of the industrialized nations opposed anything short of customs unions or free trade areas. The pressure was great, however, and in the end, Article XV was accepted, providing that new preferences could be granted "in the interest of the programs of economic development or reconstruction of one or more of [the parties]." This was subject, however, to formidable obstacles: territories of the countries included must be contiguous or within the same economic region; each preference on each good by each member must be found by the Organization to be "necessary to ensure a sound and adequate market" for a particular developing industry; if the Organization found such a preference was likely to jeopardize the trade position of others, "mutually satisfactory understandings" must be reached; and the permission was to be limited to an initial 10 years, with five-year renewals. The Article was not included, however, in the General Agreement. This was not a matter of conscious policy but simply because it was in the "Economic Development and Reconstruction" rather than the "Commercial Policy" Chapter of the Havana Charter, and only the latter was regarded as

[1] Portions of this chapter first appeared in my article, "Would Tariff Preferences Help Economic Development?" *Lloyds Bank Review,* April 1965. Permission to include that material here has been given by the editor, Mr. J. R. Winton.

necessary to protect the value of the tariff concessions which had just been negotiated in 1948, and which then constituted the General Agreement.

As it turned out, the General Agreement was not absorbed into the ITO as had been planned; during the 1954–1955 general review session of the GATT, Chile proposed that Article XV be incorporated in the General Agreement. This received little support from others and was strongly opposed by several governments,[2] reflecting the prevalent mood of those years which, as we have seen in Chapters II and III, was that at long last conditions were emerging which would make possible a sharp decrease in discriminatory and preferential practices.

But as the growth of regional economic organizations accelerated and provided new respectability to discrimination, as widespread agreement was reached among those formulating policy that economic development meant diversification and industrialization, it came as no surprise that discrimination— short of that involved in customs unions and free trade areas— should again be proposed as a conscious policy for facilitating economic growth in the less-developed countries. And, as the richer nations gradually accepted that it was their responsibility to help the poorer ones, it was to be expected that the emphasis should be on preferences from the developed to the less-developed rather than merely among the latter.[3]

EARLY POST-WAR PRECEDENTS

Early in the post-war period modest precedents of a sort were being established.[4] At the second session of the Con-

[2] See GATT, *Basic Instruments and Selected Documents, Third Supplement,* Geneva, 1955, p. 208.

[3] Less-developed countries, or "developing countries," as it has become the fashion to call them, were usually defined to mean all the world except North America, the European Economic Community, the countries making up the European Free Trade Association, Finland, Iceland, Ireland, Eastern Europe, and Japan. Usually Australia, New Zealand, and South Africa were also included in the "developed," though not "industrialized," category. Israel, Greece, Turkey, Yugoslavia, Spain, and Portugal were usually, but not always, included in the less-developed country list.

[4] It can be argued that the various pre-war metropole–overseas

tracting Parties to the General Agreement in 1948 the United States asked permission (a waiver of its nondiscrimination commitments) to accord preferential, duty-free, treatment to all imports from those Pacific islands formerly under Japanese mandate which the United States was administering under the United Nations Trusteeship system.[5] The justification was cast primarily in political terms: the islands' exports had been accorded preferential treatment by Japan; to deprive them of something like equivalent treatment in the United States would hardly be in keeping with the spirit of the United Nations and the responsibilities of the Allies as victors. The request also carried, although only implicitly, the seeds of the economic development argument that the objective of the proposed preferential access to the markets of a rich country was to help these poor islands enlarge their export earnings, a necessary condition for improving their economic welfare.[6]

Many contracting parties were worried that such a breach in the principle of nondiscrimination and of no new preferences would set a "dangerous" precedent, but the request was granted on the grounds of "exceptional circumstances" and because the United States was not seeking preferential treatment for its exports in the islands—as Japan previously had enjoyed. Approval was also made easier because it was believed that the export possibilities of the islands were so poor that other countries were not likely to be seriously hurt by the discrimination. The Contracting Parties, however, specifically reserved the right to review the waiver if at any time the preferences were found to be injurious to the trade of others.[7] Apparently no request for such a review has yet been made, the United States

---

territories relationships constituted precedents. They were, however, little drawn upon for guidance in the post-war period, apparently because their *raison d'être* included much more than the economic development of the overseas area and because they were part of a political relationship which was soon to go out of fashion.

[5] These were the Marshall, Caroline, and Marianas Islands, except Guam.

[6] See GATT, *Doc. CT2/36*, 7 Sept. 1948.

[7] See GATT, *Basic Instruments and Selected Documents*, Vol. II, Geneva, 1952, pp. 9–10.

having granted preferences only on coconut oil and copra, and the amount of trade involved having been very small.

Three years later, Italy requested a similar waiver of its most-favored-nation obligations, in order that it might continue to grant preferential treatment (duty-free entry, usually up to specified quotas) to some 50-odd specified products which Italy was then importing from Libya. As a former colony, Libya had been granted preferential treatment for its exports in Italy. Libya was now about to become an independent state; during this critical period it would face serious economic difficulties if it were abruptly to lose its preferences in its major export market. Italy also maintained that the amount of trade involved was so small—except for olive oil and some oil seeds, it was measured in only a few percentage points of total Italian imports of those goods—that no one else would be materially hurt by continuing the preferences. The waiver was initially granted for only one year, reflecting the concern of some countries over still another rupture in the nondiscriminatory rule, and was justified on the grounds that it was merely permitting the continuation of a practice that previously existed and was not likely to hurt third countries.[8] In the discussions surrounding the periodic extensions of the waiver, which have continued to date, and the periodic reports that Libya and Italy were required to make, more and more prominence has been given to the argument that this was an effective and desirable way for a rich country to help a poor one. It was argued by both parties that Libya was a very poor nation trying to improve the welfare of its people, that it was necessary to increase its export earnings if it were to be able to obtain needed imports for the hoped-for economic development, that Libya's costs often were too high to permit it to compete on world markets, and that Libya therefore needed preferential treatment. Little explanation was given as to why Libyan costs were high; it was not argued that they would later fall because of the larger market being provided. Italy said it was willing to pay a higher

[8] General Agreement on Tariffs and Trade, *Basic Instruments and Selected Documents*, Vol. II, pp. 10–11.

price for its expected imports from Libya, than if it had bought them from other sources, as a contribution to the economic growth of a former colony.

Both Italy and Libya have subsequently and regularly asserted in the GATT that the waiver was having a favorable effect on Libyan exports to Italy, on Libya's balance of payments position, and on its economic development, although almost nothing of what a skeptic would consider proof has been presented. However, the twin facts that for most of the affected goods Libya has supplied only a very small portion of the Italian imports (and so the price paid by Italy for goods exempted from duty presumably has not for this reason fallen), and that the duties to date have typically ranged between 20 and 40 percent ad valorem means that preferences could be a device in this case for significant transfers from Italy to Libya.[9]

That the waiver had not seriously harmed others is indicated by the lack of complaints and by the fact that on the average over the last several years imports by Italy from Libya of all the affected goods, taken together, have accounted for less than 2 percent of Italian imports of these commodities; this percentage has tended to fall as total Italian imports increased. Often the tariff quotas granted Libya have not been filled, reflecting supply limitations, due in part, apparently, to the failure of the Libyans to make systematic and sustained efforts to take full advantage of the preferences.

From the beginning, spokesmen for some third countries expressed concern lest the effects of the arrangements be to solidify Libya's dependence on a single market. It was therefore demanded, as a condition of extending the waiver in 1952, that Libya report periodically on what other steps it was taking to diversify its exports and to widen its markets. The Libyans regularly reported, in very general terms, that with the help of technical assistance programs from the UN and various foreign governments they were trying to increase their export capabili-

---

[9] See **GATT**, *Basic Instruments and Selected Documents, First Supplement*, Geneva, 1963, pp. 14–17, for details on the goods involved and the Italian duties.

ties but that the difficulties were great. In late 1955 a GATT Working Party concluded that Libya was having some modest success in finding other markets, partly as a result of efforts to reduce costs and partly because of concerted efforts to introduce its goods into other markets. The study implicitly concluded that Libya, as a consequence of the preferences, probably would not greatly increase its dependence on the Italian market.[10] Subsequent investigations by other GATT working parties gave only perfunctory attention to the question of the progress—or lack of it—by Libya in increasing its ability to compete in world markets.[11] The available statistical data show that while Libya's dependence on Italy as a market for the particular goods receiving preferences seemed to be increasing (Italy took 40 percent of such goods in 1959 and about 55 percent in 1962–1963), there were no clear trends—although considerable fluctuation from year to year—in the share of total Libyan commodity exports (excluding crude petroleum) flowing to Italy. These amounted to 39 percent of Libya's total in 1954, 37 percent in 1958, 31 in 1959, 36 in 1960, and 39 in 1964.[12]

Beginning in 1961, Libya's traditional foreign trade position was being swamped by the effects of its petroleum exports. The value of its total merchandise exports increased some 80-fold between 1960 and 1964 and Italy's share had dropped from nearly two fifths to only about one tenth. The discovery of large oil reserves had thus dramatically changed and reduced the role of the Italian preferences in Libya's future economic development. The waiver permitting them was due to expire at

[10] See GATT, *Basic Instruments and Selected Documents, Fourth Supplement,* Geneva, 1956, pp. 16–17, 99–102.

[11] See, for example, GATT, *Basic Instruments and Selected Documents, Seventh Supplement,* Geneva, 1959, pp. 34, 118.

[12] For some of the more informative of the reports and for details on this trade, see the following GATT documents which have been the source of most of the information in the preceding paragraphs: GATT, *Docs. L/111,* 25 Aug. 1953; *L/393,* 24 Aug. 1955; *L/401,* 6 Sept. 1955; *L/703,* 18 Oct. 1957; *L/1606,* 10 Nov. 1961; *L/1558,* 22 Sept. 1961; *L/1808,* 20 July 1962; *L/2039,* 6 Aug. 1963; *L/2034,* 18 Sept. 1963; *L/2260,* 5 Sept. 1964; and *L/2296,* 18 Nov. 1964.

the end of 1964. Shortly before then the Libyan Government stated that the huge oil revenues would permit it to proceed apace with its greatly expanded plans for diversification and increased productivity; it was therefore "legitimate to hope" that Libya would soon be able to compete internationally without special treatment. Nonetheless, with Italy's support, and after volunteering to delete about half the items currently eligible for preferences, Libya asked for a three-year extension of the waiver, asserting that it would provide needed and important help to the producers of the affected goods. The Contracting Parties granted the request, noting that other nations were not being appreciably hurt by the arrangements and that Libya had given assurances that it would continue its efforts to increase efficiency. They also noted with approval the deletion of half the items; the record does not show anyone pointing out that trade in recent years in the deleted items had been trivial or zero.

A third and more explicit step in the development of the policy that discrimination was an effective tool for facilitating economic development of the less-developed countries was taken in 1953. Australia told the Contracting Parties to the GATT that it had been studying various ways of helping the Territory of Papua–New Guinea to accelerate its rate of economic growth and had found that in addition to loans and gifts there was a need to greatly increase the incentives—both local and foreign—to invest. Such investment, Australia said, required the assurances of a certain and continuing market greater than the internal one. It therefore requested a waiver of its most-favored-nation obligation so that it could apply the principle of a "free trade area on a one-way basis"—more specifically, Australia wanted to grant duty-free entry to un-named products of Papua–New Guinea, without extending such treatment to other areas and without asking for it for Australian goods in the Territory.[13]

There was general sympathy among third countries with the stated aim of helping this less-developed area, but many were

[13] GATT, *Doc. L/133,* 19 Sept. 1953.

worried at still another breaking of the most-favored-nation rule. Several were particularly concerned at the open-end nature of the Australian request, fearing it might at some future time affect products of which they were important exporters to Australia. Australia replied that it could not identify the products in advance to receive favored treatment since one of the purposes of the preferences was to encourage investment in the production of "appropriate" *new* products. The possibility of incorporating the Trust area into the Australian customs territory was examined but was rejected on several grounds. First, no case convincing to others could be made for Australian exports being given preferences in the Territory. Second, Australia feared that this might lead to an "uneconomic drain on the limited labor resources" of the Territory; that is, the natives might move to Australia. Finally, Australia argued that to incorporate the Territory into its customs area would encourage a "dispersal" of investment effort, while the needs of the Territory would best be served if the investment were channeled only into those particular areas which gave good promise of "development." The Australian Government believed that it was a better judge than the free market as to where investment should take place; to this end, it said it would grant duty-free treatment only to those goods the production of which would contribute most to the "social and economic welfare" of the Territory.[14] The Australians made it clear at this time that they believed it was investment in primary products that would most likely meet this criteria. In contrast with what was to come a decade later, almost no objection was raised to the paternalistic aspects of all this.

The waiver was granted, but Australia was obliged to use it in such a way as not to cause material injury to others, or to protect Australian domestic producers. Before invoking the waiver on any specific good, Australia also agreed to stand ready to consult with those who might be adversely affected,

[14] See GATT, *Basic Instruments and Selected Documents, Second Supplement,* pp. 18–19, 93–95, for a report on the early discussions. See also, *Fourth Supplement,* pp. 14–16, 82–84, and *Fifth Supplement,* pp. 34–36, 114–15, for brief accounts of some of the subsequent discussions.

with a view toward coming to a settlement that would be satisfactory to all.

In the event, the Australians moved slowly and it was almost two years before they decided that the growth prospects for various timber products (unsawed logs, dressed and undressed timber, moldings and various veneers, etc.) justified the granting of preferences.[15] Canada at this time voiced some concern lest this divert some trade from its exporters but was apparently satisfied with the Australian reply that it would take many years—even with preferential treatment—before the Territory would be able to export any significant amount of timber products and that, in any case, the types of timber produced there did not compete with most current Australian imports. By early 1965 preferences had also been granted only on peanuts, passionfruit pulp and juices, and coffee.[16] As expected, the effect of the waivers on investment and on production were taking a long time to make themselves felt, but by the beginning of 1965 the trade data suggested that the preferences might be diverting some trade in coffee to the Territory and might be contributing to an increase in exports—still very small —of certain timber products to Australia.[17]

---

[15] See GATT, *Docs. L/396*, 26 Aug. 1955, and *L/375*, 13 July 1955; and *Add. 1*, 30 Sept. 1955, and *Add. 2*, 11 Oct. 1955. The choice of these products required that the waiver be amended to include unbound as well as bound items and, more importantly, that it cover not only primary products but also products "substantially derived" from primary products—manufactured goods based on local products.

[16] In the case of coffee, Uganda, and in the case of fruit, France and the U.K., on behalf of overseas territories, said their interests were threatened with damage; Australia agreed to some "concessions" on other items to compensate for this.

[17] For detailed reports on trade in the affected items, see the following GATT *Docs. L/705*, 17 Oct. 1957; *L/896*, 30 Oct. 1958; *L/1032*, 14 Sept. 1959; *L/1450*, 27 April 1961; *L/1991*, 18 April 1963; *L/2075*, 30 Oct. 1963; *L/2162*, 28 Feb. 1964; and *L/2365*, 1965.

An extremely complicated waiver, apparently closely patterned after the Australia/Papua–New Guinea one, was granted in 1960 to the Federation of Rhodesia and Nyasaland, with the object of permitting the Federation to grant preferences on 13 categories of products when originating in the dependent territories of the United Kingdom. Since the

In late 1954 the United Kingdom attempted, unsuccessfully, to generalize the Australia/Papua–New Guinea case. The U.K. proposed that the General Agreement be amended by adding a new article providing that with respect to action *any* metropolitan country might take to further the economic interests and economic development of a dependent territory, that territory would be regarded as within the customs area of the metropole, provided any such measure operated substantially to the exclusive benefit of the overseas territory concerned.[18]

The U.K.'s defense of this proposal was the now orthodox one: there were many ways in which a metropolitan country could discharge its obligations to improve the economic welfare of people in its dependent overseas territories—technical assistance, economic grants, loans, private movements of capital—to name the most common. Sometimes these sufficed. But, British spokesmen said, there also were often cases where "wanted" and "needed" industrial development [19] to be efficient required a scale of operations, and so a level of investment, exceeding that needed to meet the demands in the typically small domestic market. In the early stages of economic development, these territories as a practical matter often had no

---

Federation was dissolved in late 1963, since the waiver introduced nothing new in principle or practice, and since I have not been able to straighten out the details, no further reference is made to this here. See General Agreement on Tariffs and Trade, *Basic Instruments and Selected Documents, Ninth Supplement*, Geneva, 1961, pp. 47–49, for the text of the GATT decision. As we noted in the footnote on p. 142, there have also been some complicated preferential arrangements between the Union of South Africa and the Rhodesias and Nyasaland, which contained an element of using preferences to facilitate the economic development of less-developed areas.

[18] GATT, *Doc. L/296,* 13 Dec. 1954.

[19] At the time, they saw the problem of preferential treatment as being of particular promise in cases where the dependent overseas territories did not produce sizable quantities of raw materials for which remunerative markets existed. It was not the British notion that "industrialization" should replace existing raw materials production, but rather that help might be needed when the export possibilities in the raw material field were not at all promising.

alternative but to look to their metropole as a market. Preferences there could give them greater assurances that they would be able to get into and stay in this market and the needed investment would more likely be forthcoming. Without such investment, they argued, economic development in some dependent overseas territories might be seriously hampered and political unrest might follow.

A good bit of opposition developed in the Contracting Parties to the British request. Some of it stemmed from the continued concern over the setting of still one more precedent undermining the "no new preference" rule, a general policy many still believed to be the best guide to commercial policy and in their own national interest. This position was often most strongly held by the smaller of the relatively economically advanced countries which at that time belonged to no regional arrangements and enjoyed no preferences: Switzerland, Austria, and the Scandinavian nations. Others objected because they saw some of their exports directly threatened. Others, now including some of the new nations, stressed, more so than in the earlier most-favored-nation waiver discussions, the danger that such selective preferences could lead to greater dependence of the territory on the metropole—both as a market and as a source; it was to be expected that if the dependent overseas territories concentrated their sales in one country they would also, although there might be no legal requirement and the currency earned was convertible, tend to make most of their purchases there. If this were so, it was feared, it would make more difficult the overseas territories gaining "true" independence. It was also argued by some that such a policy and practice would leave the metropolitan country as the sole judge of what measures would benefit the dependent overseas territory. This was not seen as consonant with the new political developments. Moreover, some feared this discrimination might work to the advantage of the *dependent* less-developed countries at the expense of the *independent* ones.

For all these reasons the Contracting Parties finally decided they could not approve the original British proposal. There was much support, however, for any efforts by the richer countries to help the poorer ones expand their exports. To meet this objective while guarding against at least some of the noted costs of discrimination, the United Kingdom, but not other metropoles, was granted a waiver of its nondiscrimination obligations with respect to colonial products, agricultural and industrial, which *at the time* were wholly or largely dependent upon the United Kingdom as a market. Thus, the approval was limited only to the United Kingdom and its territories, and production of *new* goods was not to be "tied" to the metropole by preferential treatment. Provisions were also made that no "material benefits," either in domestic or import markets, could thereby come to the United Kingdom. Britain was required to obtain prior concurrence of the Contracting Parties before it introduced or increased a margin of preference under the waiver. To guard against any important trade diversion, it was also to stand ready to enter into consultations with any contracting party which believed it had suffered, or was threatened with, material damage because of any new preference. Such consultations were to have the aim of reaching a "mutually satisfactory settlement or compensatory adjustment." [20]

In the event, very little use has so far been made of the waiver, it having been invoked, apparently, only with respect to bananas and lime oil. But it is important because it placed one of the major industrial countries on record as seeing possibly great virtues in discrimination by the more-developed countries in favor of the less-developed countries as a device for facilitating the economic development of the latter.

The United Nations had assigned the trusteeship for Somaliland to Italy, and, in 1960, when arrangements were being completed for Somali to become an independent nation, Italy proposed that as part of its contribution to helping the new nation "move forward with her economic development plans," Italy continue for a time the previous arrangements under which Somali exports, chiefly bananas, had entered Italy duty free.[21] A GATT working party found that, except for bananas, Somali

[20] See GATT, *Basic Instruments and Selected Documents, Third Supplement,* pp. 21–25, for text of the decision and pp. 131–39 for the report of the Working Party on the British request.

[21] GATT, *Doc. L/1206,* 25 May 1960.

exports to Italy constituted only a very small percentage of the latter's total imports of the affected commodities and saw little danger of any serious trade diversion with respect to these goods. As regards bananas, the Italians stated that under the terms of the Rome Treaty their duty on bananas from other sources was to be reduced by something more than one half, so imports from third countries should increase even if Somali bananas continued to enter duty free.[22]

It was then unanimously agreed that the "provision of economic assistance" by Italy to Somali in the form suggested conformed to the objectives and the spirit of the General Agreement. At the same time, there was a consensus that it would not be in Somali's interest to remain "too dependent" on Italian markets—about three fourths, by value, of Somali's exports were going to Italy during the latter years of its trusteeship. The working party concluded that in order to permit a smooth transition to a "more normal trading regime" it would be desirable to provide for a gradual alignment of the Italian duties applied to Somali products with those applied to the imports of other sources. They did not, however, press for a decision on this at the time, and none has been taken. The working party did recommend, and the Contracting Parties accepted, that the preferential treatment should apply only to those products to which it had been applied under the trusteeship regime and that the decision should be "reviewed" after five years.[23] It is still too early to make even a tentative appraisal of the effects of these arrangements, but at least one

---

[22] The absolute amount of Italy's imports of Somali bananas during the first three years of the waiver was about the same as before, but they fell from 90 percent to 56 percent as a percentage of the total banana imports. See GATT, *Docs. L/2069*, 10 Oct. 1963, and *L/2168*, 2 March 1964, for the first detailed report of action under the waiver.

[23] GATT, *Basic Instruments and Selected Documents, Ninth Supplement*, Geneva, 1961, pp. 40–42, 229–31. The products included were bananas and banana flour, oilseeds, cotton, prepared or preserved meat and fish, and simply-tanned leather. At the same time, the Contracting Parties, as a routine matter, granted a waiver permitting France to extend to the entire "Kingdom of Morocco" the tariff preferences France had for many years been extending to "Morocco (French Zone)." *Ibid.*, p. 39.

more precedent for discrimination as a device for assisting in the economic development of the less-developed countries had been established.

OTHER FORCES AT WORK

But much more than precedents such as these were at work in fostering the idea that preferences from the rich countries might be an appropriate tool for facilitating the economic growth of the developing ones. In the background, especially in Latin America, was the conviction that the inter-war and post-war preferential systems of the British Commonwealth and the French Franc Zone had been costly to their exports; so, it was often reasoned, it probably would be beneficial to obtain preferences for themselves. More fundamental was the adoption by virtually all the less-developed countries of a more rapid rate of economic growth as a major national goal. Their efforts were spurred on by the accumulating evidence in the latter half of the 1950's that the gap between the rich and the poor nations seemed to be increasing.[24] But, for well-known reasons, a persistent tendency for serious balance of payments deficits to develop was proving to be characteristic of nearly all the poorer countries in which more rapid economic development was a major objective. Many of them had attempted initially to meet this problem by increasing the domestic production of import substitutes. This was often found to provide only a partial answer. There were often severe physical and technological limitations on the production of many goods in great and growing demand within the country. In other cases, the smallness of the domestic market often meant intolerably high unit costs. Such industries frequently turned out, in the early years at least, to save but little foreign exchange because they relied so heavily on imports: raw materials, processed compo-

[24] See the periodic United Nations *World Economic Survey* for data on this. For a criticism of the thesis sometimes advanced by spokesmen for the developing countries that international trade has operated as a mechanism for increasing international income inequality, see Gerald M. Meier, "International Trade and International Inequality," *Oxford Economic Papers*, Oct. 1958, pp. 277–89.

nents, and capital equipment. It was, in sum, soon recognized that to push development through import substitution could quite easily result in an uneconomic use of existing resources. As we saw in Chapters IV and V, regional economic blocs often were believed to be part of the answer to this problem, as well as the larger one of facilitating industrialization. Private investment and traditional foreign aid could also help cover the balance of payments deficits, but most nations found them inadequate, given the growth goals they had set for themselves. Many in the developed and less-developed countries alike soon concluded that one of the major tasks confronting the world trading community was to find ways for expanding trade "with particular reference to the importance of the maintenance and expansion of export earnings of the less-developed countries to the development and diversification of their economies"—in the words of the November 1958 Program of Action decision of the GATT.[25]

For the first few years after this goal had been generally accepted a good bit of detailed evidence was accumulated showing the many barriers to developing countries' exports. The emphasis in policy recommendations to meet the problem was on traditional measures for facilitating traditional exports: a general lowering of tariffs on a most-favored-nation basis, removal of quantitative restrictions, and reduction of internal

[25] For the full text, see GATT, *Basic Instruments and Selected Documents, Seventh Supplement,* Geneva, 1959, pp. 27–29. This Program had been stimulated in part by the "Haberler Report" (General Agreement on Tariffs and Trade, *Trends in International Trade,* Geneva, 1958). This, in turn, was an outgrowth of the findings reported in the GATT annual reports, *International Trade, 1954,* and immediately following years, showing that trade between developed and less-developed countries was growing much less rapidly than trade within and among the former; if the gap between "need" and "available" resources for the development programs was to be met a substantial increase in exports was required. Committee III of GATT was established in the 1958 decision cited above for the specific purpose of considering measures for expanding exports of the less-developed countries. In early 1965 the work of this committee was transferred to the Committee on Trade and Development provided for in the new GATT Chapter on Trade and Development.

taxes and charges which had often borne heavily on the established exports of the poorer countries.[26]

In fact, however, because of the preoccupation of the United States and Western Europe with the problems discussed in the previous chapters, relatively little was actually being done in these years to reduce import duties and the relevant internal taxes and, although there had been a substantial reduction in the quantitative restrictions on trade, those that remained often were on goods of the sort the less-developed countries wished to export.[27] Moreover, as we have seen in Chapters IV and V these were years when many of the less-developed countries were becoming more and more worried lest the effects of the regional economic groupings in Western Europe prove to be prejudicial to their exports.

The gloom all this fostered was deepened by the growing belief that, while there would remain for some time important possibilities for increasing earnings from the traditional exports of primary raw materials and foodstuffs, these could not be expected to match the growth of imports that would be associated with the desired or planned rates of economic growth.

With respect to farm goods, most of the less-developed country officials, probably mistakenly,[28] were less impressed by

[26] See the conclusions and recommendations in the Haberler Report, *ibid.*, and the Reports of Committees II and III, in *Basic Instruments and Selected Documents, Eighth Supplement,* Geneva, 1960, pp. 121–41; and *Ninth Supplement, op. cit.,* pp. 110–70.

[27] See Curzon, *Multilateral Commercial Diplomacy,* pp. 231–45, for some details.

For a report showing that many of the quantitative restrictions had been removed by the beginning of 1965, see GATT *Doc. L/2307 Add. 1,* 19 Nov. 1964.

[28] The GATT, in its *International Trade, 1963,* Geneva, 1964, pp. 8–17, reported that in 1961–1963, as compared with 1953–1955, the industrial areas increased their imports of farm goods by nearly 40 percent, but that the increase from the nonindustrialized countries was only about 20 percent while that from other industrialized nations soared by some 60 percent. Had the developing countries kept the same share of the markets in the industrialized countries, their export earnings in 1961–1963 would have been about $2 billion greater than they were. The

estimates of the possible absolute size of the future markets in the industrialized nations than they were by the commonly held belief that the demand for most such goods was relatively income and price inelastic in the major developed country markets;[29] and by the fear that whatever growth of demand there was in the developed areas would be satisfied largely by domestic producers because their productivity was high and because they were protected by all sorts of import barriers. As for most raw materials, many feared their exports would always be subject to possibly ruinous competition from synthetics and substitutes, and the dampening of demand associated with new procedures for recovering scrap, etc.[30] It was widely believed in the developing countries that the operation of all these factors would result in a long-run tendency toward a serious worsening of the terms of trade for producers of such goods.[31] Meager

---

GATT study concluded that much of the reason for this loss in relative position and earnings was to be found in the fact that consumption of these goods in the developing countries was increasingly appreciably faster than production. That is, the reason that the developing countries did not do better on their exports was because of inadequate supply, rather than inadequate demand.

[29] Meat and fruits and feed grains were seen as major exceptions. The income elasticity of demand for many kinds of food was generally conceded to be quite high in the less-developed countries themselves, but for reasons that are not clear to me there was a tendency to play down the contribution this type of intra-developing country trade could make to solving their balance of payments problems by reducing the large ($4 billion in 1963, excluding noncommercial deliveries) amounts they spent on imports of farm goods from developed areas.

[30] See UN, *Doc. E/Conf. 46/59*, 6 March 1964, for a recent study of this problem, with particular reference to agricultural trade.

[31] Although there was some improvement in the early 1960's, the simple commodity terms of trade of the developing countries, as a whole, deteriorated—by perhaps 10 percent—in the decade of the 1950's. For official studies of recent developments in international trade and their significance for economic development, see United Nations, *World Economic Survey, 1962, Part I, The Developing Countries in World Trade*, New York, 1963; and *World Economic Survey, 1963, Part I, Trade and Development: Trends, Needs and Policies*, New York, 1964.

For a recent, statistical study that gives no support to the view that the terms of trade have had a *secular* tendency to deteriorate for the less-

prospects were also foreseen for a large expansion of traditional manufactured exports, in particular textiles.. Recent years had shown that the major markets were often insistent on restricting the imports of just such commodities.

The policy conclusion drawn by most officials in the developing countries was that a necessary element in their process of development must be a great expansion in the production and export of new manufactured products and processed goods.[32] The idea received considerable support at this time at the policy formulation level when the Secretariat of the Economic Commission for Europe [33] estimated that for the less-developed countries to achieve a three percent per year increase in per capita income,[34] they would have to expand their total exports by some $1\frac{1}{2}$ times (from roughly $20 billion up to $50 billion per year) by 1980. The burden of their analysis was that this could be done only if, among other things, the less-developed countries as a group were able by that time to export *manufactured* goods in an amount of roughly $15 billion per year—at least a sevenfold increase over the 1961 level. At least two thirds of this, they concluded, would have to find markets in the already developed countries. Since the lion's share of the manufactured goods exports in 1961 had come from only a few countries (Hong Kong, India, Israel, and Mexico accounted for about 60 percent of the total), the problem for most was even greater than these figures suggested. Other studies in the early

developed countries or for primary goods producers, see Robert E. Lipsey, *Price and Quantity Trends in the Foreign Trade of the United States,* National Bureau of Economic Research, Princeton, 1963, Chaps. 1 and 2. See also, Meier, *International Trade and Development,* New York, 1963, Chap. 3, for a discussion of the terms of trade–economic development issue.

[32] Ragnar Nurkse provided some theoretical support for this conclusion in his *Patterns of Trade and Development,* Wicksell Lectures, Stockholm, 1959. So did Raul Prebisch, in "Commercial Policy in the Underdeveloped Countries," *American Economic Review,* May 1959.

[33] In its *Economic Survey of Europe in 1960,* Geneva, 1961, Chap. V.

[34] This is close to the five percent annual increase in gross domestic product set a short time later by the UN General Assembly as the minimum target for 1970, the end of the United Nations Development Decade.

1960's by the United Nations and the GATT secretariats,[35] while differing in many details, gave support to these general conclusions; and the thesis that the desired rates of economic growth demanded a very large expansion in the exports of manufactured goods by the less-developed countries pervaded the 1964 discussions at the United Nations' Conference on Trade and Development.[36]

SHORTCOMINGS OF ESTABLISHED COMMERCIAL POLICIES

As closer examination was given to the many-faceted problem of expanding the production and export of new manufactured goods, many concluded that ranking high in the list of obstacles [37] were the old established commercial policy rules

[35] GATT, *International Trade, 1961*, Geneva, 1962, pp. 14–19, and United Nations, *World Economic Survey, 1962, Part 1*, New York, 1963, pp. 5–9.

A recent study by Bela Balassa (*Trade Prospects for Developing Countries*, Homewood, Illinois, 1964) is fairly optimistic as to the prospects of the less-developed countries increasing their earnings from minerals and metals, of obtaining foreign capital, and of making do with fewer imports. But his work still supports the conclusion that the economic development of the less-developed areas will be hastened by lower barriers to their manufactured goods exports.

[36] They were given a prominent place in Raul Prebisch's *Towards a New Trade Policy for Development*, New York, 1964, the document designed to present the major issues and to suggest solutions to this Conference. Here, as elsewhere, Prebisch has represented the problem by stressing the "trade gap" concept. Assuming a five percent per year income growth in the less-developed countries and assuming this requires at least a six percent growth in imports, he then concludes, further assuming that past trends in world trade continue, that the "trade gap" facing the less-developed countries by 1970 will be in the order of $20 billion per year. The problem is how best to fill it. By mid-1965 this "gap" had become part of the vocabulary of all less-developed country spokesmen.

For a good discussion of the "trade gap" problem by an American official, see S. Weintraub, *The Foreign-Exchange Gap of the Developing Countries*, International Finance Section, Princeton University, Sept. 1965.

[37] For a recent, interesting statement on the problem of increasing exports of manufactured goods by the less-developed countries, see the

under which negotiations for tariff reductions were held only with the "principal supplier," requiring reciprocity in concessions, and according most-favored-nation treatment to all reductions in import barriers. The arguments, in order, were that, since, by definition, the less-developed countries could not be the "principal supplier" for the new products they had concluded it was both necessary and desirable to produce for export, tariffs on these could be lowered only when others decided to negotiate and were able to reach agreement. This meant that matters of great concern to them often did not come up for negotiation and when they did the developing countries' role was that of a mere bystander. The linear approach to tariff reductions, which was incorporated into the 1964–1966 Kennedy Round, greatly reduced the importance to the less-developed countries of the principal supplier rule. Unless covered by the "exceptions list" or made the subject of a disparity rule, goods of interest to the less-developed countries were automatically included in the tariff reductions even though the major negotiations were between the developed countries. Further, the extent of reductions on goods of interest to them under the linear approach was not heavily dependent on the bargaining power, or lack of it, of the less-developed countries.

As to the reciprocity requirement, the developing countries said they often had little to give and so could expect little if this rule remained. They "could not afford" to lower duties on many consumer goods because this would deprive them of a

---

paper prepared by Raymond Vernon for the United Nations Conference on Trade and Economic Development, UN, *Doc. E/Conf. 46/P/2*, 16 Dec. 1963. (Reproduced in *Proceedings of the United Nations Conference on Trade and Development*, Vol. IV, United Nations, New York, 1964, pp. 200–10.) Especially interesting is his discussion of the importance of ignorance, the high risks faced by entrepreneurs producing for export, and the large cost of penetrating foreign markets. For a more comprehensive statement, see the report prepared for the same conference by the United Nations Bureau of General Economic Research and Policies, UN, *Doc. E/Conf. 46/6*, 14 Feb. 1964. The latter document has been republished in *Proceedings of the United Nations Conference on Trade and Development*, Vol. IV, United Nations, New York, 1964, pp. 3–42.

needed source of internal revenue and might also jeopardize their economic development plans by using foreign exchange for what they regarded as nonessential purposes. Duties on industrial and manufactured goods and related raw materials were already often low, or needed to be kept high either as a source of revenue or as a protection for their infant industries. In any case, their trade in such products was not big enough to constitute much of a bargaining counter. Finally, they argued, in the beginning at least the benefits they would get from the lower tariffs on their new exports would not be worth much in the way of concessions by them because their exports would be small.[38] In fact, for several years the reciprocity rule had not been rigorously applied to the less-developed countries; in May 1963 the Contracting Parties to the GATT formally agreed that in the Kennedy Round full reciprocity would not be expected. The new chapter on Trade and Development added to the General Agreement in late 1964 included this as a continuing principle.

It was the most-favored-nation rule that came under the strongest attack. The mere reduction of import barriers on a most-favored-nation basis on the new goods the less-developed countries hoped to produce for export would be of little help, it was alleged, because the *new* manufacturing industries, whether making sophisticated or relatively simple goods in the less-developed countries, would often be unable at first to meet the competition from exporters in the industrially advanced countries.

THE CASE FOR PREFERENCES FROM DEVELOPED TO DEVELOPING NATIONS

Ruling out—as it usually implicitly did—the cases where this inability to compete was because of *general* inflationary condi-

---

[38] Many of these arguments are recorded in the records of the Plenary Sessions of the Contracting Parties, which are not available for citation or quotation. Indications of them emerge in GATT, *The Activities of GATT, 1959–1960*, Geneva, May 1960; *The Activities of GATT, 1960–1961*, Geneva, April 1961; and *The Activities of GATT, 1961–1962*, Geneva, July 1962.

tions, or where it was a permanent state of affairs because a given industry simply was suffering from basic comparative disadvantages, this inability to compete successfully with established exporters was seen as a temporary problem which, unless something was done, would become a permanent one. The problem was seen as the infant industry one.[39] Being newcomers, they said, meant that they would in fact have to offer comparable goods at lower prices than those of established producers in order to break into the market. Beyond this, it was commonly believed by those speaking for the less-developed countries that their inability to produce goods at competitive prices very frequently stemmed from the fact that their unit costs during the early years would be high because they were not yet in a position to take advantage of the known economies of large-scale production. They argued that if markets could be provided to permit them to reach such a level of output, they could then successfully compete. To the traditional response that if this were true the entrepreneurs (private or public) in the developing countries should themselves be willing to bear the costs either of absorbing the losses during the period of growth or of building to optimal size right off, the answer was that this overestimated the entrepreneurial initiative available in many of these areas and assumed the availability of a volume of capital which was simply beyond the reach of the local promoters.

In addition to the orthodox economies of scale considerations, many stated that during the learning process there often were very great external economies for the industries involved, some external to the firm, some external to the whole industrial sector. That is, it was argued that the private money costs of producing manufactured and semi-manufactured goods were often much greater than the real social costs. This deviation was due in part to the fact that the early producers in the less-developed countries frequently had to bear a disproportionate share of infra-structure costs. More important might be the considerable costs of educating labor and management in the

[39] A recent, excellent survey and restatement of the theoretical aspects of the many-faceted infant industry issue can be found in Meier, *International Trade and Development,* New York, 1963, Chap. 6.

basic practices and techniques of industrial work. When these persons went to another employer with their skills, the first would have to bear these costs once more—a burden not borne to anything like the same extent by his competitors in the more-developed countries. Such external economies extended also, it was often said, to the cost of developing commercial outlets and distribution channels abroad. Moreover, in the middle of the 20th century the less-developed countries not infrequently had assumed social welfare obligations, had encouraged the formation of labor unions, and had adopted wage policies which during the early stages of industrialization resulted in money labor costs exceeding productivity when the output was valued at world market prices—even though the workers' real productivity was a good bit higher than in the rural areas from which they were drawn; so the nation was better off than before.[40] As we saw in Chapter VI, producers in the developed countries feared the exact opposite: wages below the value of labor's marginal product at world prices, thus permitting market disruption. It is, of course, possible for both situations, but with respect to different goods, to exist at the same time.

It was often acknowledged that it was easy to overstate their extent, but there was little questioning that there were many instances in the less-developed countries where economies of scale are possible and where there are important temporary divergencies between social and private costs. No studies seem to have been made to determine their magnitude, but by the early 1960's it had become a virtual article of faith among many of those responsible for determining policy that the phenomena were widespread.

Although not all agreed it could in practice be successfully

[40] Spokesmen for less-developed countries often believed that the present highly-industrialized countries had been able to sell at relatively low prices and so develop markets because they were able to reach large-scale operations by exploiting their own labor, and, in some cases, also by exploiting those producing their imported raw materials. This was generally regarded as no longer tolerable or feasible. It was also argued that newcomers faced less severe competition in the earlier period because there were, relatively speaking, fewer industrialized countries than now.

carried out, there was a consensus that economic welfare could be increased in the less-developed countries by government action offsetting any "excess" of present private costs, permitting production—and exports—on the basis of the real and the long-run costs. It would, of course, be possible for the less-developed countries to attempt this by internal tax and subsidy measures, in which case the "excess" costs would be shifted from the producers of the goods in question to others within the country. This, after all, is the way an import duty helps a domestic producer overcome noncompetitive prices in the home market. Some deplored such a solution on the grounds that it would involve a transfer of real wealth from the poorer nations to the richer ones.[41] If the goods could otherwise be exported, there would be merit in this concern. Otherwise, it should be seen merely as an adjustment of prices within the producing country to reflect the real costs of producing goods, and then charging the latter. There was, however, a serious practical problem: an effort by the less-developed countries to offset the difference between the money cost to the producer and the real social cost by means of subsidies on exports only might result in the imposition of countervailing duties by importing countries.

It was also agreed that it was possible for these temporary, "excess" costs to be borne by foreign countries. There are many ways in which the traditional foreign aid programs can and have been so used. It could also be done by foreigners paying higher prices for the goods produced than they would have to pay for comparable goods imported from someone else. It was implicitly assumed by the less-developed countries —and was not often publicly challenged by the others—that such help, if not an "obligation" of the rich to the poor, could be justified on the grounds that, given the wide discrepancies in per capita incomes, total world welfare would thereby be improved. Moreover, it was usually assumed it would contribute to political stability.

All these considerations led to increasing and gradually more insistent suggestions by spokesmen for the developing countries

[41] See, for example, the French statement to the UN Conference on Trade and Development, UN, *Doc. E/Conf. 46/74*, 27 Feb. 1964, p. 17.

in the GATT, the United Nations, and elsewhere that the industrialized countries abandon the most-favored-nation rule and grant preferences to imports of manufactured and processed goods from the less-developed countries.[42] The many who quickly saw such preferences as a major device for facilitating the development of new export industries in the less-developed nations seem initially to have implicitly assumed that the only costs of moment to the preference-givers would be the real costs of the wealth transfers involved and that the world was divided into two homogeneous blocs, one made up of nations industrialized and rich, the other of countries not industrialized and poor. The problem of reaching an agreement should therefore not prove too difficult. Of this, they were soon to be disabused.

INITIAL RESPONSE, RESERVATIONS, DOUBTS OF DEVELOPED NATIONS

At first, the developed nations did not give serious consideration to the suggestions. After all, despite the fact that its significance had been greatly changed with the growth of regional blocs, most-favored-nation treatment was still regarded

---

[42] Evidence of the demand for this can be found in GATT, *The Activities of GATT*, for the years 1960 and 1963, as well as in the Reports of GATT Committee III, in GATT, *Basic Instruments and Selected Documents, Eighth Supplement*, pp. 132–41; *Ninth Supplement*, pp. 120–69; *Tenth Supplement*, 1962, pp. 167–99; and *Eleventh Supplement*, 1963, pp. 168–205.

The Secretariat of the European Economic Commission, after concluding in early 1961 that it was most desirable for the poorer countries to greatly expand their exports of manufactured goods, suggested that if the highly industrialized countries "want to help the developing countries, they could do so . . . by abolishing all customs tariffs and other obstacles to imports of manufactures from the developing countries." It went on to say that this would be at very little risk to their own industries in the short-run because few of the developing countries would be able to take advantage of it for some time but that it would nonetheless stimulate industrialization in these areas, and might be "worth more to them than much aid in the form of capital loans and grants." Economic Commission for Europe, *Economic Survey of Europe in 1960*, Geneva, 1961, Chap. V, p. 49.

by most as a cornerstone of their commercial policy and it had been strongly re-endorsed during the 1954–1955 "review" of the GATT.[43]

But the pressures from the developing nations continued, and in late 1961 the Contracting Parties to the GATT did approve a report which, in well-guarded phrases, recommended that the industrialized countries should "give sympathetic consideration" to moderating their restrictions against imports of those processed goods, semi-finished and finished components, and of the simpler industrial products which the less-developed countries could now produce.[44] This not only committed no one to anything but did not restrict the favorable treatment to the products of the underdeveloped countries. Most of the spokesmen for the less-developed countries were therefore not satisfied and in late 1962 a group of them drafted a new "Action Program" which included, along with the more traditional measures, a proposal that at the next session the Contracting Parties agree that: "Industrialized countries should also prepare urgently a schedule for the reduction and elimination of tariff barriers to exports of semi-processed and processed products from less-developed countries providing for a reduction of at least 50 percent of the present duties over the next three years."[45] Although not specified, in the context it seems clear that the authors intended this to introduce preferential treatment.

A few months later, in May 1963, a Meeting of Ministers of the Contracting Parties (which then numbered 66 countries as full members and 8 as provisional members) was held. The first item on the short agenda was "Measures for the Expansion of Trade of Developing Countries as a Means of Furthering Their Economic Development." The Ministers agreed that urgent consideration should be given to the problem of helping the less-developed countries to diversify their economies and to

[43] GATT, *Basic Instruments and Selected Documents, Third Supplement*, pp. 170–231, *passim.*

[44] GATT, *Basic Instruments and Selected Documents, Tenth Supplement*, p. 189.

[45] GATT, *Basic Instruments and Selected Documents, Eleventh Supplement*, p. 206.

increase their export earnings and export capacity. The major recommendations aimed, with many qualifications, at the non-discriminatory elimination of various trade barriers on products of special interest to the less-developed countries.[46] As expected, this was not satisfactory to many of the less-developed countries and they succeeded in getting the Ministers to agree that among the measures which should be studied promptly "would be the accordance of preferential treatment to the semi-manufactured and manufactured goods exported by the less-developed countries." [47] Shortly thereafter a GATT Working Party was set up to study the problem of preferences,[48] and those preparing for the 1964 UN World Trade Conference

[46] Since in practice temperate zone farm goods are excluded from such undertakings and most raw materials are not subject to import restrictions, the proposal applied largely to tropical foods and to selected manufactured and processed goods. As we have noted elsewhere, the European Economic Community nations could not endorse even these broad proposals—which threatened to break up the meeting. They stated officially that "more positive measures" were needed to meet the problem of the less-developed countries. Also involved in their refusal to endorse the program was that for them any such dismantling of trade barriers would deprive some of the associated states of their privileged position in the Six and could also, via its effect on the free trade arrangements among themselves and so on the products in question, change the internal balance of the quid pro quos within the Six. They therefore proposed instead that efforts should be directed to "a deliberate effort to organize international trade in products of interest to the less-developed countries." Apparently what was in mind was something on a worldwide basis, along the lines of the "managed market" arrangement which the French had developed in the mid-1950's in the French Franc Zone (see UN, *Doc. E/Conf. 46/31*, 3 Feb. 1964, Annex 1. This has since been reproduced in *Proceedings of the United Nations Conference on Trade and Development,* Vol. VIII, New York, 1964, pp. 238–403). Such a "solution" also had the advantage of being an extension and continuation of an existing policy—always a potent consideration in policy measures. Up to mid-1965, at least, no specific and detailed proposal, however, had been publicly forthcoming from the Common Market authorities.

[47] GATT, *Basic Instruments and Selected Documents, Twelfth Supplement,* Geneva, 1964, p. 44.

[48] Its terms of reference were to consider the problems and the possibilities of granting preferences on selected products (a) by the industrialized countries to the less-developed countries, and (b) by the less-developed countries to all other less-developed countries.

also asked the UN Secretariat to make a study of the matter. In these groups, and in the subsequent discussions at GATT sessions and at the World Trade Conference, a host of difficulties soon appeared. Important conflicts of interest also emerged, between those who were thought to be candidates for granting preferences and those receiving them, and among the members of each group, especially among the less-developed countries.[49]

Most of the developed countries quickly found that they had two self-interest reservations about granting such preferences. First, there were some manufactured goods from some less-developed countries the import of which they wished to discourage, not encourage, for outright protectionist reasons. This was largely the market disruption problem discussed in the preceding chapter. Second, there was much hesitancy because foreign aid, and in unknown amounts, would be involved. If a preference was effective as a preference it would be because, as compared with a nonpreferential reduction of import restrictions, it shifted imports from lower cost to higher cost sources; but it was not possible to accurately estimate the quantities involved.[50] It was recognized that if true infant industry

[49] The sources of the rest of this chapter include a series of discussions I had in the spring and summer of 1964 with various delegates to the 21st Session of the Contracting Parties to the GATT and to the United Nations Conference on Trade and Development, as well as the public discussions during the latter Conference. The most important printed sources are GATT, *Doc. L/2196, Rev. 1,* 2 April 1964; *Towards a New Trade Policy for Development,* Report of the Secretary General of the United Nations Conference on Trade and Development, UN, *Doc. E/Conf. 46/3,* 12 Feb. 1964; the report of the United Nations Bureau of General Economic Research and Policies prepared for the World Trade Conference, entitled "Trade in Manufactures and Semi-Manufactures," UN, *Doc. E/Conf. 46/6;* and UN, *Doc. TD/B/AC. 1/1,* 23 March 1965.

[50] See footnote 59 below for an estimate of the resource transfer costs. The consumer might or might not pay a lower price than before; that would depend primarily on whether the country receiving the preference found it could supply all of the market at a price below that previously ruling. If it could not, then the price and consumption would presumably stay much the same as before (since previous sources would continue to supply part of the market) and the nation granting the preference would be transferring to the less-developed countries real

conditions existed in the less-developed countries, then, after a time, the new sources might be lower cost than any originally existing, but this possibility of gain was heavily discounted by those being asked to grant preferences. Another cost, amount unknown, would be the loss of markets by a developed country to the preference-receiving country in the other developed nations' markets.[51] It was recognized that to the extent the effect of the preferences was to transfer some of the domestic market to the less-developed country suppliers and away from domestic (not other foreign) producers, the country granting the preference might, as compared with the previous situation, be getting these goods more cheaply.[52] But, it was also noted, if the preferences were of more value to the receivers than would be a most-favored-nation reduction in duties, the preference-granting countries would still be paying a higher price than if they had reduced tariffs on a nondiscriminatory basis and imported (with approximately equivalent effects on domestic producers) from other third countries. The difference would represent foreign aid. All of this uncertainty as to costs made the preference proposals unattractive to many of the developed countries. At the same time, some, but not much, skepticism was publicly voiced by officials from a few of the developed countries as to the *amount* of help that preferences could provide—a topic I return to in the concluding section of this chapter.

Although little was made of the point in the official discussions, it was noted that there might be a tendency for preferences to foster economic inefficiency in the recipient nations

---

resources equal to the value of the foregone customs receipts on imports from the favored nations. If the country receiving the preferences could now supply all the import market, the price to the consumer should fall, but by less than the amount of the preference if the preference were to have great value for the recipient. For the preference-granting nation, this would be a partial offset to the higher prices paid at the port of entry.

[51] Japan was thought by most to face the biggest risk here, at least in the short-run.

[52] That is, this would be analogous to the trade-creating effects of a customs union.

because, other things being equal, they would serve to encourage investment and growth according to the height of tariff barriers in the developed countries (that is, the margins of preference available) rather than according to comparative advantage; it was acknowledged that these two phenomena might often be positively correlated. It followed that developed countries with high most-favored-nation tariffs—and so larger margins of preference—would, under a generalized system of tariff preferences, tend to attract a relatively large share of exports from the less-developed countries, resulting, it was feared by some, in a very uneven sharing of the burden. Should the burden (adjustments plus any resource transfers) of helping the less-developed countries, it was asked, be based on levels of tariffs or on such criteria as levels of income?

There were other concerns, too. Some of the smaller industrialized nations, relying heavily on foreign trade—Switzerland, Norway, and Sweden were examples—believed that over the long-run the interests of small countries with large exports would not be well served in a world rife with discrimination and in which, as a consequence, one's bargaining power became more important. They reminded others that, despite the many breaches to the most-favored-nation rule in recent years, nondiscriminatory practices had contributed much to expanding world trade. These countries therefore took the position that if it were nonetheless decided to grant the requested preferences they must be regarded as only a sort of advance installment on a general most-favored-nation reduction of duties. They were quickly joined in this "requirement" by virtually all the spokesmen for the so-called developed nations. To have taken any other position would have meant they were prejudicing the possibility of increasing access to each other's markets via future tariff reductions.

The highly industrialized members of regional groups—the members of EFTA and the EEC—were forbidden by their rules from discriminating against other members in favor of developing countries. This was not, however, seen as an important obstacle, because the existing time schedules called for restrictions on intra-area trade to be removed by mid-1967 and it was assumed that this would be before any general preference scheme, if it were accepted, could be fully implemented. Another potential problem existed in the fact that the elimination—or sharp cut—in the common tariff on imports from the less-developed countries would be equivalent to abandoning the customs union or free trade arrangements, with respect to these goods. This could upset the internal balance of concessions within the EEC and the EFTA. The conclusion was soon reached, however, that this would not be important; more serious was the common view that the political cohesion aspect of preferential tariff arrangements, especially in the EEC, would dictate against any general preferential arrangement in favor of less-developed countries involving zero tariffs. This would limit the benefits the less-developed nations could expect.

Those developed nations, especially Britain and France, already granting preferences to some less-developed countries, had an additional reason to look askance at the proposal for preferences from all industrialized to all less-developed countries: it would violate commitments and threaten the value of the favors they were already granting. Britain at least said it was prepared to see this happen, but only if the recipients were prepared to waive their existing "rights." They were, of course, more likely (though still reluctant) to do this if, in exchange, they were given a chance to share with the other less-developed countries *new* preferential rights in other markets. It followed that a condition would have to be that all the major industrialized countries act in parallel. In particular, this made participation by the United States critical, for its was a market whose opportunities might offset losses elsewhere. Parallel action by all the major industrialized countries was also regarded as necessary in order to prevent a great concentration of imports from the less-developed countries in a few of the industrialized nations, and to ensure that the real costs that the preferences might involve would be shared among many.

The United States Government, where the orthodox doctrinaire case against preferences remained strong and was often stated, also found more immediate reasons for disliking the proposal. In 1964–1966 the most important objective of the

353

United States in the field of international economic policy was the Kennedy Round of trade negotiations. The stated U.S. goal was a linear, 50 percent reduction, over a five-year period, in import duties by the major trading nations on a most-favored-nation basis. They looked askance at anything which might interfere with the success of these negotiations. They, and others, feared that a new system of preferences would reduce the incentives for a lowering of tariff barriers on a most-favored-nation basis. A preferential reduction would not only result in the less-developed countries' ceasing to press for most-favored-nation reductions, but would create a vast new interest in preventing such reductions; after all, the only way the preferences could be honored would be by not reducing barriers to imports from all sources. In addition, there was the risk that those granting preferences would find that in opening up their markets by preferential reductions they had done about as much as it was judged politically possible to do in the way of trade liberalization.[53] Any such limitations on the scope of tariff reductions would both deprive the developed nations of some of the benefits of more liberal trade policies and, by dampening the "growth effects" of freer trade in the developed countries, would also adversely affect the exports of the less-developed nations.

The United States also argued, in a variation of this last point, that the long term interests of the less-developed countries themselves would best be served by a bigger general erosion of duties, since this would enlarge markets for *both* their traditional exports as well as for new products, by directly increasing their competitive strength vis-à-vis *domestic* (though not third country) producers. It was also argued that a successful Kennedy Round was particularly important to the less-developed countries because, if as expected it led to large reductions in duties on highly specialized and complex goods, it would provide additional export markets for the industrialized

---

[53] This tendency for preferences to deter MFN reductions was strengthened by some less-developed countries' position that the preferences might be 50 percent of MFN rates, *unless* the Kennedy Round was successful. In that case, the duties on imports from less-developed sources should be zero. See UN, *Doc. TD/B/AC. 1/1*, 23 March 1965.

countries and so make it easier for them to increase their imports of the sorts of goods the less-developed countries might produce.[54]

The United States saw other political–economic reasons for opposing the introduction of any selective, new preferential system. It warned the less-developed countries that "special trading relations are likely to carry with them special political, financial and economic relations that will impair their freedom of choice or action."[55] American officials also reminded others that existing U.S. law prohibited the granting of new preferences. They at least hinted to others that there was reason to fear that if the Congress were asked to change the law so as to authorize the granting of preferences to imports from the less-developed countries, this might encourage a veritable avalanche of "special treatment" legislation for the benefit of domestic producers who were not competitive with foreign producers. The effect of this might well be to increase the use of both tariff and nontariff safeguards and to limit, rather than expand, the market in the United States for the rest of the world. The irony would likely be that these would bear most heavily on the exports the less-developed countries were most anxious to encourage. Many of the most promising possibilities would be found in the light manufacturing and labor-intensive industries. These are often the older industries in the developed countries, ones facing stagnant demands and unemployment problems. They are therefore politically sensitive, and so prime candidates for additional protection. Although it was apparently not talked about by U.S. officials, we saw in Chapter IV that it could also be foreseen that if the United States were to make a wide breach in its general policy of most-favored-nation treatment it might prove difficult indeed for the Congress to

[54] This point was acknowledged, but not emphasized, by Raul Prebisch, in his *Towards a New Trade Policy for Development*, p. 43 (mimeographed edition). He stressed that an increase in the trade in very complex goods among the industrialized countries was desirable because it could more than offset any decline in their exports that a granting of preferences to developing countries might entail.

[55] Undersecretary of State George Ball, quoted in R. N. Gardner, *In Pursuit of World Order*, New York, 1964, p. 166.

resist the temptation to try and increase United States bargaining power by denying—or threatening to deny—most-favored-nation treatment for imports from the Common Market, as well as any other nation or group with which it was having bargaining difficulties. Such moves by Congress could quickly incite retaliatory actions and result in a substantial increasing of the trade barriers around the world, to the great cost of all.

Two events in early 1965 weakened the United States position. One was its support, noted in Chapter V, of the association agreement between Turkey and the EEC, because all recognized that this arrangement fell so far short of being a customs union as to be an old-fashioned preferential arrangement, and that American support was for political reasons. The other—more important—was the signing of an agreement with Canada to eliminate tariffs on trade in most automotive vehicles and original equipment parts; Canada intended to extend the duty-free treatment to imports from all countries, but the United States did not.[56]

Statements by officials emphasized that the automotive industries of the United States and Canada were really a single North American industry, producing identical products, in close geographic proximity, and with intimate corporate relationships. The pact, they said, was designed to promote trade and economic efficiency within this single industry by bringing about such reallocation of production between the two countries as would permit Canada to achieve substantial economies of scale

[56] For texts of the Agreements, see U.S. Department of State, *Department of State Bulletin*, Feb. 8, 1965, pp. 191–94. See also, *The New York Times*, Jan. 16, p. 1; March 26, p. 47; and April 1, 1965, p. 51; *The Wall Street Journal*, Jan. 18, 1965, p. 24; and *Automotive Products Trade Act of 1965, House Report No. 537*, 89th Cong., 1st Sess., Jan. 21, 1965.

The Canadian extension to all was more apparent than real, since it was restricted to imports by car manufacturers and there are few non-American cars manufactured in Canada. This U.S.–Canada accord may, of course, entice to Canada some European automobile manufacturers.

It should also be recorded that, in a side arrangement, United States auto makers agreed that not less than a certain percentage of the car parts sold in Canada would be manufactured there; they also agreed to invest not less than specified amounts in new plant and equipment in the Dominion.

on some components and some models, while abandoning others. Less stressed was the fact that this agreement was worked out against the background of a Canadian policy, initiated in late 1963, under which Canada rebated tariffs (ranging from 17.5 to 25 percent) on those products imported by a Canadian auto maker to the extent (dollar for dollar) that it increased over a base period its exports of other automobile products to the United States. This amounted to a substantial export subsidy and had led to demands for retaliation (imposition of countervailing duties) and to fears of re-retaliation which both governments were anxious to avoid. From the United States' point of view, therefore, the major advantage of the accord was that it disposed of a nettlesome problem and contributed to "friendly association" with Canada, a major political objective in light of the many difficulties and tensions which had developed in recent years between the two countries.

The text of the agreement was submitted to the Contracting Parties to the GATT in March 1965, and a working party was asked to examine it. To no one's surprise, it found that the United States, when it passed the necessary legislation to implement the agreement, would be violating its most-favored-nation obligations.[57] They found not convincing, or irrelevant, United States assertions that this differed from the usual

---

[57] GATT, *Doc. L/2409,* 25 March 1965.

The original pact permitted the executive branch of each signatory to make similar free trade agreements with other countries, but the United States Congress, in approving the necessary legislation in October 1965, deleted this authority for the United States President, requiring him to return to Congress for any further tariff-eliminating agreements. The United States Executive Branch had earlier rejected the suggestion of some contracting parties that the United States avoid conflicts with its GATT commitments (and, some said, avoid encouraging the EFTA countries from making "special trade deals" with the EEC) by eliminating duties on automotive products on a most-favored-nation basis. The grounds for this rejection were primarily that since United States imports of automotive products were large and its vehicle exports were subject to considerable import barriers of one kind or another in many foreign countries, American officials did not want to give away any bargaining power—especially vis à vis, the Common Market—in the midst of the Kennedy Round negotiations.

preferential schemes because there would be no trade diversion since European and Japanese cars were "not like products" and so were not competitive with American-built ones, and because the United States duty would be so low (presumably about 3.75 percent) after the Kennedy Round. More interesting for our purposes is that many of the spokesmen for the less-developed countries, while losing no opportunity to point out that the United States was failing to practice what it preached, in fact welcomed this pact. This "change of heart" toward discrimination, they said, no doubt meant that the United States would now support the much larger objective of instituting general preferences designed to facilitate the economic growth of less-developed countries.

The Contracting Parties had not, at the time of this writing, acted on the formal November 1965 request from the United States for a waiver of its most-favored-nation obligations. On the basis of waiver requests noted earlier in this chapter, one could anticipate that it would be granted, although probably subject to the condition that no serious damage be caused third parties because of trade diversion.[58] One could also safely anticipate that the broad question of preferences for furthering the growth of the less-developed countries would constitute an important part of the discussions.

LESS-DEVELOPED COUNTRIES NOT IMPRESSED

Even before this, spokesmen for the developing countries were not impressed by the noted apprehensions of the developed nations. They regarded the market disruption danger largely as a creature of the imagination and believed the advanced nations were all rich enough to easily bear whatever resource transfer costs there were to the preferences.[59] They

[58] United States spokesmen had made it known that they would be willing to enter into consultations with any contracting party which found that the accord was causing it damage because of "substantial" trade diversions.

[59] I have seen no detailed estimates of this cost, other than those implied in Reuber's study noted in footnote 86 below. The United States Government in early 1965 made a very rough calculation showing that the maximum resource transfer from all developed countries in the *near*

were not in the least worried about the "need" to take measures to ensure that the preferences were only an advance installment of a general most-favored-nation reduction because they would be quite content to continue indefinitely to receive a favored position. They shared the wish of most of the developed countries that all the latter take part in the scheme, and were convinced that this would protect them from the undesirable political consequences cited by the United States. They did not think the fate of the Kennedy Round hinged on this issue since the volume of imports that preferences might stimulate in the short-run were much too small to offset the considerations which had dictated that the Kennedy Round be held. They therefore regarded as trivial any adverse "growth effects," especially on their exports, of any less liberal trade among the developed nations. They insisted that the developed nations had the responsibility not to give in to the protectionist pressure of their less efficient producers just because a special form of shelter was being given to producers in the less-developed countries. They also believed that their potential comparative advantages were by no means limited to their traditional exports or to new, simpler

---

future probably would not exceed $600 million per year. This calculation rested on the assumption that a 15 percent margin of preference would be granted by all developed countries to all *present* exports of manufactured and semi-manufactured goods from all the developing to all the developed countries. It was also assumed that this level of exports (about $4 billion) would be maintained and that the internal prices in the preference-granting countries for these goods would not be changed. That is, that the demand in the developed countries for these goods would be completely elastic. Some of these assumptions were seen as optimistic, but, on the other hand, it was recognized that they also ignored any increase in the export levels of the less-developed countries— the very purpose of the preferences. (See UN, *Doc. TD/B/C. 2/1/Add. 1 –TD/B/AC. 1/4/Add. 1,* Annex B., June 1965). If the transfers were to be the same as the costs, one must also assume that developed nations' suppliers losing export markets had other equally attractive uses for their resources.

If one makes the same demand, supply, and margin of preference assumptions, but also heroically assumes that the dynamic effects of the policy would result in a long-term doubling of the exports of the developing countries, the resource transfer burden on all developed countries would still be only some $1.2 billion per year.

labor-intensive manufactures, markets for which might be enlarged as a result of most-favored-nation reductions. And even for these goods they wanted the price increases which they expected to be associated with preferential access.

SELECTIVE AND NEGOTIATED VS. GENERAL AND AUTOMATIC ISSUE

Despite differences among the less-developed nations which quickly came to the surface, and are discussed below, their spokesmen were as one in clinging tightly to the idea that a system of preferences could and should be worked out and that it would make important contributions to their economic welfare and growth. The first concrete, but general, favorable response by any developed country to this insistent demand was given in May 1963 at the Contracting Parties to the GATT Ministerial Meeting by the Belgian Minister of Foreign Trade and Technical Assistance. This became known as the "Brasseur Plan." As developed and expanded during the subsequent months, the essence of this plan was a system of selective, temporary, and degressive preferences, to be negotiated, commodity by commodity, among any interested parties. The initiation for such negotiations would come from the developing country or countries. Hopefully, all or most of the developed countries would take part in each negotiation, but full participation would not be necessary for each agreement. The developed countries would expect no formal reciprocity.[60]

The provision that any preferences be temporary and degressive was defended on the grounds that this would stimulate industries in the less-developed countries to improve productive efficiency and sales methods and, if actual experience indicated it was not going to be possible to make the industry or firm competitive, to curtail investment sooner rather than later, and

[60] For details of the scheme and its development, see GATT, *Press Release 750*, 17 May 1963; *Belgian Trade Review*, New York, Feb. 1964, pp. 10ff.; and the statement by Mr. P. A. Forthomme on "Preferences for Industrial Development in Developing Countries," delivered to the United Nations Conference on Trade and Development, Geneva, April 22, 1964 (mimeographed).

so reduce the cost of misdirected investment. The provision that any preferences be selective and be the result of negotiations was justified on several grounds. First, it was argued that it was the only feasible approach, because no government which was responsible to a parliament or to public opinion could be expected to undertake an open-ended commitment and agree to automatic and general preferences to all developing countries for all present and future manufactures. That is, the selective approach would permit the denial of preferential treatment to goods which were produced under "abnormal conditions" and which could lead to "market disruption." This would meet one of the major worries of the developed countries. This provision would also presumably result in no preferences being given to those goods which were otherwise already competitive and so did not "need" preferences. Second, it would reduce the waste of misdirected investment by helping to screen out preferences for goods which were thought likely to be produced "in fundamentally uneconomic conditions." In other words, the Belgians said, their proposal would help ensure that the preferences went only to genuine infant industry cases. The major purpose of the negotiations would be to establish that presumption and settle on the degree and duration of any preferences. The selective approach was also defended on the grounds that since the preferences would apply only to those with whom negotiations had been satisfactorily concluded it would permit account to be taken of the needs of the relatively less advanced among the less-developed countries.

Although not mentioned in the official documents, this approach had the great virtue to some members of the European Economic Community that it would facilitate their safeguarding the value of the existing preferences to each other and, more important, to the Associated States. The European Economic Community did not, however, formally approve the "Brasseur Plan" and differences among the Six appeared during the discussions at the 1964 United Nations Conference on Trade and Development.[61] Here France spoke in favor of the

[61] The official *European Community*, April 1964 (London issue), p. 6, reported that the European Economic *Commission* had "insisted" in

"selective" approach without specifically endorsing this particular "plan." West Germany, on the other hand, let it be known that it did not like the whole approach. West Germany believed that it had benefited little from the preferences given by the EEC to the Associated States but had paid the political price of granting preferences to some. West Germany reasoned that it might gain politically by favoring generalized preferences to all less-developed countries with little if any additional economic cost to itself.

There were also several highly industrialized countries which disliked this selective approach. Some, including the United States, did not like the political overtones of the spheres of influence they thought were inherent in it. Several of the smaller developed countries disliked it because they feared that, no matter what was said or written into formal agreements, any network of negotiated selective preferences would tend to exclude them from the markets of the less-developed countries involved, to the benefit of those larger countries which were negotiating such deals. They tended to the view that if the political pressure to grant preferences to the less-developed countries could not be resisted, which they thought it probably could not, then generalized preferences by all developed to all underdeveloped were to be preferred. To gain some political advantages, several of them were therefore ready to support, in principle, a generalized scheme, though they wished the whole question had never come up.

The less-developed countries hailed the explicit recognition in the Brasseur Plan, which they stressed had originated in a highly industrialized country, that preferences were desirable. But they found almost nothing else to their liking in this selective-negotiated approach—often for the very reasons that the plan's

---

discussions with the European Economic Community Council that the six governments should favor the idea of granting "limited preferences to certain less-developed countries to enable specific industries in the latter to become competitive."

At the May 1963 Meeting of the Ministers of the Contracting Parties to the GATT, the European Economic Community ministers recommended only that the Brasseur Plan be studied.

authors found it attractive. A major fear was that if preferences for each commodity were to be subject to negotiation few preferences would in fact be given, because the developed countries would want to protect their domestic producers or those already receiving preferences and the bargaining power of the developing nations was weak unless they bargained as a bloc. They also charged that those which were extended would be selected for reasons of interest to the industrialized nations rather than with reference to the priorities and goals, including diversification, of the less-developed countries. They believed, too, that in practice it would not prove feasible to negotiate preferences for as yet nonexistent industries. But it was often the formation of these that many of them most wanted to encourage.

Their spokesmen often shared the United States' concern that this system would probably not only solidify and extend the existing discriminatory arrangements among some developing and some developed countries, but could also easily create many new preferential blocs or regions. The result, as they saw it, could be changes in the flow of trade which were not necessarily in the direction hoped for by the developing countries. More important, it would certainly introduce new and continuing uncertainties as to the availability of markets, including those uncertainties arising from the fact that the value of a negotiated preference could easily be changed by a subsequent agreement by the preference-giving country extending it to some other developing nation. They were also much worried lest the effects be to divide and split the less-developed countries among themselves; at this time, spokesmen for the "third world" were placing great emphasis on the need for developing a stronger "unity of purpose" and "broader and more intimate cooperation" among their members so as to be in a better bargaining position vis-à-vis the other "two worlds": the western, highly industrialized market economies and the Soviet bloc.[62]

[62] For an official statement by the Secretary General of the UNCTAD, outlining the objections to the Brasseur Plan, see UN, *Doc. TD/B/AC. 1/1*, 23 March 1965, pp. 21–24.

As the discussions continued, more and more of the less-developed countries found a serious defect in the fact that this selective system was designed to withhold preferences on goods which were already competitive and to withdraw them once they became competitive. It was charged that this was looking at the problem of the less-developed countries in "infant industry" rather than in the "more appropriate" "infant economy" terms. More concretely, it was increasingly acknowledged by the developing countries that they saw preferences as a device not only to offset the temporary high cost of infant industries and the disparities between private money costs and real social costs, but also of otherwise contributing to their growth in export earnings. This last objective could be served by receiving continuing preferences—in effect price subsidies—for competitive exports.

DIFFERENCES EMERGE AMONG
POTENTIAL PREFERENCE-RECEIVERS

Spokesmen for most of the less-developed countries therefore insisted that their interests would be best served by generalized preferences, preferences extended by all developed countries to all the less-developed countries and covering all manufactured and processed goods and extending indefinitely. But if such a system were to be negotiable, it was quickly concluded, it would have to be tempered to take account not only of the fears of some of the developed countries stemming from uncertainties as to cost and that their markets might be "disrupted," but also of two major areas of conflicting interest among the potential preference-receivers.[63]

[63] There were lots of other problems on which views as to the most desirable answers differed, but they promised to be easier of solution. For example, what were to be the criteria for determining whether or not a country was to receive or to grant preferences; how should quantitative restrictions be handled in any preferential scheme; if preferences were to be of limited duration should this be a fixed term of years, or be related to competitive ability, or to per capita standards of living; should margins of preferences differ as between broad categories of goods, etc.? These are not discussed here for they had raised no new issues of major policy.

For some of the specific preference proposals by the less-developed

To help meet the cost-uncertainty worries of the developed countries, the less-developed ones soon agreed among themselves that they would find it acceptable to set a time limit— perhaps a decade, subject to renewal—on any preferences. With respect to the market disruption fears, the less-developed countries at first concluded that if the advanced countries "unreasonably" insisted on safeguards other than those provided by their own great competitive advantages, then specific exceptions for specific goods, or possibly some quota system for preferential imports, might be established. It was soon realized, however, that an exception or quota system would present extremely difficult definitional and negotiating problems, to say nothing of the subsequent administrative headaches; these problems would be multiplied into a nightmare if, to take account of the differences in competitive positions of the less-developed countries and the differences among developed nations in their fears of market disruption and as between commodities, it was found necessary to have quotas in each developed country, for each developing country, and for many specific goods, as well. After weeks of discussion at the United Nations Conference on Trade and Development, the less-developed countries reached agreement among themselves that a preferable answer would be to provide that when a country granting preferences believed imports resulting therefrom were causing "disproportionate dislocation" in its domestic markets it could appeal to the "appropriate" international authority. Following conversations with all interested parties, this international authority could, if it agreed with the complainant, authorize the temporary suspension of the preference, subject

countries, see *The Alta Gracia Charter,* drawn up by several of the Latin American countries and reproduced as UN, *Doc. E/Conf. 46/100,* 10 April 1964; and the statement by India to the Plenary Meeting of the United Nations Conference on Trade and Development, reproduced in UN, *Doc. E/Conf. 46/STA/16,* 26 March 1964. (These documents have been reproduced in *Proceedings of the United Nations Conference on Trade and Development,* New York, 1964, VI, 57–66, and II, 218–23, respectively.) Much of the substance of these had been anticipated in the paper prepared for the Conference by the United Nations Bureau of General Economic Research and Policies, UN, *Doc. E/Conf. 46/6,* 14 Feb. 1964.

to the establishment of preferential tariff quotas on imports from the less-developed country during the period of the suspension.[64]

It proved much more difficult for the less-developed countries to reach agreement among themselves on the problems of how to handle existing preferences and how to take proper account of the great differences among them in their stage of industrialization. Quite a few among them—the Malagasy and 18 African states associated with the European Economic Community and the members of the British Imperial Preference arrangements being the most important—already enjoyed preferences in some developed countries. They did not want to lose them. They had a two-pronged reply to the argument that the losses associated with sharing these with all other less-developed nations would be offset in the long run by the gains from their share of new preferences in other areas. You could not be sure; even if this did happen, it might take quite some time, and in any event their existing export industries, if specialized, would have to undergo a long and costly readjustment process. But since these existing preferences included favored access to the major markets of Western Europe, other less-developed countries were not much interested in any scheme which did not include for them preferences in these markets.

As it turned out, most of those enjoying preferences in the United Kingdom market indicated quite early that they would probably be prepared to share these, *provided* they were assured of a right to share newly created preferences elsewhere, especially in the United States and the European Economic Community. They seemingly did not regard their existing preferences on manufactured goods as of great value, but some of them suggested their attitude would have been quite different

[64] See UN, *Doc. E/Conf. 46/C2/L40,* 20 May 1964. This provision was also designed to meet another problem. If preferences could be given they could also be taken away; indeed, it would be far easier to take away a preference than it would be to raise barriers that had been lowered under most-favored-nation conditions for the simple reason that the removing of preferential reductions would redound the credit of other trading countries, while no trading country would likely conclude that it benefited from the raising of a most-favored-nation reduction.

if preferences for raw materials and foodstuffs had been involved.[65] Beyond this, in the light of the recent abortive United Kingdom negotiations looking toward its joining the European Economic Community, in which, as we noted in Chapter V, the former had agreed to a very considerable erosion of the value of the preferences, many of those still enjoying them regarded them as likely to be a short-lived asset in any case. They were not valuable enough to justify weakening the efforts of their sister less-developed countries to create a solid "third world" bloc demanding preferences from all developed nations.[66]

But the African States associated with the Common Market and enjoying preferences in the Six were not, up to the time of this writing, ready to share theirs. Although there was virtually no concrete evidence that they had as yet any significant economic value so far as exports of manufactured goods were concerned, hopes ran high that they soon would. The great difficulties these states, whose past economic transactions had been almost entirely with France, had experienced in trying to take advantage of the preferences for their tropical products and raw materials which now existed in the other members of the Common Market gave them cause to doubt whether sharing their preferences in France could be "compensated" by sharing new preferences in other industrialized countries. Moreover, since most of these states were also receiving budget subventions from Paris, any loss of export earnings resulting from giving up preferences in France would increase their "need" for larger cash grants. This possibility constituted another reason for both the Associated States and France objecting to a dilution of existing preferences. Finally, there was for both France and the Associated States quite a bit of sentimental, and so political,

---

[65] For a recent attempt to appraise the economic importance of the British preferences to the less-developed countries enjoying them, see UN, *Doc. E/Conf. 46/31*, pp. 54–63. From this study I can draw no more precise conclusion than that the preferences still have some, but probably not great, value to the less-developed countries enjoying them.

[66] This stand made it much easier for the United Kingdom to support "in principle" a system of generalized preferences.

value in them. Proposals that "appropriate compensation" be provided through "new forms" of assistance were regarded by these African states as interesting, but they did not put much value on these in the absence of specific commitments by those who would be asked to grant such help.

During the World Trade Conference of 1964 a great deal of pressure was put on the Associated African States by the other less-developed countries to agree to generalized worldwide preference system. Important here were appeals to the need for "unity" among the less-developed countries and stress on the dangers to them of what was called the "neo-colonialism" involved in bilateral preference arrangements. But by the end of that three-month meeting, agreement had not in fact been reached. Considerable publicity was given to the fact that the African States finally joined in sponsoring a proposal for preferences, but on this critical aspect it contained contradictory provisions. One section (Paragraph VII) stated that preferences "should be extended uniformly by all developed countries to all developing countries in a non-discriminatory manner" (as between developing countries). But Paragraph XIII, inserted at the insistence of the Associated African States, provided that notwithstanding the provisions of Paragraph VII, "special treatment may be granted by developed countries to the less developed amongst developing countries. . . ." [67]

The fragility of the assumption that other developing nations were prepared to stand as one in insisting that preferences be generalized was further demonstrated by Nigeria's efforts at the very time of the UNCTAD Conference—and which, as we noted in Chapter V, were later successful—to work out some sui generis type of association with the Common Market. And there were persistent rumors in 1965 that several of the Latin American states were exploring the possibility of working out

[67] UN, *Doc. E/Conf. 46/C2/L40.* See also, UN, *Doc. E/Conf. 46/C2/L50,* 2 June 1964, and *E/Conf. 46/132,* 4 June 1964, for the rapporteur's account of some of the discussion on this issue. An edited version of the last document has been published in *Proceedings of the United Nations Conference on Trade and Development,* New York, I, 1964, 143–68.

with the United States a scheme of the latter granting preferences to the former.[68]

Difficulties also arose from the fact that the less-developed countries were not homogeneous in terms of their own economic structures. They differed greatly as to their stage of industrialization and competitive ability. Indeed, the differences in these respects *among* some of them were greater than the differences *between* some of them and some of the countries regarded as developed and which were being asked to grant preferences.[69] This meant, by the same reasoning that was used to justify preferences from the developed to the less-developed, that any system of general or uniform preferences would tend to benefit primarily, if not solely, those already relatively well along on the road to industrialization. Such an effect might or might not be to the absolute disadvantage of the relatively less-developed among them, but there was within this group of nations a strong sense that any scheme of preferences should benefit them all "equally." This concern was one of the ties which bound them together, and respecting it was thought necessary if they were to present the sort of united front most of them believed necessary for wangling concessions from the developed countries.

It was easy for the potential recipients to agree that "special treatment" should be provided for the relatively less-developed. More bothersome was the question of what form this should take. Some suggested that preferences might be on a sliding scale, with the largest going to those at the lowest end of the stage of industrialization scale. Others objected to this, pointing out that, given the relatively low level of tariffs in the

[68] *The New York Times*, April 7, 1965, p. 59. See, too, *ibid.*, Aug. 15, 1965, p. 27, and Aug. 16, 1965, p. 34.

[69] These differences were reflected—though not measured—by the fact that in 1962 India and Hong Kong each exported approximately $400 million in manufactured goods to the developed countries; they, with eight others, accounted for three fourths of the total exports of manufactured goods from the developing to the developed nations. There were some 80 other nations in the group, no one of whose exports of such goods to such markets reached as much as $5 million. See UN, Doc. E/Conf. 46/6, 14 Feb. 1964, p. 10.

more developed countries, this would likely yield preferences so slight for the more industrially advanced of the less-developed countries as to make them almost valueless. This led to the suggestion of a system of national quotas in each country granting preferences and for each country receiving preferences, but this presented the prospect of an administrative nightmare. In the end, the most the less-developed countries were able to agree to in the 1964 discussions was that if preferences were to be of limited life their duration for any country should date from the time that country first began to benefit from the preferences—presumably in the form of actual exports. This provision was included in the final recommendations of Committee II of the United Nations Conference but it was not regarded as a fully satisfactory provision by most of the less-developed countries, for two reasons. One, it would be hard to administer. Two, it rested on the assumption that preferences should be withdrawn when a given industry had proven itself competitive; as we noted above, many of the less-developed countries wished to keep the subsidy that preferences might give at least until the whole nation's standard of living was at a "satisfactory" level—or, in the more poetic language of the day, until "the economy was no longer an infant." There was therefore a consensus that this problem could best be dealt with by other means. A favored device was that the less-advanced should receive technical assistance and foreign aid to enable them to "avail themselves fully" of the preferential treatment. Such financial assistance, it was suggested, should come from "the international community."

WORLD TRADE CONFERENCE RECOMMENDATIONS

By the summer of 1964 it was acknowledged that much work remained to be done in elaborating the details of any system of preferences for economic development. But the spokesmen for the less-developed countries were extremely anxious that the principle be accepted by all, or most, governments, that the rules of international trade be changed so as to provide that all developed countries should grant substantial preferences for a long period of time to all the imports of manufactured and semi-manufactured goods from all developing countries. To

this end, they formally put forward to the United Nations Conference on Trade and Development a proposal embodying this principle and incorporating the compromises noted above.[70] When this came to a formal vote in the committee which had spent the better part of two months working on the problem, it was approved by a vote of 69 in favor, 8 against, and 23 abstentions. All those voting in favor regarded themselves as potential recipients of preferences. The "no" votes were cast by Canada, Finland, Iceland, Norway, Poland (for reasons that had little to do with the main issue), Sweden, Switzerland, and the United States. Most of those abstaining had publicly expressed themselves as being in favor, "in principle," of the use of preferences to facilitate the economic development of the less-developed countries. Some of them, led by the United Kingdom, abstained because the specific proposals being voted on were not clear on some points, had far too few details on others, did not give adequate attention to the importance of continued most-favored-nation reduction of trade barriers.[71] Most of the Soviet bloc abstained only because they did not like the parts of the proposal specifically referring to what those developed countries with centrally planned economies should do.[72]

[70] UN, *Doc. E/Conf. 46/C2/REC.6,* 2 June 1964.

[71] The U.K. and others made it clear that their friendly attitude to the preferential question was conditional on their understanding that it would not interfere with the success of the Kennedy Round.

[72] It was recognized that tariff preferences would be of little significance in countries of centrally planned economies so, among other things, the proposal provided that with respect to these countries their "trade plans" should "provide for . . . a rapid increase in the proportion of manufactures and semi-manufactures" coming from the less-developed countries. To this end they also proposed that the countries with centrally planned economies reduce the margins between import prices and internal sales prices of manufactured and semi-manufactured goods imported from the developing countries. The Soviet bloc countries would not agree to this but they did agree to a separate resolution calling on them, among other things, to "take appropriate measures which would result in the diversification and significant growth of their imports of manufactures and semi-manufactures from the developing countries." UN, Conference on Trade and Development, *Final Act, Annex A.III.7*.

In February 1965 the Soviet Union informed the United Nations

In the face of this badly split vote and all the noted unresolved issues, and as a part of the intense efforts in the hectic last few days of the Conference to get a Final Act which all or nearly all the participants could sign, the Act limits itself on the operative provisions of this matter to stating that the great majority of countries agree with the "principle of assisting the industrial development of developing countries by the extension of preferences in their favor" and to asking the UN Secretary General to make appropriate arrangements for the establishment of a committee of government representatives to consider the matter "with a view to working out the best method of implementing such preferences on the basis of nonreciprocity from the developing countries, as well as to discuss further" differences of view as to the principle.[73] A three-week session of this Committee in May 1965 was devoted to a reworking of all the previous arguments. Little new in the way of facts or analysis seem to have been presented and the meeting showed that very little, if any, progress had been made in resolving the differences we have noted. But the matter was much too important to cast aside and the group recommended to the Secretary General "that consideration of all aspects of the matter be pursued further." [74]

In the meantime, most of these same governments were also working on the problem of preferences in their role as contracting parties to the GATT. At the famous May 1963 meeting, the ministers, as we noted earlier, had agreed that study should be given to the question of according preferential treatment to the semi-manufactured and manufactured exports of the less-developed countries. The ministers at this time also "recog-

---

that it had abolished customs duties on all goods imported from the less-developed countries. (*The New York Times*, Feb. 5, 1965, p. 39.) The less-developed countries welcomed this, but they had made clear earlier that they did not think this would be enough to greatly expand their exports to Russia.

[73] UN, Conference on Trade and Development, *Final Act, Annex A.III.5.* This version was adopted "without dissent," meaning that many simply reserved their position since it was understood that silence could mean "yes," "no," or "abstention."

[74] UN, *Doc. TD/B/C.2/1–TD/B/AC.1/4*, 4 June 1965, p. 15.

nized the need" for a new chapter in the GATT ("adequate legal and institutional framework") covering problems of trade and economic development—a subject to which they and the GATT Secretariat have been devoting much time since 1958.[75] Representatives of many of the less-developed countries wanted to incorporate in the new Trade and Development Chapter authority and procedures for the granting of development-inducing preferences. But the General Agreement, in contrast to the Final Act of the World Trade Conference, is not just a declarative document, it is an international agreement carrying legal rights and obligations. In light of all the unresolved differences on the question of preferences, the new chapter, finally approved in late November 1964, therefore made no reference to them.[76] The Contracting Parties did agree, however, that the matter would be kept under discussion, looking toward future proposals; a Working Group on Preferences by Industrial Countries was soon established for this purpose.[77]

In May 1965, before this group had a chance to do much work, Australia applied to the GATT for a waiver from the most-favored-nation rule to enable it to grant tariff preferences (subject to tariff quotas so as to "safeguard" Australian producers and existing foreign suppliers) on imports of *selected* manufactured and semi-manufactured goods produced in those less-developed countries which had a "competitive need" for preferences on such goods. About 60 product groups (5- and 6-digit customs categories) were on the originally proposed list, but it was anticipated that this would be periodically reviewed. The list apparently included no goods on which less-developed —as distinguished from the developed—members of the Commonwealth were receiving Commonwealth preferences. Australia's current imports of goods on the initially proposed list

[75] See Eric Wyndham White, "The GATT and Economic Development" (Secretariat of the GATT), Geneva, 1964; and GATT, *The Role of GATT in Relation to Trade and Development,* Geneva, March 1964. For a more critical view, see S. B. Linder, "The Significance of GATT for Underdeveloped Countries," UN, *Doc. E/Conf. 46/P/6,* 21 Jan. 1964.

[76] GATT, *Doc. L/2282,* 26 Oct. 1964.

[77] GATT, *Doc. L/2410,* 25 March 1965.

from all developing nations were very small—less than one million Australian pounds in 1963–1964. Most of the developing countries, nonetheless, welcomed this concrete acceptance of the principle of preferences, supported the Australian request for a waiver, but, as with the Brasseur Plan with which it had some similarities, they expressed serious misgivings over the limited coverage and the selective aspects of it.[78] At the time of this writing the Contrasting Parties have not acted upon the request.

It is too early to tell whether, as most of the developing nations hoped, the Australian request would quickly be followed by proposals from other developed countries for GATT waivers authorizing them to grant general preferences to all developing countries on all manufactured and processed goods. What seems more likely at this writing is that the major industrialized countries will first try to work out some agreed position among themselves. Given the complexities of the issues which had already been cast up, this effort could take many months and could, even then, prove unavailing.

PREFERENCES AMONG DEVELOPING COUNTRIES

In the GATT discussions, as in those at the World Trade Conference, relatively little attention was given to the question of the less-developed nations granting preferences to each other. This was chiefly because the developing countries themselves were less interested in them. For some, their existing or planned regional blocs, noted in Chapter IV, already provided much of whatever benefits there might be in. such preferences. Although it is not obviously true, the potential size of the markets to be created by these preferences were usually thought to be much smaller than those that would be created by preferences in the developed countries. Perhaps most important, the transfer of real wealth that is the consequence of effective preferences would be from one less-developed country to another—clearly of lower priority in their view than

[78] See UN, *Doc. TD/B/C.2/1–TD/B/AC.1/4,* pp. 9–10. GATT *Doc. L/2443,* reproduces the Australian request. Other relevant GATT documents were still classified at the time of this writing.

gaining acceptance of preferences by the developed to the less-developed nations. Finally, some feared that establishing a new system of intra-developing area preferences might be seen by the developed nations as a substitute for preferences from the latter to the former.

Nonetheless, the less-developed countries thought preferences among themselves might be of some value, especially via enlarging markets and permitting economies of scale in cases where regional groupings were not already doing so. Against only slight opposition, they succeeded in inserting in the Final Act of the World Trade Conference "General Principle Ten" providing that "Regional economic groupings . . . or other forms of economic cooperation should be promoted among developing countries . . . ," which, together with the more explicit "recommendations" of Committee II of the Conference,[79] the less-developed countries interpreted as giving a blessing to exchanges of preferences among themselves. Acceptance of this policy was eased by the fact that the United States had already proposed that a slightly modified ITO Article XV, mentioned on the first page of this chapter, be incorporated in the new GATT chapter on Trade and Development. Although strongly opposed to this in 1955 when Chile had made much the same recommendation, the United States Government, as we saw in Chapters IV and V, subsequently had come to have fewer objections to regionalism in general. More important, the U.S. also was acknowledging that in its traditional opposition to preferences it was enjoying fewer and fewer supporters and that perhaps the most it could salvage from its long campaign against preferences was acceptance of something like the old Article XV provisions that they be limited in time and to countries in the same economic region, or having "strong historical ties." [80] These conditions, it was

[79] United Nations Conference on Trade and Development, *Final Act, Annex A.III.8.*

[80] The World Trade Conference "recommendation," noted above, would permit preferences among any less-developed countries, not just those geographically close or tied by history. The United States entered formal reservations on this aspect of the recommendation.

hoped, would tend not only to limit the extent of the use of preferences but would increase the possibility that those who did use them might in time develop into genuine customs unions or free trade areas.[81] Moreover, in addition to a lot of loosely defined "border traffic," the Latin American Free Trade Area and the Central American Common Market, to say nothing of the regional groups in Africa, had so many exceptions to full intra-area free trade that an extensive system of selected preferences among groups of less-developed countries had in fact already been sanctioned. It still remains, in mid-1965, for the General Agreement to be amended so as to enable such exchange of preferences, but since no one seems much opposed this seems likely to take place soon. In the meantime, the GATT established in 1965 a new special Group, charged with examining the problem of expanding trade among the less-developed countries, with particular reference to the role of preferences in promoting such trade. This Group was distinct from the one working on the problem of preferences by industrial countries to the less-developed ones.

SOME TENTATIVE CONCLUSIONS

Much negotiating remains to be done, but the pressures for some kind of preferential system designed to help the less-developed countries expand their exports of manufactured goods seem irresistible. Although a firm answer cannot be given, the question must still be asked whether the costs are

[81] As in their regional blocs, the less-developed countries themselves did not anticipate letting such preferences result in much trade-creation, in the usual sense of changing the locus of production as among themselves. This was made clear by their frequent statements that in any such regional cooperative efforts "due regard" or "careful attention" should be paid to the "individual characteristics" and "different needs" of the members, so as to prevent harm and to assure "equal opportunity" for all. (See, for example, UN, Conference on Trade and Development, *Final Act, Annex A.III.8.*) This seems likely to mean that many of the preferences will be created by increasing the rates of duties on both the preference-receiving goods, *as well as on other imports,* from nonfavored nations. The first would protect domestic producers from lower-priced imports and the second would be needed to maintain needed government revenues.

likely to exceed the benefits—a calculation those fostering the proposal seem not to have made. The possible costs are many. The cost in terms of political friction has already been demonstrated: this time among the less-developed countries, between them and the developed countries, within the European Economic Community, and between the United States and some of its Western allies. It was clear to all that one cost of a new preference system would be new divisive elements in the international community.

No careful calculations seem to have been made—or, at least, published—of the likely resource transfer costs to the preference-givers of purchasing in dearer rather than cheaper markets, but that there would be some was agreed. The potential recipients had implicitly assumed that this device would increase the total amount of aid available from the richer to the poorer countries. The fact that it would be hidden encouraged their hope that it would be additional and long-lived, but there was always the possibility that there would be some offsetting decreases in other types of aid being provided. It also had been implicitly assumed by many that aid in the form of preferences would be particularly well placed in the sense that those which would in fact benefit from it were those of the greatest relative efficiency in the less-developed countries, those which were, in Hirschman's terms, "on the threshold" of becoming competitive in the world markets. But the question also has to be asked whether generalized preferences might not encourage indiscriminate investment with resulting waste and reduced supply elasticities of goods, including nonmanufactured exports, able to compete in international markets. And would even a system limiting preferences in time prevent the creation of permanent infants, with all their costs? Spokesmen for the less-developed countries often had implicitly assumed that preferences—because they opened up new possibilities and because they were evidence of a willingness on the part of the developed countries to help—would encourage domestic investors and enterpreneurs in the poorer countries to press export programs more vigorously, which might even be successful without the preferences but which would not in fact be made without the confidence borne of favored access. But as this was examined, one could also have a faint doubt. Had it not been said that the fact of preferences had led associated states of the European Economic Community to rest on their oars rather than to take hope and work harder? [82]

There was also the nagging worry lest such preferences be somewhat capricious in their effects on investments and trade flows, and in determining which developing countries would bear any burdens, because they would tend to encourage production of those goods for export to those markets in which the MFN rates—and so the possible preferences—were high. These often might not be goods or markets in which the developing countries had comparative advantages, and so economic inefficiency might be fostered in them.

Aid via preferences seemed almost certain to carry exceptionally large costs for administration. The Geneva discussions made it seem likely that any acceptable system would have some exceptions—always difficult and costly to administer. It would also have to attempt to give something called "equality of advantage" to each of the less-developed countries, which were in very different relative stages of development and so differed in their ability to take advantage of any preferences. The arrangements (country quotas, differential preferences, varying time limits to receive preferences, etc.) that had been advanced to take account of this wish and this fact could easily result in an administrative chamber of horrors.

More worrisome were the potential costs of such a preferential scheme in reducing the incentives to cut barriers on a most-favored-nation basis, thus directly limiting the markets for the developed countries. This, via adverse growth effects, could adversely affect the developing countries as well. But probably the greatest potential cost stemmed from the fact that a system of preferences along the lines envisaged was not feasible unless the United States participated. That would require a change in the law by the American Congress and probably mean subjecting the whole trade expansion program to Congressional review. The danger was real and great, for reasons noted earlier,

[82] See p. 262.

that the consequences might well be an appreciable increase in import restrictions by the United States on goods of particular export interest to the less-developed nations as well as the abandonment of most-favored-nation treatment on goods traded among the developed countries, bringing with it the threat of retaliatory increases in trade barriers all around the world.

These costs could be substantial. Were the benefits likely to be as great as had been hoped when the scheme was first put forward, great enough to offset these costs? Two major conditions must prevail with respect to any product if tariff preferences are to permit a less-developed country to export a good where otherwise it could not; if, that is, preferences are to do what was claimed for them in the way of encouraging young industries and preventing their becoming permanent infants. First, the price charged by the less-developed country must still be *below* those of the domestic producers in the developed countries being asked to give preferences. It is only in this circumstance that a tariff cut or removal has a direct influence on trade. Second, the price charged by the developing country can *exceed* that of other producers among the developed exporting countries only by an amount that is less than the tariff, or the preference, if that is smaller. If the price disadvantage is more than this margin, exporters from other countries will still be able to keep the market, even though the less-developed country has a lower tariff to hurdle. If the latter's price is below those of developed countries, then, *so far as permitting a new industry to get started is concerned,* a preferential tariff cut has but few advantages over a nonpreferential one, assuming the latter is an alternative. To the extent the price charged by the less-developed country falls within the range set by these two conditions the nation granting the preference presumably will for that reason purchase its goods. Prices at the port of entry (prior to duty collection) for imports from the less-developed country will be higher than for imports from developed countries. However, the total price, including duty, will be lower for the former than for the latter and so such goods will be preferred, to the benefit of the less-developed country.

From the record it appears that most of the preference advocates have so far overlooked the fact that the creation of the European Economic Community and the European Free Trade Association dramatically increased the importance of the first condition. Once attention is given to the fact that "the domestic producer" whose prices the less-developed countries exporters must undercut, would include in each of these major European trading blocs the most efficient producer in any one of the members, the scope of possible benefits shrinks.[83]

The second condition noted above means the higher the tariffs in the preference-granting countries, the greater are the number of goods produced in preference-receiving countries that may enjoy larger export markets and the larger the price differential that may be provided to those enjoying preferences. The heights of the tariffs in the developing countries is therefore critical. It is surprising that, so far as I can determine, those who spent so much time espousing the case for preference had not, up to mid-1965 at least, made the detailed commodity-by-commodity, country-by-country studies that would be necessary to determine whether or not the relevant tariffs were high enough so that a preferential cut in them could provide substantial help to the recipient. It is notoriously difficult to measure the heights of tariffs, but the 1963 average tariff level on manufactured goods in the major developed countries amounted to only about 15 percent ad valorem, calculated as a simple arithmetic average of the tariffs on all manufactured items. Some tariffs were much higher, but there was a heavy clustering around this average. Apart from the severe limitations on using an average for these purposes, this figure does not take account of the critically important fact that even a low tariff on a processed good, when combined with a much lower duty on imported incorporated inputs, will yield a high duty on the value added by the processing. The very scanty data available to me suggest that perhaps a 75–100 percent increase in the 15 percent figure above would be needed to take account of

[83] This "problem" exists, of course, for both most-favored-nation and preferential reductions.

this tariff structure phenomenon. These extremely rough and averaged figures only indicate that the possibilities here are of a different order of magnitude from the aid which countries have in the past often forced their own consumers to provide to their own infant industries by means of high tariffs, and which was often cited as demonstrating the effectiveness of preferences as a means of encouraging industrial growth.

If one goes on—since we are here concerned with policy—and assumes that the Kennedy Round of tariff negotiations proves moderately successful and that the level of tariffs on manufactured goods and on imported components, will be reduced by something in the neighborhood of 30 percent, the resulting simple arithmetic average level of ad valorem tariffs on all manufactured goods in the major developed countries (after the noted adjustment for the tariff structure aspect) turns out to be not much more than, say, 20 percent. Account then must be taken of the fact that there will be great reluctance for developed countries to give preferences that result in zero duties. During the 1964 World Trade Conference, where bargaining positions were being taken, the less-developed countries spoke of zero duties but frequently proposed that for most goods the preferences initially should be equal to "at least 50 percent of the most-favored-nation rate." But this is not all. The Geneva discussions had shown that any general system of preferences would have some exceptions; cotton textiles were one of the obvious examples, but it was usually assumed that there would be others as well. Calculations and considerations such as these at best only indicate the roughest orders of magnitude. What they do do is strongly emphasize the need for a careful and detailed investigation of the potential benefits from tariff preferences.

In the meantime, such considerations may have dampened a bit, but they did not extinguish, the enthusiasm in the developing countries for preferences. A part of the continuing campaign for them stemmed not only from the idea that any help, even if small, was worth having but also from the belief that a detailed investigation *would* show that there were a large number of goods for which a preferential tariff reduction would be a decisive factor in making it possible for the less-developed countries to take markets in developing nations away from both domestic producers and from producers of competitive goods in the industrial countries.[84] This might be because cost differences were such that only a small margin of preferences was needed. Or it might be because in many developed countries even the nominal tariffs on goods of interest to developing nations were relatively high. But the greatest hope was founded on the belief—which a few very limited private studies had supported [85]—and which we tried to make some allowance for above, that the effective rates of duty on the value added in the manufacturing process of the goods of particular interest to them were substantially higher than the nominal rates because such products often included large amounts of imported components subject to lower duties.

Even more important to some less-developed countries was the consideration that preferences, even when they would not make it possible for infant industries to grow up and become strong and self-reliant, would nonetheless increase sales and

[84] Presumably such instances would be most likely found in the near future where the most advanced of the less-developed countries had already demonstrated a modest, but not impressive, ability to compete in the markets of the developed countries, where the tariffs in the developed countries were relatively high, and where the supply conditions in the less-developed countries were likely to be elastic enough to permit the infants to grow up. An unpublished, unclassified, preliminary study, entitled "Trade Preferences for Less Developed Countries," dated Sept. 10, 1963, by Sidney Gardner, prepared while he was a summer intern in the U.S. State Department, found that such conditions appeared to exist for several less-developed countries and in several of the advanced countries for at least various kinds of rubber manufactures, footwear, glassware, pottery, cutlery, several kinds of furniture, and miscellaneous sporting goods. A more complete examination than he was able to do, especially if it took account of the *structure* of tariffs, would certainly show others; but the interesting thing is the relatively small number of commodities that seem obviously likely to benefit quickly. In the long run the number would be larger.

[85] See especially, G. Basevi, "The U.S. Tariff Structure: Estimate of Effective Rates of Protection of U.S. Industries and Industrial Labor," *The Review of Economics and Statistics,* (*in press,* 1965).

prices received by those who were *already* exporting,[86] or who would in any case be able to do so in the future. Such increases would help the balance of payments of the less-developed countries, would have a very beneficial effect on the profit rates of the favored exporters, and would make possible and encourage more domestic investment and growth.[87] The use of preferences to subsidize less-developed countries' producers which are

[86] The Gardner study cited in footnote 84 above found that the most important categories of goods here, important in the sense that export capabilities already existed in quite a few less-developed countries but duties were still quite high in many developing countries, were textiles, various leather manufactures, wood manufactures, some drugs, and a variety of miscellaneous light manufactures.

Except for that involved in the U.S. Government study noted in footnote 59 above, little work seems yet to have been done on estimating the possible *total* trade effects of generalized preferences. G. L. Reuber, on the assumptions that the present (pre-Kennedy Round) most-favored-nation rates average 12 percent and are maintained for imports from developed countries, that zero duties are applied to the imports of manufactured goods from the less-developed countries, and that the demand elasticity coefficient is 2, calculates that the developing countries exports of manufactured products subject to significant tariffs but *not* now subject to quantitative controls would increase in the medium term by 25 percent (or about $250 million). He estimates that similar tariff preferences, following a removal of quantitative restrictions would, under optimistic assumptions, increase these exports—textiles being important—by an additional $1.1 billion. These estimates, some think, are too low because the assumption of an average tariff of 12 percent does not take account of the fact that the real or effective rates on manufacturing, or value added, are a good bit higher than this. Further, these estimates seem to be medium run and apparently do not take into account all the dynamic affects: the effect of greater access to the markets in the developed economies on long-term investment and total production and costs in the developing nations of both new exports as well as existing ones. On the other hand, they optimistically assume there will be no exceptions and preferences based on zero duties on goods from developing countries. See G. L. Reuber, *Canada's Interest in the Trade Problems of the Less-Developed Countries,* Private Planning Association of Canada, Montreal, 1964, pp. 23–29.

[87] Some skeptics feared that in many of the less-developed countries aid via higher profits might end up as higher consumption or "low priority" investments rather than investments of the sort wanted by the planning authorities, unless these higher profits were taxed away.

already able to compete in world markets, was of course in keeping with the infant *economy* concept and the obligation of the rich to help the poor that was frequently set forth in international forums. But it was not publicly stressed, for it put the question of preferences as a straightforward foreign aid proposal; this the developing countries were reluctant to do.

My conclusions can be summarized briefly.[88] There is a case for government action to offset some of the high money costs of producing certain manufactured goods in less-developed countries. A case can be made for the industrialized nations giving aid for this purpose. Tariff preferences are properly seen as a device for extending such aid and not only as a commercial policy measure. They can provide some aid. The conclusion I hold most strongly is that combining aid and commercial policy in this way is an extremely complex undertaking and that the political-economic costs over and beyond the resource transfers of such a major departure from MFN practices will be great and varied. There is therefore an urgent need for far more extensive empirical investigations than so far seem to have been done of the actual potentialities of such preferences facilitating the industrialization and growth of the developing nations. The task is immense. It should include an examination of the tariff *structures* in the developed nations, permitting the calculation of real, rather than nominal tariffs, and so the possible effective margins of preference;[89] estimates of costs of producing manufactured goods in the developing nations, and so their ability to benefit from such preferences; and a careful examination of various kinds of preference arrangements. Such a huge task is justified only because the issue is an extremely important one for commercial policy, for international aid policy, and for the political relations among and between the developed and developing nations.

[88] This chapter has benefited (though they may say not enough) in ways that make specific attributions difficult from some as yet unpublished work on preferences by H. G. Johnson and by J. Pincus.

[89] See, H. G. Johnson, *The Theory of Tariff Structure, With Special Reference to World Trade and Development,* Etudes et Travaux de l'Institut Universitaire de Hautes Etudes Internationales, No. 4, Geneva, 1965.

CHAPTER VIII

Summary of Findings and Conclusions

T WENTY YEARS after World War II discrimination according to source was a widely used and in most policy-formulating circles a thoroughly respectable policy instrument. Unconditional-most-favored-nation treatment was under attack from all sides. Although differing in critical details, the less-developed countries were as one in wishing to emasculate the principal on a wide range of transactions. The outstanding economic–political developments in Western Europe, the EEC and EFTA, rested on discriminatory policies. Even the United States and Canada, the great champions in recent decades of nondiscrimination, had at the end of the period and as a matter of conscious policy blatantly violated their earlier strictures.

The impressive theoretical work in the 1950's on customs unions, the theory of the second-best as applied to international trade, had destroyed the easy theoretical defense of nondiscrimination, which had guided and comforted those who, in the 1940's, had drafted the major rules for international trade and payments—rules that had as their object a multilateral, nondiscriminatory, freer trading world. But this new work provided no simple new guide to those making policy; for it said that if an economy were prevented from simultaneously obtaining all the conditions for maximizing economic welfare then the effect of discrimination, whether it would increase, or worsen, or leave welfare unchanged, would depend on the *particular* circumstances. Thus released doctrinally, government officials often found that the specific circumstances of their situation, which were most pressing on them at the moment, argued for discrimination.

Nonetheless, had this study been written a decade ago the conclusion would have been that discrimination was declining, not increasing, and that there had been a resurgence of support at the policy level for unconditional-most-favored-nation treatment. The post-war record up to then had shown that the very widespread balance of payments discrimination against the dollar, and the discrimination against all nonmembers inherent in the EPU–intra-OEEC trade liberalization scheme, had brought with them many benefits. They had permitted some additional trade, they had facilitated an increase in the hard currency reserve holdings by discriminating countries, and they had probably fostered some increases in production and productivity. All of these were commonly regarded by the policy makers as necessary pre-conditions for the nondiscriminatory multilateral trading world which had been their stated goal. The widespread discrimination against Japan had successfully provided protection to several industries already in difficulties in many nations.

But the experience of these years had also shown that many of the recognizable benefits tapered off with time. In particular, there was a general sense that the higher levels of trade and production that had by then been achieved did not require continued discrimination for their maintenance in most countries. More important in determining policy was that at the same time the costs were becoming more apparent, and greater. These costs were often subtle and diverse. International friction in all sorts of places was proving once again to be a handmaiden of discrimination. Exporters who were discriminated against found the potential cost to them steadily going up as time passed and as others solidified their positions in the sheltered markets. Government authorities in discriminating countries became increasingly conscious of the cost of denying themselves the privilege of buying in the cheapest foreign markets—costs that were reflected not only in the real cost of higher-priced goods for domestic consumption and investment, but also in the extra burden such higher costs put on their exports. By the mid-1950's there was also a growing concern lest prolonging the discriminatory shelter result in perpetuating high costs, because new investments were being made whose economically profitable survival would demand continued shelter.

It also happened that some of the more powerful—economically and politically—of the partner nations in the EPU–OEEC arrangements were the ones being called upon to finance the weaker members, and this in a fashion which gave the former fewer options or alternatives than they would have liked or than might otherwise have been available. A greater cost to some was that continued membership in these institutions greatly increased the risks, and so the costs, of making their currencies convertible, a step they believed to be in their national interest. As the years went by, those few nations which did not discriminate against Japanese exports found increasingly burdensome the cost to them of the policy of those which did, because it was resulting in a sharp concentration of Japanese competition.

Thus it came about that, in the mid-1950's, there was emerging something of a consensus among the free world governments that the cost to the partners, as well as to the others, of the widespread discrimination probably had come to exceed the benefits, and that both economic and political considerations argued for less use of this device, though a quick, complete dismantlement of all the discriminatory machinery was not appealing to most. So it was that in the 1955 general review of the General Agreement on Tariffs and Trade it was concluded, after lengthy consideration of various proposals to make continued discrimination easier, that Article I of the Agreement, committing its members to unconditional-most-favored-nation treatment, as well as the other provisions proscribing and restricting discrimination, should not be altered in any substantively important manner.

It was not to be long, however, before governmental attitudes toward discrimination were to change. If there were to be a general review of the GATT in 1965, all those sections dealing with this matter, especially Article I (the general unconditional-most-favored-nation clause) and Article XXIV (the customs unions and free trade areas section), would be much altered, probably beyond recognition. By all odds, the most important reason for this shift was that a great many of those in authority in many countries had become convinced that their national interests, defined to include political and broadly defined economic goals, would be better served by joining regional blocs of one kind or another than by working toward a multilateral, worldwide, nondiscriminatory system. A sophisticated economic rationale for a regional approach was developed by scholars and theoreticians, in and out of governments. It was demonstrated that under certain conditions both the members and the nonmembers would benefit in terms of an increased flow of goods and services available for individual consumption. Those who were responsible for having their governments adopt regional policies rarely if ever had at their disposal the facts necessary to be sure that the conditions required to bring about these happy results for either or both groups were present in their case. But a great many *believed* they were. This belief was soon much strengthened throughout the free world by the twin facts that the West European countries had formed themselves into regional economic groups and they had prospered. That there was as yet little indisputable evidence that these two events were causally related—or were not—gave little pause to those determining policy. Moreover, although the members of the European regional blocs were paying something for their own discriminatory policies, in terms of some *unwanted* protection, some high cost imports, some inefficient production, some undesired limitations on other foreign policies, and some increased international irritations; to date, these had not in fact been very important. Certainly they have bulked small compared to the benefits the participants anticipated, or believed they were already receiving as indicated by their rising incomes, trade, investment, and consumption. And so, in contrast with the earlier discriminatory policies designed to cope with balance of payments difficulties, there has been little *internal* pressure for abandoning these regional efforts.[1] Indeed, regionalism has become for many the new faith, an *ideé fixé*.

The many regional communities, markets, and free trade areas involving the less-developed countries reflected not only their hope of reaping some of the potential benefits of large-scale production and increasing the productivity of existing enterprise, but, even more, the great value placed by their

[1] This is not to deny that some, General de Gaulle comes first to mind, have the greatest reservations about some of the political aspects of the EEC.

officials on increasing the level of industrialization and on creating *new* industries in their areas. As a consequence, they incorporated more provisions than the West European ones designed to limit the trade-creating effects and to increase the trade-diverting ones. That is, they are especially discriminatory. The high cost this is likely to entail to the members in terms of economic efficiency, however, has contributed less to the slow progress made to date in consummating them than to the difficulties of working out regional preferential arrangements that would result in little if any shifts in the locus of existing production *within* the group and that would also ensure that any benefits of the union (especially in the form of increased industrialization) were equitably spread among the members.

There was never any serious likelihood that the fact that these regional groups, in developed and less-developed areas alike, violated their members' nondiscriminatory commitments, vis-à-vis nonmembers, would stop their formation. There was far too much doubt that nonmembers would in fact suffer when both the static and dynamic effects were considered for that. Moreover, there was a great deal more than commercial policy and, indeed, than the usual economic welfare considerations, involved. Full economic union was the goal of some; in toting up the costs and benefits of this ambitious enterprise the possible costs to nonmembers via adverse effects on their exports were destined to be given little weight. Many governments in the less-developed areas, as we have just noted, put great value on the industrialization and economic diversification that trade-diverting, partial preferential arrangements clearly could foster *in each member* and so they were not to be deterred because there was such diversion. Beyond all such "economic" matters, regionalism was also—sometimes primarily—a thing desired for political reasons; these could offset many economic costs—especially those borne by others.

Nonetheless, at an earlier period it had been agreed by most of those involved that the goal should be nondiscriminatory multilateral trade on a worldwide basis; machinery had been set up to see that rules and obligations to foster this objective were honored. This meant two important things. First, those forming regional blocs went to greater pains than they otherwise would have to avoid from the outset policies which would do great damage to others. Second, nonmembers were given an unprecedented opportunity to be heard.

In examining the regional plans of others, nonmembers often found cause to be deeply worried and an immense amount of effort was spent, most if it in connection with the European Economic Community, in efforts so to amend or modify the particular regional arrangements so as to reduce the extent of damage that nonmembers feared they would otherwise suffer. These many and prolonged confrontation and justification sessions generated considerable friction, and they did lead to some modification of the arrangements, most notably those between the Six and the Associated Overseas States, designed to decrease the discrimination against other less-developed countries. They seemed to have had almost no effect on the Community's agricultural policy or the level of its original common external tariff—major determinants of the amount of discrimination. However, to the formation of the EEC and the resulting prospect of the United States losing markets must go a big part of the credit for the latter's taking the initiative in a major new effort substantially to reduce trade barriers all around the world. Should this prove successful, and adding one thing to another there seems on balance to be no reason why the formation of the six nations into the Six and the seven into the Seven, should reduce that probability for industrial goods, then although some discrimination will remain the net effect may yet be to enlarge the size of the foreign markets for the rest of the world as compared with what they would have been had there been no EEC and EFTA. If it does *not* so happen, then effective trade barriers will have been raised, especially since restraints against imports of many farm goods are clearly higher as a consequence of the creation of the Six. And there is no convincing evidence to date that the growth effects of these unions will offset this so far as the impact on the exports of the rest of the world is concerned.

Because the developing countries typically were such small

elements in the exports of nonmembers, because it was believed that many of these regional groups would not come to fruition, and because it was the fashion of the times to welcome almost any efforts—even those thought likely to be ill-advised—of the developing countries to help themselves; because of all these things the possible cost to third countries of regionalism in the developing areas has been largely ignored at the policy formulation level. The less-developed countries have in fact been given virtually blank checks in these matters by the rest of the world.

The extensive spread of regionalism so thoroughly diluted the commitments of many nations to nondiscrimination that two other major attacks on most-favored-nation policy generated far less opposition than relatively minor breaches had done in the first post-war decade. Although the possibilities of benefits to members were not of the same order of magnitude as those associated with forming customs unions or free trade areas, there was far less questioning of these later developments than there had been of the earlier common market proposals. The attitude toward discrimination had changed. It was no longer *assumed* that it was undesirable.

From the very beginning of the period studied a great many countries had discriminated against Japan for outright protectionist reasons and in violation of the spirit, and often the letter, of their international commitments. Among the costs of this, that had become more onerous with the passage of time, was the development and refinement of a particularly odious form of trade restrictions, the so-called "voluntary export restrictions." The policy also served to concentrate Japanese competition on those who did not discriminate and made more difficult the incorporation of Japan into other international arrangements which both Japan and, often, those discriminating against its exports, wished. The effort to provide some new "safeguards" against Japanese imports in the hope that this would lead to a relaxation of the prevailing discrimination against it led to widespread endorsement in the late 1950's of the proposition that the phenomena of "sharp and substantial" increases of imports of "particular goods" from "particular sources" at prices "substantially" below those prevailing in the importing country should be recognized as creating an undesirable situation known as "market disruption." The goods in mind, though often not specified, were labor-intensive manufactured products made in low-wage countries. It was further agreed that it was proper to take, under international auspices, special measures restricting such imports, so as to avoid such a situation.

This very important new doctrine, or modern variation of the hardy cheap foreign labor argument for restricting trade, was defended primarily on the grounds that it would prove less costly to economic efficiency than the next actual alternative: a perpetuation and expansion of the existing maze of unilaterally imposed severe restrictions by many nations which, whether justified or not, believed that Japan was an "unfair" competitor, especially in labor-intensive goods, primarily because it was able to pay lower wages per unit of output than other countries. It was also defended on the grounds that, for a variety of institutional reasons, Japanese pricing methods for some exports might in fact be ones, entirely apart from any labor exploitation issue, that would call for such a sudden and sharp withdrawal of resources from the affected industry in the importing country as to create not only intolerable political problems but also a much larger reduction in the level of economic activity than would be necessary if the adjustment were spread out over a longer period of time. The heart of the support for the doctrine, however, came from governments that simply wanted to protect weak domestic industries.

The great significance of the emerging avoidance of market disruption policy did not lie in its relevance to the so-called Japanese problem. The structure of the Japanese economy was by this time changing so much that one could foresee Japan slowly moving out of the production of low-cost, labor-intensive manufactured goods in favor of heavier products and more capital-intensive, complex light goods. It is the less-developed countries—the third world—that are likely to feel the brunt of this policy. Most of the less-developed countries as a matter of highest policy are trying to create at least a few "modern" sectors in which they hope to produce manufactured goods with the most up-to-date techniques and with labor's physical productivity approaching or equal to that of the industrially advanced nations. Alongside these high productivity pockets are the larger traditional sectors, where both productivity and wages are low. So long as the low wages in the latter sectors act as a depressant on the wages that are paid in the former, the producers in the modern sector *may* be able to offer goods on the world market at prices below the ruling ones. And being latecomers, there are powerful reasons for their doing so. The avoidance of market disruption policy, then, threatens to become a policy-justifying discrimination against just those activities in the less-developed countries that are high on their long-term development goals and in which they may well have the greatest comparative advantages.

The one major concerted effort to date to implement this doctrine, the long-term arrangement for cotton textiles, was frosted with general commitments to expand, in an "orderly fashion," to be sure, imports from the countries being discriminated against. Nonetheless, it came as no great surprise that the early experience under the arrangement has been most unsatisfactory from the less-developed countries' point of view. In the long-run it may turn out that the greatest cost of them was not that their textile exports expanded less than they had been led to hope, or even that the developed countries were using the time the new shelter provided not to move resources out of the affected industry in an orderly and politically tolerable way, but to reorganize, re-equip, and in general to resuscitate the affected industries. The most important cost may be all the other import restraints that will follow from international acceptance of the principle that special shelter against imports from low-wage countries is right and proper. So far, except for textiles, these have remained largely possibilities, although fearsome ones. The international trading community still has time to discourage any expansion of these discriminatory practices. One of the great tasks ahead of the Contracting Parties to the

General Agreement is to insist on definitions of "sharp increases of imports," "prices substantially below those prevailing," and "serious damage"—which will relegate this problem to a footnote in the future history of foreign trade.

But in the middle of the 1960's it was the less-developed countries themselves that seemed most determined to foster the greater use of discrimination as a tool of policy. Not only were they in the process of creating all manner of preferential arrangements among themselves in the form of regional markets, communities, and free trade areas and demanding that the rules for establishing them be especially lenient in their case, but their spokesmen were insisting that high on the agenda of all manner of international economic gatherings be the proposal that all developed countries extend preferences to the imports of all manufactured goods from all less-developed countries. One effect of such policy will likely be to widen the area for application of the avoidance of market disruption policy.

Neither the idea nor the practice of developed countries granting import preferences to certain products from the less-developed countries as a means of aiding the latter's economic transformation was new. There was also general agreement in the middle of the 20th century that it was a "good thing" that the less-developed country should aspire and work toward a significant, say, three percent per capita per year, increase in national income. It was acknowledged that this would require a considerable increase in the value of exports, that some of these should be in manufactured or processed goods, and that such goods would face severe competition from those countries which had a long head start in the modernization process. There was no doubt that receiving preferential treatment would be of some help in meeting these important problems. Although there were many differences among them as to approach, method, types, and extent, and these may—though it is unlikely —still prove insurmountable, a very large majority of the governments of the world went on record in 1964 as believing that some such preferential system was both feasible and desirable. This was less surprising than the fact that it was done before a careful appraisal had been made, or apparently even attempted, of whether the benefits were likely to exceed the costs.

It thus has come about that, in the summer of 1965, the world is caught up in a headlong flight toward a massive recrudescence of discrimination. Both theory and experience have demonstrated that a blind doctrinaire adherence to a policy of nondiscrimination is to deny the world many opportunities to improve the uses to which it puts its resources, including not only the amount of real goods and services available for consumption but also a variety of valued "noneconomic" objectives. Neither theory nor experience, however, can give comfort to those who would embark on a discriminatory policy solely on the basis of some likely, or even certain, short-run benefits to the participants, or who would ignore the economic costs, to the participants and to others, of the noneconomic objectives that discrimination may often further. This study has found that in all instances there were many costs of discrimination and that while some of the benefits taper off with time, it would be prudent to assume that the costs will continue to increase. Over and beyond the costs sorted out, there is a potentially huge one that seems to have been virtually ignored by the policy makers in recent years because it was still in the future. Will not ever-widening discrimination and the erosion of the most-favored-nation principle sharply curtail the willingness of nations to negotiate, and then to honor, trade barrier reductions? Why negotiate what are regarded as mutually advantageous cuts in barriers if what you receive stands a good chance of being effectively withdrawn by subsequent discriminatory cuts by your partners?

The world will be well served by holding to the general policy of nondiscrimination, requiring that departures from it be justified in each case. It will also be well served by continuing to demand that any such departures be subject to international approval and supervision. Despite all the outright violations of the IMF and GATT nondiscrimination rules, and the even more frequent bending of them, the two decades since the end of World War II have demonstrated that such rules and such institutions not only means that retaliation is less likely, but also that if a nation or a group of nations wants to discriminate they have to give more attention than they probably otherwise would to long-run as well as short-run consequences, to the impact on others as well as on themselves, and to secondary as well as primary effects. This surely is in the interests of the world's welfare.

Index

Index

INDEX

with EEC, 265; and trade with EFTA, 266; and German accession to GATT, 272; and market disruption restraints against, 304, 313; and preferences to developing nations, 363, 371, 371n. *See also* individual members

"Spaak report," 147n, 200n

Spain, 14, 249n, 299, 311n, 313, 324n

"static consumption effects," 122–23

"static production effects," 122–23, 159, 267, 269–70. *See also* trade-creation; trade-diversion

Sterling Area, 29n, 37n, 41, 49; and dollar pool, 67–75, 114. *See also* United Kingdom

Stockholm Convention, 140, 191, 194, 196, 217, 217n, 218, 231. *See also* European Free Trade Association

"supplemental levy," 213, 215

Surinam, 233n

Sweden, 126n, 127, 135, 137, 156n, 226n, 303n, 311, 311n, 352, 371

Switzerland, 120n, 218, 226n, 296, 303n, 308; and preferences for economic development, 333, 352, 371

Syria, 144

"target price," *see* "indicative price"

tariff alignment, *see* alignment of tariffs

tariff disparities, 156n, 159n, 179–81, 179n, 282

tariff levels, external, of regional blocs, 159–88 *passim;* source of internal conflicts, 159–60, 164–65; measurement problems, 160, 160n, 168–69; and increase in effective levels, 166; and alignment problem, 135–38, 146, 161, 170–73, 175n, 252; weighting problem, 167–68; GATT efforts to cut, 170–88 *passim;* of ECSC, 135–38; Yaoundé Convention cuts, 254, 254n, 390. *See also* particular regional blocs

tariffs, structure of and real rates, 20, 160n, 168n, 246n, 271, 271n, 380–84. *See also* tariff disparities

Tanganyika (Tanzania), 141, 256, 294n

Tasca, H. J., 23n

tea, suspension of duties on, 253n

Thailand, 143

Thorbecke, E., 259n, 267n

"threshold price," 202

tinbergen, J., 151n, 267n

Tobago, 294n

Togo, 294n

Torquay, session of GATT, 70–75, 79

trade-creation, and regional groups, 16–17, 121–24, 145–55 *passim,* 159, 163n, 267, 351n, 376n, 389

trade deflection, 135, 161, 161n, 163–64, 234–35

trade-diversion and regional groups, 11, 16–17, 121–24, 145–55 *passim;* and European Coal and Steel Community, 125–39 *passim;* sometimes desired, 151–54, 220–21; and tariff levels, 159; and agricultural policies, 197–222 *passim;* effects of EEC and EFTA, 262–70; and U.S.–Canada automobile accord, 357–58, 358n, 389

Trade Expansion Act of 1962, 176–77, 227n, 238n, 309, 390

"trade gap," and case for preferences, 337–41, 341n

412